CONFESSIONAL LUTHERAN DOGMATICS

Gifford A. Grobien, Editor

II

Holy Scripture

by

Jack D. Kilcrease

Published by
The Luther Academy
Ft. Wayne, Indiana

Jennifer H. Maxfield, Technical Editor

© 2020 by The Luther Academy, 6600 North Clinton St., Ft. Wayne, IN 46825
To order copies of Luther Academy books contact Logia Books c/o the above address

Biblical references, except where noted, are from the English Standard Version of the Bible, copyright © 2000, 2001 by Crossway Bibles, a division of Good News Publishers, 1300 Crescent Street, Wheaton, IL 60187, USA. All rights reserved.

Library of Congress Catalog Number: 89-84112

ISBN: 978-1-935035-26-8   (Volume II, paperback)
        978-0-9622791-0-2   (13-Volume Set)

Printed in the United States of America

To my wife, Dr. Bethany Kilcrease

CONTENTS

PREFACE TO THE GENERAL INTRODUCTION

by Gifford A. Grobien, General Editor
Confessional Lutheran Dogmatics

In his General Introduction to this series Robert Preus reminds the reader that no dogmatics nor even the Lutheran Confessions themselves could claim to be a perfect or ultimate explanation of Holy Scripture. Rather, like the Confessions, the volumes of the Confessional Lutheran Dogmatics are to lead readers into the Scriptures, which themselves continue to teach the truth, mercy, and love of God to a broken world. Confessional Lutheran theology not only articulates the theology of Scripture but relies on the same "thought pattern" and even on the terminology of the Confessions, in order that the scriptural way of thinking and speaking be made clearer, more deeply understood, embraced, taught, and followed. Even when facing new questions and challenges presented in changing historical and cultural circumstances, such a reliance on and continuous attention to the Scriptures characterizes confessional Lutheran theology.

Thus it is with great pleasure that the Luther Academy releases this volume on Holy Scripture, the eighth to be published in a series of thirteen volumes. In keeping with this purpose of a confessional dogmatics, author Jack Kilcrease leads the reader deeply and confidently into reading and studying the Scripture by addressing topics such as revelation, inerrancy, inspiration, canonicity, and hermeneutics. With his noteworthy scholarship, Dr. Kilcrease also engages classic and contemporary views of Scripture. His challenging and stimulating treatment will encourage readers by its penetrating analysis and faithful presentation, both in affirming what can be received from these views and in exposing where and how they fall short. Throughout, he upholds the Christological center of Scripture, as to its source: the words written by prophets and apostles, and by the Holy Spirit, attesting the truth of Christ; its content: the witness to Christ's person and work; and its purpose: the justification and salvation of men on account of and in Christ.

I give thanks for this addition to the Confessional Lutheran Dogmatics series and for its role as an important resource for seminaries, pastors, and scholars around the world. I am also pleased to mark one more step in completing this dogmatics series, a joyful task to which the Luther Academy remains committed.

GENERAL INTRODUCTION

by
Robert D. Preus, General Editor, 1984–95
Confessional Lutheran Dogmatics

For some time now those of us in the Lutheran church who have interested ourselves in the Lutheran Confessions, taught from them, and conducted research in these great symbolic writings have recognized the need for a dogmatics resource based upon the outline and thought pattern of the Lutheran Confessions. Such a resource, heretofore available only in Leonard Hutter's little *Compendium Locorum Theologicorum*, would address theologians of our day with a truly confessional answer to the theological issues we are facing in Christianity and in our Lutheran Zion today. We were in no way interested in replacing as a textbook in our Lutheran Church—Missouri Synod Francis Pieper's monumental *Christian Dogmatics*, which has served students in our church body and others for three generations. Such an endeavor would have been unnecessary and unproductive. The authors of the various monographs in this Confessional Lutheran Dogmatics series come at their respective subjects from somewhat different vantage points and backgrounds and personal predilections as they practice dogmatics. It was decided, therefore, to issue a series of dogmatics treatises on the primary articles of faith usually taken up in traditional dogmatics since the sixteenth century—the Augsburg Confession, Phillip Melanchthon's *Loci Communes*, and Martin Chemnitz's *Loci Theologici*, for example.

But why the approach from the Lutheran Confessions? Are not these musty old creeds and symbols irrelevant to our day, and would not a series of monographs written from the point of view of confessional Lutheran theology be equally irrelevant to the theological issues presently confronting the church? It is because we must respond to such a question with an emphatic *No* that we presume to issue the forthcoming volumes. The Confessions, whose theology is taken directly from the Scriptures, are indeed relevant to our day, just as are the Scriptures themselves which are always "profitable for doctrine, for reproof, for correction, for instruction in righteousness" (2 Tm 3:16). There has been a real call and need for just the kind of dogmatics series here proposed, that is, a confessional Lutheran dogmatics. First of all, no dogmatics book of any kind has been published by orthodox confessional Lutheran theologians (along the lines of Elert, Pieper, Hoenecke, and Hove) within the last generation. During the same time, however, there has been a renewed interest in the Lutheran Confessions, in their function in giving form to our Lutheran presentation of doctrine, and to some extent even in norming that doctrine: note the excellent studies of Edmund Schlink, Holsten Fagerberg, Leif Grane, Peter Brunner, Wilhelm Maurer, Friedrich Mildenberger, Hermann Sasse, and others as well as the many recent books and studies written in connection with anniversary observances of the Book of Concord, the Augsburg Confession, etc. Thus, it would appear that there is need not only for a dogmatics resource in our day, but one that is strictly and consciously confessional in its presentation of doctrine and its assessment and analysis of modern theological trends throughout the Christian church. This series, of which the present volume is a part, is written to fill this need, and it is the hope and prayer of the editors that the present volume will to some extent accomplish this aim.

The volumes making up Confessional Lutheran Dogmatics are not a theology of the Lutheran Confessions; they are rather a series in dogmatics. They differ from other dogmatics books in that they are patterned strictly after the theology of the Book of Concord as they address the issues of today. They follow not only the theology of the Book of Concord, as the texts of Francis Pieper and Adolf Hoenecke and other confessional Lutheran dogmaticians have done, but, unlike these dogmaticians, the authors of the present volumes follow the actual pattern of thought (*forma et quasi typus*, ὑποτύπωσις) of the Lutheran Confessions. Such a procedure is according to the principle of the Confessions themselves; creeds and confessions are indeed a pattern and norm according to which all other books and writings are to be accepted and judged.[1] This fact will account for the agreement in both doctrine and formulation that the reader will observe within the present entire dogmatics series; the authors bind themselves not only generally to the theology of the Book of Concord, but to its content and terminology (*rebus et phrasibus*).[2]

There is another reason for the doctrinal agreement which will be apparent among the authors of the Confessional Lutheran Dogmatics. It is this: all the authors share the concept of doctrine, unity of doctrine, consensus in doctrine, and purity of doctrine consistently articulated in our Confessions. All of the Lutheran Confessions see doctrine as a singular, organic whole. Christian doctrine is like a body (*corpus doctrinae*) with parts (*partes*) or joints (*articuli*) and ligaments and members (*membra*). The plural "doctrines" is rarely used in the Confessions, as in Scripture, but rather the singular "doctrine." In the church, if one member suffers the whole body suffers; according to the organic, unitary nature of Christian doctrine, if one article or member fails, the whole body of doctrine is adversely affected. Luther said, "One article is all the articles, and all articles are one."[3]

As a confessional Lutheran dogmatics, the present volume will consciously and scrupulously draw its doctrine from Scripture. All the Confessions, beginning with the creeds and concluding with the Formula of Concord, claim

---

1. See SD RN.10.

2. Preface, *The Book of Concord: The Confessions of the Evangelical Lutheran Church*, trans. and ed. Theodore G. Tappert (Philadelphia: Fortress Press, 1959), 13.

3. *Lectures on Galatians*, 1535 (AE 27:38; WA 40/2:47.32–33).

to be and are direct explications of Sacred Scripture. As such, their purpose is never to lead us away from Scripture, nor to summarize the Scriptures in such a way as to make their further study unnecessary. They are written to lead us *into* the Scriptures. This is exactly what their function has been in the history of the church, whether we think of the many commentaries written on the early creeds by the church fathers or the expositions of our Confessions by the reformers and their successors. The reader will therefore notice that the present work in dogmatics engages in much more direct and extensive exegesis than other works in dogmatic theology of our day, except the immense *Church Dogmatics* by Karl Barth. This is altogether proper and called for in a confessional Lutheran dogmatics text.

The present work is a kind of *loci communes*, the recapitulation of the main themes of Scripture on the basis of the confessional Lutheran outline and pattern of thought. The Lutheran Confessions themselves never claim to be the final work on the understanding and exegesis of the Scriptures; we recall Luther's statement on *oratio, meditatio, tentatio*[4] with its blasts against theological know-it-alls and how often this statement of Luther's was repeated by the post-Reformation theologians in their dogmatics works. The Confessions always lead deeper into the Scriptures, especially as new issues arise in new cultures and succeeding generations which must be faced only with theology drawn from the Scriptures and patterned after the Lutheran Confessions.

The volumes in this series are dedicated to Francis Pieper, a great confessional Lutheran dogmatician of our church, in the hope and prayer that they will help to achieve what he did so much to accomplish in his day—namely, doctrinal unity and consensus in the doctrine of the Gospel and all its articles among all Lutherans and a firm confessional Lutheran identity so sorely needed in our day.

---

4. *Preface to the Wittenberg Edition of Luther's German Writings*, 1539 (AE 34:285; WA 50:659.4).

PREFACE

As the "faith that was once for all delivered to the saints" (Jude 1:3), the Christian faith is perpetually the same in its essence. Nevertheless, in each generation the discipline of theology must seek new ways to expound the articles of the faith and apply their truths to the present context. In our situation today, standing between the failed epistemic and utopian projects of modernity and the brave new world of postmodernity, the doctrine of Holy Scripture faces significant challenges.

Since the Reformation, debates over the authority of Scripture have become central to the question of Christian doctrine and identity. In the sixteenth century the question of the authority of Scripture was overwhelmingly associated with a larger debate about the authority of church tradition and the teaching authority of the Latin church's magisterium which had been going on in various forms since the High Middle Ages. In the mid-seventeenth century, beginning with Baruch Spinoza and Thomas Hobbes and continuing through the works of Herman Reimarus and Johann Salomo Semler, Enlightenment-era rationalism did not merely question the authority of Scripture in relationship to churchly authority but treated Scripture in various degrees as another false and heteronomous authority that sought to crush human authenticity, rationality, and autonomy.

The impact of this Reformation- and Enlightenment-era discourse remains with us today. Even now in the first decades of the present century these debates fundamentally define how modern Christians engage the doctrine of Holy Scripture. Although the conflicts over Scripture in these two eras may seem disconnected, both relate fundamentally to questions of certainty and freedom.

For the late medieval church the Holy Scriptures did not give certainty because like any text they are open to interpretation; the institutional church was thus necessary as a means of clarifying the Bible. One could gain certainty and freedom through submission to the legal order the Roman Church sought to impose on both state and society. The Roman Church claimed for itself infallible teaching authority and also the ability to vouchsafe the sacraments that gave the faithful the spiritual energy (grace) necessary to fulfill the Church's commandments. The sacraments removed guilt and gave human beings a free will sufficient to obey God's Law and merit salvation. The price of this freedom was submission to the institutional church as the conduit of grace.

As should be obvious to all students of the Lutheran Confessions, the freedom and certainty offered by the Roman Church entailed legalism and Enthusiasm. These benefits were contingent on obeying the Law, or at least a particular version of the Law (legalism), and they were to be gained from an individual (the pope) or group of individuals (a council) who claimed to have the Spirit apart from or merely alongside the external Word (Enthusiasm).

If the late medieval church, like today's Roman Catholic Church, offered freedom and certainty by way of legalism, the Enlightenment offered freedom and certainty on the basis of a form of antinomianism. From the perspective of the Epicurean tradition that was revived during the Renaissance with the rediscovery of Lucretius's *De Rerum Natura*, both the Roman magisterium and the Bible of the Reformation were heteronomous laws that destroyed both freedom and certainty. Indeed, for many thinkers of the Enlightenment no certainty could be found in the pages of the Bible. In their minds the Roman magisterium and the myriad of Protestant confessions that had arisen from the Reformation all disagreed about what the actual content of the Bible was. Moreover, both the pope and the Bible demanded submission to claims that could not be tested rationally. As a result, the claims of authority made by the Christian tradition at large were perceived as destroying human freedom, authenticity, and certainty.

For Enlightenment thinkers a better alternative to irrational religious authority was found in philosophical foundationalism and the discoveries of the Scientific Revolution. In particular the knowledge provided by philosophical foundationalism was beyond doubt since it was founded on truths that no rational human could deny if he genuinely investigated them. Such knowledge was autonomous in that it came from within the person's own experience and thoughts. Knowledge was to be accepted only if it was based on one's own perception of the truth, not on a divinely guided church or inspired book that demanded submission to an external authority. The supernatural history the Bible recounted could be rejected out of hand as mythological because it conflicted with the reason and experience of contemporary people.

The corollary of autonomous knowledge was an ethic based on "human rights." Much like foundational rational ideas, human rights were presumed to be universal and self-evident. Again, because the autonomous human knower could use his reason to discern his rights, he did not need a magisterium or an inspired book to tell him he had these rights. The Enlightenment paradigm of rights rather than commandments or the natural law of the premodern and early modern tradition made ethics fundamentally about asserting oneself against those who would seek to take away one's freedom, rather than about conforming to a cosmic order of justice. Individuals were under no obligation to submit to any external authority they had not established by their own autonomous choice (social contract, democracy, etc.). Therefore, in the realms of both the epistemic and the ethical, the Enlightenment paradigm taught that individuals were a law unto themselves and could ignore any external authority that sought to crush their human authenticity.

The certainty and freedom offered through papal legalism was thus inverted into the certainty and freedom of the self-legislating individual (Kant). The

Enthusiasm is equally evident in these positions. The Roman pontiff claimed, as he does still today, to have the Spirit within his own heart and to stand judge over the Word. The autonomous individual of the Enlightenment claims to possess the gift of reason within his own heart, which allows him to decide freely for or against the truthfulness of any proposition asserted by an external authority, including the Word of the Bible.

Moreover, both the Catholic and Enlightenment theories of certainty and freedom are grounded in an essentially circular argument. The pope claims ultimate authority as the arbiter of truth because he interprets the Bible to teach as such, but one can know that the Bible authorizes the papacy only on the word of the pope. Likewise, the Enlightenment autonomous knower grounds the authority of reason in reason itself. Even Descartes' attempt to ground reason in God was circular: in order to establish God's existence, the French philosopher first had to assume the reliability of his own reason apart from God.

The Roman Catholic and Enlightenment alternatives of legalism and antinomianism as the basis of certainty and freedom continue to frame options in the contemporary West. The secular culture of the West has continued its descent into moral chaos in the service of what Charles Taylor famously referred to as "expressive individualism." Postmodernism has demonstrated that a rationality grounded in the autonomous knower is impossible, thereby opening up the possibility that the world itself is unknowable as anything more than the gray soup of Derrida's *différance*. In the postmodernist amplification of secular modernity, any moral claim or claim of objective knowledge represents a form of potential enslavement of the autonomous self. Indeed, even the claim that the self exists is for many postmodern thinkers an unbearable form of oppression.

In view of the anarchical antinomianism of postmodern secularism the Roman Catholic Church has renewed its false promises of certainty and freedom through submission to the papacy. This claim on the part of Catholics is not infrequently grounded in a narrative of the advent of modernity and postmodernity which asserts that the expressivist individualist chaos of the contemporary West never would have come to fruition without Luther's refusal to recant at Worms. In recent years many conservative Evangelicals have fallen prey to this false promise that civilization can be restored by the Roman magisterium alone, leading to many high-profile conversions to Catholicism.

Similarly, Roman Catholics often have seen this narrative of Luther as the founder of expressive individualism being validated by the fact that many forms of Protestantism have re-interpreted Luther's doctrine of *sola scriptura* in the service of the Enlightenment's autonomous rationality. In this scheme the individual's right to interpret the Bible in the light of his own subjectivity (one thinks in particular of the Baptist doctrine of immediacy of believers before God) is equated with the Enlightenment's autonomous knowledge based on philosophical foundationalism. Just as the Enlightenment grounded authority in the independent judgement of interior reason, many Protestant denominations ground authority in the individual's own subjective judgment regarding the meaning of Scripture as guided by the Spirit in the deepest recesses of his heart. The law of the pope's heteronomous subjectivity is thus replaced by the self-legislation of each believer.

In view of this modern and postmodern war between autonomous individualism and heteronomous authority, it is imperative for Lutheran Christians to raise the question: How in this context are we to confess coherently the Scripture principle of the Reformation? Indeed, how can we assert the authority of the Bible without falling into the ditch of either papal traditionalism or Enlightenment rationalism? What must be clearly apprehended is that the followers of both Catholicism and the Enlightenment labor within the boundaries established by the *opinio legis* and do not take into consideration the centrality of the Gospel. Lutherans historically have recognized that if one knows nothing but the Law, one invariably is forced into the yoke of either legalism or antinomianism. Paradoxically, in seeking to abandon the Law, antinomianism acknowledges the Law's ultimate authority by defining itself in opposition to it.

Neither Roman Catholicism nor the Enlightenment could accept Luther's doctrine of *sola scriptura* because of their implicit and explicit legalism. Catholicism could never bear the idea that although the Bible contains the Law of God, it does not see the Law as a way of salvation or a blueprint for an earthly kingdom of God. Because the Bible does not provide an outline for how to climb the ladder of merit up to eternal fellowship with God, Catholics needed to invent a pope to apply the law to every new circumstance.

Likewise, the expressive individual of the Enlightenment must resist Luther's doctrine of the supreme authority of the Bible in order to create his own law. The Bible imposes moral authority in the form of commandments spoken from Sinai rather than a social contract constructed on the basis of the aggregate of humanity's autonomous preferences. Likewise, it promises a kingdom beyond history rather than a utopia constructed by humans in history. For Enlightenment thinkers, the Bible is also oppressive because it demands that one believe in miracles or other historical events that go beyond the verification of reason and the experience of the individual.

In contrast, Luther and the other authors of the Book of Concord proposed an evangelical rather than a legal basis of certainty and freedom. Indeed, for the Lutheran confessors of the sixteenth century, unilateral divine grace is the overarching framework that defines human life within the twin poles of creation and redemption. Although Luther and his fellow authors affirmed that the Law is the eternal holy will of God, the Law remains penultimate to the power of the Gospel. From the perspective of the Gospel, the cultural, scientific, and political achievements of both the medieval church and the post-Enlightenment West can be appreciated as instances of the appropriate applications of the Law in the provisional circumstance of the old creation. Nevertheless, because the

Law is penultimate, none of these civilizational achievements can ever give the ultimate certainty and freedom granted by Holy Scripture comprehended through the Gospel.

For Lutheran confessional theology the Bible is the inerrant Word of God, which brings with it the presence of the risen Jesus, commending His eschatological promise of salvation. It is only through the eschatological promise of the Gospel that genuine certainty and freedom are granted. The certainty granted by the Gospel is grounded not in the circular arguments of the inner gift of the Spirit or of reason but in the objective reality of Christ's resurrection. The resurrection is God's final verdict on Jesus and the truth He proclaimed. In the resurrection the old creation and its preliminary projects are revealed to be provisional and relativized.

The Spirit active through the promise of the risen Christ does not grant humans a kind of interior enlightenment. Rather, the Spirit draws us from subjectivity to the objectivity of the vindicated risen Christ and His promise of the infallibility of the witness of the prophets and the apostles compiled in the Scriptures. The Word of God not only grants certainty of its truthfulness through the work of the Spirit but also gives the certainty of its own eschatological fulfillment in the forgiveness and eternal life of believers. This certainty is based on the fact that the center of the Bible is a divine promise and not a demand. As an unconditional and categorical promise the Gospel is always true and therefore qualifies and illuminates each particular and conditional statement of the Bible. As God's Word sacramentally present in human words, the Bible also possesses the divine power to fulfill all that it promises. The Word of God gives unconditional certainty because God works in His infinite power through the Word in order to grant what it speaks: judgment, forgiveness, and eternal life.

The evangelical certainty of Scripture grants genuine freedom. This authentic freedom is not a freedom of the will that is necessary to cooperate with grace and merit salvation, as the medieval church taught. Neither is it the freedom to live as a self-legislating godling as the Enlightenment conveyed. Instead, evangelical freedom breaks out of the prison of the *opinio legis* by both fulfilling the Law and transcending it. This freedom is unconstrained by the condemnation of the Law because certainty is granted by the inerrant Scriptures and God's promises in them.

The Scriptures seen from the perspective of the Gospel thus grant a twofold freedom, negative and positive. Negatively, the Scriptures grant freedom from the judgment of the Law in our relationship with God. This negative freedom comes from both the fulfillment of the Law in Christ and the fulfillment of the Law through the sanctification of the inner person to be completed at death. Positively, the Gospel grants the freedom to live out the Law in our earthly relationships unencumbered by the burden of trying to establish our relationship with God through the Law. This obedience of faith granted by the

Scriptures is framed by the promise of grace and therefore does not confine the believer to the delusion of the *opinio legis*.

Both freedom from the Law before God and freedom for the Law before humanity are guaranteed by the absolute truthfulness of the Scripture in its presentation of the history of salvation as well as the Law and promise attached to that history. As a result, the *opinio legis*'s *aporia* between submission and autonomy is overcome by a free and joyful submission to the works of the Law in a believing life proleptically secured by the eschatological promise of the Gospel. This free submission also grants the ability to confess everything the Scriptures teach as inerrant and true. Contrary to the claims of the Enlightenment, the assertion that Scripture is absolutely truthful and must be trusted is not a form of epistemic oppression but a grant of freedom. Every fact to which the Bible witnesses ultimately lends itself to inculcating and explicating the Christ and His Gospel of freedom. Every commandment God issues drives individuals to Christ or assures the redeemed that their faith-wrought obedience is God-pleasing.

In view of the unique challenges Christians face in the present context, it is my hope that these efforts to expound and defend the historic Lutheran doctrine of Holy Scripture have the practical effect of enhancing the proclamation of Law and Gospel in the contemporary church. Thank you to the editor of the series, Gifford Grobien, and copyeditor Jennifer Maxfield for patiently working with me to complete the volume, and to the Luther Academy board for their input and the opportunity to contribute to the Confessional Lutheran Dogmatics series.

Jack D. Kilcrease
Grand Rapids, Michigan
Feast of Pentecost, 2020

ABBREVIATIONS

References to versions of the Bible:

LXX   Septuagint
KJV   King James (Authorized) Version
NIV   New International Version
ESV   English Standard Version

References to the Book of Concord:

CA   Unaltered Augsburg Confession
Ap.   Apology of the Augsburg Confession
SA   Smalcald Articles
Tr.   Treatise on the Power and Primacy of the Pope
LC   Large Catechism
FC   Formula of Concord
      SD   Solid Declaration of the Formula of Concord
      RN   Rule and Norm of the SD

References to the editions and translations of the Book of Concord:

Bente   *Concordia Triglotta. The Symbolical Books of the Ev. Lutheran Church, German-Latin-English.* Translated and edited by F. Bente, W. H. T. Dau, and The Lutheran Church—Missouri Synod. St. Louis: Concordia Publishing House, 1921.

References to the Book of Concord are to the confession, article, and paragraph number.

References to Luther's works:

WA   *D. Martin Luthers Werke. Kritische Gesamtausgabe.* 69 vols. Weimar: Hermann Böhlaus Nachfolger, 1883–1993.
WADB   *D. Martin Luthers Werke. Deutsche Bibel.* 12 vols. Weimar: Hermann Böhlaus Nachfolger, 1906–61.
WATr   *D. Martin Luthers Werke. Tischreden.* 6 vols. Weimar: Hermann Böhlaus Nachfolger, 1912–21.
AE   *Luther's Works.* American Edition. 82 vols. Edited by Jaroslav Jan Pelikan, Hilton C. Oswald, Helmut T. Lehmann, and Christopher Boyd Brown. St. Louis: Concordia Publishing House, 1955–86.

Other references:

ANF   *The Ante-Nicene Fathers*. Edited by Alexander Roberts and James Donaldson, 10 vols. Peabody, MA: Hendrickson Publishers, 2004.

BF   *Summa Theologiae*. 60 vols. Black Friars Edition. New York and London: McGraw-Hill, 1964–.

NPNFa *Nicene and Post-Nicene Fathers*. 14 vols. First Series, edited by Philip Schaff. Peabody, MA: Hendrickson Publishers, 2004.

NPNFb *Nicene and Post-Nicene Fathers*. 14 vols. Second Series, edited by Philip Schaff and William Wace. Peabody, MA: Hendrickson Publishers, 2004.

ST   *Summa Theologiae* of Thomas Aquinas

THE WORD OF GOD
AND THE CONCEPT OF REVELATION

INTRODUCTION

In describing the basic *principia* of theology Johann Gerhard spoke of a principle of being (*principium essendi*) and a principle of knowledge (*principium cognoscendi*). God is the principle of being in that He is the ground of all reality and the object of theological investigation. Likewise, Holy Scripture is the principle of knowledge because it is the means through which the triune God reveals Himself and His promise of salvation to humanity.[1]

Although Gerhard preferred to begin with the principle of knowledge and move on to the principle of being,[2] he acknowledges that the principle of knowledge presupposes the principle of being. In this sense, although the dual *principia* are distinct from one another they are inexorably dependent on one another: Scripture is not an isolated authority but brings with it the reality of God who has addressed us through it.

In expounding the doctrine of Sacred Scripture we will follow Gerhard's insight regarding the structure of God's revelation. However, we will examine this structure in a somewhat different order. We will begin with God and His reality as an eternal speaker. Then we will describe His activity in creating a linguistic creation and human beings as His hearing and speaking creatures. All of this is necessary groundwork for explicating God's definitive address to humanity in Sacred Scripture.

THE SPEAKING GOD AND HIS LINGUISTIC CREATION

Our basic starting point for talking about God's Word as it is present in its inspired and written form in the Bible is the recognition that as creatures we exist and suffer the address of a speaking God (*Deus loquens, Deus dicit*). Insofar as we are God's creatures we are addressed by God in His act of creation and receive our being from that same address (Genesis 1; John 1). Since we are being

---

1. Johann Gerhard, *On the Nature of Theology and Scripture*, trans. Richard Dinda (St. Louis: Concordia Publishing House, 2006), 43. Also see a discussion of Gerhard on these points in Richard Schröder, *Johann Gerhards lutherische Christologie und die aristotelische Metaphysik* (Tübingen: Mohr Siebeck, 1983), 49–50.

2. Gerhard, *On the Nature of Theology and Scripture*, 43.

addressed by God already in our creation, the dogmatic question relating to Sacred Scripture ultimately will be "How are we being addressed by God?" and not "Are we being addressed by God?" To answer this question we must first examine the ontological structure of God as a speaker from all eternity and creation as His created speech in time.

The Godhead speaks from all eternity. Jesus Christ is the eternal Word of God (John 1). This is the truth with which any confessional Lutheran account of Sacred Scripture must begin, just as the Book of Concord and the Augustana begin with this affirmation in the ecumenical creeds.[3] The Word of God is not something created but rather is eternal. In that God is eternal and unchanging (Nm 23:19; Mal 3:6; Heb 13:8), in all eternity He is never a speechless or inactive God (*Deus mutus, Deus otiosus*). From all eternity the Father speaks forth a linguistic image of Himself in the person of His Son (Jn 1:1–3; Heb 1:3; Col 1:15). Though the Father is the source of divinity (*fons totius divinitas*), He nevertheless knows and addresses Himself from all eternity in the person of His Son (Mt 11:27; Lk 10:22). As Hermann Sasse observes:

> The God of the Bible is a speaking God, from 'and God said: let there be light' on the first page of the Bible to 'he speaks, the one who witnesses: yes, I am coming soon' on the last page . . . The false gods are dumb, but the Lord speaks. . . . No one can understand the biblical teaching of God's speaking, whether it be his spoken or written Word, if he is not clear that speaking is a characteristic of the true God in contrast to the other false gods, whose worship is forbidden in the First Commandment.[4]

As a speaking God, God is by nature a relational God. God is not relational in an amorphous or abstract sense, but concretely so through His Word. In speaking Himself forth God also returns Himself to Himself in the living unity of the Spirit. As Athanasius once noted, the life of the Trinity is relational rather than centered. By centered we mean an object that is determined by a quality internal to itself. The Father is not the Father because He possesses some sort of quality internal to Himself. Rather, the Father is the Father because He has a Son, just as the Son is the Son because He has the Father.[5] The Spirit likewise possesses His reality as Spirit due to the relationship between the Father and the Son. God's reality as Trinity is therefore something non-centered and is rather relationally constituted. By relationally constituted we mean a reality that is

---

3. See *Concordia Triglotta: The Symbolical Books of the Evangelical Lutheran Church, German-Latin-English*, trans. and ed. F. Bente, W. H. T. Dau, and The Lutheran Church— Missouri Synod (St. Louis: Concordia Publishing House, 1921), 31–35 (hereafter cited as Bente). Unaltered Augsburg Confession I (hereafter cited as CA; Bente, 42–43).

4. Hermann Sasse, *Sacra Scriptura: Studien zur Lehre von der Heiligen Schrift*, ed. Friedrich Wilhelm Hopf (Erlangen: Verlag der Evangelische-Lutherische Mission, 1981), 11. Cited and translated in Peter Nafzger, *"These Things Are Written": Toward a Cruciform Theology of Scripture* (Eugene, OR: Pickwick Publications, 2013), 68–69.

5. Athanasius, *Against the Arians* 1.4.12; *Nicene and Post-Nicene Fathers*, ed. Philip Schaff and William Wace, Second Series, 14 vols. (Peabody, MA: Hendrickson Publishers, 2004), 4:313 (hereafter cited as NPNFb). "The word 'Father' is indicative of the Son."

determined by another. Within the Godhead the personhood of each person subsists in and through the life of the other persons.

As a relational God, God speaks forth an equally relational creation. A non-relational God would not have created a world to relate to, or at minimum such a God would not be immutable. By His act of creation He would metamorphose into a relational God, when He had not been one before. He would be dependent on something outside Himself to be Himself and therefore lack aseity. Such a god would be less than ultimate in the sense that Scripture has defined the constitutive nature of divinity.

Though God is sovereign and therefore properly called King of kings and Lord of lords (Rv 19:16) and the author of the Law (Exodus 20), He is also the self-giving God of the Gospel. It is important to recognize that God's address of Law and promise to His creatures in time is rooted in God's own eternal reality. Just as the Law demands correspondence to a pattern of righteousness in time, so too God perfectly corresponds to Himself in the persons of His Word and Spirit in eternity. In and through His Word and Spirit He exercises absolute sovereignty. Likewise, the Gospel is a unilateral and unconditional promise of grace and love. To make a promise to another person means to pledge oneself completely to the other: "I swear by myself . . ." (Gn 22:16; Jer 49:13; Is 45:23; Heb 6:13). To fulfill a unilateral and unconditional promise, a person must give his whole self to the other to whom the promise is made.[6] A knight sworn to protect his lord will stay on watch as the lord eats or relaxes. He will remain awake as the lord peacefully sleeps. In effect he will donate his person and make his activities conform to the person of the lord. Ultimately a promiser must become a servant in order to make certain that the promise is fulfilled. Making a promise is thus an act of self-donation and self-objectification.[7]

For this reason, out of love, the Father eternally pledges and surrenders the fullness of His being in the begetting of the Son (Jn 1:1–5; Heb 1:1–5).[8] Due to their infinite glory in eternity the Son and the Father are free to fully give the fullness of their being to one another in the dual procession of the Spirit (Rom 8:9; Gal 4:6; Phil 1:19; 1 Pt 1:11).[9] Because God possesses such a character

6. See Oswald Bayer, *Living By Faith: Justification and Sanctification*, trans. Geoffrey Bromiley (Grand Rapids: Wm. B. Eerdmans, 2003), 53. Bayer writes, "God's being is [a] gift and promise as he gives himself wholly and utterly to us."

7. See similar arguments in Jack Kilcrease, "Kenosis and Vocation: Christ as the Author and Exemplar of Christian Freedom," *Logia: A Journal of Lutheran Theology* 19, no. 4 (2010): 21–34.

8. See similar description in Hans Urs von Balthasar, *Theo-Drama*, trans. Graham Harrison, 5 vols. (San Francisco: Ignatius Press, 1983–98), 4:323–27. Also see Peter Leithart, *Deep Comedy: Trinity, Tragedy and Hope in Western Literature* (Moscow, ID: Canon Press, 2006), 89.

9. Augustine, *On the Trinity* 15.17; *Nicene and Post-Nicene Fathers*, ed. Philip Schaff, First Series, 14 vols. (Peabody, MA: Hendrickson Publishers, 2004), 3:215 (hereafter cited as NPNFa); Martin Chemnitz, *Loci Theologici*, trans. J. A. O. Preus, 2 vols. (St. Louis: Concordia Publishing House, 1989), 1:142–45; Francis Pieper, *Christian Dogmatics*, 3 vols. (St. Louis: Concordia Publishing House, 1951), 1:424–27; Carl Beckwith, *The Holy Trinity*, vol. 3 of Confessional Lutheran Dogmatics (St. Louis: The Luther Academy, 2016), 244–63.

in eternity He is able to be the God of the Gospel in time and pledge Himself to the human race beginning with the *protoevangelium* (Gn 3:15). Such a pledge eventually culminates in the full self-communication of God's Word in the incarnation (*genus majestaticum*)[10] and Christ's subsequent presence in the embodied promise of the sacraments.[11]

As creator, God narrates creation into existence through His Word (*creatio per verbum*).[12] As the Father speaks forth the Son in eternity as His uncreated Word, similarly in time He speaks forth the temporal order as His created speech.[13] God reveals His will and grace in time not only through audible words given to the prophets and apostles but also through the natural order which He has established by His speech. As communicators of His will and His grace, creatures reflect in time the relation the Father possesses in eternity to His uncreated Word. Just as the Father eternally begets the Son and stands in relationship with another within His own being in eternity, so too He freely speaks forth creation and enters into relationship with creatures in time.[14] As Luther observes: "By speaking, God created all things and worked through his Word. All his works are words of God, created by the uncreated Word."[15]

As God's created speech, creatures carry within themselves the character of both Law and grace. Much like the gospel of the new creation, the original creation is a result of God's unilateral grace. God speaks forth His creatures freely and graciously by an act of fiat without any effort on their part (Mt 5:45).[16] Likewise, as God's created speech, creation mirrors God's eternal reality as the author of the Law. In bringing about creation God has established a structure and logos of being within which creatures necessarily act (*ius naturale*). This structure serves to channel the creatures' response of praise for being given all good things by God's unmerited favor (1 Tm 4:14).

THE NARRATIVE STRUCTURE OF CREATED BEING

God's act of creation does not occur within an abstract or distant "once upon a time," but happened within a definite narrative of the six days of creation as they

---

10. SD VIII (Bente, 1041); Martin Chemnitz, *The Two Natures in Christ*, trans. J. A. O. Preus (St. Louis: Concordia Publishing House, 1971), 241–86; Johann Gerhard, *On the Person and Office of Christ*, trans. Richard Dinda (St. Louis: Concordia Publishing House, 2009), 203–87.

11. See Johann Anselm Steiger, "The *Communicatio Idiomatum* as the Axle and Motor of Luther's Theology," *Lutheran Quarterly* 14 (2000): 125–58.

12. See Gustaf Wingren, *The Living Word: A Theological Study of Preaching and the Church*, trans. Victor Pogue (Philadelphia: Muhlenberg Press, 1960), 72–75.

13. See this notion in Bayer's interpretation of Luther: Oswald Bayer, *Martin Luther's Theology: A Contemporary Interpretation*, trans. Thomas Trapp (Grand Rapids: Wm. B. Eerdmans, 2008), 101–4.

14. See similar argument in Balthasar, *Theo-Drama* 5:61–99.

15. *Lectures on Genesis*, 1535–45 (AE 1:47; WA 42:35).

16. Bayer, *Martin Luther's Theology*, 95–100. Also see Luther's comments in *Lectures on Genesis*, 1535–45 (AE 8:39; WA 44:607).

are recorded in book of Genesis. Within the dynamic narrative of the six days of creation, God speaks creation into existence. Beyond its protological narrative, creation continues in the present as a dynamic narrative that is ever being spoken forth by the divine narrator (*creatio continua*). Therefore, according to the Bible the essence of creatures (that is, what they are most fundamentally) is not determined by a Platonic or Aristotelian form. Rather, it is determined by God's address within the dynamic narrative of Genesis 1.

Although the narrative-ontological character of creation can be established by Genesis itself, it also can be discerned from the analogy of everyday life. If someone is asked the question "Who are you?" he likely would tell his life story. Going beyond his individual life story, other constitutive elements of his identity are self-evidently narrative in his character. For example, if he were a German his identity would be determined in part by World War II. This would be the case whether he liked it or not. The historical narrative of World War II would project a kind of determination onto his existence.[17] In his limited human freedom he could of course place himself in a position standing for or against the reality of his nation's identity as determined by its history. Nevertheless, one cannot escape that history: it shapes the individual irrespective of whether his individual response is positive or negative.

The essence of a creature thus is not determined by an internal source that exists independently over and against God. Rather, creation is radically dependent upon God's word of address. Creatures are determined by the divine address whether they desire it or not. Hence the identity, indeed the mere existence of all creatures as such, much like the persons of the Trinity, is something determined by a reality external to itself. A creature's identity as a distinct entity is constituted relationally in both its origin and its continuing existence through the address of God's Word.

Since created being receives its reality from its narrative, God did not make the whole of creation in a single instant but rather as a dynamically unfolding narrative that would determine the essence of all future beings within creation. Had God created the world in a single instant, creation would lack a story and therefore an essence which is dependent on God's original address. As we have observed already, the essence of all creatures lies in their story narrated by God. Our individual reality as distinct entities fits into and is determined by God's overall narration of reality. In their existence (that is, in the classical philosophical sense), creatures may be alienated from their essential nature due to the reality of sin. Nevertheless, the narrative of Genesis 1 still determines creatures in their reality. Even as fallen, creatures are deemed fallen precisely because they do not correspond to what God has established by His Word in the first six days.

---

17. See Werner Elert, *An Outline of Christian Doctrine*, trans. Charles Jacobs (Philadelphia: United Lutheran Publication House, 1927), 22–25.

HUMANITY AS GOD'S HEARING
AND SPEAKING CREATURES

Within the linguistic creation, humans possess a unique role as God's hearing and speaking creatures. Indeed, this unique role is the basis of the righteousness of faith, which constitutes the original righteousness and holiness lost in the Fall. Historically this righteousness has been identified by confessional Lutherans as the *imago Dei*.[18] This interpretation is accurate based on the biblical evidence from the description of sanctification being a restoration of the *imago Dei*: "put on the new self, which is being renewed in knowledge after the image of its creator" (Col 3:10; also see Eph 4:24).[19]

Righteousness (צֶדֶק, δικαιοσύνη) is never an abstract property (for example, a color) but is always a relational term and the following of a concrete standard within that relationship. This is particularly true in the original Hebrew usage in the Old Testament.[20] Rather, human righteousness in the state of integrity (*status integritas*) and now in the time of grace (*tempus gratiae*) is a response rooted in the listening to and proper hearing of God's perpetual address with faith. To "hear" in the Old Testament frequently means to obey.[21] Likewise, as Paul notes (Rom 14:23) along with Luther[22] and Gerhard,[23] all sin is essentially unbelief, and therefore conversely all righteousness is rooted in the hearing of faith (Hebrews 11). This fact is discernible from the Genesis narrative itself, in that Adam and Eve acted disobediently and fell specifically because they did not believe God's Word (Genesis 3). Faith looks outside itself (*extra nos*) to life hidden in the Word. Likewise, love, to which faith gives rise, looks outside itself to the neighbor and his needs.

Through this righteousness the person of faith is constituted in a de-centered existence which mirrors that of the Trinity. As Luther observes in *On the Freedom of a Christian*: "We conclude, therefore, that a Christian lives not in himself, but in Christ and the neighbor. *He lives in Christ through faith, and in his neighbor through love.*"[24] Indeed, just as the person knows God and is drawn out of his own incurvature (*incurvatus in se*) through the Word *extra*

---

18. See Ap. II (Bente, 109); *Lectures on Genesis*, 1535–45 (AE 1:162; WA 42:121).

19. See A. L. Graebner, *Outline of Doctrinal Theology* (St. Louis: Concordia Publishing House, 1949), 58.

20. In particular, the Hebrew term denotes right relationship, particularly (though not exclusively as some claim) in faithfulness to a covenantal relationship. See discussion of etymology and word usage in Alister E. McGrath, *Iustitia Dei: A History of the Christian Doctrine of Justification*, 2d ed. (Cambridge, UK: Cambridge University Press, 1998), 8.

21. Philip Davies, "Ethics in the Old Testament," in *The Bible in Ethics: The Second Sheffield Colloquium*, ed. John Rogerson, Margaret Davies, and Mark Daniel Carroll (Sheffield, UK: Sheffield Academic Press, 1995), 164.

22. See *Lectures on Genesis*, 1535–45 (AE 1:147; WA 42:110); *On the Freedom of a Christian*, 1520 (AE 31:361; WA 7:32).

23. Johann Gerhard, *On Sin and Free Choice*, trans. Richard Dinda (St. Louis: Concordia Publishing House, 2014), 15.

24. *On the Freedom of a Christian*, 1520 (AE 31:371; WA 7:69); emphasis added.

nos, God knows Himself through His Word. Likewise, just as the person of faith returns love to God and his neighbor as a result of this knowledge (Rom 12:1; Heb 13:15; 1 Jn 4:19), God the Son returns Himself to the Father through the love of the Spirit. The life of faith thus mirrors the responsive life of the Trinity. As Hermann Sasse observes:

> The Christian faith understands the nature of the human person from this vantage. Man becomes "person" through the call of God. "I have called you by name." [Isaiah 43:1] This is how the personhood of man is established. God's creative Word has called everything into existence: "He bears all things through is powerful Word." [Hebrews 1:3] In this mystery of the world, this is not "nature," or something independent, which exists of itself. It is rather "creature," something that God has called into existence out of nothing. Therein man has a part in all creation. But this distinguishes him from the rest of the world. He is a creation "according to the image of God." God has created man to be person, to be an "I" who can hear the word of God. Man is an "I" whom God stands over against as a "thou," who can answer to him and is answerable to him. This distinguishes man from other creatures. So the person of man is conjoined with the person of God. Only because God is person and has set himself as a person over against man, therefore there is life as personhood. Not as though God and man stand over against each other as equals! God is the creator and man a creature. The boundaries are not blurred. Man does not have life as a person because man is a divine essence. He has such life because the creator created him as a "thou." The divine call alone makes man a person. Because it is so, no philosophy may decipher the mystery of the human person, the mystery of the "I." It cannot be understood from nature, or from a participation in a realm of the intellect. It can be understood only from the word of the creator: "I have called you by name."[25]

In these remarks Sasse echoes and develops some of Luther's own thoughts on the subject as expressed in his *Disputation Concerning Man* (1536).[26] Luther begins the disputation by making the observation that Aristotle is in some measure correct to define human beings as rational animals (although he seems to express some mild doubt about applying the category "animal" to humans). When human beings are relationally defined over against the background of the rest of the created order, they stand out as the only creature that possesses reason. The human faculty of reason is "something divine" since it actualizes itself in human dominion over creation, which mirrors God's own sovereignty over the world. Such dominion over and responsibility for creation was not destroyed by the Fall but remains to the present.[27] The implication here is that the *imago Dei* present in human rationality ("something divine") remains in part even after the Fall. Later we will see a similar notion in Gerhard's treatment of the subject.

---

25. Hermann Sasse, "What Is the State?" (1932), trans. Matthew Harrison (unpublished manuscript, 2015), 12–13.

26. See classical discussion and an attempt to deduce the whole of Luther's theology from this discourse in Gerhard Ebeling, "Disputatio de homine," in *Lutherstudien*, vol. 2, parts 1 and 2 (Tübingen: Mohr Siebeck, 1977).

27. *Disputation Concerning Man*, 1536 (AE 34:137; WA 39/1:175).

It is interesting to observe here that Luther implicitly endorses aspects of the medieval tradition's appropriation of ancient Greek faculty psychology (reason, will, memory)[28] as a means of identifying the *imago Dei*, at least *coram mundo*.[29] Nevertheless, there is a major distinction here. Whereas the medieval tradition largely followed Aristotle regarding the primacy of reason and therefore also claimed that the interior contemplative life was superior to the active life,[30] Luther reversed all this. For Luther, reason is not to be turned inward in the form of mystical contemplation but rather directed to activity external to itself in vocation in the kingdom of the world (*regnum mundi*). It is precisely this activity of working within the world as God's viceroy that is most natural and primal, insofar as it was Adam's vocation in the state of integrity. Over against the interior and centered conception of the authentic human self found in the medieval tradition, Luther views reason itself as externally oriented to practical action within the orders of creation (*status, ordines, regimina, Stände, Schöpfungsordnung*).[31]

Although Luther partially agrees with Aristotle and the earlier scholastic tradition about the importance of reason, human beings ultimately are not defined by their use of reason. In terms of their self-knowledge and destiny, humans are not centered but creatures constituted and destined for someone outside of themselves. In a real and meaningful sense, human beings come to know themselves only on the basis of what God has revealed about them in His Word. They do not know themselves through reason "*a priori*, but only *a posteriori*" through the Word of God *extra nos*.[32]

Indeed, we may go a step further than Luther and observe (with Sasse above) that as a creature of God even reason itself is dependent on the Word for its existence. Contrary to what Enlightenment thinkers believed, reason lacks any autonomous existence over against God and His Word, but rather is radically dependent on them. After all, for reason even to exist as a faculty of humanity it must be narrated into existence through God's Word. Even on an intercreaturely basis, our ability to think and use rational categories is dependent on language. Such language is not something created by our inner autonomous and disembodied faculty of reason; it is received from outside ourselves from the surrounding culture. In this, the inner reality of reason is dependent on our prior address through the external Word.

28. *Summa Theologiae* of Thomas Aquinas 1a, 93, 1–9 (hereafter cited as *ST*); Thomas Aquinas, *Summa Theologiae*, Black Friars Edition, 60 vols. (New York and London: McGraw-Hill, 1964), 13:49–85 (hereafter cited as BF).

29. *Disputation Concerning Man*, 1536 (AE 34:137; WA 39/1:175).

30. *ST* 2a2æ. 182, 1–4; BF 46:67–83.

31. See orders of creation in Luther in *Lectures on Genesis*, 1535–45 (AE 1:103–6; WA 42:78–81). Also see classic discussions of the orders in Adolf von Harless, *A System of Christian Ethics*, trans. A. W. Morrison (Brighton, IA: Just & Sinner, 2014), 416–99; Johann Michael Reu, *Christian Ethics* (Columbus: The Wartburg Press, 1935), 256–354.

32. *Disputation Concerning Man*, 1536 (AE 34:137; WA 39/1:175).

Luther goes on to consider the causes (formal, material, instrumental, final) Aristotle outlined as a basis for understanding the existence of various creatures.[33] If one applies these categories to humanity and then juxtaposes what the Bible says about humans and what philosophy knows about them, one will discover that humans come to know themselves only from God's address in Scripture. For this reason *coram Deo* humans must have a very different definition than they do *coram mundo*.

Luther points out that philosophy does not know the formal or material cause of human existence since it does not know the biblical narrative of creation and the vocation of Adam in the Garden of Eden.[34] Neither does philosophy know anything about original sin (*peccatum originale*).[35] Finally, philosophy knows nothing about the redemption in Christ or humanity's final eschatological redemption through the resurrection of the dead and the renewal of creation (*causa finalis*).[36] Indeed, even our temporal existence does not find its meaning within itself, as Aristotle supposes, but rather based on what it will be: "Therefore, man in this life is the simple material of God for the form of the future life . . . [j]ust as the whole creation which is now subject to vanity [Rom 8:20] is for God the material for its future glorious form."[37] Our temporal life is radically and externally oriented toward the future life. Our present temporal life is merely the matter (in Aristotle's sense, *causa materialis*). Its form (again, following Aristotle, *causa formalis*) is our eschatological existence in the new heaven and the new earth.[38]

Ultimately, since human self-knowledge and destiny is defined by God's address and the trusting reception of it, the theological definition of humans is summed up by "Paul in Romans . . . as 'Man is justified by faith.'"[39] In the end, humanity is not defined by an inner faculty of rationality but by its response to the external and audible word of the Gospel.

At this point another significant divergence between Luther and the medieval tradition suggests itself. Augustine[40] and Aquinas[41] both describe the eternal Word of God as reflected in the inner faculty of human reason. The human subject is able to reflect on himself through reason, analogical to the Father's eternal act of self-reflection resulting in His begetting of God the Son. Augustine and Aquinas here prioritize disembodied reason over the spoken word in both God and His image in humanity, thereby following the general

---

33. *Disputation Concerning Man*, 1536 (AE 34:138; WA 39/1:176). Also see description of Aristotle's four causes in Aristotle, *The Metaphysics*, Book 5, trans. Joe Sachs (Santa Fe: Green Lion Press, 2002), 77–108.
34. *Disputation Concerning Man*, 1536 (AE 34:138; WA 39/1:176).
35. *Disputation Concerning Man*, 1536 (AE 34:138–39; WA 39/1:176).
36. *Disputation Concerning Man*, 1536 (AE 34:139–40; WA 39/1:177).
37. *Disputation Concerning Man*, 1536 (AE 34:140; WA 39/1:177).
38. *Disputation Concerning Man*, 1536 (AE 34:139; WA 39/1:176).
39. *Disputation Concerning Man*, 1536 (AE 34:139; WA 39/1:176).
40. See Augustine, *On the Trinity* 9; NPNFa 3:125–33.
41. *ST* 1a, 34, 1–3; BF 7:25–42.

trend of the Greek philosophical tradition. The older Melanchthon also took over this explanation in his treatment of the Trinity in *Loci Communes 1559*.[42]

As Francis Pieper observed, one of the major difficulties with this analogy is that it is utterly lacking in biblical support.[43] Not only does it lack positive biblical sanction, it directly contradicts what Scripture says about the Trinity. John calls Jesus God's "Word" (John 1) and not God's "Thought." Although one may object that John uses the term Logos, which can mean "reason" as well as "word," another may respond that John's prologue is essentially a retelling of Genesis 1, where God acts and creates by His external speech act and not His interior contemplation. Hence, John speaks of the Word not as something internal to the Father but something "with God" (Jn 1:1), through which God acts externally to create and redeem (Jn 1:3, 14).

Not only does John describe Jesus as the eternal Word of God, Jesus in the Gospel of John describes the Holy Spirit as the revelation of the "hearing" between the Father and the Son. The Father speaks in eternity, and such locution constitutes the reality of the Son. Likewise, the Spirit reveals to believers what is spoken in eternity and what therefore constitutes the hearing between the Father and the Son: "He will not speak on his own authority, *but whatever he hears* he will speak, and he will declare to you . . ." (Jn 16:13; emphasis added).

When Luther developed his own trinitarian theology more fully in the 1530s, particularly in sermons and disputations, he followed this more biblical model and rejected the Greek/medieval prioritization of disembodied and centered reason. We have already observed that Luther regards the *imago Dei* as rooted in God's address ("justified by faith"). This conception finds an interesting echo in his trinitarian theology. In his Trinity Sunday sermon of 1538 the Reformer describes God according to the biblical paradigm as one who speaks (the Father), one who is spoken (the Son), and the hearing between them (the Holy Spirit).[44] God is thus constituted by an eternal Word-event and not an act of self-reflection.

Last, the definition of the *imago Dei* offered above both clarifies and resolves an apparent tension in the teachings of Scripture and the historic Lutheran tradition. As noted earlier, the Lutheran Confessions consistently teach that original righteousness (*iustitia originalis*) lost in the Fall constitutes the *imago Dei*. For this reason it is also asserted that the image of God has been utterly lost. This notion is supported by certain passages of Scripture (see the aforementioned Col 3:10 and Eph 4:24).

---

42. Philipp Melanchthon, *Loci Communes 1543*, trans. J. A. O. Preus (St. Louis: Concordia Publishing House, 1992), 21. Note that Concordia Publishing House mistakenly published *Loci Communes 1559* as *Loci Communes 1543*.

43. Pieper, *Christian Dogmatics* 1:399–400.

44. See discussion in Paul Hinlicky, *Luther and the Beloved Community: A Path for Christian Theology after Christendom* (Grand Rapids: Wm. B. Eerdmans, 2010), 130–35. The section of the sermon Hinlicky refers to can be found in *Sermon for Trinity Sunday* (WA 46:433).

Nevertheless, there are other passages of Scripture which seem to suggest that the *imago Dei* is present even after the Fall (notably, Gn 9:6; Ps 39:6; Mt 22:15–21; 1 Cor 11:7; Jas 3:9).[45] Gerhard agrees with the Lutheran Confessions that the original righteousness constitutes the image of God. Nevertheless, he posits that there is a remnant of the original image in humans in the form of conscience and right-reason which makes civil righteousness possible.[46] As was observed earlier, in his *Disputation Concerning Man* Luther seemingly takes the same position in that he insists reason is both "something divine" (suggesting it is in some sense reflective of God's image) and the basis of civil righteousness.[47]

Our characterization of the *imago Dei* as original righteousness ultimately is rooted in humanity's capacity to hear and communicate as a result of God's address, and this interpretation resolves these tensions. Although humanity in the state of sin and condemnation has become deaf to God's gracious address in creation and redemption (an argument Luther makes in his sermon of 1538 on Mk 7:31–37),[48] nevertheless in both conscience and in nature God's address in the form of Law is still perceptible, even if it is strained. God is, as Paul observes, "clearly perceived . . . in the things that have been made" (Rom 1:20), and His "law is written on their [humanity's] hearts" (Rom 2:15). Thus, through a knowledge of the structure of the visible creation (*notitia Dei acquisita*) as well as through the inner conscience (*notitia Dei insita*), God's word of Law is still capable of partially being heard.[49]

Therefore, insofar as God continues to address His creatures indirectly by His word of Law, weakly perceived in nature, they continue to respond in the form of civil righteousness. It could also be said that humans respond as well in the permutations of idolatrous works righteousness (*opinio legis*) that are to be found in the various world religions.[50] Nevertheless, since this Law is imperfectly perceived due to the damage sin has caused to our noetic capacities, it remains partially veiled, as Luther observes in the Great Galatians commentary (1535).[51] Israel could not stand God's unmediated (*Deus nudus*) and fully condemning address of Law as it was experienced at Mt. Sinai (Exodus 20). As a result, the people sought Moses as a buffer and a veil (Exodus 34; 2 Corinthians 3). So too, Luther observes that the force of the Law is only partially known to unconverted humans. Indeed, the full force of total condemnation is not felt by them, and they thereby come to believe falsely that the Law is

---

45. Johann Gerhard, *On Creation and Providence*, trans. Richard Dinda (St. Louis: Concordia Publishing House, 2013), 325–26.
46. Gerhard, *On Creation and Providence*, 326.
47. *Disputation Concerning Man*, 1536 (AE 34:137; WA 39/1:175); CA 18 (Bente, 51).
48. See *Sermon on the Twelfth Sunday after Trinity Sunday* (WA 46:493–95). See discussion in Bayer, *Martin Luther's Theology*, 106–8.
49. See Robert Preus, *The Theology of Post-Reformation Lutheranism*, 2 vols. (St. Louis: Concordia Publishing House, 1970–72), 1:175.
50. See Pieper, *Christian Dogmatics* 1:9–21.
51. *Lectures on Galatians*, 1535 (AE 26:322; WA 40/1:500).

manageable and doable. They do not know the true theological use of the Law.[52] Their response to God's address of Law in creation and their consciences is to be hardened in works righteousness. Hence, in that which is below us *coram mundo*, the *imago Dei* is present insofar as we are able to respond to God's address of the Law through active and civil righteousness. Viewed from the perspective of *coram Deo*, we are deaf, unbelieving, and unresponsive to God's address of totalizing judgment and totalizing grace. For this reason God does not recognize His image in us and we are wholly sinful (Rom 7:18; 1 Cor 2:14).

THE WORD OF GOD AND THE
ESCHATOLOGICAL MOVEMENT OF TIME

As discussed earlier, God spoke creation into existence as a narrative. Any narrative presupposes the distance of space and the movement of time, within which the various agents can interact with each other and their relationship can develop. Both the *diastasis* (separation) of space and the movement of time provide an environment within which God can address His hearing and responsible creatures, and within which they can respond.

In this movement and distance of created being, the analogy of the trinitarian life is quite clear. In the life of the Trinity the "movement" (understood analogically) of begetting and procession as well as the distance between the diverse identities of the persons provide an environment within which Father, Son, and Holy Spirit may act upon and respond to one another.[53] Likewise, the reality of space creates the analogical distance within which God can address His creatures as other. The reality of time provides a movement within which God's relationship within His creation moves toward an eschatological fulfillment. This movement and fulfillment were prefigured already in the seven days of the original creation which culminated in an entry of creation into God's own rest (Genesis 1–2; Hebrews 2–3). In that it is God's own presence that finally gives rest, such final eschatological rest corresponds analogically to the *perichoresis* of the differing persons within the Trinity (Jn 14:11; 1 Cor 2:10–11).[54] Just as each person of the Trinity dwells in and perfectly donates Himself to the others, so too creation's eternal rest will be granted by a loving act of divine indwelling (Rv 21:3).

Thus, the *diastasis* of space and the movement of time provide an eschatological depth dimension within which the life of faith is lived out through trust in the Word. The *diastasis* of space and time possesses two aspects in the relationship between faith and the Word. There is the distance between

---

52. *Lectures on Galatians*, 1535 (AE 26: 322–23; WA 40/1:500).

53. Balthasar, *Theo-Drama* 5:91–95.

54. See a brief explanation of *perichoresis* in Alister McGrath, *Christian Theology: An Introduction* (Oxford: Blackwell, 2001), 325; and Roderick T. Leupp, *The Renewal of Trinitarian Theology: Themes, Patterns & Explorations* (Downers Grove, IL: InterVarsity Press, 1995), 70–75.

the divine and human subjects. Faith must have an object in the other. Such a "distance" is of course analogical insofar as God is infinite and therefore omnipresent: "for 'in him we live and move and have our being'" (Acts 17:28). This relationship is mediated through the divine Word of address as Law and Gospel, wherein the divine speaking subject operates upon the hearing and responsive human subject. Likewise, there is an ultimate fulfillment of the divine-human relationship in the movement of time. This fulfillment is prefigured in the six days of creation culminating in humanity's participation in God's indwelling presence and heavenly rest (Hebrews 3–4). The full and unmediated revelation of God's being (*Deus nudus*) remains "distant" in the future.

THE WORD OF GOD AND DIVINE HIDDENNESS

The analogical distance between God and His creatures manifests itself not merely in the ontic distinction between divine and human subjects but also in the barrier of divine hiddenness. Prior to the eschatological fulfillment of creation God's being is disclosed to humans paradoxically as simultaneously hidden and revealed (*Deus absconditus, Deus revelatus*). As Luther states in *The Bondage of the Will* (1525),[55] faith presupposes a dimension of hiddenness. God as the object of human faith and trust must not be simply other than His creatures. That is to say, God's hiddenness goes beyond the fact that He is ontologically distinct from His creation. Likewise, this quality goes beyond the fact that God is incomprehensible and transcendent, a fact agreed upon by all creedally orthodox Christian theologians. Rather, for Luther, God must actively hide from His creatures in order to make room for faith: "In order that there may be room for faith, it is necessary that everything which is believed should be hidden."[56]

Luther recognized that in Scripture God hides Himself in two distinct ways. The British church historian B. A. Gerrish refers to these two distinct forms of God's hiddenness as Hiddenness 1 and Hiddenness 2.[57] According to Hiddenness 1 God hides in the event of revelation, particularly in the cross. Although Gerrish does not discuss it at much length, as we will see below Luther also speaks of God adopting other creaturely covering in His act of revelation.

For this reason the Word of God is necessary for the relationship of faith. Although the Word of God certainly does give propositional information about

55. For a discussion of *The Bondage of the Will* and the debate with Erasmus, see the following sources: Gerhard Forde, *The Captivation of the Will: Luther vs. Erasmus on Freedom and Bondage*, ed. Steven Paulson (Grand Rapids: Wm. B. Eerdmans, 2005); Robert Kolb, *Bound Choice, Election, and the Wittenberg Theological Method: From Martin Luther to the Formula of Concord* (Grand Rapids: Wm. B. Eerdmans, 2005), 11–66.

56. *Bondage of the Will*, 1525 (AE 33:62; WA 18:632).

57. B. A. Gerrish, "To the Unknown God: Luther and Calvin on the Hiddenness of God," *Journal of Religion* 53 (1973): 263–93.

God to the believing subject, most importantly it directs the believer to the promise (*promissio*) of God's action in, under, and through His creaturely masks (*larva Dei*). Faith ascertains that God is present and active within the creaturely covering. The believing subject gains access to the knowledge of God present under the covering by passively hearing and trusting in God's Word concerning His activity within this covering.

As a result the passive life of faith (*vita passiva*) is different than the active life based on vision. Vision is active insofar as it sees, analyzes, and acts upon the sensory object before it. Faith passively hears and trusts in the object of faith, which it can only hear but not see. As Luther observes in the Great Galatians commentary (1535): "Thus faith is a sort of knowledge or *darkness that nothing can see*. Yet the Christ of whom faith takes hold is sitting in this darkness as God sat in the midst of darkness on Sinai and in the temple."[58] Elsewhere Luther observes: "The ears alone are the organs of a Christian."[59]

For Luther, Hiddenness 1 pertains not only to the means of grace operative within the order of the church but also to the whole of creation. As Luther writes: "The whole creation is a face or mask of God" (*larva Dei*).[60] This is particularly the case in the state of integrity, when Adam and Eve perfectly believed God's Word and therefore enjoyed His perpetual bounty communicated to them through the medium of the whole of the created order.

As Paul asserts: "For his [God's] invisible attributes, namely, his eternal power and divine nature, have been clearly perceived . . . *in the things that have been made*" (Rom 1:20; emphasis added). Seen from this perspective, creatures as means through which God manifests His goodness to His creatures are analogous to the visible words (*verbum visibile*) of the sacraments. Borrowing from Augustine's definition of sacraments (*sacramentum*),[61] Luther speaks in the Large Catechism of sacraments as concrete and visible elements to which God attaches a Word.[62] In the sacraments of the New Testament, the word of promise that attaches to the visible elements (bread, wine, water) conveys the presence of the risen Christ and His mediation of salvation to sinners. Nevertheless, even in the state of integrity and subsequently in the kingdom of the world outside the means of grace, God also attaches words to His creatures in order to inform believers what created goods He wishes to mediate to them. All goods within creation are the result of God's speech and activity. Trust in God and obedience to His commandments means abiding by God's Word concerning when and where He will communicate the good. In this regard Luther observes: "We need the wisdom that distinguishes God from his mask [i.e., creature]. . . . When a greedy man, who worships his belly, hears that 'man does not live by bread alone, but by every Word that proceeds from the mouth of God' (Matt. 4:4) he

---

58. *Lectures on Galatians*, 1535 (AE 26:129–30; WA 40/1:229); emphasis added.
59. *Lectures on Hebrews*, 1517–18 (AE 29:224; WA 57/3:221).
60. *Lectures on Galatians*, 1535 (AE 26:95; WA 40/1:173–75).
61. Augustine, *Tractates in the Gospel of John*, 80.3; NPNFa 7:344.
62. LC IV (Bente, 737).

eats the bread but fails to see God in the bread; for he sees, admires, and adores only the mask."[63]

Luther explicates this notion in a number of places. One of the most interesting and provocative examples in Luther's writings can be found in the Genesis commentary of the 1530s. In one passage Luther takes it upon himself to defend a medieval heretical group known as the Anthropomorphites. According to Luther this group insisted that God must be spoken of as having "eyes, ears, arms."[64] God, says Luther, must be referred to in this manner because "it is . . . insane to argue about God and the divine nature without the *Word or any covering.*"[65] When God reveals Himself, He covers Himself and presents Himself in, under, and with the creaturely medium of His revelation:

> When God reveals Himself to us, it is necessary for Him to do so through some such *veil or wrapper* and say: "Look! *Under this wrapper* you will be sure to *take hold of Me.*" When *we embrace the wrapper*, adoring, praying, and sacrificing to God there, we are said to be praying to God and sacrificing to Him properly.[66]

Therefore, speculates Luther, before the Fall Adam and Eve would have been free from the danger of idolatry and would have used creation as a medium through which to receive and worship God: "Our first parents worshiped God early in the morning, when the sun was rising, *by marveling at the Creator in the creature* or, to express myself more clearly, because they were urged on by the creature."[67]

One should not seek God above these wrappers, maintains Luther, because this is "insane."[68] Indeed, "those who want to reach God apart from these coverings exert themselves to ascend to heaven without ladders . . . Overwhelmed by his [God's] majesty, which they seek to comprehend without coverings, they fall to their destruction."[69] The wrapper still covers over God, and His presence remains unrecognized "without the Word."[70] Because God is covered by a wrapper and comprehended through His Word alone, the believer must accept the dissonance between vision (the sight of the covering or wrapper) and the Word which gives the knowledge of God within.

There is thus no such thing as a bare Word from God. God always speaks His Word in reference to some material thing. In *That These Words of Christ, "This Is My Body," Etc., Still Stand Firm Against the Fanatics* (1527), Luther himself make this observation over and against his early Reformed opponents when dealing with the issue of the validity of the sacraments:

---

63. *Lectures on Galatians*, 1535 (AE 26:95; WA 40/1:173).
64. *Lectures on Genesis*, 1535–45 (AE 1:14; WA 42:12).
65. *Lectures on Genesis*, 1535–45 (AE 1:13; WA 42:11); emphasis added.
66. *Lectures on Genesis*, 1535–45 (AE 1:15; WA 42:12); emphasis added.
67. *Lectures on Genesis*, 1535–45 (AE 1:15; WA 42:13); emphasis added.
68. *Lectures on Genesis*, 1535–45 (AE 1:13; WA 42:11).
69. *Lectures on Genesis*, 1535–45 (AE 1:14; WA 42:11).
70. *Lectures on Genesis*, 1535–45 (AE 1:13; WA 42:11).

God . . . sets before us no word or commandment without including with it something material and outward, and proffering it to us. To Abraham he gave the word including with it his son Isaac [Gen. 15:4ff.]. To Saul he gave the word including with it the slaying of the Amalekites [1 Sam. 15:2f.]. And so on. You find no word of God in the entire Scripture in which something material and outward is not contained and presented. If we followed the fanatical spirits, we have to say that all these material, outward things were of no avail and simply nothing.[71]

Luther's argument regarding the necessity of the sacramental mediation of God's Word and presence has much support elsewhere in the Bible. Luther was particularly fond of making reference to Moses' encounter with YHWH on Mt. Sinai.[72] As may be recalled, it was initially God's intention to address Israel directly at the foot of the mountain and not through the use of a mediator. In Exodus 20 He does so by speaking the Ten Commandments directly to those gathered there. The Israelites are so horrified by the sound of God's own voice that they insist Moses ascend the mountain and receive the Law on their behalf. We are told that Moses enters into a dark cloud and speaks with God. Later, after the apostasy with the golden calf, Moses returns to speak with YHWH and wishes to see His face (Exodus 33). God warns Moses that no one can see His face and live, but He will permit him to see His "back" (Vulgate: *posteriora*),[73] or as Luther translates it, "hindquarters" (*hintennach*). Even though Moses does not see God's face directly, he still glows with the divine glory (בָּבוֹד). As a result, the prophet is forced to wear a covering when reading to the assembly of Israel the divine commandments delivered to him on Sinai. Israel can only hear God's Word; they cannot look upon God's transcendent glory without a covering and an audible word (Exodus 34).

Ultimately this encounter between God and His creatures through the Word and under a covering finds its greatest fulfillment in the incarnation and work of Christ.[74] In discussing the divine hiddenness in the incarnation, the young Luther contrasts what he referred to as the theology of glory (*theologia gloriae*) with the theology of the cross (*theologia crucis*). In the Heidelberg Disputation (1518) Luther distinguishes between two different sorts of theologians: theologians of glory and theologians of the cross.[75] Regarding the theologian of glory Luther writes:

---

71. *That These Words of Christ, "This Is My Body," Etc., Still Stand Firm Against the Fanatics,* 1527 (AE 37:135–36; WA 23:261–62).

72. *Lectures on Genesis,* 1535–45 (AE 7:103; WA 44:375).

73. *"Tollamque manum meam et videbis posteriora mea faciem autem meam videre non poteris"* (Ex 33:23, Vulgate). Also referred to obliquely in *Heidelberg Disputation,* 1518 (AE 31:52; WA 1:354): *"Visibilia et posteriora Dei."*

74. See a similar discussion in Jack Kilcrease, *The Self-Donation of God: A Contemporary Lutheran Approach to Christ and His Benefits* (Eugene, OR: Wipf & Stock, 2013), 105–10.

75. See the following books on the subject: Walther von Loewenich, *Luthers Theologia Crucis* (München: Kaiser Verlag, 1954); Herman Sasse, "The Theology of the Cross," in *We Confess Anthology,* trans. Norman Nagel (St. Louis: Concordia Publishing House, 1998), 35–45.

> That person does not deserve to be called a theologian who looks upon the "invisible" things of God as though they were clearly "perceptible in those things which have actually happened (Rom. 1:20)" [or the more correct translation: "things that are made";[76] cf. 1 Cor 1:21–25]. This is apparent in the example of those who were "theologians" and still were called "fools" by the Apostle in Rom 1:[22]. Furthermore, the invisible things of God are virtue, godliness, wisdom, justice, goodness, and so forth. The recognition of all these things does not make one worthy or wise.[77]

In other words, the theologian of glory looks to God apart from His Word and speculates about Him on the basis of His glorious attributes as they are visibly manifest in and through the coverings of His mighty works of creation (Psalm 19; Romans 1). By observing and identifying with God's hidden power and glory as it is manifested in the temporal realm, the theologian of glory believes that he may enter into fellowship with God through analogously embodying that glory. This quest to embody the divine glory may take the form of knowledge of the divine being or glorious external works that embody divine righteousness.

Note that Luther does not claim the theologian of glory does not have (from a purely epistemic perspective) a valid knowledge of God: "Yet that wisdom is not of itself evil, nor is the law to be evaded; but without the theology of the cross man misuses the best in the worst manner."[78] Rather, the Reformer's criticism is that by attempting to echo the divine being through knowing (that is, knowing God's transcendent glory) and doing (that is, mighty external deeds of righteousness), the theologian of glory seeks deification by becoming like God in His glory. He abuses the knowledge of God's glory he possesses, and through it becomes conceited.[79]

By contrast, the theologian of the cross holds to the flesh of Jesus where God is real and present in an absolute sense. Nevertheless, God's full and absolute presence is hidden in suffering and weakness, something seemingly in contradiction to His glorious nature:

> The manifest and visible things of God are placed in opposition to the invisible, namely, his human nature, weakness, foolishness. The Apostle in 1 Cor. 1:25 calls them the weakness and folly of God. Because men misused the knowledge of God through works, God wished again to be recognized in suffering, and to condemn "wisdom concerning invisible things" by means of "wisdom concerning visible things," so that those who did not honor God as manifested in his works should honor him as he is hidden in his suffering (*absconditum in passionibus*). As the Apostle says in 1 Cor. 1:21, "For since, in the wisdom of God, the world did not know God through wisdom, it pleased God through the folly of what we preach to save those who believe." Now it is not sufficient for anyone, and it does him

---

76. Kurt Marquart, "Luther and Theosis," *Concordia Theological Quarterly* 64 no. 3 (2000): 195. This is a strange translation, not only because it is grammatically incorrect and because it is obviously a quote from Rom 1:20 (which is cited), but because, as Marquart points out, it makes no sense in terms of Luther's obvious intention.

77. *Heidelberg Disputation*, 1518 (AE 31:52; WA 1:354).

78. *Heidelberg Disputation*, 1518 (AE 31:55; WA 1:363).

79. *Heidelberg Disputation*, 1518 (AE 31:53; WA 1:362).

no good to recognize God in his glory and majesty, unless he recognizes him in the humility and shame of the cross. Thus God destroys the wisdom of the wise, as Isa. 45:15 says, "Truly, thou art a God who hidest thyself." So, also, in John 14:8, where Philip spoke according to the theology of glory: "Show us the Father." Christ forthwith set aside his flighty thought about seeing God elsewhere and led him to himself, saying, "Philip, he who has seen me has seen the Father" (John 14:9). For this reason true theology and recognition of God are in the crucified Christ, as it is also stated in John 10 (John 14:6), "No one comes to the Father, but by me." "I am the door" (John 10:9), and so forth.[80]

In other words, the theologian of glory tries to become like God through corresponding to His eternal glory. By contrast, the theologian of the cross becomes a receptive and hearing creature through the Word of the cross. As Isaiah foretold, there was nothing attractive to ordinary human vision about the crucified Jesus (Is 53:2). Neither does His visible manifestation in weakness and condemnation give Him the appearance of the almighty God, who is defined by His attributes of glory, power, and righteousness.

Moreover, the knowledge of Christ comes by hearing and not by vision, that is, the "preaching" of the cross mentioned by Paul. Luther's point here is not that God's being becomes transparent in the cross; this is a mistake commonly made by modern proponents of the theology of the cross.[81] Many argue that the cross reveals a God who is vulnerable and capable of suffering in and of Himself. In contrast to this, Luther argues that God in Himself, apart from any covering, is in fact glorious and powerful, a fact ascertainable by His self-revelation in the glorious works of creation and His self-testimony in Scripture. Nevertheless, Luther insists that God is completely and wholly present in the cross, yet utterly "hidden in . . . suffering."[82] Again, we do not see God but only hear the Word, just as the Israelites could only look on Moses' veil and hear the Word.

Nevertheless, in the case of the incarnation, God does not just make a covering but in fact covers Himself with His very opposite (*sub contrario*) in order to humble the pride of sinners. By nature, theologians of glory wish to see and thus correspond to His eternal glory through their works and knowledge rather than by humbly and graciously receiving Him under the coverings and wrappers He has ordained.[83] Luther writes in *The Bondage of the Will*: "Thus God hides his eternal goodness and mercy under eternal wrath, his righteousness under iniquity. This is the highest degree of faith, to believe him merciful when he saves so few and damns so many, and to believe him righteous when by his own will he makes us necessarily damnable."[84] Regarding this humble receptivity of faith Luther writes: "I myself was offended more than

---

80. *Heidelberg Disputation*, 1518 (AE 31:52–53; WA 1:362).
81. The most glaring example of this is Jürgen Moltmann, *The Crucified God: The Cross of Christ as the Foundation and Criticism of Christian Theology*, trans. R. A. Wilson and John Bowden (Minneapolis: Fortress Press, 1993).
82. *Heidelberg Disputation*, 1518 (AE 31:52–53; WA 1:362).
83. *Bondage of the Will*, 1525 (AE 33:61; WA 18:632).
84. *Bondage of the Will*, 1525 (AE 33:62; WA 18:633).

once, and brought to the very depth and abyss of despair, so that I wished I had never been created a man, before I realized how salutary that despair was, and how near I was to grace."[85] As Luther realized, faith and receptivity to the divine Word are the proper stance of the creature in relation to divine hiddenness.

Although God's action on His creatures through words and coverings takes its most complete and profound form in the Word of the cross (1 Cor 1:18), this has nevertheless been His mode of interaction with His creatures from the beginning. In Genesis 1 God attaches the word "very good" to all He has made. Likewise, in His address to Adam and Eve in the same chapter we read that "God blessed them. And God said to them, 'Be fruitful and multiply and fill the earth and subdue it and have dominion over the fish of the sea and over the birds of the heavens and over every living thing that moves on the earth'" (Gn 1:28). Later God promises Adam: "You may surely eat of every tree of the garden" (Gn 2:16). In these cases God attaches a word of promise that He will channel specific goods to our first parents through their dominion in creation, their fertility, and their consumption of the fruits of the garden.[86] Later, in addressing Noah and his sons, God attaches a word to all animals that they will now be a means through which humans can feed and sustain themselves in the post-diluvian age (Gn 9:2–3). Still later He attaches a word through the distinction of clean and unclean animals given to Israel (Leviticus 11). Finally, in the era of the New Testament God again attaches a word of promise to unclean animals that they are now clean: "Rise, Peter; kill and eat" (Acts 10:13).

With regard to God's institution of the orders of creation, this phenomenon can also be seen in God's institution of the orders of family and the state. In Genesis 2, when God brings together the man and the woman we are assured that through marriage and its consummation "they shall become one flesh" (Gn 2:24). Jesus further explicates this by stating, "So they are no longer two but one flesh. What therefore God has joined together, let not man separate" (Mk 10:8–9). In giving the Ten Commandments God gives a promise of life to those who obey their parents (Ex 20:12), and by extension to those who exercise civil authority (Romans 13, etc.).[87]

Seen from the perspective of the mediated nature of God's interaction with creation, the Ten Commandments take on a new character. As we have previously observed, Scripture tells us that the root of all righteousness is faith in God's Word. In his discussion of the Ten Commandments in the Large Catechism Luther observes that the First Commandment possesses the character of both Law and Gospel. A god, states Luther, is anything in which we put our trust. God bids us put our trust in Him because He is the author

---

85. *Bondage of the Will*, 1525 (AE 33:190; WA 18:719).
86. Oswald Bayer, "Worship and Theology," in *Worship and Ethics: Lutherans and Anglicans in Dialogue*, ed. Oswald Bayer and Alan Suggate (New York: Walter de Gruyter, 1996), 149.
87. LC 1.4 (Bente, 621). Luther writes: "In this commandment belongs a further statement regarding all kinds of obedience to persons in authority who have to command and to govern. For all authority flows and is propagated from the authority of parents."

of the good. In our sin we may be tempted to think that creatures themselves are authors of the good, but this is false. Instead, God mediates the good to us through the channels of His creatures, and thereby reveals Himself as the singular proper object of our total and unconditional trust.

> For even though otherwise we experience much good from men, still whatever we receive by His command or arrangement is all received from God. For our parents, and all rulers, and everyone besides with respect to his neighbor, have received from God the command that they should do us all manner of good, so that we receive these blessings not from them, *but, through them,* from God. For creatures *are only the hands, channels, and means whereby God gives all things,* as He gives to the mother breasts and milk to offer to her child, and corn and all manner of produce from the earth for nourishment, none of which blessings could be produced by any creature of itself.[88]

There is a clear difference between the believer who trustingly receives God's goodness through the created "channels" and the unbeliever who thinks the channel is the source of the good in and of itself, thereby making it into an idol. God testifies in His Word that He is the author and communicator of the good in, under, and through the channels. Objectively, the word and the visible created elements together convey to the believer the benefits given by God, much like in the sacraments of the New Testament.

As Luther observes, the First Commandment is also a word of Law insofar as it commands us to trust in God and promises retribution if we trust in creatures instead of the Creator as the author of the good. For this reason faith fulfills the Law: "with respect to the First Commandment, which we have had to explain at length, since it is of chief importance, because, as before said, where the heart is rightly disposed toward God and this commandment is observed, *all the others follow.*"[89] Faith fulfills the whole Law by trusting in God's promise of the good and by fleeing idols.

The implication seems to be that not only does the obedience of faith act out of gratitude for God's gifts, it also recognizes the manner in which creatures communicate the good as God's "hands, channels, and means." The believer recognizes when and where God desires to mediate a specific good: He has attached a word of promise and command so that His hearing and responsible creatures may find a particular good in that specific place.

Creatures are given the gifts of God even if they receive these gifts in an unbelieving manner (Mt 5:45). Nevertheless, in receiving these gifts without faith and gratitude they call down God's wrath upon themselves (Romans 1, etc.). In the same manner the sacraments of the New Testament are also objective insofar as the reality of the sacraments adheres to the visible sign.

---

88. LC I.1 (Bente, 587); emphasis added.
89. LC I.1 (Bente, 593); emphasis added.

Nevertheless, he who receives them without faith "eats and drinks . . . judgment on himself" (1 Cor 11:29).[90]

Beyond the fact that humans are ungrateful in their reception of the good, they also disobey God when they seek the good apart from God Himself and the means through which He has promised it: "Learn, therefore, from these words how angry God is with those who trust in anything but Him, and again, how good and gracious He is to those who trust and believe in Him alone with the whole heart."[91] For example, in establishing the order of marriage (Gn 1:28; 2:24), God promised that He will channel the good through the committed relationship between a man and woman. Seen in this light, what the Sixth Commandment condemns is unbelief. Sinners do not believe in God's promise with regard to where the goods connected with marriage are to be found. In their unbelief, fallen humans pursue other forms of sexual activity apart from marriage between a man and a woman. They thereby attempt to gain some of the goods of marriage (i.e., children, companionship, sexual fulfillment, etc.) apart from the channel to which God has attached His word of promise. In this, sinful humans rely on their own inner faculties to discern the good and its location. In their unbelief they seek the good where God has placed nothing but a promise of His destructive wrath. Such divine wrath manifests itself both through the logical and natural consequences of bad behavior within the structure of the present creational order (*ius naturale*; the major theme of the book of Proverbs), as well as through God's eternal condemnation at the end of time (1 Cor 6:9; Rv 22:15).

All of this clarifies what Luther means when he states at the beginning of his explanation of each commandment that we should "fear and love God so that we . . ." In fearing God, the believer recognizes and heeds the word of wrath attached to circumventing the means God has established to communicate the good. In faith the believer flees from this wrath to the place where God has promised to share the gifts of creation. In this manner the person of faith finds God and His grace in, with, and under the means He has established through His Word to communicate the good. Having received the good through the means God has ordained, the person of faith loves Him out of gratitude (1 Jn 4:19).

From the beginning of creation the pattern of the temporal life of faith is shaped by flight from God's wrath to the place of His Word of grace. The situation in the state of integrity was in fact no different, because God placed within the Garden of Eden both the tree of life and the tree of the knowledge of good and evil (Gn 2:9). Adam and Eve were meant to flee from the tree of the knowledge of good and evil to God's grace and goodness as manifested in the

---

90. See commentary on this verse in R. C. H. Lenski, *The Interpretation of St. Paul's First and Second Epistles to the Corinthians* (Peabody, MA: Hendrickson Publishers, 1998), 480–83; Gregory Lockwood, *1 Corinthians* (St. Louis: Concordia Publishing House, 2000), 408.

91. LC I.1 (Bente, 589).

tree of life and the other trees. In these wrappers God manifested His goodness and grace by attaching to them His words "very good" and "you may eat" in order to designate them as channels of the good. Likewise, Israel was bidden not to approach Sinai due to the manifestation of God's wrath (Exodus 19–20). Instead it was exhorted to approach God's gracious and forgiving presence in the tabernacle. In the era of the New Testament humanity is bidden to flee from the coming judgment to the grace found in the Word and Sacrament ministry of the church (Acts 2:38–40).

This brings us to the second dimension of divine hiddenness, which B. A. Gerrish refers to as Hiddenness 2. God and His goodness are indiscernible apart from the "Word or any covering."[92] This is the case not only because it is impossible to see past the wrappers or words God has given us and into His hidden being (*Deus ipse*), but because God manifests Himself in seemingly (though not actually) contradictory ways through His masks (*larva Dei*). In one place He attaches His word of Law and condemnation (as in the government, for example in Romans 13). In other spheres of His activity He promises His unconditional love and grace (as in the Word and Sacrament ministry of the visible church). Again, such a situation obtained in the state of integrity with the distinction between the tree of life and the tree of the knowledge of good and evil.

Hence, prior to the eschatological fulfillment of creation God hides under masks, some of which are Law and others grace. Although God binds Himself to act according to the Law and the Gospel when He is encountered in any of these specific masks, He may move and change in which masks He wishes to interact with His creatures in accordance with His hidden electing will: "There is no god beside me; I kill and I make alive; I wound and I heal" (Dt 32:39; also see 1 Sm 2:6; Isaiah 45). This is the case because He is free and unbound as He exists above and beyond these masks. As Luther writes in *The Bondage of the Will*: "But God hidden in his majesty neither deplores nor takes away death, but works life, death and all in all. *For there he has not bound himself by his word, but has kept himself free over all things*."[93] Indeed, God's electing and free nature is shown in His proper name: "I will be who I will be" (Ex 3:14; my translation). God more clearly explains this to Moses when He proclaims His name before him on Sinai: "I will make all my goodness pass before you and will proclaim before you my name 'The Lord' [a condensation of "I will be who I will be"]. *And I will be gracious to whom I will be gracious, and will show mercy on whom I will show mercy*" (Ex 33:19; emphasis added).

Apart from God's grace, humans typically attempt to rationalize exhaustively all of God's actions according to the rubric of the Law (*opinio legis*). They assume that if they are obedient to God or to whatever idols they have set up in the place of the true God, they will be able to coerce God into being

---

92. *Lectures on Genesis*, 1535–45 (AE 1:13; WA 42:11).
93. *Bondage of the Will*, 1525 (AE 33:140; WA 18:684); emphasis added.

gracious to them. In *The Bondage of the Will* Luther describes these persons as existing under the light of nature (*lumen naturae*).[94] Since these individuals think of themselves as righteous, their experiences give rise to the quest of theodicy: "Why do bad things happen to good people?"[95] What they come to recognize only under the light of grace (*lumen gratiae*) with the revelation of original sin (Romans 5) is that there are no "good" people.[96]

In the meantime, the more thoughtful individuals among the unregenerate conclude either that God is uninvolved in the world (Epicureans, Deists)[97] or that because He does not properly reward righteousness He does not exist at all (atheists). They thus reveal their divine ambition (*ambitio divinitatis*). Instead of God being the communicator of the good and humans the passive receivers of it, humans generate the good through their works which God passively receives. Likewise, in the minds of those who operate within the *lumen naturae*, it is God who must justify Himself before human beings through His righteousness, rather than humans who must justify themselves before the bar of God's Law. Hence Luther's proper definition of theology ("the sinning human being and the justifying God"[98]) reverses itself.

The mystery of divine hiddenness nevertheless remains even for those regenerated by faith in the Gospel. Although the revelation of original sin and its logical corollary of divine wrath makes sense of temporal human suffering and ultimately damnation, the logic of God's electing grace remains a mystery (Rom 11:33). Indeed, although the Law is God's eternal and immutable will for His creatures (*lex aeterna*),[99] God's wrathful and gracious activities in creation cannot be reduced to the structure of the Law. As Luther observes, God does not merely judge non-compliance with the Law but propagates the human species in such a way as to spread original sin to each and every person.[100] Each person is fated to be a sinner from conception, and therefore also an object of divine wrath (Ps 51:5; Jer 13:23; Romans 5; Eph 2:3). Moreover, despite the universality of original sin, the Law of wrath and judgment is applied unevenly. Some are elected and saved, and others are not (Rom 8:29–30; 9:11; Eph 1:4–5, 11–12; 1 Pt 1:20).

Luther argues that the paradox of God's condemning and gracious electing activities within creation will be resolved only in the light of glory (*lumen gloria*) after the last judgment.[101] Here the distance of time mentioned earlier, like the

---

94. *Bondage of the Will*, 1525 (AE 33:289–92; WA 18:784–85).

95. See the most sophisticated versions of this attempt in Gottfried von Leibniz, *Theodicy*, trans. E. M. Huggard (New York: Cosmo Classics, 2010).

96. *Bondage of the Will*, 1525 (AE 33:291; WA 18:785).

97. *Bondage of the Will*, 1525 (AE 33:291; WA 18:785). See literary version of this view in Voltaire, *Candide* (New York: Dover Publications, 1991).

98. *Commentary on Psalm 51*, 1532 (AE 12:311; WA 40.2:328). Cited from Bayer, *Martin Luther's Theology*, 37.

99. See SD III (Bente, 935). Also see *Antinomian Disputations* (WA 39/1:348).

100. See *Bondage of the Will*, 1525 (AE 33:174–77; WA 18:706–10).

101. *Bondage of the Will*, 1525 (AE 33:292; WA 18:785).

distance of space, also serves as a horizon of divine hiddenness. In the light of glory the veil of God's masks will be taken away and we will see Him and His truth "face to face" (1 Cor 13:12). Just as the transition from the *lumen naturae* to the *lumen gratiae* was marked by the simple solution to the philosophical problem of human suffering in the reality of original sin (i.e., all have sinned so all deserve suffering), we likewise will find an easy solution to the problem of election.[102] Nevertheless, until the dawn of the *lumen gloriae* one can find God's Word of grace attached to the concrete reality of the Word and Sacrament ministry of the church. Since God has placed His Word of grace there, we can be absolutely certain we have God's favor when we cling to the means of grace and flee from the terrible wrath of *Deus absconditus*.[103]

Returning to the state of integrity, one can discern the same situation in Eden. As we have previously observed, in the original creation uncorrupted by sin, humans righteously believed in every audible word that God attached to the visible coverings and wrappers of His creatures. Trusting in God and His Word, they were perpetually enveloped in God's gracious address to them. Their default experience of God was not, as with fallen humans, the perpetual condemnation under the Law (*das Urerlebnis*, Rom 1:18).[104] Nevertheless, divine hiddenness was still a reality for them. Hiddenness 1 existed insofar as God used the medium of His audible and visible words as a cover to interact with them in the garden. Moreover, although Hiddenness 2 was not their normal experience of God, it still lay for them as a possibility beyond the barrier of the tree of the knowledge of good and evil. Outside of the barrier presented by the commandment not to eat from this tree lay the possibility of encountering the hidden God. In their unbelief they would fall under God's wrath and also become deaf to the promises He had attached to His creatures.

According to Luther in his Genesis commentary, obeying the command not to eat from the tree of the knowledge of good and evil would have functioned as an act of worship and devotion: "Only this he [God] wants: that he [Adam] praise God, that he thank him, that he rejoice in the Lord, and that he obey him by not eating from the forbidden tree."[105] In describing the tree of the knowledge of good and evil as such, the Reformer goes on to speculate that the tree itself was not a single tree but more like a grove of trees that could have served as a

102. *Bondage of the Will*, 1525 (AE 33:291; WA 18:785). For a discussion of election in the Lutheran Confessions, see SD XI (Bente, 1063–95).

103. *Bondage of the Will*, 1525 (AE 33:291; WA 18:785). Also see comments in Bayer, *Martin Luther's Theology*, 213.

104. See description of the *Urerlebnis* in Werner Elert, *The Structure of Lutheranism: The Theology and Philosophy of Life of Lutheranism, Especially in the Sixteenth and Seventeenth Centuries*, vol. 1, trans. Walter Hansen (St. Louis: Concordia Publishing House, 1962), 17–28. Also see Gustaf Wingren, *Creation and Law*, trans. Ross McKenzie (Philadelphia: Muhlenberg Press, 1961), 174. Wingren observes about fallen humanity: "We might say that man's conscience has a continual foretaste of the Last Judgment."

105. *Lectures on Genesis*, 1535–45 (AE 1:106; WA 42:81).

chapel.[106] Adam and his descendants would have gathered together and Adam would have preached on the divine Word given to him that prohibited the consumption of fruit from the tree.[107] In this way the pattern of later Christian worship and proclamation was also established: fleeing from the place of God's condemnation to His Word of grace.

It is important to observe that the Word and Sacrament ministry of the church began even in the state of integrity. According to Luther, in giving the commandment not to eat from the tree God also thereby established the office of the ministry. In Gn 2:15–17 Adam is given the Word of God prior to the creation of Eve. Since, as the Reformer observes, the text does not indicate that the Word was given a second time to the woman, it necessarily follows that Eve received the Word of God from Adam. Eve thus functioned as the first church, whereas her husband occupied the role of the first minister of the Word: "Adam alone heard it [the command not to eat from the tree of the knowledge of good and evil], he later informed Eve of it. If they had not fallen into sin, Adam would have transmitted this single command later to their descendants."[108]

As can be observed from this account, the giving of the Word has always been associated with the establishment of the office of the ministry.[109] Contrary to the assumption of much of Anglo-American Evangelicalism, the Word of God is not an abstract authority, unembedded from the concrete life and history of the order of the church and therefore given over to the capricious private interpretation of individuals. Rather, the Word of God is properly understood only when read, studied, and proclaimed in the sphere of the church as constituted by a Word and Sacrament ministry centering on the unconditional promise of the Gospel. Although this pattern does not establish an infallible institutional church ministry as is supposed in Roman Catholicism, it nevertheless means that the locus of proclaiming, interpreting, and testing the Word occurs in or in relation to the ministry of Word and Sacrament.

The establishment of the office of the ministry in the state of integrity was necessary because creation had an eschatological destiny even prior to the Fall. Luther writes in the Genesis commentary:

> But the church was established first because God wants to show by this sign, as it were, that man was created for another purpose than the rest of the living beings. Because the church is established by the Word of God, it is certain that man was created for an immortal and spiritual life, to which he would have been carried off or translated without death after living in Eden and on the rest of the earth without inconvenience as long as he wished.[110]

---

106. *Lectures on Genesis*, 1535–45 (AE 1:105; WA 42:79–80).

107. *Lectures on Genesis*, 1535–45 (AE 1:106; WA 42:80).

108. *Lectures on Genesis*, 1535–45 (AE 1:105; WA 42:80). Also see David Scaer, "Ordaining Women: Has the Time Come?" *Logia: A Journal of Lutheran Theology* 4, no. 2 (1995): 83–85.

109. Basically the point made in the CA XXVIII (Bente, 83–95).

110. *Lectures on Genesis*, 1535–45 (AE 1:104; WA 42:79).

For Luther, then, the earthly state of integrity was the first stage of God's purposes for His creation, which would be fulfilled later by the integration of humanity into heavenly existence. Even in the state of integrity, humanity at some later appointed time would have entered into heaven and thereby would have enjoyed God's eternal rest.[111]

Luther's interpretation, and much of the patristic and medieval tradition before him, has strong support in texts like Hebrews 3–4. Paul also implicitly supports this inference in his remark that Adam's prelapsarian earthly body was only a preliminary stage to the eventual reception of a spiritual body (1 Cor 15:45–46). The book of Daniel describes the final eschatological kingdom of God in terms of a great mountain filling the whole of creation. This image seems to signify the presence of God at Zion as the new Eden, expanding and giving rest to the whole of creation at the end of time (Dn 2:35).[112] Indeed, the Book of Revelation appears to echo this fulfillment prefigured in Eden and the seventh day of creation: "Behold, the dwelling place of God is with man" (Rv 21:3). In these passages we see the eschaton represented as a universal *perichoresis* of the divine presence.

Since such an eschatological fulfillment of creation transcends God's original self-giving presence in Eden, it is logical to infer that the realization of heaven on earth (God's unmediated presence) was God's original goal for His creation from the beginning. Scripture is clear that God's purposes are consistent and cannot be thwarted (Is 14:27; Prv 19:21; Jb 42:2). From this principle we can infer that even if the Fall had not occurred, God's goal for creation would have been the same.

Moreover, this eschatological destiny of creation reflects the analogical similarity to the distance and relationality within the life of the Trinity. As we saw earlier, the distance of space and time corresponds to the analogical distance between the persons within the Godhead and the "movement" of begetting and procession. Such distance and movement finally find their end in the mutual interpenetration of the differing persons of the Trinity (*perichoresis*, Jn 14:11; 1 Cor 2:10–11). In the same manner God's goal is to communicate Himself and His presence to humanity by indwelling the new creation while simultaneously maintaining His ontic distinction from it.

In this final fulfillment of creation God's self-communication will be perfected. Thus, He will require neither a word nor covering to mediate His relationship with humans. Although we now interact with God through a word and covering, "through a glass darkly," at the final fulfillment of creation the mask and covering will be taken away and we will see Him "face to face" (1 Cor 13:12). Therefore, until the final eschatological unmediated revelation of divinity (*Deus nudus*), the office of the ministry must function. For the time being,

---

111. *Lectures on Genesis*, 1535–45 (AE 1:104; WA 42:79).

112. G. K. Beale, *The Temple and the Church's Mission: A Biblical Theology of the Dwelling Place of God* (Downers Grove, IL: InterVarsity Press, 2004), 144–53.

then, we "know in part and . . . prophesy in part" (1 Cor 13:9). This incomplete knowing also applied to the state of integrity, when the two forms of divine hiddenness were already operative. Indeed, God's revelation of Himself through His Word is necessary only insofar as He is hidden: "How then will they call on him in whom they have not believed? And how are they to believe in him of whom they have never heard? And how are they to hear without someone preaching?" (Rom 10:14).

THE WORD OF GOD AND HUMAN LANGUAGE

In the light of our discussion of the revelation of the Word of God we are confronted with the relationship between the uncreated and eternal Word of God and human language. Whereas God's Word is infinite and eternal, the human words that carry the freight of God's truth are finite and created. Through many centuries Christian theologians have contemplated how God is knowable in time by His creatures.

First, we should recognize that the Bible uses diverse forms of speech to describe God. In some of the statements the Bible makes about God He is described as being, or being like, a temporal entity such as a king, a rock, or a shepherd (Ps 24:10; Dt 32:4; Ps 23:1). Many would view these statements as metaphors or similes. Nevertheless, as Luther notes, on a certain level they are actually quite literal in that God is a "spiritual king," rock, and shepherd.[113] Other statements about God are clearly literal. God's commandments are literal descriptions of His eternal statutory will. Likewise, that God is both three and one is a literal statement (Mt 28:19; Jn 1:1; 5:18; 8:58; 10:33; 2 Cor 13:14; Phil 2:2–11, etc.).

Beyond these more easily classifiable linguistic expressions, Scripture teaches that God possesses certain attributes which are described using language that does not fall strictly into a category of either literal or metaphorical speech. Taking its inspiration from the Neoplatonic philosopher Proclus in his book *The Platonic Theology*,[114] Christian theologians historically have distinguished between two sets of attributes: negative and positive.

First, the Bible defines what God is by saying what He is not, namely, a finite limited creature. This method of speaking of God is called apophatic or negative (*via negativa*).[115] When the Bible says that God is infinite and eternal (1 Kgs 8:27; Ps 90:2; Is 6:3; Acts 17:28; Rv 1:8) it speaks of God in negation of what creatures are. To say that God is infinite is really to say He is not finite. Infinity does not mean the multiplication of finitude so as to stretch on forever, but rather a negation of finitude. Likewise, to say that God is 'simple' (*simplex*)

---

113. *That These Words of Christ, "This Is My Body," Etc., Still Stand Firm Against the Fanatics*, 1527 (AE 37:171–75; WA 26:271–74).

114. See Proclus, *The Six Books of Proclus, the Platonic Successor, on the Theology of Plato*, trans. Thomas Taylor (London: A. J. Valpy, 1816).

115. See brief description in McGrath, *Christian Theology*, 188.

is only to say that God is not compounded of different attributes but in fact is His attributes.[116] It does not mean there are no positive distinctions within the being of the one God, as is sometimes claimed.[117]

Second, there is what is called kataphatic or positive theology. Kataphatic theology speaks of what God's attributes are rather than what they are not.[118] In the Bible God is called wise, good, and loving (Ps 136:1; Jb 12:13; 36:5; Rom 11:33; 1 Jn 4:8). The difficulty with these scriptural statements is that they describe God as possessing qualities that also can be found in creatures. It would be hard to argue that God, who is infinitely different from His creation, possesses these qualities in quite the same manner as His creatures.

Thus, the ontological distance between God and His creation sets up a significant dilemma for human language about God. On a pastoral level this question is not insignificant. At the heart of the Word of God are the Law and the Gospel, which are themselves rooted in the divine attributes of holiness and mercy. On the one hand, if one argues that these terms mean something entirely different when applied to God's attributes than when they are applied to creatures (equivocal), the question necessarily arises how it is possible for words to tell us much of anything meaningful about God. On the other hand, if these words mean the same thing when applied to God and to His creation (univocal), God would be dragged down to the level of His creatures.

In the history of Western Christian thought, Scripture's language about God's attributes often has been characterized as analogical. This conception often has been embedded within the structure of the larger metaphysical theory of the analogy of being (*analogia entis*) as articulated by Thomas Aquinas and the Thomistic tradition in general.[119] According to this view, God expressed His eternal qualities (goodness, wisdom, etc.) in making His creatures. God possesses such qualities absolutely and simply. That is to say, God is neither derived nor compounded of qualities, entities, or causal forces that pre-exist Him.[120] Logically, then, creatures who are dependent on God's creative activity can possesses such transcendental qualities only derivatively and analogically. There is a similitude between God and His creatures that exists within an infinite dissimilitude.[121]

---

116. See discussion of Richard Muller, *Post-Reformation Reformed Dogmatics: The Rise and Development of Reformed Orthodoxy, Ca. 1520–1720*, 4 vols. (Grand Rapids: Baker Academic, 2003), 3:38–44.

117. See example in Paul Hinlicky, *Divine Simplicity: Christ the Crisis of Metaphysics* (Grand Rapids: Baker Academic, 2016).

118. McGrath, *Christian Theology*, 188.

119. See recent treatments of the doctrine of the analogy of being in the following: Erich Przywara, *Analogia Entis: Metaphysics: Original Structure and Universal Rhythm*, trans. John Betz and David Bentley Hart (Grand Rapids: Wm. B. Eerdmans, 2013); Thomas Joseph White, ed., *The Analogy of Being: Invention of the Antichrist or the Wisdom of God?* (Grand Rapids: Wm. B. Eerdmans, 2011).

120. *ST* 1a, q. 3, art. 7; BF 2:41–47.

121. *ST* 1a, q. 13, art. 6; BF 3:67–71.

This account of the analogical relationship between uncreated and created being serves as a platform for a description of how human language can carry the freight of God's infinite incomprehensibility. When we apply creaturely predicates to God (goodness, wisdom, power, etc.), such language can function only analogically.[122] In other words, God can be spoken of as "wise" only as long as the theologian understands that when Scripture applies this word to God, it is within a larger framework of a similarity within an infinitely greater dissimilarity. Analogy therefore represents a dialectic of affirmation and negation. The similarity between God and creatures is an affirmation, whereas their infinite dissimilarity is a negation.[123]

As Robert Preus correctly observes, the question of analogy can be broken down into two different aspects.[124] The first question is about the relationship between God's being and those finite creatures He has made. This might be described as the ontological or metaphysical question. On this level it is difficult for Christian theology to deny in a broad sense what Thomistic tradition teaches: God is properly what His creatures are secondarily and by derivation. God is wisdom itself, and creatures are wise only insofar as they mirror God's wisdom. Moreover, it is undeniable that God is like His creation in some ways, and unlike it in other ways.[125]

Preus observes that the second question regarding analogy is a linguistic one. That is to say, when the human words of the Bible speak specifically of God's attributes, they display these attributes by means of similarity (affirmation) and infinite dissimilarity (negation) with those attributes. Of course, much of the language of Scripture about God is undeniably analogical. An example of this can be found in discussions of the Trinity. Although Luther was often cautious in his late trinitarian disputations about suggesting that there could be any exact analogy between the Trinity and creaturely existence,[126] even he was forced to admit in a number of later sermons on the same doctrine that analogy must be used in the same manner that a father stammers so that his small children can understand him.[127] The "persons" of the Trinity and their relations with one another (i.e., begetting, procession) are clearly neither univocal or equivocal terms, but analogical. Therefore, the question we seek to answer is narrower: is analogy an appropriate way to describe divine attributes?

122. *ST* 1a, q. 13, art. 1–6; BF 3:47–71.

123. See a good summary of Aquinas's position in Richard Cross, "Duns Scotus and Suarez at the Origins of Modernity" in *Deconstructing Radical Orthodoxy: Post-Modern Theology, Rhetoric, and Truth*, ed. Wayne Hankey and Douglas Hedley (Burlington, VT: Ashgate Publishing, 2005), 67–68.

124. Preus, *The Theology of Post-Reformation Lutheranism* 2:43–44.

125. See observation in Paul Hinlicky, *Beloved Community: Critical Dogmatics after Christendom* (Grand Rapids: Wm. B. Eerdmans, 2015), 74–75.

126. Christine Helmer, *The Trinity and Martin Luther* (Bellingham, WA: Lexham Press, 2017), 101–3.

127. Helmer, *The Trinity and Martin Luther*, 239–41.

In order to answer this question we will build on the framework discussed previously of Luther's Hiddenness 1 and Hiddenness 2. First, as we have already shown, Luther in his Genesis and Galatians commentaries asserts that God interacts with His creatures only through other creatures. God does not confront His creatures according to His naked reality (*Deus nudus*), but in, under, and through various masks (*larva*) and wrappers (Hiddenness 1). Indeed, it is a key biblical and confessional principle that we never encounter God apart from means. In His activity through the channels of His creatures we are confronted by God's attributes directly through what He actually performs in His works.

Therefore, God's acts through His masks do not represent a kind of visible simile for His invisible activity. As we have already seen, there is not a likeness and unlikeness in God's actions through His creaturely masks. Rather, God concretely acts and manifests His attributes through the channels of creation to communicate the good to His creatures. Thus, God displays His attributes through His created channels concretely and directly.

This mediated quality of our knowledge of God and His attributes is true not only within the order of creation but within the order of redemption. God's revealed Word of Law and promise manifest in the Bible and the Word and Sacrament ministry of the church are not like and unlike God's wrath and mercy, but directly enact them on the hearers of the Word. If we do speak of an affirmation and negation in God's manifestations in His masks, wrapping, and channels, it would be of the positive word of promise that God has attached to creatures as a channel of the good (affirmation) and the hidden reality of God concealed behind the medium as the author of the good (negation).

This pattern of simultaneous manifestation through the word and concealment under the created mask is supremely true in the cross, the central revelation of God in Scripture (1 Cor 2:2). In the revelation of God in the crucified Jesus all analogy breaks down. Jesus is God Himself, not an analogy or representation of God. He fully possesses the divine attributes in His created humanity (Col 1:19). Moreover, although God becomes fully visible in Jesus (Jn 14:9), His transcendental attributes do not appear in an analogical similarity and dissimilarity. Rather, God's glory appears under the form of His very opposite (*sub contrario*). God's wisdom appears under the form of foolishness (1 Cor 1:18–2:31), the divine life under the form of death (Acts 3:15), and the eternal righteousness under the form of sin (2 Cor 5:21). We know that this is the author of life Himself under the form of death because the Father has witnessed to it in a word that contradicts all seeing: "Surely he was the Son of God!" (Mt 27:54).

If our first set of objections to analogy involved Hiddenness 1, the second involves Hiddenness 2, that is, the reality of *Deus absconditus* above the many divine masks. The fact that we recognize and understand God's attributes only through His created masks is further complicated by the fact that in these means God's attributes confront us in ways that often appear contradictory and are not easily synthesizable by human reason. For example, St. Paul speaks of the wisdom and power of God as displayed gloriously through creation in such a manner that even fallen human reason can recognize it (Rom 1:20). Paul nevertheless also states that in an even deeper manner we are confronted with the wisdom of God in Jesus and His cross in a way that appears not as glorious but as foolish and weak (1 Cor 1:18–2:31).

Paul's conflicting manifestation of God's attributes of wisdom and power does not mean that there are two kinds of power or wisdom in God. There is one God and one power and wisdom in God. Nevertheless, for Luther the unity of God's attributes lie in His eternal hidden being (*Deus absconditus*, Hiddenness 2) existing above the temporal manifestations of God in His masks and wrapping (Hiddenness 1). The unity of the eternal attributes of God is not knowable in this life; it is an object of faith. We cannot remove the masks of God. Faith hears the Word as we are confronted with it in the differing masks, and trusts in the unified saving purpose of God behind His many masks. Faith can trust in this unity because God has shown us His true heart in Christ.[128]

Most importantly, God's attributes of holiness and mercy confront humanity under the forms of two distinct and non-synthesizable words: the Law and the Gospel. Although in the sphere of active righteousness (*coram mundo*) the Law and the Gospel certainly do not contradict one another (first and second use of the Law), in the sphere of passive righteousness (*coram Deo*) the Law and the Gospel are opposite manifestations of God's single will.[129] Through His word of Law God wills unrelenting and absolute death, wrath, and judgment. In His word of the Gospel He wills unilateral and unconditional mercy. Although we can perhaps glimpse the unity of these two divine attributes in the cross (Rom 3:26), the Lutheran symbolic writings are absolutely clear that God acts in completely different ways in His two words.[130]

Luther's belief in the hidden unity of God above His works stands in contrast to Aquinas's understanding of analogy as the means by which faith in the present gains access to God's eternal being above His works. The implication of analogy is that the temporal manifestation of His works is a kind of image of God's eternal being. Through these images humans are given a means to peer into eternity. Thus, when augmented by divine grace and illuminated by the light of revelation, human reason becomes competent to "think-into" both revelation and created order, thereby synthesizing the various manifestations of God into a unified vision of how the divine being relates to the world.[131]

As is clear from both Aquinas's writings and subsequent Roman Catholic theology, this use of analogy has a disastrous effect on the proper distinction

---

128. LC II.3 (Bente, 695).

129. "Therefore, the Law and the Gospel are contrary doctrines [concerning salvation]." *Lectures on Galatians*, 1535 (AE 26:208; WA 40/1:337).

130. Ap. IV (Bente, 121).

131. See summary in Yves Congar, *A History of Theology*, trans. Hunter Guthrie (Garden City, NY: Doubleday, 1968), 93, 97–98.

between Law and Gospel, and therefore also the doctrine of justification. When the sinful human mind looks past the external Word to peer into the eternal unity of the divine attributes of holiness and mercy, Law and Gospel become mixed together corruptly by human conjecture. If God's justice is synthesized with His grace, then it ceases to be absolute and full judgment. Rather, God's Law is adjusted so as to make it doable. The blatant example of this is the early modern Jesuit moral theory of probabalism.[132] Likewise, for the Thomistic tradition God's grace cannot be a unilateral and total gift of salvation but must involve some fulfillment of the Law by the power of grace.[133]

Another analogical approach to the Word of God can be found in the theology of the twentieth-century Reformed theologian Karl Barth.[134] Much like that of Aquinas, Karl Barth's analogical theology of the Word is concerned primarily with making God knowable while preserving His transcendence. Unlike Aquinas, Barth rejects all natural theology and considers the exclusive revelation of God to be found in Jesus Christ. Thus on the one hand, God's act of entering creation in the incarnation of Jesus Christ makes a genuine impact on the creaturely realm. Because of His incarnation in Christ, God may be thought about and known by created beings. On the other hand, revelation is not a direct manifestation of God Himself. Rather, it is only an analogical echo of God's own infinite and eternal being. Even in the event of the revelation the Word of God still remains wholly other.

For Barth, revelation is about God: "God reveals Himself. He reveals Himself through Himself. He reveals *Himself.*"[135] Because the revelation of the Word is about God, it is not about human consciousness or other forms of speculative knowledge. Knowledge of God is always totally disruptive. It comes about not on the basis of immanent possibilities within creation but on the basis of a divine act: "If we really want to understand revelation in terms of its subject, i.e., God, then the first thing we have to realize is that this subject, God, the Revealer, is identical with His act, in revelation and also identical with its effect."[136]

Barth argues that because God is triune, the event of God's act of revelation reflects the structure of the Trinity. Therefore, just as God is actualized in His

---

132. Probabilism allows a person to choose a course of action that has some moral support, even if there are other options that have greater moral grounding. See James Franklin, *The Science of Conjecture: Evidence and Probability before Pascal* (Baltimore: The Johns Hopkins University Press, 2001), 69–76.

133. See brief summary in *The Canons and Decrees of the Council of Trent*, trans. Theodore Alois Buckley (London: George Routledge & Co., 1851), 30–50; David Farina Turnbloom, *Speaking with Aquinas: A Conversation about Grace, Virtue, and the Eucharist* (Collegeville, MN: Liturgical Press, 2017), 58–61.

134. Much of the material in this section will appear in an expanded and modified form in "The Challenge of Karl Barth's Doctrine of the Word of God" in an upcoming volume of *Concordia Theological Quarterly*.

135. Karl Barth, *Church Dogmatics*, trans. G. T. Thomason, G. W. Bromiley, and T. F. Torrance, 4 vols. (Edinburgh: T&T Clark, 1936–77), I/1:296.

136. Barth, *Church Dogmatics* I/1:296.

eternal being as triune, He acts in time to reveal Himself in a triune manner. Father, Son, and Holy Spirit are "Revealer, Revelation, and Revealedness."[137] There is then a threefold form of God's temporal manifestation as the Word in the form of the man Jesus, the Bible, and the preaching of the church.[138] God "repeats in His relationship *ad extra* a relationship proper to Himself in His inner divine essence."[139] Indeed, "He makes a copy of Himself."[140]

Barth's way of thinking about revelation has several implications for how human language is understood as a vehicle of God's Word. First, since revelation as it is comprehended by creatures is a temporal and creaturely echoing of the divine being, it can by no means be directly identical with God's own eternal being and therefore must necessarily be analogical. God's being infinitely transcends human words, so there can be only a dialectical similitude between the created and uncreated word: "Pressed by the revelation of God we are pushed on to the word 'analogy.'"[141] The creaturely echo of God's act is similar to God's own eternal being. In spite of this, His being remains mysterious; indeed, the act of revelation is one of "veiling."[142] Although this language sounds very much like the "veiling" and "covering" we discussed in Luther earlier, it is by no means the same concept. Rather, there is a "likeness and unlikeness . . . a partial correspondence and agreement"[143] between the divine act of revelation and the creaturely analogue. God by way of analogy remains free and revealed simultaneously. He reveals Himself, yet is not enslaved by His act of revelation.

The second implication of thinking of revelation as an analogical representation of a divine act follows from the first. Because God remains free in His revelation, the analogical similitude between the created word and its divine referent is always the result of divine initiative. Creation in and of itself lacks any inherent ability to reveal God. This is one of the several reasons Barth does not favor the Thomistic doctrine of the analogy of being.[144] Of itself, human language does not have an inherent capacity to convey the divine being. What therefore must happen is a divine act of grace that will exalt human language and make it capable of witnessing to the divine being. It is "not that language could grasp revelation," writes Barth, but rather that revelation "could grasp language."[145]

Ultimately Barth defines the revelation of the Word of God in what might be described as Christomonistic terms.[146] It is not simply the case that the

---

137. Barth, *Church Dogmatics* I/1:295.
138. See short description in Barth, *Church Dogmatics* II/1:870–71.
139. Barth, *Church Dogmatics* III/2:218.
140. Barth, *Church Dogmatics* III/2:218.
141. Barth, *Church Dogmatics* II/1:225.
142. Barth, *Church Dogmatics* II/1:225.
143. Barth, *Church Dogmatics* II/1:225.
144. See comment in Barth, *Church Dogmatics* I/1:ix.
145. Barth, *Church Dogmatics* I/1:340.
146. See helpful observation in Richard Muller, "A Note on 'Christocentricism' and the Imprudent Use of Such Terminology," *Calvin Theological Journal* 68 (2006): 253–60.

message of the Bible centers on Jesus (something confessional Lutherans would doubtless agree with): for Barth, Jesus is the only true revelation of God.[147] Hence, Scripture is authoritative not because it is the Word of God but only because it is a witness to Christ as the Word of God.[148]

Barth's view of Scripture is defined overwhelmingly by his understanding of the person of Christ and how the two natures in Christ relate to one another. Much like the rest of the Reformed tradition, Barth rejects the Lutheran belief in the full communication of the divine attributes to the human nature of Christ (*genus majestaticum*).[149] Instead, he insists that there is a *communicatio gratiarum*, wherein the human nature of Christ does not contain the fullness of God's presence but by the power of divine grace echoes and reflects God's glory as an analogical copy.[150] Since Christ's humanity is an analogical copy of God's being in eternity, the theologian may peer into God's eternal being and see that it is configured around the covenant of grace enacted in the death and resurrection of Jesus.[151] Likewise, just as the humanity of Jesus does not possess the real presence of God's glory but merely represents it analogically, the Bible is not the Word of God but is a mere witness to it.[152]

Barth's analogical theology of the Word is problematic for reasons similar to why that of Aquinas is problematic. First, from the perspective of Hiddenness 1, Barth's theology fails to accept fully the Lutheran notion of the sacramentality of the Word which ultimately is rooted in the full communication of Christ's divinity to His humanity (*genus majestaticum*). God makes Himself fully available through the media of His revelation while paradoxically concealing Himself. As we have seen, this is supremely true of the person of Christ, who possesses the fullness of divine glory and yet simultaneously conceals that glory under the form of its opposite (*sub contrario*).

Thus, in the medium of the Word God does not give analogical echo of Himself but gives His very self in the promise of grace. Gerhard aptly observes: "The Holy Spirit speaks to us in and through Scripture. The voice and way of speaking of the Holy Spirit, therefore, sounds in those very words of Scripture."[153] In criticizing Barth, Gustaf Wingren also observes: "Even in the passage and even in preaching, *communicatio idiomatum* holds sway. . . . The Word, the Bible, carries within itself Christ's coming as its general aim, to which all tends . . . It is in the simple words, in what is human in the Bible, that God's power is hidden; divine and human must not be separated."[154]

147. Barth, *Church Dogmatics* I/1:119.
148. Barth, *Church Dogmatics* I/2:457.
149. Barth, *Church Dogmatics* IV/1:143. Also see brief discussion in Barth, *Church Dogmatics* IV/2:82–83.
150. See lengthy discussion in Barth, *Church Dogmatics* IV/2:91–115.
151. Barth, *Church Dogmatics* II/2:94–195.
152. Barth, *Church Dogmatics* I/2:507–9; Barth, *Church Dogmatics* I/2:529–33.
153. Johann Gerhard, *On the Legitimate Interpretation of Holy Scripture*, trans. Richard Dinda (Malone, TX: Repristination Press, 2015), 20.
154. Wingren, *The Living Word*, 208.

In addition, much like for Aquinas, the ultimate effect of Barth's attempt to remove the masks of God is to destroy the dialectic of the hidden and revealed God (Hiddenness 2) as well as the distinction between Law and Gospel. In Barth's mind, through the analogical Word the theologian is allowed to climb into eternity and see God's unity looming above the diversity of His temporal work. This thinking-into eternity effectively eliminates any kind of dialectical manifestation of God's being (hidden/revealed, Law/Gospel) in His works.[155]

For Barth, God cannot operate in two different manifestations (hidden and revealed) and according to two different words (Law and Gospel). Instead, for Barth, God is manifested in a single and unitary Word (i.e., God's covenant of grace in Jesus Christ) above the duality of Law and Gospel. As a result, as with Aquinas, Law is collapsed into grace and grace into Law.[156] As we have previously observed, this conflation effectively creates a higher synthesis of the sinner's relationship with God being structured on a grace-induced submission to the Law.

For Barth, the passive human reception of grace is thus not the goal of the divine-human relationship but a first step to establishing a relationship based on performative righteousness. The believer is to engage in an "act of responsibility, offering himself as the response to the Word of God, and conducting, shaping and expressing himself as an answer to it. He is, *and is man, as he does this.*"[157] Thus, *coram Deo* the freedom of the Gospel is not the goal of the Law's determination of the divine-human relationship. Rather, grace's aim is fundamentally to activate human agency and place it in the right direction. Humanity is ultimately defined by "willingly corresponding to the claim laid upon us by the Word of God."[158] As a result, creation's essence and identity is not to be found in receiving (*vita passiva*) but rather in doing. In one of the later volumes of *Church Dogmatics* Barth very bluntly states regarding this ontic determination that "the statement 'I am' demands further explanation. It means: '*I do*.'"[159] Elsewhere, Barth even went so far as to reverse the reformational order of Law–Gospel, historically shared by both Lutheran and Reformed theologians, into the order of Gospel–Law.[160]

Again, all of this is a byproduct of Barth's analogical concept of the Word. If one is permitted to use analogy to think-into God's reality above the duality of His two words of Law and Gospel, one ultimately will come to see God's grace universally revealed in Christ as a law of God's general relationship with the world. Such a relationship is defined exhaustively by grace, without any

---

155. See similar observations in Wingren, *The Living Word*, 208–9.
156. Wingren, *The Living Word*, 208–9.
157. Barth, *Church Dogmatics* III/2:175; emphasis added.
158. Barth, *Church Dogmatics* III/2:181.
159. Barth, *Church Dogmatics* III/2:181; emphasis added. For a good summary of how Barth views divine and human agency, see George Hunsinger, *How to Read Karl Barth: The Shape of His Theology* (New York: Oxford University Press, 1993), 185–224.
160. Karl Barth, "Gospel and Law," in *Community, State and Church: Three Essays*, ed. Will Herberg (New York: Doubleday, 1960), 71–100.

hiddenness or wrath. Ironically, this exhaustive self-definition of God as grace turns all knowledge of God functionally into Law. Grace becomes a law insofar as it discloses the Law of God's relationship with the world and then demands that the sinner conform his behavior to it. By contrast, the confessional Lutheran sees God's will dialectically revealed in two words. Although faith does lead to the fruit of obedience in the kingdom of this world (*coram mundo*), the divine-human relationship (*coram Deo*) is defined fundamentally by the fleeing of the repentant sinner from the word of God's wrath to the word of His grace.

Thus, in the light of our objections to both Aquinas and Barth, the Neoplatonic procedure of affirmation and negation through analogy is highly problematic for confessional Lutheran theology.[161] If we are to retain the procedure of negation and affirmation, it could perhaps be modified in the following manner: Lutheran kataphatic or positive theology is an explication of how God manifests His transcendental attributes in, under, and through His creaturely masks (Hiddenness 1). Likewise, Lutheran apophatic or negative theology would then be concerned not only with God's limitlessness in relationship to His creatures, but with the hidden unity of the divine being above His many masks (Hiddenness 2).

THE TRIUNE MANIFESTATION OF THE WORD IN THE LIFE OF THE CHURCH

Finally, within the order of the church God discloses His being and will in a threefold manner through His Word, and the divine Word manifests God's triune existence. First, in revealing His Word God reveals the truth about His being and character. For this reason the Word of God necessarily possesses a propositional dimension. This reality may be seen by the analogy of normal human experience. Any address necessarily reveals the speaker. Likewise, there is content to what the speaker speaks insofar as words signify things. As we have seen, in disclosing His word of Law and grace to Adam in the primal state, God revealed His identity as the one true God who had created Adam and given him all good things by His gracious fiat. He also revealed His character as wise, gracious, and loving.

Within the trinitarian shape of divine disclosure, the propositional dimension of the Word of God corresponds to the Father. As the font of divinity (*fons totius divinitas*), He is the object to which the eternal Word corresponds. Likewise, just as the Father is the ultimate source of the Son and the Spirit, the propositional content of the Word is the supreme source of the other two dimensions of the Word.

---

161. See a similar approach to my argument here in Lowell Green, *Adventures in Law and Gospel: Lectures in Lutheran Dogmatics* (Ft. Wayne: Concordia Theological Seminary Press, 1993), 47–53.

The second dimension of God's Word is its self-communicative sacramental efficacy. Within the trinitarian life this dimension corresponds to the Son, who is the creative and effective self-communication of the Father. This sacramental dimension possesses an efficacious-event quality insofar as it changes and shapes the creature's existence through suffering God's creative presence and activity in the Word.

Again, this effective and sacramental character of the Word is not disconnected from the propositional character of the Word. The Word is effective precisely because the Spirit works through the disclosure of the reality of who God is and what His will is for humanity. Likewise, the Son is a true Word that communicates who the Father is (Jn 14:9; Col 1:15; Heb 1:3). Nevertheless, the Son does not merely represent the Father (as in Arianism[162]) but is also the perfect embodiment and self-communication of the Father in that He possesses the fullness of the communicated divine essence (Jn 1:2; Col 1:19; *homoousios*). The Hebrew word דָּבָר discloses both of these dimensions, connoting word, event, or deed in its many uses through the Old Testament.[163]

Recognizing both the propositional and effective dimensions of the Word is important in view of the propensity of many twentieth-century radical revisionist Lutheran theologians (notably Rudolf Bultmann[164] and Gerhard Ebeling[165]) to claim that the Word of God is pure "event" (*Wortereignis*) that confronts sinners with a new existential reality.

For Bultmann in particular this move is crucial, since most biblical doctrines must be deemed mythological, and denied.[166] Nevertheless, according to Bultmann, that many of the core doctrines of the New Testament are actually mythical does not discredit the Christian faith. The Christian faith has an abiding core which can be "demythologized."[167] Ultimately for Bultmann and for those who follow him, Christianity is not about believing specific truth claims but rather about a new existential reality encountered in Jesus' call to decision.[168] In this view, when Jesus calls sinners to the kingdom of God, the

162. See the following: Lewis Ayres, *Nicaea and Its Legacy: An Approach to Fourth-Century Trinitarian Theology* (Oxford: Oxford University Press, 2006); R. P. C. Hanson, *The Search for the Christian Doctrine of God: The Arian Controversy, 318–381* (Grand Rapids: Baker Academic, 2006); Rowan Williams, *Arius: Heresy and Tradition* (Grand Rapids: Wm. B. Eerdmans, 2002).

163. Horst Dietrich Preuss, *Old Testament Theology*, trans. Leo G. Perdue, 2 vols. (Louisville: Westminster John Knox, 1995–96), 2:81; Edgar Jones, *The Greatest Old Testament Words* (London: SCM Press, 1964), 59–62.

164. See in particular Rudolf Bultmann, *Begriff der Offenbarung im Neuen Testament* (Tübingen: Mohr, 1929).

165. See in particular Gerhard Ebeling, *The Problem of Historicity in the Church and Its Proclamation*, trans. Grover Foley (Philadelphia: Fortress Press, 1967).

166. See in particular Rudolf Bultmann, *Jesus Christ and Mythology* (New York: Hymns Ancient and Modern Ltd., 2012).

167. See Rudolf Bultmann, "On the Problem of Demythologization (1952)," in Rudolf Bultmann, *New Testament and Mythology and Other Basic Writings*, trans. and ed. Schubert M. Ogden (Minneapolis: Fortress Press, 1984), 95–130.

168. See Sasse's critique of Bultmann in Hermann Sasse, "Flight from Dogma: Remarks on Bultmann's 'Demythologization' of the New Testament," in Hermann Sasse, *The Lonely Way:*

essence of what He taught is not the literal coming of God's eschatological rule. Rather, it is the coming of a new orientation of human existence to the future.[169] Incidentally, Bultmann interprets Paul's contrast between Law and Gospel in the same manner.[170]

Though Bultmann is certainly correct that the Word of God is living and therefore actualizes a new existential situation for the believer, this in no way detracts from its propositional content or the necessity of believing it. Moreover, as we will explore further in a later chapter, God's truth cannot be discounted as mere mythology, the husk of which can be removed in order to expose the kernel of truth within (kerygma). God's saving action through the Word is always embodied and incarnate in a specific worldview and specific claims about His supernatural activity in history.

The intersecting nature of the effective and propositional content of the Word of God can be observed particularly in the theology of John's Gospel.[171] John emphasizes that Jesus is God's eternal Word (Jn 1:1–2). Jesus' identity as the Word means that He is a creative and effective Word. As John explains in His Christological prologue, Jesus is the Word spoken of in Genesis 1 who created the world (Jn 1:3). In becoming incarnate Jesus speaks forth a new creation in the same manner in which He brought about the old one. This fact is quite clear from John's use of the motif of the seven signs or miracles, corresponding to the seven days of creation,[172] as well as other creational imagery: Jesus as true man on the sixth day of a new creation (Jn 19:5), Jesus as Second Adam giving birth to the church as the new Eve (Jn 19:34), the garden motif (Jn 18:1; 19:41, etc.).

Nevertheless, this effective and creative nature of Jesus' identity is not the only aspect of Jesus as the Word. Jesus' revelation is also understood as a propositional truth about the Father and about Himself: "Whoever has seen me has seen the Father" (Jn 14:9; also see Jn 12:45; 18:37).[173] Indeed, this propositional knowledge of who God truly is and the nature of His will for humanity (Law and Gospel) is the precondition for existential and creative efficacy of the Word of God: "You will know the truth, and the truth will set you free" (Jn 8:32; compare with Gal 5:1). The propositional truth communicated by

Selected Essays and Letters, Volume 2 (1941–1976), trans. Matthew Harrison et al. (Concordia Publishing House, 2002), 93–116.

169. See in particular Rudolf Bultmann, *History and Eschatology: The Presence of Eternity* (New York: Harper & Brothers, 1962); and Rudolf Bultmann, *Jesus and the Word*, trans. Louise Pettibone Smith and Erminie Huntress Lantero (New York: Scribner, 1958).

170. See Rudolf Bultmann, *Theology of the New Testament*, trans. Kendrick Grobel, 2 vols. (Waco, TX: Baylor University Press, 2007), 1:259–345.

171. See similar observation in Oscar Cullmann, *Salvation in History* (New York: Harper & Row, 1967), 137.

172. Andreas J. Köstenberger, L. Scott Kellum, and Charles Quarles, *The Cradle, the Cross, and the Crown: An Introduction to the New Testament* (Nashville: B & H Academic, 2009), 305.

173. See my lengthy argument and discussion about these themes in Jack Kilcrease, "The Self-Donation of God: Gerhard Forde and the Question of Atonement in the Lutheran Tradition" (Ph.D. diss., Marquette University, 2009), 66–74.

Jesus ("God so loved the world . . .") translates into the effective reality of the life of faith (i.e., freedom from the condemnation of the Law).

Luther himself recognized a distinction between the propositional and effective dimensions of the Word of God.[174] The Luther scholar David Steinmetz summarizes this point well in writing:

> Luther draws a distinction between two kinds of words in order to make clear what the Bible means when it speaks of the Word of God. There is, of course, the *Heissel-Wort*, the Call-Word, the word which people use when they apply names to things which already exist. The biblical story of Adam in the garden is a fine example of this. He names all the biblical creatures. He does not create them; he only sorts them out and gives them labels. But there is a second kind of word, the *Thettel-Wort* or Deed-Word, which not only names but effects what it signifies. Adam looks around him and says, "There is a cow and an owl and a horse and a mosquito." But God looks around him and says, "Let there be light," and there is light.[175]

As Steinmetz later points out, the church is entrusted with the Word of God, and consequently God's Deed-Word (Christ) appears in and under human words written in Scripture and proclaimed in the divine service (*Gottesdienst*).[176] Moreover, the Deed-Word the church proclaims has power only because its Call-Word content describes who God is (triune) and what He has done in Christ.

Third, the Word of God is necessarily liturgical and doxological. This aspect of the Word corresponds within the trinitarian life to the Spirit, through whom the Son returns Himself to the Father in an eternal doxology. Likewise, through their actions and their confessions of faith, believers praise God by accepting the truth of His Word. As Luther states in *On the Freedom of a Christian*, the highest praise anyone can give another is to believe that he is truthful.[177] This doxology of faith is a direct response to the knowledge of God and His gracious self-communication. Likewise, we find in the liturgical literature of the Old Testament (namely, the Psalms) praise of Yhwh in response to who He is and what He has graciously done in creation and in the history of the people of God. Ultimately such praise is able to be spoken precisely because God has disclosed Himself and worked in the hearts and minds of His people. The power of the Spirit enables believers to respond to God with words that He has graciously communicated to them.[178]

Ultimately this threefold content of the Word finds a further echo in the structure of the disclosure of the Word of God. First, beginning with Adam,

---

174. See *That These Words of Christ, "This Is My Body," Etc., Still Stand Firm Against the Fanatics*, 1527 (AE 37:149; WA 23:282).

175. David Steinmetz, "Luther and the Two Kingdoms," in *Luther in Context* (Bloomington: University of Indiana Press, 1986), 115.

176. Steinmetz, "Luther and the Two Kingdoms," 115–16.

177. *On the Freedom of a Christian*, 1520 (AE 31:350; WA 7:25).

178. Luther makes a similar point about the giving of God's name in baptism in the Large Catechism. See LC I.2 (Bente, 593–603).

God revealed His Word to His prophets and apostles. Insofar as the giving of the Word is an act of self-communication, it corresponds to the Father's eternal begetting of the Son. Likewise, Adam and later prophets and apostles proclaim the Word of God they have received to other human beings, in human words. Such a communicated and incarnate Word of God mirrors the eternal begetting of the Son and His incarnation into human reality within time. Finally, this proclamation elicits the praise of God, thereby manifesting the glorifying power of the Spirit (Jn 16:13–14).

FLIGHT FROM THE EXTERNAL WORD: THE FALL AS ENTHUSIASM[179]

As Luther observes in his Genesis commentary, Satan in the form of the serpent brought about the first sin precisely by fostering unbelief in the external Word: "Unbelief is the source of all sins; when Satan brought about this unbelief by driving out or corrupting the Word, the rest was easy for him."[180] Luther's statement here is clearly in accordance with Scripture in that "everything that does not come from faith is sin" (Rom 14:23) and "without faith, it is impossible to please God" (Heb 11:6). Since belief is a passive receptivity to God's Word, it represents a self-consciousness of the human being's status as a creature that possesses its existence as a result of the divine address (Genesis 1). Conversely, unbelief is then also a refusal to accept one's status as a creature and a receiver of the good from an external divine source.

In Genesis 3, Satan fosters unbelief in a twofold manner. First he directs Eve away from God's external Word of promise, to God's hidden being and intention above and beyond His Word. He does so first by questioning the external Word: "Did God actually say, 'You shall not eat of any tree in the garden'?" (Gn 3:1). As previously observed, God bids His creatures to seek Him in the external means He has established. As in the era of the New Testament, God made Himself tangible to His creatures in His promise of life and freedom to Adam and Eve: "Be fruitful and multiply and fill the earth and subdue it, and have dominion . . ." (Gn 1:28). The whole of creation was offered to our first parents as a visible word of God's self-donating love and favor.

There is no gap here between God's will for humanity and His self-manifestation in His various words and coverings. Adam and Eve's faith in God's manifest grace recognizes that there is a unity between His external audible and visible words and the divine will. As Luther shows, in return God seeks only the spontaneous doxology of His creatures channeled through their obedience to the external commandment not to eat of the tree of the knowledge of good and evil.

---

179. Much of this section is based on my discussion of the Fall in my doctoral dissertation: Kilcrease, "Self-Donation of God."

180. *Lectures on Genesis*, 1535–45 (AE 1:147; WA 42:110).

According to Luther's interpretation of the Hebrew of Gn 3:3, Eve's answer to Satan about what God had actually commanded suggests that the temptation to unbelief regarding the unity of God's external Word and His actual will is already beginning to show. As the Reformer understands it, Eve adds the word "perchance" to her answer when quoting God's commandment: "lest perchance we die."[181] She thus begins to speculate about what God might actually do, rather than assuming that there is an absolute unity between what the invisible God wills and what the external Word says.

Luther observes that such speculations about whether God's Word is true have plagued the church throughout its history. For example, Arius thought it was "perchance" the case that God was not constituted by a Trinity of persons.[182] Similarly, many look away from the clear meaning of God's promises and speculate that "perchance" "This is My Body" could mean something other than what the words actually say.[183]

The examples Luther offers here are particularly apt insofar as they touch on the gap between the external Word and the reality it represents. As we shall see later, this gap is the necessary presupposition of Enthusiasm. In the case of Arianism, the gap is between the uncreated God and His finite, created Word, the pre-existent Christ. In other words, for Arius the Son is not *homoousios* with the Father; consequently, God and His eternal Word do not correspond perfectly with one another. There is ultimately an infinite gap between the thing signified (the Father) and the Word that signifies it (the Son). Likewise, Zwingli and Calvin's insistence that Christ's body was physically distant from the simple words "This is My Body" also opens up a gap between the truth (Christ's body present in a semi-local heaven) and the word that expresses it (the Words of Institution and the host). As noted before, this gap finds its basis and corollary in the Reformed teaching on the *communicatio idiomatum*, where again the signified (the divine nature) is ontologically distant from the visible signifier (the human nature), rather than being present in and through it (i.e., the Lutheran *capax* and *genus majestaticum*). Finally, as already observed, this same distancing of God from His Word is one of the major problems with the Thomistic and Barthian theories of revelational analogy.

Claiming special knowledge of God's hidden will above His Word, Satan then asserts that, contrary to His Word, God does not wish Adam and Eve well. Rather, instead of giving them all things as He had promised (Gn 1:28–29; 2:16), He desires secretly to withhold from them divinity: "For God knows that when you eat of it your eyes will be opened, and you will be like God, knowing good and evil" (Gn 3:4). The irony is that they are already like God. They are made in God's image and exercise His dominion within creation. Only in doubting what

---

181. *Lectures on Genesis*, 1535–45 (AE 1:155; WA 42:117); emphasis added. Some newer interpreters suggest a better translation might be "lest we die." Either way, Luther must be thought correct in his understanding of the general direction of the conversation.

182. *Lectures on Genesis*, 1535–45 (AE 1:156; WA 42:118).

183. *Lectures on Genesis*, 1535–45 (AE 1:157; WA 42:118).

God already had told them explicitly could they find Satan's words plausible and tempting.

Luther suggests that Satan's tempting statement could be understood in at least two different ways. First, Satan may be stating that God is to be resented for withholding divinity from them. The second interpretation, and the one Luther favors, is that the serpent is praising God and therefore saying it is logical to assume that if God is good He would also wish humans to share in the divine quality of the knowledge of good and evil.[184]

With either interpretation, the nature of Satan's subversion of God's Word is clear. Having claimed that a gap stands between the external Word and God's will, Satan places himself within this fictional gap he creates in the imagination of Adam and Eve. In doing this he makes himself into an alternative mediator to the true minister of the Word, Adam. As Luther writes: "Satan imitates God. Just as God had preached to Adam, so he himself also preaches to Eve. . . . Therefore, just as from the true Word of God salvation results, so also from the corrupt Word of God damnation results."[185] God had given Adam His Word which he was to preach to Eve, the first church. Such a Word bid them find God's blessings by fleeing from divine hiddenness manifested in the tree of the knowledge of good and evil and to the promises of life and freedom present in the other trees of the garden, most particularly in the tree of life. In contrast, Satan does not rely on the external Word but on his supposed secret knowledge of the divine from within his own heart. He is the supreme Enthusiast in that he appeals to his own internal authority at variance with the external Word. Whereas God's Word bids humanity to flee from the tree of the knowledge of good and evil to the tree of life, Satan insists on the very opposite by his internally wrought authority. In doing this Satan, not unlike God, attaches a word of promise to a tangible object, the fruit of the tree of the knowledge of good and evil.

Beyond the attack on the Word of God attached to the tree of the knowledge of good and evil, note that Satan's act of temptation also touches on the narrative-linguistic structure of reality we have observed already in our discussion of Genesis 1. In his act of false mediation the serpent effectively re-narrates reality as it was established in the earlier chapters of Genesis. Whereas in Genesis 1–2 God establishes humanity in life and freedom through His gracious Word of promise, the false mediator Satan substitutes a false narrative of reality. Within this false narrative God does not freely speak the good into existence. Rather, humans must grasp at it by their own powers and works. Rather than passively receiving the good through faith in the Word, by their own initiative our first parents believe that they must stretch out their hands to take hold of the good they have been denied in the form of the forbidden fruit.

---

184. *Lectures on Genesis*, 1535–45 (AE 1:158; WA 42:119).
185. *Lectures on Genesis*, 1535–45 (AE 1:147; WA 42:111).

Logically, this grasping is rooted in the Enthusiasts' sense that there is a gap between God's Word of grace and His true, hidden intentions beyond the Word. Enthusiasm literally means "God-within-ism,"[186] and Luther uses the term for any human attempt to internalize authority. When humans stand before the abyss of the hidden and unbound divine will, they have no other recourse but to attempt to oppose and coerce God by taking control of the good for themselves. Apart from His self-binding in the Word of grace, God's will and power appear as a threat to human existence insofar as God with His infinite power is under no obligation to be gracious to humans. Ultimately, faced with this situation, Adam and Eve no longer trust in God's Word and therefore doubt His willingness to communicate the good. For this reason they must become gods themselves (Gn 3:4).

In the Smalcald Articles (1537) Luther commented that he saw very little difference between the spiritualists, the pope, and Satan in the Garden of Eden.[187] All took up the office of the ministry without a proper call and drew people away from those who had received a regular call. All claimed the ability to know God's hidden will and drew people away from the external Word.[188] Luther thus posits that Enthusiasm and unbelief are the originating sin. Without recourse to the Word, Enthusiasts claimed to have bridged the gap between the word and the object it represents, God preached and God not preached.[189] The spiritualists as well as the papacy had "swallowed the Holy Spirit, feathers and all."[190] As a result, they claimed the ability to judge "good and evil" apart from and indeed even against the external Word through the power of the intangible Spirit.

For Luther it is crucial to recognize that Enthusiasm is not simply the work of Satan but also something to which he converts human beings: "the old devil and old serpent, who also converted Adam and Eve into enthusiasts, and led them from the outward Word of God to spiritualizing and self-conceit . . ."[191] Scripture teaches that we are to "trust in the Lord with all your heart, and do not lean on your own understanding" (Prv 3:5). But Eve does in fact trust her own internal understanding rather than the Lord and His external Word: "So when the woman saw that the tree was good for food, and that it was a delight to the eyes, and that the tree was to be desired to make one wise, she took of its fruit and ate" (Gn 3:6). Eve relies on her own intellectual and visual assessment of the value of the fruit rather than the word that God had attached to them.

---

186. Michael Horton, *The Gospel Commission: Recovering God's Strategy for Making Disciples* (Grand Rapids: Baker, 2011), 259.

187. SA III.viii (Bente, 495–96).

188. See CA V (Bente, 45).

189. *Against the Heavenly Prophets in the Matter of Images and Sacraments*, 1525 (AE 40:149; WA 18:139).

190. *Against the Heavenly Prophets in the Matter of Images and Sacraments*, 1525 (AE 40:83; WA 18:65).

191. SA III.viii (Bente, 495–96).

She thus is converted by Satan to Enthusiasm insofar as she accepts an internal source of authority rather than the external Word.

Beyond this, Eve seeks to gain inner wisdom (חָכְמָה) from consuming the fruit. Again, instead of listening to the external Word of God, she desires to possess wisdom through the internal knowledge of good and evil. The Hebrew word דַּעַת, typically translated as "knowledge," does not denote merely a casual knowledge of information, like one knows a security code or the date of a birthday. Rather, דַּעַת usually denotes a deep participatory knowledge. It is the euphemism the Old Testament consistently uses to describe sexual intercourse. Male and female "know each other" in sexual intercourse insofar as they literally participate in each other's bodies. Indeed, they "become one flesh" (Gn 2:24).

Hence, Eve seeks not just information about the distinction between good and evil but an internalized participatory knowledge of it enclosed within the seat of her own heart. Such inner knowledge stands as an alternative to God's external Word. In a sense she does receive such knowledge. Having possessed a participatory knowledge of the good through God's own sacramental mediation of it to her and her husband, they now also possess a participatory knowledge of evil through actively experiencing the reality of evil wrought by their own sinful choices.

Ultimately this internalization of authority on display with both Satan and our first parents is key to the phenomenon of Enthusiasm. This phenomenon may exhibit itself in the crass form of the megachurch pastor, the false prophet, or the Roman pontiff, all of whom claim to possess a special, inner spiritual revelation from God. It also can exist in the subtler form of exalting the authority of one's thoughts, reason, emotions, or longings over the external Word of God. Even if these subtler Enthusiasts do not claim to possess an inner revelation from God, they nevertheless rely on a god within: for the subtle Enthusiast, the inner person and his own perceptions take over the divine authority of the external Word. His inner thoughts and feelings come to take the place of God as the supreme object of trust. Instead of being oriented outside of himself to the external Word, the Enthusiast becomes curved in on himself (*incurvatus in se*) by his reliance on the inner god.

Ultimately Enthusiasm fails, not only because of its unverifiable subjectivity and the implausible nature of its claims (seer stones, golden plates, Mary's assumption into heaven, etc.), but also because the very structure of reality is oriented to God's external address in the Word. Any claim humanity makes regarding the ability of its inner faculties to discern the truth must ultimately rely on God and His creative power in the Word. It is therefore self-contradictory to claim an independent ability to discern the truth over and against the external Word, since the Word is the very source of creaturely existence and all creaturely truth-discerning faculties (reason, intuition, feeling, etc.).

Adam and Eve's unbelief in the Word changes their relationship with God. As Luther comments in the Great Galatians commentary (1535), faith "is something omnipotent."[192] As he observes, on the one hand the "omnipotence" of faith lies in that it "recreates" God within us. That is to say, faith and unbelief cause us to perceive God differently within our hearts and minds. But beyond this, in an objective sense, faith and unbelief place humans in the realm of God preached or the realm of God unpreached, respectively. In unbelief Adam and Eve fled from the sphere of God's grace to the sphere of His wrath and hiddenness. Humanity thus comes to stand in a new relationship with God, omnipotently "recreating" God by their unbelief. God, who was once encountered as gracious, has now become wrathful. Indeed, as Luther observes, Satan's temptation ultimately results in the creation of a "new god."[193] By the power of their false belief God becomes precisely what Adam and Eve believe Him to be.

In that Adam and Eve reject the Word of God in their unbelief, they become deaf to every word that God has attached to His creation. To draw upon Jeremiah and St. Stephen's rather odd yet apt description, in their state of sin they possess "uncircumcised ears" (Jer 6:10; Acts 7:51). Whereas God had attached the word "very good" to the whole of creation, our first parents are now deaf to this gracious word. They feel shame in looking upon their physical bodies which God had deemed "very good," and therefore must cover them (Gn 3:7). Likewise, whereas God had guaranteed their life and freedom within creation, the whole creation and God Himself have become untrustworthy (Gn 1:28–29). Indeed, as a condemning "mask of God"[194] the whole experience of fallen humans within creation becomes a "continual foretaste of the Last Judgment."[195] Luther himself observes: "After their conscience had been convicted by the Law, Adam and Eve were terrified by the rustling of a leaf . . . We see it to be so in the case of frightened human beings. When they hear the creaking of a beam, they are afraid that the entire house may collapse; when they hear a mouse, they are afraid that Satan is there and wants to kill them."[196] Indeed, "by nature we have become so thoroughly frightened that we fear even the things that are safe."[197]

By leaving the sphere of grace humans enter into the sphere of Law, wrath, and hiddenness. Just as in their pre-lapsarian existence they were determined by God's Word of grace, so now they are determined by His condemning Word of Law. In such a state "the wrath of God is revealed from heaven against all ungodliness and unrighteousness of men, who by their unrighteousness

---

192. *Lectures on Galatians*, 1535 (AE 26:227; WA 40/1:360).
193. *Lectures on Genesis*, 1535–45 (AE 1:148–49; WA 42:112).
194. *Lectures on Galatians*, 1535 (AE 26:95; WA 40/1:173).
195. Wingren, *Creation and Law*, 174.
196. *Lectures on Genesis*, 1535–45 (AE 1:170; WA 42:127).
197. *Lectures on Genesis*, 1535–45 (AE 1:170; WA 42:127).

suppress the truth" (Rom 1:18). Such a demand for self-justification drives humans all the more into sin. Indeed, as Paul tells us, "for apart from the law, sin is dead" (Rom 7:8). Luther makes the similar observation that when God confronted Adam, He did so with His condemning word of Law, and therefore Adam had no other recourse but to engage in self-justification:

> But because the hope of the forgiveness of his sins is not yet available, he feels and sees nothing but death itself because of his transgression of the command. However, because nature is unable to avoid death, Adam cannot be brought to a confession of all his sin . . . Moreover, because he hates punishment, at the same time he hates God's justice and God himself.[198]

In effect Adam and Eve are bound to continue to claim that they hold within the seat of their own hearts the true knowledge of good and evil over against the judgment of God's external Word. To justify themselves they hide and then finally blame each other and Satan (Gn 3:8–13). They must do so in order to protect themselves from the unbounded threat of the Law. Nevertheless, their self-justification is blasphemy. By rejecting God's accusation they make God a liar.[199] "If we say we have not sinned, we make him a liar, and his word is not in us" (1 Jn 1:10–11).

Ultimately, only by doubling down on Enthusiasm is self-justification possible. The Enthusiast must rely on self-judgment over and against the judgment of God's Word, thereby becoming all the more curved in upon himself (*incurvatus in se*). This is because God's Word finds everything within the sinner unacceptable, including the Enthusiast's conceit of inner truth and righteousness: "For I know that nothing good dwells in me, that is, in my flesh" (Rom 7:18).

In the light of this desperate need it becomes clear how Satan's counternarrative of tragic devolution applies to the Enthusiast's sense of self and authenticity. Through the act of unbelief the Enthusiast becomes a microcosm of the macrocosm of Satan's false narrative. The orientation of the Enthusiast is toward himself as the supreme object of trust. He looks to his own deified heart as the ultimate criterion of truth and the source of the good. He does not receive a share in God's image, life, and rule from outside of himself in the external Word, but rather imagines himself to be a god. Hence, for the Enthusiast to move out from the center of his inner divine heart to the external Word and world there is a tragic movement, from his own perspective, from authenticity and truth to inauthenticity and falsehood.

This reality is illustrated perfectly by what we find in God's confrontation of Adam and Eve in Genesis 3. When God confronts the two with their sin, they reject God's judgment as inauthentic. Instead, they make excuses and therefore rely on their own self-judgment. The external Word seems to them neither the

---

198. *Lectures on Genesis*, 1535–45 (AE 1:177–78; WA 42:132–33).
199. *Lectures on Genesis*, 1535–45 (AE 1:177–79; WA 42:132–33).

criterion of truth nor the source of the good. In their minds goodness and truth are to be found in their inner self-judgment. Hence, the movement from their interior sense of themselves as the supreme good to the external world and Word seems a kind of falling away from authenticity to inauthenticity.

Because the self-justifying Enthusiast is under constant assault by the judgment of the Law (Rom 1:18), he must necessarily remain focused on himself and not on his neighbor's needs. He does not live a reality external to himself, that is, "in Christ [or the Word] through faith, and in his neighbor through love,"[200] but instead lives an existence centered on himself. He must resist the external Word because it condemns him and his inner sense of righteousness. Moreover, he cannot truly be concerned about his neighbor: being driven by the Law and its hypocritical self-righteousness, he can be concerned only about his own fortunes. Though such individuals may display outward righteousness, ultimately it can be only for the sake of their inner self-righteousness.

Seen from all these differing angles, Enthusiasm operates from a worldview that is inherently tragic. In characterizing this worldview as tragic we are invoking the classical definition of tragedy partially explicated in Aristotle's *Poetics*.[201] Simply put, tragedy is defined as a narrative that begins well and ends badly.[202] As has already been observed, Satan's re-narration of reality and the Enthusiast's life-form embody this tragic narrative structure. Creation as a finite good is a tragic falling away from the infinite good of God's fullness of being. Likewise, the external Word is a tragic falling away from God's invisible, spiritual Word, which Satan claims to know. Finally, the Enthusiast's own inner sense of divinity and self-justifying truth must view the external world and Word as an inauthentic falling away from the supreme authenticity of his own inner world, sense of truth, and righteousness.

As we observed in an earlier section, such a view of the relation between the eternal Word of God and the means of grace is present in Aquinas's synthesis of Aristotle and the Bible (i.e., reason decodes the external Word), Calvin and Zwingli's rejection of the simple meaning of the Words of Institution, and Barth's revelational Christomonism. In these theologies the visible and audible words of God were to be thought of as an analogical echo and a tragic falling away from the infinite and eternal Word. That is to say, for the Thomist and the Reformed, God's Word is not sacramentally present in, under, and through human words; it is merely echoed in them. As we have already explored in detail, in both Thomism and Reformed theology (both Calvinist and Barthian), this judgment is both implicitly and explicitly rooted in the principle that the finite is not capable of the infinite (the *non-capax*). As a result, the theologian

---

200. *On the Freedom of a Christian*, 1520 (AE 31:371; WA 7:69).
201. Aristotle, *Poetics*, trans. Joe Sachs (Newburyport: Focus Publishing, 2006). In particular, Aristotle speaks of the tragic character flaw that propels persons in high places to fall.
202. See Leithart, *Deep Comedy*, 37–41. Leithart also has pointed me here to George Steiner, *The Death of Tragedy* (New York: Oxford University Press, 1961), 8. I greatly appreciate Leithart's argument, and much of my argument will be informed by his.

who treats the Word in this analogical manner imagines himself standing between the separated Word and the object the Word represents. From this disembodied vantage point he compares the two, thereby discerning the true spiritual meaning of the Word. This procedure can be seen particularly in the Barthian and Thomistic theories of revelational analogy. Analogical theories of revelation thus invariably lead to a form of Enthusiasm by their separation of God from His external Word.

2

SCRIPTURE AND HISTORY:
THE CRUCIFORM MOVEMENT OF THE WORD[1]

THE CHRISTOLOGICAL FOUNDATION
OF SACRED SCRIPTURE

As we observed in the previous chapter, God's solution to the problem of sin is the proclamation of the Word. This is fitting, insofar as the root of sin is Enthusiasm and unbelief in the Word. In His sermon to our first parents God first proclaimed the Law as a means both to coercively re-solidify their disrupted creational relationships and to remove the possibility of Enthusiastic self-justification. God is by nature gracious and self-giving, and therefore this condemning sermon, although necessary, is alien to His heartfelt desire to communicate the good graciously and freely. Hence Luther refers to God's condemning work through His Word as His "alien work" (*opus alienum*): "Therefore his compassion is more abundant because it is a part of God's nature, since wrath is truly God's alien work, in which he engages contrary to his nature, because he is forced into it by the wickedness of man."[2]

Having completed His alien work, God is now free again to enter into His proper work (*opus proprium*). God speaks forth the word of the Gospel: "I will put enmity between you [Satan] and the woman, and between your offspring [or seed] and her offspring [or seed]; he shall bruise your head, and you shall bruise his heel" (Gn 3:15). For this promised redeemer to destroy the power of Satan He must be divine, since humans after the Fall clearly remain under Satan's power and it is beyond their power to overcome him.[3] Likewise, the one spoken of must necessarily be human, in that He is the Seed of the woman and represents humans who are condemned to eternal death by God. Third, He must be born of a virgin, since we are told that He is the Seed of the woman, not of the man. As David Scaer notes, in the cultural understanding of the ancient Near East women did not have "seed" and in actuality did not contribute biologically

---

1. Though our arguments are somewhat different, we should give credit to the following work as inspiring the title and some of the content of this chapter: Peter H. Nafzger and Joel P. Okamoto, *"These Are Written": Toward a Cruciform Theology of Scripture* (Eugene, OR: Pickwick Publications, 2013).

2. *Lectures on Genesis*, 1535–45 (AE 2:134; WA 42:356). Also see discussion of alien and proper work in Karl Holl, *Gesammelte Aufsätze*, 3 vols. (Tübingen: Mohr, 1928), 1:75–77, 3:562–67.

3. Gerhard, *On the Person and Office of Christ*, 35.

to reproduction.[4] The "Seed of the woman" is highly suggestive of virgin birth, insofar as reproduction is spoken of solely as the act of the woman. Fourth, the promised one will suffer the "bruise" of the serpent on His heel but will deliver the deathblow by "bruising" the serpent's head.[5] Thus, the whole narrated promise of the Gospel is contained in *protoevangelium*.[6]

In the giving of the *protoevangelium* the Lord demonstrates that although He is faithful to His previously established visible and auditory words, they do not exhaust His will or His possibilities as God. Adam and Eve deviated from God's protological order by fleeing from the place of God's grace to the place of His judgment. By doing so they placed themselves outside the sphere of God's grace and in the sphere of His condemning word of Law and hiddenness. If God's will were exhausted by the Law or the protological order of creation, humanity would be doomed to eternal death.

Although the Law is God's holy Word and God cannot deny Himself (2 Tm 2:13), it is only one aspect of His will. The Law is the eternal will of God (*lex aeterna*),[7] but it does not exhaust the content of His eternal will. Within the temporal order God has bound Himself to act through of some of His masks as Law and through others in accordance with His grace. But above His self-binding He remains free to actualize new possibilities within His creation through His almighty Word. As Luther states: "God hidden in his majesty . . . *has not bound himself by his word, but has kept himself free over all things.*"[8] Indeed, God designates His name as "I will be who I will be" (Ex 3:14; my translation).

For this reason the triune God is the God not only of creation but of new creation. If this were not the case, within the post-Fall world He would be nothing but a condemning God in faithfulness to His original word of Law. But God is not defined exhaustively by His role as the author of the legal order of the original creation. As in eternity the Father transcends His own singularity in the relational acts of eternal begetting and procession, similarly in time God also may surpass Himself as creator by entering into the new possibilities as redeemer. Likewise, much as He spoke forth the original creation gratuitously by His eternal Word, through the word of the Gospel He speaks forth the new

---

4. David P. Scaer, *Christology*, vol. 6 of Confessional Lutheran Dogmatics (St. Louis: Luther Academy, 1989), 34–35. Luther makes the same observation in *On the Last Words of David*, 1543 (AE 15:318–21; WA 54:70–74).

5. "Bruise" seems to be the most plausible translation here. Some commentators have argued for "strike."

6. See Chemnitz, *Loci Theologici* 1:37. Chemnitz writes: "At the very beginning, when the Son of God announced to our first parents the mystery of the promise of the Gospel which had been hidden from eternity in the bosom of the Father, He gave a brief summary of the Gospel in Gn 3:15."

7. SD III (Bente, 935). Also see Luther's statement in Martin Luther, *Second Set of Antinomian Theses*, Theses 47 and 48 in *Only the Decalogue Is Eternal: Martin Luther's Complete Antinomian Theses and Disputations*, ed. and trans. Holger Sonntag (Minneapolis: Lutheran Press, 2008), 81; WA 39/2:350.

8. *Bondage of the Will*, 1525 (AE 33:140; WA 18:685); emphasis added.

creation. He possesses a will and possibilities that go beyond the promulgated moral law, which therefore open up new eschatological possibilities for creation through His Word of grace.

Through speaking His word of the Gospel God donates Himself to His creatures in the deepest manner possible. In the original creation God donated Himself to humanity by attaching supernaturally perceptible words to His created speech as a means of sharing the good with them. Through these media God made Himself into the tangible and graspable servant of humanity through the promise of the good. Indeed, one who makes an unconditional promise to another subjects himself to that other in order to fulfill the promise. In speaking of the gratuitous promises of the good through creation Luther writes: "For here we see *how the Father has given Himself to us, together with all creatures . . .*"[9]

In the *protoevangelium* God donates Himself in a new way to Adam and Eve through the promise of a Savior. As the Father gave this Savior to humanity tangibly in and through His creaturely words, now after the fall into sin God donates and objectifies Himself in an even more profound way through the promise of the incarnation and death of His eternal Word and Son. Although God acted and continues to act and give access to the good through His various creaturely masks, He is not incarnate in them. In the promise of Christ, though, God identifies Himself with humanity and its plight totally by an act of self-binding. In this sense the giving of the *protoevangelium* is itself the beginning of Christ's *kenosis.* Even before He becomes flesh in Christ, through the promise He stands in solidarity with human beings under sin and death. Likewise, as God's eternal Word, Christ is present through the power of the Spirit in all the supernaturally audible words God gives to humanity. This solidarity given through God's Word drives the whole historical process of the history of salvation as it is recorded in Sacred Scripture. Salvation history culminates in the communication of the fullness of His divine glory to the man Jesus, and by taking upon Himself the curse of death He had imposed on the old creation.

God's speaking forth of the *protoevangelium* is a disruptive, apocalyptic event. Giving the unilateral promise of grace represents a disruptive break in God's word of judgment spoken over Adam and Eve. Whereas in His word of Law God judged and demanded, out of the inexhaustible well of His gracious heart He gives unilateral grace. There is nothing God finds desirable about humanity that causes Him to speak His Word of grace. Humans in their state of sin in no way merit God's favor.

THE NEW NARRATIVE OF CREATION

Although God's redemptive speech-act transcends the protological order and the manifestation of His will within it, it nevertheless contradicts neither. It is the same eternal Word, Christ, which speaks forth both. It would be more

---

9. LC II.1 (Bente, 683); emphasis added.

appropriate to state that God's actions in redemption stand in a "dramatic" coherence with His earlier deeds and words. By dramatic we mean that it is dialectically continuous with God's previous acts. When the plot of any good drama is contemplated from the perspective of its end, the course of the actions and the decisions of the characters can be seen to be a logical and coherent whole. This is true even though the character did not behave mechanically so as to make the end of the story absolutely inevitable. Each person's decisions make sense in the light of his character, even if those decisions were not the only ones available. Indeed, there even may be elements of surprise and even occasional disruption in movement in the plot.[10]

The same is true of God in the history of salvation as it is recorded in Sacred Scripture. God's graciousness and self-donation through the *protoevangelium* is not the only option open to Him as the sovereign God. Nevertheless, seen from the perspective of God's entire redemptive plan centered in Christ, this act stands as coherent with His previous gracious actions in creation. As Luther observes in his personal confession of 1528, God's self-donating gift in His Word through creation prefigures His self-donation in Christ:

> These are the three persons and one God, *who has given himself to us all wholly and completely,* with all that he is and has. The Father *gives himself to us,* with heaven and earth and all creatures, in order that they may serve us and benefit us. But this gift has become obscured and useless through Adam's fall. Therefore the Son himself *subsequently gave himself and bestowed all his works,* sufferings, wisdom, and righteousness, and reconciled us to the Father, in order that restored to life and righteousness, we might also know and have the Father and his gifts.[11]

Likewise, in speaking forth a new promise and a new creation God remains faithful to His original creation. The words that command and bless which He has attached to His creatures remain true. The word of the Gospel does not negate the words of creation and Law but rather opens the ears of God's hearing creatures who have become deaf through sin to His supernaturally perceptible words. Hence, the Gospel gives rise to vocation in creation and necessitates the third use of the Law.[12] In the same manner, although the *protoevangelium* represents a disruption in God's judgment and condemnation, it does so by promising that Christ will fulfill God's previous word of Law and judgment on the cross.

In speaking His redemptive word God establishes a counternarrative to the mangled and tragic narrative of the original creation. In order for creation to be redeemed, its story once tragically mangled by sin must be spoken forth again in order to establish a new narrative of creation. As was observed in the previous chapter, creation receives its essence from its narrative.

---

10. For this description of the dramatic see Robert Jenson, *Systematic Theology,* 2 vols. (New York: Oxford University Press, 1997–98), 1:64.
11. *Confession Concerning Christ's Supper,* 1528 (AE 37:366; WA 26:505); emphasis added.
12. SD IV (Bente, 939–51).

Like the old narrative, this new narrative is formed by the pattern of God's effective address of Law and Gospel. Whereas the old narrative succumbed to the tragic power of sin and the condemnation of the Law, the new narrative will be the story of the eternal triumph of divine grace. To achieve this triumph the eternal Word of God became flesh in order to enter into the curse of the Law as a new Adam. Fulfilling and destroying that curse by His divine power, He may speak forth a new creation in the power of His resurrection. It is fitting that the eternal Word undertook this role, in that it was He who spoke forth the first creation (Heb 2:10). In the incarnation, death, and resurrection, Christ creates the world again by the divine power and glory communicated to His flesh (Col 1:19).[13]

The content of the promise of the Gospel that drives along, structures, and actualizes the new narrative of creation encompasses and transcends the promise of blessing given to humanity in the first creation. As previously noted, before the Fall Adam and Eve were given the promise of life and freedom (Gn 1:28; 2:15–17). After the Fall they were given the same promises in a different form by the *protoevangelium*'s prophecy of the destruction of Satan's power by the Seed of the woman (Gn 3:15). Through fulfilling the Law, Christ will give freedom from the curse of the Law, and eternal life.

Regarding temporal promises of life and freedom, throughout Genesis God promises the patriarchs that He will multiply their descendants and give them dominion in the land of Canaan. N. T. Wright demonstrates that these promises to Israel according to the flesh echo those made to the first man and woman at the end of the account of creation in Genesis (Gn 1:28), thereby suggesting that Abraham and his descendants are replacements for Adam and Eve.[14]

With the reference to the same Seed mentioned to Eve, Abraham and his descendants also implicitly receive the promise of the *protoevangelium* (Gn 22:18). God's renewal of His primal promises of life and freedom to Adam and Eve in the testament given to Abraham (Genesis 12, 15, 17) finds its final fulfillment in Christ. Indeed, the promise to Abraham of temporal life and freedom can find its true and full fulfillment only in the death and resurrection of Christ. In mere temporal blessings, the full expression of God's grace manifest in the *protoevangelium* is still limited and marred by the curse of sin, death, and the Law.

The Sinaitic covenant made God's blessings dependent on obedience to the Law (Exodus 19–20, 24). Since Christ is the only Israelite to remain faithful to the Sinaitic covenant, it is proper to say that He is the only object of God's blessings under the terms of the old covenant. Moreover, as the true Israelite He

---

13. For the fittingness of the incarnation see Martin Chemnitz, Polycarp Leyser, and Johann Gerhard, *The Harmony of the Four Evangelists*, trans. Richard Dinda (Malone, TX: Repristination Press, 2009), 1:67–68.

14. N. T. Wright, *Christian Origins and the Question of God*, 4 vols. (Minneapolis: Fortress Press, 1992–2013), 3:720. Wright lists the examples of Gn 12:2; 17:2–8; 22:16; 26:3, 24; 28:3; 35:11; 47:27; 48:3.

is also the only true replacement for Adam and Eve, or as Paul says, the "second Adam" (Romans 5, 1 Corinthians 15). Hence He is the true Seed of blessing promised to the patriarchs. He is the one who gives life and freedom, not only to Israel but to the nations. Indeed, Abraham was promised that his Seed would bless all nations, something that could happen only in Christ's redemption and not in the geographically limited life of Israel according to the flesh.

Finally, the promise to Israel of life and rest (Ex 33:14; Dt 12:10) finds its final fulfillment in the resurrection of the dead and the renewal of all creation (Isaiah 26, 66; Daniel 12; 1 Corinthians 15; Revelation 20–22). The completion of the Abrahamic covenant thus entails not only a release from the guilt and power of sin but also the realization of the original goal and purpose of creation to enter into a final heavenly rest. Jesus' saving work thus also brings creation into that eternal rest prefigured by the Sabbath (Mt 11:28; Hebrews 2–4; Revelation 20–22).[15]

From all this we can recognize that the promise of the Gospel and the new creation do not cancel the promises of blessing of the old creation, but fulfill and expand them into an even greater promise of blessing. The incorporation of the old creation into the new creation is analogous to the *enhypostasis-anhypostasis* Christology of the Fifth Ecumenical Council.[16] In this description of the relationship between Christ's two natures the Council posits that His divine person (*hypostasis*) incorporates into itself (*enhypostasis*) a unit of non-personal human nature (*anhypostasis*). In other words, Christ's human nature subsists in the already existing person of the Son of God, who is, properly speaking, the subject of the incarnation.

By analogy, then, the promise of Christ's new narrative of creation assumes the existence of and incorporates into itself the old creation and God's promises of blessing. Nevertheless, the proper *hypostasis* of the old creation is the new creation and its neutralization of sin and the condemnation of the Law which marred the original creation. Although the old creation continues to subsist as an actual reality, it nonetheless becomes a tragic subplot of the overarching narrative of redemptive promise actualized by Christ in His life, death, and resurrection.

---

15. See a discussion of new creation through recapitulation in Gottfried Thomasius, *Christi: Person und Werk: Darstellung der Evangelisch-lutheranischen Dogmatik vom Mittelpunkt Christologie aus*, 2 vols. (Erlangen: Andreas Deichert Verlag, 1886–1888), 2:216–18; and Gustaf Wingren, *Gospel and Church*, trans. Ross McKenzie (Philadelphia: Fortress Press, 1964), 95–101. See Irenaeus of Lyons, *Against the Heresies* 3.18, in *Ante-Nicene Fathers*, ed. Alexander Roberts and James Donaldson, 10 vols. (Peabody, MA: Hendrickson Publishers, 2004), 1:448 (hereafter cited as ANF).

16. Chemnitz, *Two Natures in Christ*, 30, 68–72; John Meyendorff, *Christ in Eastern Christian Thought* (Washington, DC: Corpus Books, 1969), 38–40, 59–64. For the text of the Fifth Ecumenical Council see Heinrich Denzinger, *The Sources of Catholic Dogma*, trans. Roy Deferrari (St. Louis: B. Herder, 1957), 85–90.

Sacramentality of Salvation History

Much as God channeled the good to humanity before the Fall by attaching a word of promise to all His creatures, in the act of electing Israel God attaches a word of promise to a specific family and its national history. Such promises find their fulcrum in Christ and His establishment of the means of grace by His dominical command and promise. As we observed earlier, Luther taught that God never gives an auditory word without attaching it to a concrete physical object: "God . . . sets before us no word or commandment without including with it something material and outward, and proffering it to us."[17] The ministry of the Word within the church (as distinguished from the ministry of the sacraments) is not one of the bare Word but of the proclamation of the Word that God has attached to the persons and the events of salvation history culminating in Christ. And so Scripture as God's inspired and inerrant written Word serves a role of preserving, interpreting, and proclaiming the words God has attached to the history within which He brings about redemption in Christ. It is not inappropriate to describe the Gospel proclaimed by the church as a "narrated promise."[18] For this reason there is a sacramental quality to salvation history. Just as God's activity in the sacraments is not transparent apart from the Word, so too the meaning and presence of God's activity through salvation history is not knowable to believers apart from its Spirit-wrought interpretation and proclamation by specifically designated inspired prophets and apostles. Just as apart from the promises attached to the sacraments faith has nothing to grasp and cannot receive any of their benefits, apart from God's promises of judgment and redemption attached to various events in salvation history one cannot receive their gracious and saving benefits. Indeed, one cannot even understand why the invisible God has performed these historic actions apart from the Word. As the Reformed theologian Kevin Vanhoozer observes: "Only speech disambiguates behavior. Only God's word disambiguates God's deed."[19] Confessional Lutheran theology thus must reject the position of theologians like Wolfhart Pannenberg who hold that apart from the interpretation of Scripture, the revelatory meaning of salvation history is discernible through human reason.[20]

---

17. *That These Words of Christ, "This Is My Body," Etc., Still Stand Firm Against the Fanatics*, 1527 (AE 37:135–36; WA 23:261).

18. See Ronald Thiemann, *Revelation and Theology: The Gospel as Narrated Promise* (1987; reprint, Eugene, OR: Wipf & Stock, 2005). Though the phrase "narrated promise" is an apt description, we would certainly not endorse everything that Thiemann argues for in this work.

19. Kevin Vanhoozer, *Remythologizing Theology: Divine Action, Passion, and Authorship* (Cambridge, UK: Cambridge University Press, 2012), 213.

20. See Wolfhart Pannenberg et al., *Revelation as History*, ed. Wolfhart Pannenberg and trans. D. Granskou (New York: Macmillan, 1968), 135–39. Also see a similar problematic claim that the facts of history are self-interpreting in John Warwick Montgomery, *Where Is History Going? Essays in Support of the Historical Truth of the Christian Revelation* (Grand Rapids: Zondervan, 1969), 164.

Through the proclamation of salvation history as it is recorded in Scripture the fruits of redemption are offered to the whole of humanity. Scripture witnesses to and proclaims the faithfulness of God in His two words of Law and Gospel as they are manifested in the history of Israel and culminate in Christ's death and resurrection. In this Law–Gospel history God confronts the whole of humanity with its sin "in Adam," while at the same time giving the promise of universal redemption "in Christ" (Romans 5). Thus, this recorded history of Scripture possesses a universal authority and significance.

That Scripture is intended to function as a sacramental witness to the course of God's Law and promise as they find fulfillment in Christ can be shown from the genres the ancient authors drew upon as they were prompted by the inspiring work of the Holy Spirit. For example, regarding the meaning and purpose of the Pentateuch, P. J. Wiseman famously observed that there are similarities between ancient Near Eastern family histories and the book of Genesis (the Wiseman thesis). He posited that Genesis was constituted primarily by a compendium of cuneiform family records originally written by the patriarchs and compiled by Moses.[21] Incidentally, at least in some of his comments recorded in Table Talk Luther seems to have endorsed a similar idea.[22]

In his book *The Structure of Biblical Authority* the Reformed scholar Meredith Kline also has observed the similarities between ancient treaty forms and the covenantal formulas of the Pentateuch. In the ancient Near East, covenantal relationships between sovereigns and vassals were recorded in histories narrating the development of the relationship between the two parties. Kline therefore interprets the whole of the Scriptures as functioning within its ancient setting to witness to the covenantal relationship between God and His people.[23] This would be true not only of the Pentateuch and its laws but also of the historical books, wherein God acts in judgment and salvation on the basis of His faithfulness to His unilateral testament in the Gospel. By extrapolation the Psalms also might be interpreted in this manner, insofar as they offer praise or lament based on God's acts of judgment or redemption within the structure of the covenantal order.[24]

In a similar vein, Vanhoozer correctly observes that Scripture functions within the economy of salvation as a medium whereby the relationship between God and His people is facilitated by means of Law and Gospel:

21. See P. J. Wiseman, *Ancient Records and the Structures of Genesis: A Case for Literary Unity*, ed. D. J. Wiseman (New York: Thomas Nelson Publishers, 1985). In support of Wiseman, see R. K. Harrison, *Introduction to the Old Testament* (Grand Rapids: Wm. B. Eerdmans, 1971), 542–50.

22. See *Table Talk Recorded by Veit Dietrich, 1531–1533* (AE 54:40–41; WATr 1:120–21); *Table Talk Recorded by John Mathesius, 1540* (AE 54:373; WATr 4:620). Many thanks to the Rev. David Jay Webber for directing me to these comments.

23. Meredith Kline, *The Structure of Biblical Authority* (Grand Rapids: Wm. B. Eerdmans, 1972), 27–44.

24. Kline, *Structure of Biblical Authority*, 45–67.

> The covenant relation [between God and His people] would not exist were it not for these texts [the Bible]—God's law and promises fixed in writing—that constitute it. This is how the Law and the Prophets present themselves: as part and parcel of the communicative relation between God and his people, not some independently observed record of alleged divine activity. Scripture is the means whereby God interacts socially (covenantally) through messages.[25]

From a confessional Lutheran perspective Kline and Vanhoozer's approach is helpful because it suggests that Scripture by its very genre is meant to proclaim God's promises of judgment and grace as well as His faithfulness to them. However, Kline may be criticized for interpreting the covenantal structure of scriptural authority primarily in accordance with a Reformed conception of the church as a legal order.[26] Indeed, Kline posits that the Scriptures came to be written down only when Israel became a nation that needed a national constitution.[27] For this reason he and Reformed theologians who have been influenced by him (notably his student Michael Horton) interpret the Bible as a sort of "legal constitution."[28] Unfortunately, this interpretation prioritizes the Law over the Gospel in the definition of the church's identity and mission. It also contradicts Wiseman's insight that the structure of Genesis gives evidence of having been written down in part at a time when Israel was established on the basis of the promise rather than Law (Gal 3:18).

By contrast, the confessional Lutheran will see the witness of Scripture as focused primarily on the Gospel, although not to the detriment of a proper understanding of the Law. The church lives on the basis of the promise, not on the enforcement of a legal covenantal order, whether by the enforcement of the Mosaic Law or, at the time of the Reformation, the establishment of one of Calvin's consistories. This priority of the promise becomes particularly clear when one takes into account the insight from Wiseman's thesis about the origins of Genesis as family histories. The Old Testament is the story of a family, and later a nation, which God called into existence by His creative power, and to which He then attached His word of promise. The entire historical narrative of the Old Testament is centered on the progress of the Seed promised first to Eve and later to the patriarchs.[29]

---

25. Vanhoozer, *Remythologizing Theology*, 214–15.

26. John Leith, *An Introduction to the Reformed Tradition: A Way of Being the Christian Community* (Louisville, KY: Westminster/John Knox, 1980), 146–71.

27. Kline, *Structure of Biblical Authority*, 76–102.

28. Michael Horton, *The Christian Faith: A Systematic Theology for Pilgrims on the Way* (Grand Rapids: Zondervan, 2011), 151–55. In fairness, Horton's treatment, much like his theology in general, is more Gospel-centered than the average Reformed account.

29. Bringing together Wiseman's and Kline's insights into this synthesis might possibly reconcile von Rad's claim that the center of the Old Testament is "recitation" of God's historic deeds with Eichrodt's contention that the central concept is covenant. See Walther Eichrodt, *Theology of the Old Testament*, trans. J. A. Baker, 2 vols. (Philadelphia: The Westminster Press, 1961–67); Gerhard von Rad, *Old Testament Theology: Single Volume Edition*, trans. D. M. G. Stalker, 2 vols. (Peabody, MA: Prince Press, 2005).

As the Scriptures make clear, every step of the way God's creative testamental Word creates and guarantees the reality and continuation of the Israelite family of the promise. God first reconstituted the church in the Garden of Eden through the *protoevangelium*. He gives the same promise to Abraham and thereby constitutes the people of God through the creation of faith in the patriarch's heart. From this point on God creates and preserves the Seed every step of the way through miraculous intervention based on His promise. He causes the matriarchs to become pregnant even when they are infertile. God surpasses even this miracle by the virginal conception of Christ. In doing this God actualizes the Seed by His own miraculous creative power and not by the enforcement of a legal code.

Beyond God's preservation of the Seed by His own supernatural intervention, He saves Israel from destruction, exile, and slavery because of the promises given to the patriarchs. Finally, in Christ they and the whole of humanity are saved from sin, death, the devil, and Law by a unilateral action of God incarnate in the cross and the empty tomb. Ultimately, the church and its "constitution" are *sui generis* among human communities. It is a community based on and regulated by the creative power of the grace found in the promise of the Gospel (a "testamental" order, that is, a unilateral promise), and not an order based on enforced laws (a "covenantal order"—a legal order based on bilateral promises of fealty).[30] Though God addresses us through all His creatures, He has chosen to address us through Scripture with one end in mind: salvation in Christ. Such an address opens our ears so that we might hear Him clearly in all His other creatures and be obedient to Him.

Christ as the Author of Scripture

From the above it should become clear that, as Luther observes, "All of Scripture . . . is pure Christ."[31] And again he writes: "Take Christ out of the Scriptures, and what will you find left in them?"[32] In this same vein Gerhard states:

> Because "the end of the Law" and the nucleus of the Gospel is Christ (Rom 10:4), the ultimate scope [*scopus*] and, therefore, the center of Scripture, to which all things are related, is Jesus Christ . . . Just as man is the epitome of the entire universe and the center of created nature, so Christ is the epitome and center of all Scripture, the Alpha and Omega, with whom all things in Scripture begin and in whom they all end.[33]

Indeed, supporting this idea Jesus states regarding the Old Testament: "You search the Scriptures . . . it is they that bear witness about me" (Jn 5:39). This

---

30. For contrasts between covenant and testament, see summary in Scott Murray, "The Concept of *Diatheke* in the Letter to the Hebrews," *Concordia Theological Quarterly* 66, no. 1 (2002): 41–60.

31. *On the Last Words of David*, 1543 (AE 15:339; WA 54:89).

32. *Bondage of the Will*, 1525 (AE 33:26; WA 18:606).

33. Gerhard, *On the Nature of Theology and Scripture*, 85.

is the case not only because all the history recorded in Scripture is driven to the one goal of Christ or because the testimonies of the inspired prophets and apostles all center on Christ. Rather, it is proper to say that Christ Himself is the author of Scripture and is present in His inspired Word. Jesus states in His promise of inspiration: "The one who hears you hears me" (Lk 10:16). The inspired apostolic word not only represents the will of the risen Christ but mediates His presence, for "I am with you always, to the end of the age" (Mt 28:20).

Although Gerhard holds that it is the whole triune God who is the cause of the inspiration and writing of Sacred Scripture, it is in particular the Son as the Word of God who is the speaking agent of all divine revelation:

> The Son, the second person of the Deity, is called ὁ λόγος, "the Word," and in Chaldaic Bibles "Memrah" because he is that person through whom the Father spoke to our first parents and to the patriarchs and who, in the form that he later assumed in the fullness of time, appeared to the saints in the Old Testament at various times and spoke to them in a similar fashion.[34]

Indeed, then, in all divine revelation it is God's eternal Word who speaks. Consequently, the inspired words of the Bible must properly be thought to be those of Christ. Although the inspiration of the Scriptures is typically attributed to the working of the Spirit (2 Tm 3:16; 2 Pt 1:21), as David Scaer pointed out, the Holy Spirit is always the Spirit of the Son (Gal 4:6).[35]

For this reason, Jesus Himself states, the Spirit is never untethered, as in Enthusiasm, but is always a conduit for the speech of the risen Christ: "When the Spirit of truth comes, he will guide you into all the truth, for he will not speak on his own authority, but *whatever he hears he will speak,* and he will declare to you the things that are to come. He will glorify me, *for he will take what is mine and declare it to you*" (Jn 16:13–14; emphasis added). Christ is the actual author through speaking His Word to the prophets and apostles in the power of the Spirit. In the Old Testament the Spirit acted so as to manifest the presence of the pre-incarnate Christ as the Word. In His revelation of the Old Testament He anticipated the incarnation of Christ and pointed to it through types and rectilinear prophecy. Indeed, as we have seen, there would be no revelation of the Word of God in the history of salvation without the giving of the *protoevangelium*. In His earthly life Christ promised and gave the Spirit to the apostles as His inspired instruments for the writing of the New Testament (Lk 10:16; Jn 16:13–14).

From this conclusion it also follows that since the Holy Spirit is always the Spirit of the pre-incarnate Son (*Filioque, per Filium*), His work must always necessarily be tethered to the work of the cross. As Scaer further observes, Paul identifies the inspired Word of God he preaches as an apostle as the "word of

---

34. Gerhard, *On the Nature of Theology and Scripture*, 53.
35. David Scaer, "Inspiration in Trinitarian Perspective," *Pro Ecclesia* 14, no. 2 (2005): 148–54.

the cross" (1 Cor 1:18). The Corinthians had sought transcendent divine wisdom and spiritual gifts through their charismatic and Enthusiastic experience—through an experience of the Holy Spirit apart from Christ and His cross. Paul counters this approach by claiming that the Spirit is always anchored in the risen Jesus and His cross. [36] Whereas the Corinthians had become Enthusiasts and theologians of glory by holding up their wisdom, glory, and righteousness, the true work of the Spirit always mediates the Word of the cross, which "destroy[s] the wisdom of the wise, and [thwarts] the discernment of the discerning" (1 Cor 1:19).

For John as well, the Holy Spirit is always the Spirit who speaks in harmony with the apostolic testimony that "Jesus Christ has come in the flesh" (1 Jn 4:2), and therefore also implicitly that in that flesh "he is the propitiation for our sins, and not for ours only but also for the sins of the whole world" (1 Jn 2:2). Hence, the Spirit that inspires the Scriptures through the prophets and the apostles is always the Spirit of Jesus, crucified and raised: "the testimony of Jesus is the spirit of prophecy" (Rv 19:10).

In order to explicate this fact the Gospel writers highlight the presence of the Spirit at every stage of Christ's redemptive *kenosis*. It is the Spirit that caused the Virgin Mary to conceive, placing the eternal Word in solidarity with the flesh of fallen Adam (Mt 1:23; Lk 1:26). The Spirit is given publicly to Christ at His baptism, where He voluntarily enters into solidarity with sinners confessing their sins (Mt 3:13–17; Mk 1:9–11; Lk 3:21–23). Christ's solidarity with sinners culminates on the cross. In His redemptive death He accepts full responsibility for the sins of humanity. Through the Spirit He offers Himself to the Father: "Christ . . . through the eternal Spirit offered himself without blemish to God" (Heb 9:14). And "Father, into your hands I commit my spirit!" (Lk 23:46).[37] Finally, it is the Spirit who raises Christ from the dead and gives to Him the eternal testament of forgiveness (Rv 5:3–5). Christ bestows on the apostles the same Spirit through the channel of the Gospel of forgiveness conditioned and shaped by His work of the cross, both as He breathes on them (Jn 20:19–23) and at Pentecost (Acts 2).

The manifestation of the Spirit and His gifts of revelation and inspiration thus always are conditioned on the basis of the word and work of the Son. In the history of salvation the Holy Spirit's work of revelation and inspiration begins with the *protoevangelium* and ends with the apostolic witness to the cross and empty tomb. The Spirit is not an amorphous gift, bestowing on the prophets and apostles a kind of mystical experience that might ultimately reveal anything about God's will. Rather, being ordered to and conditioned by the work of the Son, the Spirit reveals and presses the Son's own cruciform existence on the

---

36. Scaer, "Inspiration in Trinitarian Perspective," 153.

37. In the Luke quotation, some might object that Jesus is offering His human spirit. This is an irrelevant point. Because of the hypostatic union, Jesus' "human spirit" is always united with the eternal Word and hence also with the Holy Spirit, which proceeds from Him.

pattern of the revelation of the Scriptures and on those redeemed creatures who receive them (Mt 16:24; Rom 6:4; Col 2:12).[38]

Tentatio: **The Cruciform Movement of the Word in the History of Salvation**

As we observed in the last section, Christ has been present in the external Word in the power of the Spirit from the beginning of creation. In the giving of the *protoevangelium* He enters into a *kenosis*, wherein He becomes a redemptive servant to Israel and ultimately the whole of humanity. Such a *kenosis* through the Word necessarily leads to the suffering of opposition and persecution. In speaking the *protoevangelium* God promises the woman not only that her own Seed would destroy the power of Satan but that there would be opposition and strife from the seed of the serpent. In John's Gospel Jesus seemingly makes an allusion to this verse in describing as children of the devil those who oppose Him and His embodiment of revealed truth of God (Jn 8:44).

As we have observed, the Seed of the woman is Christ, and we might add by proxy, those who are mystically united with Him by faith (*totus Christus*).[39] As God's eternal Word who spoke through the prophets and the apostles, Christ is God's supreme prophet. He is not an Enthusiast who discovers truth from within Himself. Rather, from all eternity He receives Himself as the Father's Word. In time this eternal reality is manifested in the fact that the incarnate Christ hears and believes the Father's external Word in Scripture and through the revelations given to Him at key points in His ministry. He obeys what is revealed to Him by the Father through the Word, accepts His plan of redemption, and patiently awaits "the hour" when His vocation will be fulfilled.[40] Moreover, as we have already observed, those whom God has elected to serve as prophets and apostles participate secondarily in the prophetic ministry of Christ through His act of inspiration and revelation to them. Like their master, they obey God's Word and suffer opposition because of it.

Since the pre-incarnate Christ predicted to Eve that there would be strife between her Seed and that of Satan, the Word of God given to the prophets and apostles is not mere heavenly information that comes into the world unopposed. Rather, as Luther puts it:

> The most unvarying fate of the Word of God [is] to have the world in a state of tumult because of it. . . . The world and its god cannot and will not endure the Word of the true God, and the true God neither will nor can keep silence; so when these two Gods are at war with one another, what can there be but tumult in the whole world?[41]

---

38. Scaer, "Inspiration in Trinitarian Perspective," 152–54.
39. See Tyconius, *The Book of Rules*, trans. W. S. Babcock (Atlanta: Scholars Press, 1989), 2–14.
40. Balthasar, *Theo-Drama* 4:231–40.
41. *Bondage of the Will*, 1525 (AE 33:52; WA 18:626).

Just as Christ is the supreme prophet, Satan is the arch-Enthusiast. Since the foundation of all reality is the Word of God, Satan can only oppose and contradict what God has already established as true. The same is true with his children, who violently oppose the Word and throw the world into a tumult with their rage.

Herein lies what Paul calls the "mystery of lawlessness" (2 Thes 2:7). As Paul tells the Thessalonians, the "mystery of lawlessness" is already in the world, even if the "man of lawlessness" is still to come (2 Thes 2:8).[42] "Lawlessness" cannot be understood as anything less than another name for Enthusiasm, in that one who is lawless rejects his accountability to God's external Word in favor of his own inner law. The "lawless one" exalts himself over everything, meaning he makes himself and his own inner truth into a god (2 Thes 2:4). In a similar vein, John observes "sin is lawlessness" (Jn 3:4), and Paul states that "whatever does not proceed from faith is sin" (Rom 14:23). Sin is therefore in its essence that which turns one away from faith in the external Word. In turning from the external Word the person of sin is oriented toward his own inner sense of truth, thereby becoming an Enthusiast and lawless.[43]

The power of lawlessness has been at work since the Fall and yet remains mysterious. It is mysterious because, although God's Word is living and therefore always efficacious, it nevertheless has a differentiating effect. The proclamation of the Word removes the inborn Enthusiasm of some, thereby justifying and sanctifying them. Others, however, harden themselves upon hearing the Word.

John highlights this differentiating effect in his Gospel, where the discourses of Jesus repel many people while creating faith in others (notably in John 6). As we can observe in Jesus' Parable of the Sower in the Synoptic tradition (Mt 13:1–23; Mk 4:3–20; Lk 8:1–15), the Sower (the Son) spreads His seed (the Word and Spirit) indiscriminately. The Farmer does not pretend to sow His seed (i.e., Calvinism), but filled with overflowing love He spreads it everywhere. Some seed falls on good soil and other on bad. The mystery is why some soil remains bad, when the same universally loving Farmer could very well dig it up and cultivate it. The reality, though, is that some seed (the Word) is choked off and repelled by the soil, whereas in other soil it bears fruit. Herein lies the mystery of lawlessness, as well as the grace of election.[44]

Even if lawlessness in human history remains a mystery, it is a very real and potent force opposing the Word of God. Both Luther[45] and Melanchthon[46]

---

42. I must credit my understanding of this distinction to a conversation I had with Dr. Charles Gieschen, who uses it in his forthcoming commentary on 1 and 2 Thessalonians.

43. SA III.viii (Bente, 495–96).

44. SD XI (Bente, 1063–95).

45. See John Headley, *Luther's View of Church History* (New Haven: Yale University Press, 1963).

46. See Peter Fraenkel, *Testimonia Patrum: The Function of Patristic Argument in the Theology of Philip Melanchthon* (Geneva: Librairie E. Droz, 1961), 61–62, 69, 100–118.

recognized that the history of creation and salvation is the story of the war between those who believed God's Word and Enthusiasts standing in opposition to it. Because within the post-lapsarian world God's Word always suffers opposition, the history of salvation is an arena of testing, suffering, and bearing the cross for those who receive the Word with faith and proclaim it. Since Christ was present in the Word given to the prophets and apostles from the time of the *protoevangelium* onward, through resistance to His Word He also kenotically suffers perpetual testing and opposition (Mt 11:12–19).

Drawing on Psalm 119[47] Luther wrote of the true knowledge or understanding of God's Word coming to an individual through the guidance of the Spirit in prayer (*oratio*) and through contemplation of the written Word of God (*meditatio*). He taught that when the Spirit had manifested the truth of God's Word to the person, he was bound also to proclaim that truth. In proclaiming God's truth, he also must submit to the final stage of interpretation: *tentatio*. *Tentatio* means suffering, temptation, and testing. When tested by opposing forces, the theologian may come to recognize he has been mistaken and has fallen under the influence of a spirit that is not of Christ. Even if one is truthful and genuinely has apprehended God's truth, he still will be placed in a position to be attacked by the devil, the world, and his own sinful nature. The person of faith will endure this suffering, and God's Word will establish itself as true in both judgment and salvation.[48] As should be evident, the inspired prophets and apostles received God's revelation by the working of the Word and the Spirit, as do non-inspired interpreters, who likewise must submit to testing, suffering, and opposition.

Such testing and suffering of opposition occurs in two stages. The first stage is the opposition God's self-revelation must suffer from the unwilling human subject under the thrall of sin. Norman Habel observes in his famous article on prophetic commissions that there is an established pattern throughout the Old Testament in how God calls His prophets. Most important to our discussion is the fact that upon hearing God's call, the sinful mind of the prophet revolts. God then reassures the prophet with His grace and gives him a miraculous sacramental sign to affirm the validity of the call. Through this God overcomes the prophet's resistance and establishes him as a willing vessel for His revelation.[49]

---

47. *Preface to the Wittenberg Edition of Luther's German Writings*, 1539 (AE 34:285–88; WA 50:658–60).

48. See good descriptions in Oswald Bayer, *Theology the Lutheran Way*, trans. Jeffrey Silcock and Mark Mattes (Grand Rapids: Wm. B. Eerdmans, 2007), 33–36; Bayer, *Martin Luther's Theology*, 32–37; Reinhard Hütter, *Suffering Divine Things: Theology as Church Practice*, trans. Doug Stott (Grand Rapids: Wm. B. Eerdmans, 2000), 72–76; John Kleinig, "*Oratio, Meditatio, Tentatio*: What Makes a Theologian?" *Concordia Theological Quarterly* 66, no. 3 (2002): 255–68; Pieper, *Christian Dogmatics* 1:186–90; and Martin Nicol, *Meditation bei Luther* (Göttingen: Vandenhoeck and Ruprecht, 1984), 91–101. Both Nicol and Bayer note the influence of monastic practices of reading on Luther's method.

49. See Norman Habel, "The Form and Significance of the Call Narratives," *Zeitschrift für*

This pattern of prophetic call also holds true for Jesus' call of the apostles in the Gospel resurrection narratives. After Jesus is resurrected the apostles initially resist the good news given to them by the women returning from the empty tomb. But they finally come to accept the resurrection and their apostolic vocation when confronted by the presence of the risen Christ, His word of assurance, and the visible signs He offers them.

God's Word thus kenotically suffers opposition even from the sinful flesh of the prophets and apostles. But by its hidden divine power the Word overcomes such opposition and establishes itself as the truth. The prophet or apostle is drawn out of his own inborn Enthusiasm to God's external self-communication through the Word and the Spirit. It follows that in establishing the prophets and apostles in their offices as His amanuenses[50] God subjects them and their words to the same testing and opposition. In Deuteronomy God sets forth through Moses the criteria for true prophecy: a true prophet must prophesy in the name of the Lord, and what he prophesies must come true (Dt 18:18–22).

The first criterion means the word the prophet speaks must stand in continuity with God's previously established revelation. In revealing Himself, God attaches His name to His revelation: "I am the God of Abraham, Isaac, and Jacob" (Ex 3:6). Indeed, through Moses the preamble to God's entire revelation is the disclosure of His name (Ex 3:14). In revealing Himself, God thus attaches His name to specific historical events and persons.

In fact, God and His revelation are identifiable only because of His connection to specific historical events. The Old Testament scholar Albrecht Alt notes that in contrast with the pagan gods of the ancient Near East, who typically are identified by their connection with a geographical location (Baal of Peor, etc.), the God of the Bible identifies Himself primarily with persons and historical events.[51] One might even say that although historical events do not ontologically alter God's eternal and immutable being, they nevertheless are incorporated into His identity. Much as in the incarnation, wherein God the Son incorporates an anhypostatic humanity into His already existing person, so too without somehow evolving or adding onto His being (as in the case of Hegelian-inspired theologies[52]), God nevertheless identifies Himself with the history in which He creates and redeems.

This pattern is most evident when YHWH identifies Himself to Moses through His connection to the patriarchs and their history. He tells Moses both that He is the God of his ancestors and that He will fulfill promises made to them. For this reason Moses' proclamation of God's Word stands or falls on the basis of the historical continuity of God's faithfulness (חֶסֶד) to His promises.

die Alttestamentliche Wissenschaft 77 (1965): 297–323.

50. Robert Preus, *The Inspiration of Scripture: A Study of the Theology of the Seventeenth Century Lutheran Dogmaticians* (St. Louis: Concordia Publishing House, 2003), 54.

51. Albrecht Alt, "God of the Fathers," in *Essays on Old Testament and Religion*, trans. R. A. Wilson (Oxford: Basil Blackwell, 1966), 3–66.

52. For example, Moltmann, *Crucified God*, and Jenson, *Systematic Theology*.

God was faithful to His promises to the patriarchs. He gave them children and prosperity, and finally led Israel out of Egypt.

Deuteronomy thus presupposes that the previous revelations (with which a true prophet must stand in continuity) have been validated.[53] Indeed, God remained faithful to the patriarchs and Israel in spite of many barriers. Such barriers provided a means of testing what God had declared would come to pass (the infertility of the matriarchs, the power of Pharaoh, etc.). Throughout the books of Exodus and Numbers, Moses' own ministry suffered continuous opposition and testing (Exodus 32, Numbers 12 and 16, etc.). Nonetheless, God validated Moses' prophetic ministry and his speaking of God's Word by effective signs, especially in the form of the judgment of the prophet's opponents. Thus, to prophesy in God's name is to invoke all previous revelations to which He has attached His name.[54] This is important, because although many false prophets can give miraculous signs (Dt 13:1–5; Mt 24:24), their words will always be out of harmony with God's previously established revelation (Mt 5:15–16).[55]

Deuteronomy 18 points to the second criterion of a true prophet: because God's Word is almighty, what the true prophet proclaims proves and vindicates itself by "coming to pass." The person of faith will recognize the fulfillment and validity of the Word, because the power of the Word will both effect the objective realities upon which faith stands (i.e., the salvific events of history) and open the hearts and minds of the faithful to recognize their objective reality (Rom 8:16; Gal 3:2).

Similarly, faith active in hope may also anticipate God's future faithfulness based on past and present faithfulness (Rom 4:18–22; Heb 11:1). God created faith in Abraham's heart through the word proclaimed to him (Genesis 12, 15), and strengthened it by protecting him and giving him offspring in his old age. Finding God to be trustworthy, Abraham believed that in the future God would fulfill His promises to give his descendants the land of Canaan and send them the Messiah (Genesis 12, 15, 17, 22). Likewise, the prophets of the Old Testament performed signs and made prophetic statements that were fulfilled within the immediate experience of their audiences. This verification of their divine calling in the present also validated what they spoke regarding the future coming of Christ and the era of the New Testament.

Hence, the self-establishing validity of the Word of God can take a variety of forms. Although some might wish to interpret the fulfillment of the Word spoken of in Deuteronomy 18 as referring exclusively to predictive prophecy, this need not be the case. Indeed, if that were true it would be impossible to believe any of God's prophets until what they had spoken came true. In many cases this fulfillment would be decades or even centuries in the future, at which point it would be too late to respond to God's promise of salvation or judgment.

---

53. *Lectures on Deuteronomy*, 1523–1525 (AE 9:188; WA 14:684–85).
54. *Lectures on Deuteronomy*, 1523–1525 (AE 9:187; WA 14:684).
55. *Lectures on Deuteronomy*, 1523–1525 (AE 9:129–31; WA 14:647).

Nevertheless, because God's Word is creative and effective, its "coming to pass" may be either in the present or in the future.

For example, in the miracles of prophets in the Old Testament we often find that the prophets prayed to God (1 Kgs 17:21–22; 18:41–19:8) or announced a miraculous event God would perform (Exodus 7–12). Subsequently the miraculous event came to pass in accordance with the prayer or the word that been announced previously. The same is true of the proclamation of the Law and Gospel. The Word of God is proclaimed and the hearers are convicted and justified by the divine power of the Word. Thereby the Word of God causes what it says, whether judgment or grace, to come to pass. Finally, the efficacy of God's Word may find its fulfillment in prophecies that have come to pass regarding the future. Some prophecies are fulfilled in the short term, others in the long term. With most of the prophets, prophecies regarding the distant future are accompanied by prophecies concerning the immediate future (Isaiah 1–39 vs. 40–66; Ezekiel 1–32 vs. 33–48, etc.). The fulfillment of the immediate prophecies reveals God's presence in the prophet and validates the truth of the future prophecy.[56]

The ministry of Christ is the supreme fulfillment of all prophecy and therefore the epitome of Deuteronomy's criteria of true prophecy. Indeed, the preamble of Moses' authorization of all future prophecy is a prediction of Christ as a "prophet like me [Moses]" (Dt 18:18).[57] Christ fulfilled Moses' criteria by prophesying in the Father's name (Jn 5:43; 12:28; 17:1) and affirming the authority of God's previous revelations in the Old Testament (Mt 5:17; Jn 5:39, 45–47; 10:35). Likewise, Christ's words "came to pass" in the performance of miracles, by convicting consciences and creating faith in His hearers, and finally by the fulfillment of His prophecy of the resurrection. In the resurrection the Father placed a stamp of approval on all Christ said and did (Acts 2:22–36). This approval included Christ's affirmation of the authority of the Old Testament and also of the apostles as His infallibly inspired witnesses.

Moreover, all these objective validations of God's Word were received by the apostles and the early church through the divine power of the words Christ proclaimed. By the creation of faith a "cloud of witnesses" (Heb 12:1) gained new hearts and minds to be able to perceive and receive the objective fulfillment of Christ's word (Lk 24:32; Jn 24:29). Christ gave the apostles divine power to perform miraculous signs in order to validate their own ministries in the sight of their original hearers (Acts 2; Heb 2:2–3), who in turn could witness to the validity of their offices and the authority of the canonical New Testament they produced.

---

56. *Lectures on Deuteronomy*, 1523–1525 (AE 9:188–89; WA 14:684–85). Luther sees not just predictive prophecy but also miracles as a fulfillment of this criterion. According to Luther, God never gives new doctrines without objective signs.

57. See *Lectures on Deuteronomy*, 1523–1525 (AE 9:176–86; WA 14:675–83) and Carl Friedrich Keil and Franz Delitzsch, *Biblical Commentary on the Old Testament*, vol. 3: *The Pentateuch*, trans. James Martin (1865; reprint, Peabody, MA: Hendrickson Publishers, 1996), 934–36.

In spite of this glorious fulfillment, God's Word must always withstand opposition from His fallen creatures. Testing must precede validation. As in the life of Christ, humiliation always precedes glory, and trial always precedes vindication. Indeed, the reality of testing and opposition to God's Word reveals the deep kenotic dimension to the act of revelation. Through His Word God not only reveals Himself, His will, and His purpose but is sacramentally present in it by the power of the Spirit (Mt 18:20; 28:20; Gal 3:2). God's eternal Word, without losing its uncreated power and glory, kenotically makes itself available and tangible through the medium of finite human words. By making Himself known and tangible through His revelation in means, God opens Himself up to rejection, blasphemy, and abuse by His creatures.

Indeed, one suspects that this is the motivation behind Aquinas and Barth's previously discussed theories of revelational analogy. If God makes Himself to be known in a merely analogical echo, then He does not fully open Himself up to the possibility of blasphemous abuse, misuse, or rejection of His Word. If God does not fully identify Himself with the means of grace, then He is saved from being rejected and abused when they are rejected and abused.

Aquinas and Barth's revelational analogy is of course the logical corollary of their thoroughly Leonine view of the incarnation, wherein the *communicatio idiomatum* is little more than notional.[58] Nevertheless, as Luther notes, a God who does not communicate Himself fully to the flesh of Christ and suffer abuse is ultimately of no use to us.[59] And a God who has not communicated Himself fully to the external Word as both propositional truth and effective presence is of no use to His sinful creatures in need of "grace and truth" (Jn 1:14). If God is not fully present in His Word then He remains distant and hidden from His creatures, and they cannot grasp Him for the sake of their salvation. Just as the very Word of God made flesh submitted Himself to abuse and blasphemy on the cross and yet triumphed in the resurrection, in giving His external Word God submits Himself to abuse and opposition, and yet triumphs in either the creation of faith or the hardening of judgment.

This self-gift of God in the revelation of the Word manifests itself in a number of ways, most particularly in the aforementioned biblical theme of the revelation of the divine name.[60] Johann Michael Reu observes: "So His [God's] name is much like His Word—in fact, it is the shortest form of His Word; and

---

58. See my description in "Thomas Aquinas and Martin Chemnitz on the Hypostatic Union," *Lutheran Quarterly* 27, no. 1 (2013): 1–32.

59. Regarding Zwingli's attempt to separate the two natures in Christ, Luther writes: "Beware, beware, I say, of this alloeosis, for it is the devil's mask since it will finally construct a kind of Christ after whom I would not want to be a Christian, that is, a Christ who is and does no more in his passion and his life than any other ordinary saint. For if I believe that only the human nature suffered for me, then Christ would be a poor savior for me, in fact, he himself would need a Savior. In short, it is indescribable what the devil attempts with this alloeosis." *Confession Concerning Christ's Supper*, 1528 (AE 37:209–10; WA 26:319).

60. See Robert Hayward, *Divine Name and Presence: The Memra* (Lanham, MD: Rowman & Littlefield, 1982).

whatever we do to God's Word we are also doing to His name."[61] Indeed, as we observed earlier, throughout the history of salvation God's Word has always been accompanied by the revelation of His name. The revelation of God's name does not give human beings a mere label to place on Him but defines God's identity in relationship to specific persons and events ("I am the God of . . ." etc.).

Going a step further, it can be argued that the name of God is in actuality synonymous with the Word of God.[62] The revealed name of God in Ex 3:14 is often translated as "I am what I am" (Ex 3:14), but might be translated more properly "I will be who I will be," or even "I am the one who brings into being" (אֶהְיֶה אֲשֶׁר אֶהְיֶה, condensed into YHWH). Moreover, we are told in Genesis 1 that the first words God utters are "Let there be." As Charles Gieschen has shown, many early Jewish interpreters of the text made a connection between the Word of God and the divine name because they possess the identical verb "to be."[63] That there is an intentional connection between Genesis 1 and Exodus 3, and not just one in the imaginations of the later interpreters, seems highly plausible not only because of the linguistic similarity between the verb "to be" and the divine name, but also because God's identity and agency are tied inexorably to one another throughout the Old Testament.

If we accept this identification, the implications are clear. God's name identifies Him as the sovereign one. Such sovereignty expresses itself in His ability to establish external relationships with His creatures as He so desires through His Word. This is true both in creation ("I am the one who brings into being") and in redemption ("I will be who I will be"). Thus, in speaking His Word God narrates into existence the events of the history of salvation, as He did the original creation. He also attaches His name to these historical events and persons as a means of revealing Himself and the covenant/testament faithfulness (חֶסֶד) He displays in them.

God's name/Word also is identified throughout the Old Testament with His glory (כָּבוֹד). Indeed, the tabernacle/temple is described interchangeably as the place of the dwelling of the glory of YHWH (Exodus 40) and YHWH's name: "He [Solomon/the Messiah] shall build a *house for my name*, and I will establish the throne of his kingdom forever" (2 Sm 7:13; emphasis added; also see Dt 12:5, 11; 1 Kgs 5:5; 8:16; Chr 6:5).[64] This identification also is made in Exodus by an act of poetic parallelism. When Moses is told he will see God's hypostatized

61. Johann Michael Reu, *An Explanation of Dr. Martin Luther's Small Catechism* (Minneapolis: Augsburg Publishing House, 1964), 138.

62. Charles Gieschen, *Angelomorphic Christology: Antecedents and Early Evidence* (Leiden: Brill, 1998), 103–7; Charles Gieschen, "The Real Presence of the Son before Christ: Revisiting an Old Approach to Old Testament Christology," *Concordia Theological Quarterly* 68 (2004): 105–26. Also see Johann Gerhard, *On the Law*, trans. Richard Dinda (St. Louis: Concordia Publishing House, 2015), 118.

63. Gieschen, *Angelomorphic Christology*, 74.

64. See discussion of the relationship of God's name and glory in J. Gordon McConville, "God's Name and God's Glory," *Tyndale Bulletin* 30 (1979): 149–63.

glory (כָּבוֹד), YHWH explains: "I will *make all my goodness pass before you* and will proclaim *before you my name 'The Lord.'* And I will be gracious to whom I will be gracious, and will show mercy on whom I will show mercy" (Ex 33:19; emphasis added).

In giving His Word God thus gives Israel His very self in the form of His name and His presence as a manifestation of His covenantal/testamental faithfulness (חֶסֶד). Luther shows in his Large Catechism that the ultimate goal of giving the divine name is that people might call upon it in faith.[65] As the Lord of the promise, God gives His name and presence to His people, and as a kenotic servant He allows them to call upon it for redemption. The giving of the name is the giving of the very self to the creature of faith.

If God gives only an indirect echo of Himself in revelation without giving genuine access to His being (as we have argued in the case of Thomistic and Barthian analogy), then people cannot take hold of, grasp, and call upon God's name as their ultimate object of trust. Indeed, when Paul describes justification by faith he states: "For the Scripture says . . . 'everyone who calls on the *name of the Lord* will be saved'" (Rom 10:11, 13; emphasis added). As Michael Horton observes, part of the background of this often-cited formulation in the Bible, "calling upon the name of the Lord," may be the ancient Near Eastern practice of a lesser noble being given his liege lord's name so that he might call upon it in a time of distress.[66]

Insofar as the giving of the divine name is also coterminous with the giving of the whole of God's Word, it functions not only as Gospel but also as Law. We are commanded to call on God's name alone and not that of any false god. Similarly, as Luther states in the Large Catechism, those who misuse God's name and do not keep it holy subject themselves to divine judgment. We keep God's name holy when we do not abuse it but use it trustingly to call upon Him and praise Him for the salvation He gives.[67]

Again, as we saw earlier, the giving of God's Word is a kenotic act. It is intended to be a means of salvation, but in entering into a sinful and fallen world the Lord also necessarily opens Himself up to the possibility of abuse in the form of blasphemy by His historical revelation. People who do not know God's name cannot blaspheme it. But people who do not know it cannot call upon it in faith either. God suffers the abuse of those who use His name to blaspheme Him, but ultimately He will vindicate His name in judgment, and thereby will establish the truthfulness of His address of Law and promise. Likewise, He overcomes the sinful opposition of those in whose hearts He creates faith, and thus also establishes the truth of His revelation.

As should be clear from this entire discussion, the kenotic movement of the Word/name forms a cruciform pattern. Throughout the scriptural history the

---

65. LC I.2 (Bente, 593–603).
66. Horton, *Christian Faith*, 108–9.
67. LC I.2 (Bente, 593–603); LC III.1 (Bente, 707–11).

Word of God is given in the form of the divine name, which leads to blasphemy and opposition and is followed by glory and vindication. This same pattern actualizes itself in a final way in the life history of God's living Word, Jesus, in His death and resurrection.

As we have seen previously, the divine name is identical with God's hypostatized presence. The tabernacle/temple that contains the divine presence is called a "house for my name" (2 Sm 7:13). In affirming His promise to Abraham and His redemptive relationship with Israel, God gives Moses His name in Exodus 3. By giving His name to Israel He unilaterally and redemptively binds His reality to their fate. God attaches His name to the patriarchs and ultimately to the nation, so that He comes to be known as the "God of Israel" (Jgs 11:21; 2 Sm 12:7; 23:3; 1 Kgs 8:23; 2 Chr 11:16; Ps 68:8, etc.).

It follows that because God freed and exalted Israel in the exodus, the divine name is exalted (Ex 9:16). Conversely, God's name is cursed among the nations when Israel sins and violates the Sinaitic covenant (Ez 36:20). Because God binds His Word/name to Israel, its exile becomes His own exile (particularly from the temple, Ezekiel 8–11). God's judgment of Israel means He must place His name and presence under the very judgment He has inflicted. The giving of the Word/name thus entails an exchange of realities between Israel and God, a prefiguration of both the *communicatio idiomatum* of the incarnation[68] and the "happy exchange" (*der fröhlicher Wechsel*) between Christ and the believer facilitated by the proclamation of the Word.[69] The judgment of exile, which forms the whole narrative arch of the Old Testament, prefigures God's own crucifixion in the person of His Son. Shadrach, Meshach, and Abednego as God's witnesses in the fiery furnace prefigure Christ's descent into hell (Daniel 3).

In the end Yhwh will redeem Israel not for their sake but for the sake of His name (Ez 36:22). God's name and presence, which had suffered blasphemy and opposition, would come out of exile (Is 40:3–5; Ez 37:27; Zec 2:10–11; Mal 3:1) and be exalted (Is 45:23). There will be a final moment of universal reconciliation where all the nations recognize His name and will give true worship (Is 45:23). If the nations worship God's name, it is only logical to think they have received the promise of the Gospel, which entails their reception of the divine name so that they may call upon it for salvation. The identification of Israel through the giving of His Word/name is a necessary stage in the exaltation of His name/Word. Humiliation comes before glory, trial before vindication. Just as the exile and rejection of God's name/Word prefigure the crucifixion, the return from exile prefigures God's final triumph and exaltation in His Son's resurrection.

God's Word/name was to be exalted through the Davidic line: David inherits the promises given to Abraham, through whom God had promised to

---

68. See Steiger, "*Communicatio Idiomatum,*" 125–58.
69. *On the Freedom of a Christian,* 1520 (AE 31:351; WA 7:55). See discussion in Bayer, *Martin Luther's Theology,* 225–29.

bless all nations (Gn 12:2). Before Abraham's election, the one who receives the blessing of the coming Seed is Noah's son Shem (Gn 9:26–27). Shem, whose name literally means "name,"[70] inherits the promise of the *protoevangelium*. Abraham then inherits God's promise to Shem to bring about the reconciliation of the Gentiles (suggested by Gn 9:26–27), and is told that his name will be great (Gn 12:2). All the nations will be blessed and reconciled in the Seed of Abraham, as Shem's descendant (Gn 22:18).

This promise directly parallels God's statement in Isaiah 45 that the exaltation of His name would coincide with the reconciliation of the nations. Elsewhere, David as the representative Israelite is told that his name will be made great: "I will make for you a great name, like the name of the great ones of the earth" (2 Sm 7:9). This will come about because God will establish the eternal throne of the Messiah. David states in his prayer in response to the oracle: "This is the instruction of all mankind" (2 Sm 7:19). He goes on to prophesy that by God fulfilling His promise, His name also will be exalted among the nations (2 Sm 7:26). In other words, by way of the exaltation of David's Seed and name, which embody the destiny of Israel, God's own name will be exalted, thereby fulfilling His Gospel promises to Adam, Eve, and Abraham about the coming Seed. The exaltation of Israel and of Yhwh's name merge into a single reality, that is, a single person. As the New Testament shows us, this single person is the Word made flesh, Christ. He is the name/Word of God, who donates Himself to His people in grace. As in the era of the Old Testament, such a self-gift necessarily entails the suffering of humiliation, blasphemy, and opposition.

This pattern is particularly evident in the Gospel of Matthew. Not only does Matthew begin his narrative by highlighting Jesus' descent from Abraham and David, he identifies Him with God's name and presence: "You are to give him *the name Jesus* [God is our salvation] because he will save his people from their sins. . . . they will *call him 'Immanuel' (which means 'God with us')*" (Mt 1:21, 23 NIV; emphasis added). This naming is paralleled at the end of the Gospel, where Jesus attaches a promise to His name and presence in Word and Sacrament: "Go therefore and make disciples of all nations, baptizing them *in the name of the Father and of the Son and of the Holy Spirit*, teaching them to observe all that I have commanded you. And behold, *I am with you always*, to the end of the age" (Mt 28:19–20; emphasis added). Indeed, Jesus' name is identified with His presence elsewhere in the Gospel: "For where two or three are gathered in my name, there am I among them" (Mt 18:20).[71]

Moreover, Jesus is not just the presence and name of God, He is the Word of God. In the Sermon on the Mount Jesus stands on the mountain and addresses the people directly as Yhwh attempted to do in Exodus 19–20. Jesus is identified

---

70. Scott Hahn, *Covenant by Kinship: A Canonical Approach to the Fulfillment of God's Saving Promises* (New Haven: Yale University Press, 2009), 98.

71. See discussions in Charles Gieschen, "The Divine Name in Ante-Nicene Christianity," *Viliae Christianae* 57 (2003): 124–25; David Scaer, *Discourses in Matthew: Jesus Teaches the Church* (St. Louis: Concordia Publishing House, 2004), 172, 202.

with the very voice of God. Indeed, as the very voice of God, Jesus' words are eternal and divine: "Heaven and earth will pass away, but my words will not pass away" (Mt 24:35, paralleling Is 40:8). Matthew implicitly characterizes Him as the living Torah by organizing Jesus' teachings into five great discourses corresponding to the five books of Moses.[72] In many circles in Second Temple Judaism (particularly the Pharisees), to study Torah was seen as a means of entering into God's own presence in parallel with the temple.[73]

Jesus as the living Torah and name of God made flesh not only serves as God's definitive self-revelation but also becomes the occasion upon which Israel and the nations commit the ultimate act of blasphemy. As Jesus illustrates in a number of His parables late in the Gospel (Mt 21:33–46; 22:1–14), God's self-objectification in the incarnation is the culmination of the whole history of Israel rejecting the prophets and the Gentiles trampling upon Israel. The testing and opposition suffered by the prophets in the Old Testament becomes definitive in the testing and opposition of the Word/name made flesh.[74] Nevertheless, much as God vindicated His Word/name in spite of sinful opposition in the Old Testament, so too Christ is resurrected and exalted at the end of the Gospel. God thus conclusively defines His relationship to humanity through His Word against all opposition. The "I will be who I will be" (YHWH) has chosen to become "God is our salvation" (Jesus) in spite His rejection by sinful humanity (Acts 2:36; Phil 2:9–11; Heb 1:4).[75]

In Jesus the whole history of the strife between God's Word and Enthusiasm—the Seed of the woman and the seed of the serpent—comes to its climax. Throughout the history of salvation the Word of God was spoken, thereby either hardening or redeeming its hearers by its effective power. Although hardening in response to God's Word remains ever mysterious, it nevertheless becomes the occasion for the Word to manifest its power and truth through its self-vindication.

The ultimate fulfillment of this cruciform movement of the Word is the living Word, Jesus, who was rejected by those hardened by His preaching. In

---

72. Christopher Gilbert, *A Complete Introduction to the Bible* (New York: Paulist Press, 2009), 207.

73. Wright, *Christian Origins* 1:236–27. Gerhard Barth further comments: "The presence of Jesus in Matthew's congregation is here described as analogous to the presence of the Shekinah ... the place of Torah is taken by ... Jesus; the place of the Shekinah by Jesus himself." Gerhard Barth, "Matthew's Understanding of the Law," in Günther Bornkamm, Gerhard Barth, and Heinz Joachim Held, *Tradition and Interpretation in Matthew*, trans. Percy Scott (Philadelphia: The Westminster Press, 1963), 135.

74. See David Turner, *Israel's Last Prophet: Jesus and the Jewish Leaders in Matthew 23* (Minneapolis: Fortress Press, 2015).

75. One also sees this motif in the Johannine tradition. Christ and His followers witness to the truth and are "cast out" of the synagogue. The man born blind exemplifies this motif (John 9). Finally, Jesus is Himself "cast out" of Jerusalem in the crucifixion. Nevertheless, in being cast out, Jesus "casts out" the ruler of this world (Jn 12:31). See an interesting discussion of this in Peter Leithart, *Deep Exegesis: The Mystery of Reading Scripture* (Waco, TX: Baylor University Press, 2009), 174–80.

spite of this rejection culminating in His crucifixion, Jesus was vindicated by the power of His resurrection. Indeed, this cruciform pattern is hardwired into the whole structure of the scriptural history. Arthur Just has argued that in explicating the Scriptures to His disciples on the road to Emmaus, the risen Jesus pointed primarily to the fitting nature of the rejection of the Son of Man. In the Bible, humiliation comes before glory and trial before vindication.[76]

Ultimately, then, this cruciform movement of the Word is fitting in that the Spirit facilitates revelation. As we have already seen, the Holy Spirit is always the Spirit of the Son, and consequently always is channeled through His crucified and risen person. Therefore, wherever the Spirit is manifested He imprints the cruciformity of Christ's person on all His works, including in the history of salvation and in the revelation of God's Word in Holy Scripture.

IS SCRIPTURE MYTHOLOGICAL?

In accordance with historic confessional Lutheran theology, our discussion up to this point has assumed that the history of salvation recorded in the Bible is inerrant and absolutely true. Although in the next chapter we will discuss the reality of the inerrancy and verbal inspiration of Scripture, in the midst of a discussion of the Bible and history it would be wrong to ignore the challenge of those who claim that the scriptural history is mere myth.

The question of whether Scripture can be considered mythological is in many ways rather difficult. This is not because confessional Lutheran theology operates under any doubt that the Bible is factually true, but because the term "myth" is notoriously difficult to define. In the light of this dilemma it might be helpful to start with a brief discussion of where the idea originated that the Bible was mythological. Although many rationalist theologians of the Enlightenment challenged the idea that the Bible was absolutely truthful and pointed to many things in it that they regarded to be mythic elements, the notion that the scriptural history is best characterized as myth was popularized and applied comprehensively by the early nineteenth-century biblical scholar D. F. Strauss.

Early in his career Strauss was heavily influenced by the philosophy of G. W. F. Hegel.[77] Hegel taught that the New Testament account of God dying in the person of Jesus was a myth that symbolized what his philosophy taught literally. Specifically, Hegel claimed that in a "speculative Good Friday" God had completed the development of history by uniting Himself as the absolute being with absolute nothingness.[78] Although Strauss eventually rejected

---

76. Arthur Just, *Luke*, 2 vols. (St. Louis: Concordia Publishing House, 1996–97), 2:1021–36.

77. Peter Hodgson, "Editor's Introduction: Strauss' Theological Development from 1825 to 1840," in David Friedrich Strauss, *The Life of Jesus, Critically Examined*, trans. George Eliot (Philadelphia: Fortress Press, 1972), xxii.

78. G. W. F. Hegel, *Faith and Knowledge, or the Reflective Philosophy of Subjectivity in the Complete Range of Its Forms as Kantian, Jacobian, and Fichtean Philosophy*, trans. Walter Cerf and H. S. Harris (Albany: State University of New York Press, 1977), 190–91. Also see discussion

Hegel's interpretation of what the "mythology" of the New Testament actually symbolized,[79] he nevertheless retained the notion of the Christian religion as mythological in his magnum opus, *The Life of Jesus, Critically Examined.*

In his *Life of Jesus* Strauss characterized the Bible in general and the New Testament in particular as mythological.[80] In doing this he sought to overcome the strife that had developed between rationalist biblical exegetes and followers of traditional Christian orthodoxy during the eighteenth century. As should be evident, orthodox Christian exegetes viewed the Gospels and the Bible in general to be literally true supernatural history. Put simply, the Bible gave a truthful account of historical events and God's supernatural role in them.[81]

Interestingly, many of the rationalist exegetes accepted the historicity of the Gospels and other biblical stories. Nevertheless, they were committed to a categorical rejection of miracles on philosophical grounds, which caused certain theological problems since the Bible is filled with miraculous events. To maintain simultaneously the general historical truthfulness of the Bible and their rejection of miracles, the rationalist exegetes argued that the biblical authors were primitive and did not understand the laws of nature. Consequently, they had faithfully recorded naturalistic events they believed were miracles, but that in fact were not. In some cases they had embellished these events, but only very slightly.[82]

One example of an event thought to have been embellished, in the interpretation of rationalist exegete Heinrich Paulus, is Jesus' feeding of the five thousand. Paulus claimed that Jesus did not actually miraculously multiply the loaves and fishes. Instead, Christ simply shared the food He Himself had brought with the disciples in front of the five thousand. Inspired by His example, the five thousand brought out food they had been hiding away and shared it with one another. Thus, what appeared to be a miracle was in fact a naturalistic event.[83]

Strauss thought both approaches to the Bible were problematic. As a child of the Enlightenment he could not accept the claim of historic Christian orthodoxy that God intervened supernaturally in the ordinary course of world events. And he found the approach of the rationalist theologians problematic because it did not take seriously what the scriptural texts actually said, namely, that miraculous events had occurred historically. Strauss proposed a third

in Deland Anderson, *Hegel's Speculative Good Friday: The Death of God in Philosophical Perspective* (Missoula: Scholars Press, 1996).

79. See David Friedrich Strauss, *In Defense of My Life of Jesus Against the Hegelians*, trans. Marilyn Chapin Massey (Hamden, CT: Archon Books, 1983).

80. Strauss, *Life of Jesus*, 52–94.

81. See example of this view in works such as the following: E. W. Hengstenberg, *Christology of the Old Testament*, 4 vols., trans. Theodore Meyer and James Martin (Grand Rapids: Kregel, 1956).

82. Strauss, *Life of Jesus*, 46–49.

83. See Heinrich Eberhard Gottlieb Paulus, *Das Leben Jesu als Grundlage einer reinen Geschichte des Urchristentums*, 2 vols. (Heidelberg: C. F. Winter, 1828), 1:357–60.

approach: that Scripture in general and the Gospels in particular were in fact mythic and symbolic stories portraying higher theological truths, most fundamentally that Jesus was the Messiah, even though the facts of His life did not fit into Jewish Messianic expectation.[84]

In the twentieth century Strauss was followed in this same mythological trajectory by the existentialist theologian and New Testament scholar Rudolf Bultmann. As we have already observed, Bultmann characterized the New Testament as largely myth because it portrayed the occurrence of supernatural events. He also asserted that the New Testament authors made metaphysical and cosmological claims no modern person could take seriously (angels and demons, pre-existent Son, three-storied universe, etc.).[85]

Bultmann, however, did not think the New Testament authors should be criticized for having taken over Jewish and Hellenistic myths as ways of explicating what had happened in the life of Jesus. As people of their time these authors simply used categories that people of their time would understand.[86] Nevertheless, such categories are not our categories and their plausibility maps are not ours, and it would therefore be irresponsible to maintain Christian doctrines that rest on a mythological worldview in the contemporary world.[87]

Still, Bultmann thought there was a kernel of genuine theological truth in the Bible (kerygma) which could be recovered by removing the mythological husk. He believed it is the task of theology to decode the primitive mythological symbols one finds in the writings of the New Testament and translate them into an idiom which can be understood better by modern people,[88] notably Heidegger's version of existentialism.[89] As a result, the New Testament's message of the kingdom of God and the resurrection of Christ must now be de-literalized. In the preached Word concerning Jesus, God confronts the hearer with a decision about the orientation of his existence. One can decide for a new existential orientation to the future (the de-literalized kingdom of God and resurrection) or remain trapped in an orientation toward the past (the de-literalized present evil age).[90] As Vanhoozer points out, Bultmann's claim that one genuinely encounters God in the preaching of the church is extremely odd considering his previous commitments to demythologization. Having declared all supernatural interventions in time mythological, Bultmann apparently does not seek to demythologize the supernatural intervention of God in the preached Word.[91]

---

84. Strauss, *Life of Jesus*, 52–92.
85. Bultmann, *Jesus Christ and Mythology*, 20–21, 35–36.
86. Bultmann, *Jesus Christ and Mythology*, 11–18.
87. Bultmann, *Jesus Christ and Mythology*, 38–39.
88. Bultmann, *Jesus Christ and Mythology*, 18. Also see Bultmann, "On the Problem of Demythologization," 95–130.
89. Bultmann, *Jesus Christ and Mythology*, 45–59.
90. Bultmann, *History and Eschatology*, 152–53.
91. Vanhoozer, *Remythologizing Theology*, 16–17. Also see Rudolf Bultmann, "How Does God Speak to Us through the Bible?" in *Existence and Faith: Shorter Writings of Rudolf*

In view of our commitment to a theology grounded in the Bible and the Lutheran Confessions, we should make a number of observations about Strauss and Bultmann's characterization of the Bible as mythological. The first and most obvious point is that this characterization of the Bible is often loose and derives primarily from their belief that both miracles and supernatural entities are not real. This central claim of their work remains unproven, however. To some extent both authors seem to feel that in view of their audience's presumed plausibility maps they do not need to prove this supposition. Such modes of thought are rooted in high modernist worldviews that are by no means self-evident. Indeed, as we will see there is much empirical evidence for the existence of miracles, and such worldviews ultimately fail to account for the data of reality in some very significant ways.[92]

When such theological judgments are taken on the terms of the presuppositions of the authors, they prove to lack coherence. That is to say, if one has already made an intellectual commitment to the existence of the Christian God (granted, something more true of Bultmann[93] than of Strauss[94]), then one is logically compelled to accept the possibility of miracles and the existence of supernatural entities. Placed in a syllogistic scheme, the logic of this position is clear and utterly convincing. Major premise: God can do anything (Jer 32:27). Minor premise: Miracles fall into the category of "anything." Conclusion: Miracles are possible, and consequently historical reports of miracles cannot be ruled out a priori.

Second, Strauss's implicit definition of myth as more or less any narrative that contains supernatural elements, whether miracles or supernatural entities, is problematic. Such a definition is extremely imprecise and heuristically deeply unhelpful. A wide variety of narratives contain such elements, and anthropologists or literary theorists doubtless would not want to characterize all such narratives as myths.

Although at times Bultmann seems to share Strauss's definition, when pressed on the issues he gave a more precise definition: "[Mythology is] the use of imagery to express the otherworldly in terms of this world and the divine in terms of human life, the other side to this side."[95] When this definition is applied

---

Bultmann, ed. and trans. Schubert M. Ogden (New York: Living Age Books, 1960), 166–70.

92. See R. Douglas Geivett and Gary Habermas, eds., *In Defense of Miracles: A Comprehensive Case for God's Action in History* (Downers Grove, IL: InterVarsity Press, 1997); Craig S. Keener, *Miracles: The Credibility of the New Testament Accounts*, 2 vols. (Grand Rapids: Baker Academic, 2011).

93. As we have seen above, Bultmann oddly does seem to believe in the Christian God. Since he denies most of the works of this God, it is unclear why he believes.

94. See Strauss's idiosyncratic views of God and theology in general in David Friedrich Strauss, *The Old Faith and the New: A Confession*, trans. Mathilde Blind (New York: Holt, 1873).

95. Rudolf Bultmann, "New Testament and Mythology," in *Kerygma and Myth: A Theological Debate*, ed. Hans Werner Bartsche, trans. Reginald Fuller (London: SCPK, 1953), 10. Cited in Bruce Waltke, "Myth, History, and the Bible," in *The Enduring Authority of the Christian Scriptures*, ed. D. A. Carson (Grand Rapids: Wm. B. Eerdmans, 2016), 546.

to the Bible it yields the notion of a transcendent God who does not actually interact with the world but who humans drag down to the temporal world, so to speak, through the symbolism of myth. This of course utterly contradicts the central claims Scripture makes about the incarnational and sacramental interaction between God and His creation.

It also follows that what Bultmann is suggesting with his program of demythologization is a form of Enthusiasm. In other words, much like Satan in the Garden of Eden, Bultmann is advocating that we move past the external Word by removing the mythological husk to find the kernel of truth inside. He claims to have the tool (i.e., Heidegger's analysis of human life) that is able to remove this husk and enable the discernment of this kernel of truth. Here again is the pattern we examined in the last chapter: the Enthusiast separates the external Word from the thing it signifies. He then places himself in between the two and claims that through some special spiritual insight from within his own heart he can relate the opaque external Word to a higher meaning beyond it.

Last, neither definition of mythology and its relationship to Scripture takes into consideration the origins of the term μῦθος in the Greek philosophical tradition and its differentiation from philosophical contemplation and discourse (λόγος). The Greeks seem to have been the first to make a clear distinction between rational philosophical thought and mythology,[96] and consequently their definition of myth may be viewed as foundational. By exploring the ancient mythological worldview rejected by the Greek philosophical tradition, we will seek to evaluate whether or not the Bible falls into the category of myth.

The Ancient Mythological Worldview

Early Greek myth reflected a worldview that represents what many have called ontotheology (Heidegger).[97] In this view God/gods are beings among other beings. Those entities characterized as gods are differentiated from mortals not because they are the uncreated basis of all created being. Rather, like mortals they are beings among other beings, who simply happen to be immortal and supremely powerful. This definition of divinity stands in profound contrast with Scripture, wherein God is not a mere being but is the basis of all being through His identity as one who creates out of nothing (*creatio ex nihilo*). By contrast, in early Greek mythology (and indeed in all pre-biblical ancient Near Eastern mythologies[98]) the world has always existed and possesses order and stability

---

96. Kathryn Morgan, *Myth and Philosophy from the Presocratics to Plato* (Cambridge, UK: Cambridge University Press, 2004), 3. Although the Greek philosophical tradition was anti-mythological, it still utilized myth.

97. See Martin Heidegger, "The Onto-theo-logical Constitution of Metaphysics," in *Identity and Difference*, trans. Joan Stambaugh (New York: Harper and Row, 1969), 42–74. Also see the interesting studies of the following two authors: Jean-Luc Marion, *God without Being*, trans. Thomas Carlton (Chicago: University of Chicago Press, 1991) and Merold Westphal, *Overcoming Onto-theology: Toward a Postmodern Christian Faith* (New York: Fordham University Press, 2001).

98. Paul Copan and William Lane Craig, *Creation Out of Nothing: A Biblical, Philosophical,*

because it is dominated by certain gods, frequently identified with natural forces, who have stabilized it by the application of their power.

Indeed, Homer and Hesiod describe a world filled with divinity. Such gods fight with one another in order to impose their wills on one another. In the mythic universe of Hesiod and Homer, Zeus is the supreme deity.[99] But this is the case only because he is the most powerful deity. He was not originally the most powerful deity but earned his position by overthrowing his father Cronus and consigning the Titans to Tartarus (i.e., Greek hell).[100]

One can find a similar worldview implicit in ancient Near Eastern mythology, which likely served as an influence on Hesiod and therefore indirectly on the pre-philosophical Greek world.[101] For example, the Babylonian creation myth of the Enuma Elish portrays Marduk and the gods of order defeating the primal sea serpent Tiamat and her compatriots. Creation does not come about by the grace and peace of God's "let there be" but from a violent imposition of order by Marduk and his allies on Tiamat and the gods left alive after her defeat. For this reason German scholarship has dubbed creation myths of this nature (common throughout the ancient Near East) *Chaoskampf*.[102] Having been defeated by Marduk, protesting their subjection to labor, and demanding rest, the defeated gods petition the victor to create humanity as their slaves that they might receive from them rest.[103] This dynamic serves as another interesting contrast to Genesis 1–2, wherein God as infinite and eternal possesses His own "rest," which He shares with humans by establishing the Sabbath day.

Within the mythological worldview there is only Law and no Gospel. For ancient pagans the structure of the world as it exists after the Fall is basically the world as it has existed eternally. Of course, within the mythological worldview there are fluctuations between times of chaos and times of order (e.g., Norse Ragnarök,[104] Stoic Ekpyrosis,[105] etc.). Nevertheless, there is no moving beyond the endless cycles of time.

Creation myths are therefore something of a misnomer, in that the gods of most ancient mythologies create nothing. The gods are trapped in the possibilities of the present fallen world and can suppress its chaos only

---

and Scientific Exploration (Grand Rapids: Baker Academic, 2004), 34.

99. See Ken Dowden, *Zeus* (New York: Routledge, 2006).

100. Hesiod, *Theogony*, trans. Richard Caldwell (Indianapolis: Hackett Publishing, 1987), 27–86.

101. Hesiod, *Theogony*, 22–27.

102. See David Toshio Tsumura, *Creation and Destruction: A Reappraisal of the* Chaoskampf *Theory in the Old Testament* (Winona Lake, IN: Eisenbrauns, 2005).

103. See Leonard W. King, *Enuma Elish: The Seven Tablets of Creation; The Babylonian and Assyrian Legends Concerning the Creation of the World and Mankind*, vol. 1 (New York: Cosimo Books, 2007).

104. See John Stanley Martin, *Ragnarök: An Investigation into Old Norse Concepts of the Fate of the Gods* (Assen: Van Gorcum, 1972).

105. Michael Lapidge, "Stoic Cosmology," in *The Stoics*, ed. John Rist (Cambridge, UK: Cambridge University Press, 1978), 161–86.

temporarily in order to bring forth order in the creation myth through violence. There is no transcendent God who, having once called the world out of nothing, possesses the ability speak forth a new creation that stands beyond limited and depressing possibilities of the world under the curse of sin, death, the devil, and the Law (2 Cor 4:6).

In these worldviews goodness and order come from violent legal imposition, not from God's gracious fiat. We use the term "legal" because, just as temporal rulers within the fallen world impose order through coercive violence, within these ancient mythological systems the gods seem to do a very similar thing. But the mythological worldview rejects not only the Gospel, but in its fullest sense also the Law. For pagans the law is not the transcendent will of an eternal God but rather the arbitrary decision of whatever god happens to be in power. Indeed, most ancient Greek religious practice had little to do with morality and much to do with placating the capricious will of the gods through sacrifice.[106] Seen from this vantage point, the Law can never genuinely accuse the sinner, because the sinner can simply escape its judgment by fleeing from the curse of one god to the blessing of another. Odysseus in the Odyssey is successful despite being hated by Poseidon because he has found favor in the sight of Athena.[107]

The ultimate horizon within which the mythological worldview operates is one of extreme nihilism. There are no absolute goods and evils, only an endless cycle of power struggles without an ultimate meaning. Because there is no final basis for transcendental moral judgments and unilateral grace, there can be no genuine eschatology. Just as there is no God who creates out of nothing on the basis of grace alone, there can be no new creation wrought by the effective word of the Gospel. Similarly, since there is no transcendental Law of God (*lex aeterna*), there will be no final reckoning of the violence and injustice done throughout history. Instead, there is nothing but tragedy, insofar as the little order that can be established always falls back into chaos (Hesiod's five ages, etc.).[108]

Hence, within the horizon of a purely mythological worldview, history understood as a linear series of developments is impossible. History in the biblical and modern sense of the term presupposes that the particular and the new are genuine possibilities. Myth, by contrast, assumes there is no linear history but rather an endless cycle of recurrence. Within the endless expanse of time the old possibilities of an eternally fallen world are rearranged endlessly. History is therefore cyclical, not linear, in that all that is, always has been and always will be. The gods and humans merely recycle what always was, in their attempt to hold the fabric of the universe together under the threat of the return of primal chaos.

---

106. Eckart Otto, "Law and Ethics," in *Religions of the Ancient World: A Guide*, ed. Sarah Iles Johnston (Cambridge, MA: Harvard University Press, 2004), 91.

107. See Homer, *The Odyssey*, trans. Robert Fagles (New York: Penguin Classics, 1999).

108. Stephanie Nelson, *God and the Land: The Metaphysics of Farming in Hesiod and Vergil* (Oxford: Oxford University Press, 1998), 68–76.

As the mid-twentieth-century scholar of world religion Mircea Eliade shows, cultures that labor under the mythological worldview tend to establish religious rituals aimed at restoration of the primal order (*Urzeit*).[109] This tendency makes sense in view of these cultures' cyclical view of history. That is to say, in the mythological worldview the event of creation happens only insofar as a god or some other powerful supernatural entity violently imposes order on the chaos of an already-existing cosmos. Since creation is a cycle of a tragic falling away from the primal order followed by its temporary restoration, religious ritual seeks to reenact the primal myth of the imposition of order as a means of recapturing it. For example, in ancient Babylon in a spring festival (Akitu), the king annually would confess the nation's sins and receive again his sovereignty from the gods. Later the Babylonian king would participate in ceremonies reenacting the creation myth of the Enuma Elish, that is, the story of creation being forged out of chaos by Marduk's victory. Such a ritual had the aim of renewing the cosmos.[110] Ultimately, religious ritual does not offer new eschatological possibilities for creatures but rather returns creation to a primal order from which it had fallen away.

Since divine power is identified with force, there is a very interesting intersection between the political and the religious in cultures that operate with a mythological worldview. First, outside the Bible, divinity is never truly divine in the biblical sense because there is no absolute boundary between creature and creator. This absence of distinction allows for the possibility of god-kings who are divine simply because they exercise absolute political power. By contrast, in the biblical worldview God is God because He possesses the ability to create out of nothing in contradistinction to creatures. This means that God is God precisely because He has the power of unilateral grace and not simply the supreme power to impose His will on things that already exist. Second, since within the mythological worldview the divine is identified with a raw power that establishes order out of chaos in endless cycles of time, no genuine eschatology can offer creation new redemptive possibilities and relativize the power of political authorities as in the Bible. Rather, political power becomes divine in a way that no one can ever hope to escape through endless cycles of time.

The Bible as True Myth: Beyond Myth and Metaphysics

Our brief contrast of mythology with the biblical worldview is based on a very general description of what the Greek philosophical tradition referred to when it first began to reject myth (μῦθος). We cannot provide an exhaustive study of what has been understood by the term "myth." Our main goal here is to address whether what we find in the Bible is mythological, and to explore

---

109. Mircea Eliade, *The Sacred and the Profane: The Nature of Religion*, trans. Willard Trask (Chicago: Harcourt, 1987), 20–116.

110. See Julye Bidmead, *The Akitu Festival: Religious Continuity and Royal Legitimation in Mesopotamia* (Piscataway, NJ: Gorgias Press, 2002).

briefly what constitutes a genuinely mythological worldview within the ancient world. Considering how common it is to view the Bible as mythological, it is surprising how resoundingly this notion is dispelled by our brief study. Beyond the obvious structural differences we have noted, it is ultimately the power and sacramentality of the Word of God that dispel this erroneous understanding.

First, as we have already seen, the God of the Bible is not a being among other beings. He is the basis of all created being, in and of Himself. In this sense the early Christians were rightly accused of atheism by the Romans.[111] In a word, there are no divine beings in the created world. One can very easily climb to the top of Mt. Olympus and discover it is empty. Similarly, when one reads Genesis 1 over and against its ancient Near Eastern background, one is struck with how naturalistic it is in its orientation. The forces of nature are merely impersonal. They are not gods, nor are they filled with the presence of various gods. Although God does exist, He transcends the created world and is not part of it. He is not one entity among many within it, He is the foundation upon which every created being stands.

This is one of the many reasons Strauss and Bultmann's rejection of miracles as mythological is thoroughly unfounded. The Bible's claims of miracles have nothing to do with the natural capacities of the visible creation or with deities dwelling within it. These claims are about the almighty power of God's Word, which transcends creation. Humans cannot move beyond the visible creation and see what God is capable or not capable of. Rather, they must trust that insofar as God's Word can do all things, what He testified to in Scripture regarding His previous works must be trustworthy.

As we have already seen, God's power as God is the power He exercises by His eternal Word. The power of His Word to create is central to His identity as both creator and redeemer. As Luther notes in the Large Catechism, all things possess a radical dependence on God and His grace for their existence.[112] Grace rather than Law is most fundamental to the ontological order of creation. The same reality pertains to redemption, wherein God calls creation into existence anew through the work of His eternal and incarnate Word. The gods of the mythological worldview exercise authority not through their word but through the blunt force of their power, like the impersonal forces of nature.

God rules in both judgment and grace through His Word. Having created all things out of nothing, God's Word is able to offer creation new eschatological possibilities. As we have seen, after the giving of the *protoevangelium* the whole story of Scripture is constituted by the history of God narrating into existence a new creation through His eternal Son. As one who pre-exists His creation and calls it into being, God by His gracious fiat may create possibilities for His creation beyond the boundaries of the present fallen world. He does not merely

111. Harry Boer, *A Short History of the Early Church* (Grand Rapids: Wm. B. Eerdmans, 1976), 46.

112. LC II.1 (Bente, 679–83).

exercise a raw power capable of pressing things into order out of a primal chaos. Instead, He is capable of new actions and new creation: "Behold, I am doing a new thing" (Is 43:19), and again: "Behold, I am making all things new" (Rv 21:5).

A recognition of the transcendent power of God's Word brings to the fore a deep irony in the idea that the Bible is mythological. If the charge has been made noisily by liberal theologians like Strauss and Bultmann, it has been shouted all the more loudly by materialist and atheist critics of Christianity since the seventeenth century, like Spinoza and d'Holbach.[113] Interestingly, those who reject the Christian God and the miraculous history of salvation in favor of metaphysical naturalism and materialism actually accept something quite similar to the ancient mythological worldview.

In the materialist/naturalist worldview, nature itself is eternal and must eternally repeat itself due to its finite possibilities and infinite duration. This worldview may be manifested in the theory of an infinite number of Big Bangs followed by an infinite number of Big Crunches (the so-called Oscillating Universe Theory)[114] or even by an explicit reference to a myth of eternal recurrence (Nietzsche).[115] The agents of creation are the forces of nature themselves, which are defined as creative by virtue of their raw power. Such forces often were identified by the ancients as gods themselves, and within the materialist/naturalist worldview they are functionally indistinguishable from the pagan mythological concept of deity. It could even be argued that materialists/naturalists venerate technology for the same reason the ancients venerated sacrifice. In the contemporary world, technology rather than sacrifice and ritual pacifies and manipulates the power of nature to the fulfillment of human desires.

In contradistinction to this worldview, because Scripture speaks of a God who creates from nothing, it also can speak of a genuine history of salvation and not a "myth of the eternal return" (Eliade).[116] A God who creates out of nothing by His Word must necessarily be before all things, and therefore logically must also form a boundary before time and after time as well. Such a boundary establishes time as linear (that is, it has a beginning and an end) rather than cyclical.[117] A God who can call things into being from nothingness also can narrate into existence genuinely new and unique events, the presupposition of all genuine history. Eliade himself has noted that the Bible breaks with the

---

113. See a discussion of modern materialism and naturalism in Jonathan Israel, *Radical Enlightenment: Philosophy and the Making of Modernity, 1650–1750* (Oxford: Oxford University Press, 2001).

114. P. J. Steinhardt and N. Turok, *Endless Universe* (New York: Doubleday, 2007).

115. See Lawrence Hatab, *Nietzsche's Life Sentence: Coming to Terms with Eternal Recurrence* (New York: Routledge, 2005).

116. Mircea Eliade, *The Myth of the Eternal Return: Cosmos and History*, trans. Willard Trask (Princeton: Princeton Univerity Press, 2005).

117. See this emphasis in Oscar Cullman, *Christ and Time: The Primitive Christian Concept of Time and History*, trans. Floyd Filson (London: SCM Press, 1962); Cullman, *Salvation in History*.

religion of mythology in a revolutionary manner, in favor of history.[118] Because God can create the genuinely new, reality need not be mere recycling of what has come before.

For this reason the sacraments of the old and new covenants are not rituals aimed at restoring the *Urzeit* with its triumph of legal order over chaos. They are instead effective promises, proclaiming God's redemptive victory in the historical past and giving access to the future eschatological reality that Christ has enacted proleptically in the present. The Passover, in other words, points back to the exodus and prefigures Christ, just as the Lord's Supper points back to the crucifixion and forward to the eschatological feat of the Lamb.

This point brings us back to the second part of our thesis: namely, that Scripture is anti-mythological not only because of the eternity, power, and transcendence of the Word of God, but also because of the sacramentality of the Word. To appreciate this fully, we observe the nature of the Greek philosophical reaction to myth. Plato and the Greek philosophical tradition in general rejected Hesiod and Homer's mythological worldview. They sought to escape the ontotheology of the poets by positing a world of being above the world of becoming. Within the Greek philosophical tradition this principle of being took on a variety of shapes: the theory of the Forms (Plato), the prime mover (Aristotle), or the Logos (Stoicism).[119] Nevertheless, ultimate reality was not to be defined as a finite being among beings but as something that transcended the temporal world, much like the God of the Bible. In this respect the church fathers correctly saw that through both conscience and reason the Greek philosophers had come to some inkling of the true God's existence (Acts 17, Romans 1–2).[120]

Still, this understanding was not much of an improvement over the tragic worldview of the poets. Plato viewed the world of appearances as a tragic falling away from the prime unity and spiritual reality of the pre-temporal world of the Forms. Personal eschatology was a matter of reversing the soul's tragic fall from the pre-temporal bliss of the spiritual world, that is, yet another myth of the eternal return.[121]

Truth ultimately was to be found in in disembodied conceptual realities above the temporal realities of history, language, and culture. Indeed, Plato and the entire subsequent Greek philosophical tradition taught that truth is attained by moving beyond μῦθος (myth, narrative, etc.) to λόγος (pure, unadulterated conceptual thinking). He thus sought to overcome the essential relativism and

---

118. Eliade, *Sacred and the Profane*, 110–11.

119. See Francis A. Grabowski, *Plato, Metaphysics, and the Theory of the Forms* (London: Bloomsbury Academic, 2008); Theodore Scaltsas, *Substances and Universals in Aristotle's "Metaphysics"* (Ithaca: Cornell University Press, 2010), 124; Antonia Tripolitis, *Religions of the Hellenistic-Roman Age* (Grand Rapids: Wm. B. Eerdmans, 2002), 37–38.

120. Constantine Carvanos, *The Hellenic-Christian Philosophical Tradition* (Belmont, MA: Institute for Byzantine and Modern Greek, 1989).

121. Plato *Phaedrus* 249d–257b, in *Plato: The Complete Works*, ed. John Cooper (Indianapolis: Hackett Publishing, 1997), 527–33.

nihilism of mythology identified earlier. As we observed, from the perspective of the mythological worldview there are only relative goods, not absolute and eternal good that can measure the relativity of history and creation. By moving beyond the relative, the particular, and the historical, Plato and the other post-Socratics sought to find the eternal and the universal outside of creation.

Although this impulse to locate divine truth in something transcendent was essentially correct, Plato and the entire Western philosophical tradition have failed at this task of finding truth beyond history, language, and culture. In pursuing truth unadulterated by temporality, they could not help but employ language, narrative, and history. Plato's rejection of myth simply gave rise to new myths. He sought the eternal, pre-temporal, and pre-linguistic truth, but could do so only through the medium of dialogue.

Ultimately, for human creatures it is not possible to ascend above the created world to the realm of the eternal by their own efforts. Humans are culturally and linguistically bound creatures, and there is no moving beyond their historically and linguistically constructed manner of engaging reality. This fact has been broadly recognized by various forms of postmodern philosophy, particularly post-structuralism. For this group of thinkers there are no pure, atemporal, pre-linguistic truths. Even if there were a God, He cannot be reached, and therefore we must *de facto* accept historical relativity and, implicitly, nihilism. The Western philosophical tradition thus has come full circle. To postmodernism, the nihilism, relativism, and provisionalism of the poets and the sophists are the only logical options left.[122]

In contradistinction to both myth and metaphysics, the Bible offers the sacramentality of the Word. God's eternal Word is not only so great and infinite that it transcends and bounds creation, it also is capable of entering into the created realm and fully communicating itself to the finite (*finitum capax infiniti*). From within this total self-communication, as we have seen, God enacts new eschatological possibilities for creation through the history of salvation and Christ's new narrative of creation. In the event of the incarnation, the universal and eternal God, without ceasing to be universal and eternal, incorporates a particular human existence into Himself. By fully communicating Himself to a part of the finite creation, He invests the life of Jesus and the history of salvation recorded by the Bible with a universal and eternal significance. From this vantage point we can see that the way to overcome what the postmodern theorists rightly observe about the relativity of the finite, historical, and linguistically bound nature of human existence is not to revert to the philosophical quest for truth unadulterated by temporality. Rather, we should believe, teach, and confess all the more strongly the confessional Lutheran *capax*. It is in, under, and through God's audible and

---

122. See Jean-François Lyotard, *The Postmodern Condition: A Report on Knowledge*, trans. Geoff Bennington and Brian Massumi (Minneapolis: University of Minnesota Press, 1984); Richard Rorty, *The Linguistic Turn: Essays in Philosophical Method* (Chicago: University of Chicago Press, 1992).

visible words within creation and history, manifest in the Bible, that the eternal and infinite Word of God gives humans a share in His truth.[123]

For this reason Oswald Bayer describes Christian theology, and by implication the Bible, as occupying a place suspended between "metaphysics and mythology."[124] Metaphysically speaking, the Bible is concerned with an infinite God who transcends all creaturely existence. Nevertheless, the Bible also deals with a concrete, historical narrative of Jesus, in which the eternal and infinite God fully communicates Himself to the finite. In speaking, acting, and becoming incarnate in history, God is not swallowed up into the finitude of history. That is, God does not metamorphose into a mythological character, a being among beings. Moreover, God's history with creation is unique, concrete, and particular. It does not give "free rein"[125] to mythological fantasy but is grounded in an actual historical reality within which God acts, commands, and makes promises. In a word, the scriptural history is sacramental and incarnational, not mythological.

Hence, the biblical history represents the real presence and incarnation of the truth, transcending both the metaphysics of the philosophers and the mythology of the poets. One could say, along with C. S. Lewis, that the Bible is a "true myth."[126] Lewis defined myth in a broader sense than we have above. Simply put, for Lewis myth is any imaginative narrative that expresses the human quest for and partial apprehension of abstract transcendental truth.[127] The history of salvation culminating in the life of Christ is a "true myth," because it is the true reality and presence of God Himself, coming to humanity in a genuine historical narrative and not one that is merely allegorical or imaginative. The Bible does not merely reflect the human quest for the truth: it is God in person directly communicating the truth through genuine history. In the incarnation the abstract God and His abstract truth become concrete and literal history: a true myth.[128]

As we have already seen, human beings are storied creatures. God created the whole universe through speaking forth a single grand narrative over the protological week (Genesis 1). Humans find their identity and life in a story narrated by God. For this reason humans understand and process reality as

---

123. See a similar approach in Johann Georg Hamann, "Metacritique on the Purism of Reason (1784)," in *Hamann: Writings on Philosophy and Language,* ed. Kenneth Haynes (Cambridge, UK: Cambridge University Press, 2009), 205–18. Also see Bayer's discussion in Oswald Bayer, *A Contemporary in Dissent: J. G. Hamann as Radical Enlightener,* trans. Roy Harrisville (Grand Rapids: Wm. B. Eerdmans, 2012), 156–70.

124. Bayer, *Theology the Lutheran Way,* 8.

125. Bayer, *Theology the Lutheran Way,* 9.

126. See John Warwick Montgomery, ed., *Myth, Allegory, and the Gospel: An Interpretation of J. R. R. Tolkien, C. S. Lewis, G. K. Chesterton, and Charles Williams* (Minneapolis: Bethany House, 1974).

127. See C. S. Lewis, "Myth Became Fact," in *God in the Dock: Essays on Theology and Ethics* (Grand Rapids: Wm. B. Eerdmans, 2014), 57–58.

128. Lewis, "Myth Became Fact," 58–61.

narrative. This truth is reflected in the fact that all cultures generate myths and literature. They do this not simply because telling stories or performing plays is enjoyable and entertaining, but as a means of self-understanding. Characters in myth, literature, and drama are abstractions of human nature as it exists in the real world. By abstracting themselves from their daily lives and placing the self in a narrative, humans can analyze their existence and come to some form of self-understanding. Much like fallen human reason is able partially to apprehend God and His existence (Romans 1–2), humans in reflecting on the literary may partially apprehend the truth of human existence.

Nevertheless, Scripture is something quite different from a mere myth, play, or other literary production. As we have observed already, all human beings live out their existence and have their identity within a grand historical narrative that God narrates. The Bible and its history give us access to this narrative of creation and redemption which is ontologically foundational to the whole of reality. As we are confronted by this history in the proclamation of the church through Law and Gospel, we find ourselves either in the tragic narrative of Adam or in Christ's new narrative of creation. We stand in solidarity with the Seed of the woman, or with that of the serpent.

Adam and Christ are concrete historical figures who are protologically and eschatologically determinative of our existence. This is true whether we are conscious of it or not. Indeed, we do not fully comprehend ourselves as humans until we understand ourselves as standing under the determination of their narrative identities. Unlike myth and literature, Adam and Christ are not mere abstractions or imaginative representations of human nature. One might say they are the real presence of human nature, condemned under sin and the Law or redeemed and glorified under the Gospel (Romans 5).

The same is true of the being of the triune God as He manifests Himself in the scriptural history. God is in part knowable through human reason and conscience, even in our fallen state (Romans 1–2). Nevertheless, such knowledge is a mere abstract conceptual representation of God. Fallen humans are able to deduce such non-saving knowledge of God indirectly from the divine fingerprints in creation and the human soul. By contrast, when one turns to the Scriptures one discovers a direct knowledge of God. Indeed, God as He comes to us in His Word centered in Christ is not merely reflected or represented, as in the analogical concept of revelation, but is encountered directly through His real presence. This is so, not only because God has infallibly inspired the Scriptures so that they give a direct knowledge of the divine, but because God is present in His Word.

Likewise, through Christ's testimony concerning the Father and the Spirit, as well as through their testimony concerning Him (Jn 5:30–38; 15:26), God is unveiled in, under, and through the media of creation and redemption: the Father through the mask of creation, the Son through the mask of the incarnation, and the Holy Spirit through the mask of the means of grace.

These creative and redeeming activities do not merely represent or reflect God's eternal being: they directly manifest it. In directly manifesting Himself God reveals His will for humanity, and in the process reveals the true nature of human identity and destiny.

As humans are confronted with the real knowledge and presence of God and humanity through Scripture, faith is created and believers are drawn out of their natural Enthusiasm. Instead of projecting their inner self-understanding and their own self-developed concepts of divinity onto God and humanity, they are drawn out of their self-incurvature to recognize the real presence of both humanity and divinity in Christ. Christ is the true, complete, and final revelation of God. He is also the Second Adam and the head of the new humanity.[129]

From the historical reality of God's revelation we must conclude that it is important not only that God has acted and spoken in history to create and redeem His people, but that He has left a true and inerrant witness to this fact. Such a witness is a condition *sine qua non* of the church's Word and Sacrament ministry. For that reason we will turn in the next chapters not only to the question of the inspiration and inerrancy of Holy Scripture, but also to the canonical boundaries within which that inspired and inerrant witness is to be found.

---

129. Luther states that the subject of Scripture and all true theology is "the sinning human being and the justifying God." *Commentary on Psalm 51*, 1532 (AE 12:311; WA 40/2:328). Cited from Bayer, *Martin Luther's Theology*, 37.

3

THE WRITTEN WORD OF GOD:
THE INERRANCY OF SACRED SCRIPTURE

THE FUNCTION OF SCRIPTURE
WITHIN THE ECONOMY OF SALVATION

Thus far in our study we have observed that the Word of God is the foundation of the entire structure of the life of God and created reality. From all eternity God has been constituted as triune through the speaking forth of His Word in the unity of the Spirit. At the beginning of His works in time, God spoke forth the original creation through His unilateral grace. Our first parents rejected the goodness that God channeled to them through His visible and audible words within original creation, thereby succumbing to the temptations of Satan's Enthusiasm. Adam and Eve thus fled from the places where God had attached His Word of grace to the location where He had attached His word of wrath.

After the tragic fall into sin God began the process of redemption by again speaking forth His Word in the form of the *protoevangelium*. Through the *protoevangelium* the pre-incarnate Christ entered into a redemptive solidarity with humanity under sin and the judgment of the Law. This identification with humanity culminated in the final and absolute solidarity of the incarnation and the cross. Christ's victory of the resurrection is the final and definitive battle in the apocalyptic war between God's external Word and Satan's deceitful Enthusiasm.

The result of His redemptive process and victory is God's new narrative of creation. However, God not only recreates the world through the speaking of His Word, He also gave a revelation of Himself and His will through the medium of the redemptive events of the history of salvation. The content of this divine self-revelation and its outworking in time was recorded infallibly by the prophets and apostles in the production of the God-breathed (θεόπνευστος) Scriptures (2 Tm 3:16).

Sacred Scripture is not merely a written record of God's historical revelation. Rather, Scripture is a sacramental medium and a form of revelation in itself. As such, it is appointed by God to possess a specific role within the economy of salvation and the life of the church. Indeed, as we have already seen, Scripture makes sense only as a particular medium of divine address when considered from the overall perspective of God's communicative agency within eternity and time.

The ultimate goal of the inspiration and writing of Holy Scripture is the oral proclamation of the Word within the life of the church. In turn, the ultimate purpose of the proclamation of the Word is to give Christ and His promise to creatures of faith. The written Scriptures, like sacraments, are nothing less than a delivery system for the truth and presence of the crucified and risen Christ (Mt 18:20; Lk 10:16; Jn 6:63; 2 Tm 3:15).[1] Robert Preus observes that such a view is in accordance with the teaching of the Lutheran scholastics, who understood Scripture "assumes its true significance only when viewed soteriologically, [that is] when considered as an operative factor in God's plan of salvation."[2]

Therefore, contrary to the assumptions of much of modern Protestantism (whether liberal or conservative), the Bible is not an abstract authority, properly understood by rational and autonomous human beings within the sphere of their own subjective solitude (2 Pt 1:20). It is not a compendium of abstract bits of heavenly information that can be picked apart and assembled in order to say virtually anything. Rather, Scripture's proper purpose is to be proclaimed and understood in the midst of the church and its sacramental life of forgiveness. Consequently, the presence of the risen Christ and the forgiveness He offers in the midst of the church is the lodestar for any proper understanding of the purpose and meaning of Holy Scripture.

This fact comes into particular focus when one considers that before it was written down as Sacred Scripture, the Word of God was first transmitted orally within the assembly of Israel and the liturgical-sacramental life of the early church. Luther frequently observed that the Word of God was written down only so that it might be preserved and therefore orally proclaimed with greater certainty.[3] Even if one ignores the role that Holy Scripture possesses in the Word and Sacrament ministry of the church, it should be noted that in the ancient world all written texts were intended for oral performance insofar as reading was almost never done silently.[4] Therefore, as an ancient text, Scripture is by definition meant for oral proclamation.

Jesus authorized the apostles as His infallible witnesses (and therefore as the infallible authors of Scripture) simultaneous with His authorization of the Word and sacraments of the church (Mt 28:19–20; Lk 10:16; Jn 16:13; Acts 1:8). This correspondence suggests that the authority of Holy Scripture and the authoritative ministry of the church are not separable but function properly only when understood in the light of one another. Some might object that

---

1. Johann Baier, *Compendium Theologiae Positivae*, ed. C. F. W. Walther, 3 vols. (Grand Rapids: Emmanuel Press, 2005–6), 1:117–18; Gerhard, *On the Nature of Theology and Scripture*, 333.

2. Preus, *Inspiration of Scripture*, 170; cited from Webster, *Holy Scripture*, 40.

3. *First Sunday in Advent* (WA 10/1:2.48). "The church is a mouth-house, not a pen-house." Cited from Mark Thompson, *A Sure Ground on Which to Stand: The Relation of Authority and Interpretive Method of Luther's Approach to Scripture* (Carlisle, UK: Paternoster Press, 2004), 75.

4. Ben Witherington III, *New Testament Rhetoric: An Introductory Guide to the Art of Persuasion in and of the New Testament* (Eugene, OR: Cascade Books, 2009), 1–2.

the commissions cited above are authorizations merely of the preaching of the Word, not of the writing of the New Testament itself.[5] This is an incorrect interpretation for a number of reasons.

First, Jesus' authorization of the Word and Sacrament ministry of the apostles came along with His call for the apostles to be universal ("to the ends of the earth," Acts 1:8) and infallible witnesses ("those who hear you, hear me," Lk 10:16). If Jesus had intended their witness to be constituted merely by their oral preaching and not the writing of the New Testament documents, then the Lord's prophecy would have failed. This is because the apostles did not literally reach the ends of the earth. But Jesus' prophecy has not failed: the apostles' infallible witness has reached the "ends of the earth" in the form of the written New Testament. We must understand His authorization of their ministry to include writing.[6] In the same manner, John, the Beloved Disciple, also "abides" until Jesus comes (Jn 21:22) through the witness of his Gospel.[7]

Second, although the preserved written testimonies of the apostles are infallible, the writings of those who succeeded the apostles in ministry were not. Contrary to what the Roman Catholic Church claims, the New Testament does not assert the infallible teaching authority of the post-apostolic church. Although Matthias could have the apostolic office transferred to him and Paul could be granted the apostolic office, they nonetheless had to fulfill the criterion of being witnesses to the resurrection (Acts 1:22). Because no subsequent bishop of the church can fulfill this criterion, the apostolic office and witness is *sui generis* and could never be transferred to later generations.

Without written Scriptures the post-apostolic church would be fairly likely to mangle the witness of the apostles as a result of its fallibility, thereby preventing the apostles' pure witness from reaching the "ends of the earth." Having a written witness which preserves the apostles' infallible testimony is thus the *sine qua non* of the fulfillment of Jesus' prophecy that the apostles would be His witnesses to the ends of the earth through the Word and Sacrament ministry of the church. Hence, the meaning and purpose of the written Word of God are inexplicable apart from their appointed role within the context of the church's ministry.

THE RELATIONSHIP OF HISTORICAL REVELATION AND THE WRITTEN WORD OF GOD

As should be clear from the discussion of the previous chapter, God's historical acts of revelation are distinct and yet not separate from God's revelation in

5. Robert Bellarmine and many early modern Roman Catholic apologists made this argument. See Gerhard, *On the Nature of Theology*, 51–58. See a modern objection along the same lines in James Barr, *Holy Scripture: Canon, Authority, and Criticism* (Philadelphia: Westminster, 1983), 12.

6. Gerhard, *On the Nature of Theology*, 53.

7. Richard Bauckham, *Jesus and the Eyewitnesses: The Gospels as Eyewitness Testimony* (Grand Rapids: Wm. B. Eerdmans, 2008), 393.

its written form.[8] Scripture is a means whereby God mediates His historical acts of revelation and their redemptive benefits to believers.[9] For this reason, while categories of "revelation" and "the Word of God" are applied validly to Sacred Scripture in and of itself, Scripture nevertheless does not exhaust these categories. Robert Preus observes with regard to the teaching of the Lutheran theologians of the seventeenth century: "The dogmaticians do not equate Scripture and the Word of God. Scripture is the Word of God, but the Word of God is not Scripture."[10] God has been revealing Himself, acting, and addressing His creation long before there was a written Scripture.[11] For example, the exodus and God's revelatory speeches to Moses on Mt. Sinai occurred first, and only later were written down by Moses as Holy Scripture. Hence, such historical acts of divine self-disclosure constitute a form of the Word of God distinct from and prior to the written Scriptures. As Preus observes in summarizing the position of the Lutheran scholastics regarding this question: "The dogmaticians never called revelation Scripture: the two terms were never equated as if Scripture was God's only revelation."[12]

However, such a distinction regarding the forms the Word of God has taken historically should by no means call into question that the Scriptures are the single source of revelation to the Christian church. As stated above, the revelation of the Word of God as a historical event is distinct but not separate from Scripture. The post-apostolic Christian church has no access to those revelatory events of history apart from their recording in the Scriptures. It is for this reason that the Scriptures are the sole foundation and touchstone of all preaching and teaching of God's truth (Eph 2:20).[13]

It cannot be stressed enough that Scripture's ability to mediate these events to believers is dependent upon its being inerrant and fully inspired. This is the case for a number of reasons. First, without fully inspired Scriptures, God's historical acts of revelation would remain hidden, lost, or at minimum mangled beyond recognition. Modern theologians who reject the inspiration or at least the full inspiration of the Scriptures effectively claim that after having revealed Himself in history God laid down no provision to vouchsafe His revelation to future generation. Such a decision on God's part would constitute an act of extreme ineptitude, something obviously inconsistent with the analogy of faith. Hence, even among pagan nations "[God] did not leave himself without witness" (Acts 14:17). But especially in His sphere of supernatural revelation,

---

8. Preus, *The Inspiration of Scripture*, 29–33.

9. Baier, *Compendium Theologiae Positivae* 1:80. Baier cites Quenstedt emphasizing that Scripture is the single source and medium of revelation to the contemporary Christian church. Obviously, before Moses began to write the Pentateuch there was a revelation of the Word of God.

10. Preus, *Inspiration of Scripture*, 23.

11. Martin Chemnitz, *Examination of the Council of Trent*, trans. Fred Kramer, 4 vols. (St. Louis: Concordia Publishing House, 1971–86), 1:49; Pieper, *Christian Dogmatics* 1:193.

12. Preus, *Inspiration of Scripture*, 39.

13. David Scaer, "Apostolicity, Inspiration, and Canonicity," *Concordia Theological Quarterly* 44, no. 1 (1980): 46.

"the Lord God does nothing without revealing his secret to his servants the prophets" (Am 3:7).

Second, as we have already seen in the previous chapters, God has attached the audible and written words of Scripture to the events of salvation history as a means of revealing His acts of judgment or grace, in, under, and through them. This is similar to the manner in which He attaches audible words to the visible words of the sacraments as a means of informing the believer what salvific benefits he will receive through the physical elements. If Scripture were in error even in small matters, it would lack a sacramental character. A prerequisite for God to make promises regarding certain historical events is that those events must genuinely have occurred. If they did not happen, it would be equivalent to a minister of the Word speaking the Words of Institution over an empty chalice and plate. In a word, God cannot attach His promises to objects that are not there or to events that did not occur.[14]

As sacramental, Scripture does not merely witness to these events but gives a participatory knowledge (דַּעַת) of them: "taste and see that the Lord is good" (Ps 34:8; also Jer 31:34; 1 Cor 2:16; 2 Cor 4:6; 1 Jn 5:10). One dies as a sinner as a result of the knowledge of divine wrath, both in God's Law and in historical acts of judgment (Rom 7:9; 1 Cor 1:20–24; Gal 2:19–20). Likewise, one is resurrected and redeemed through the knowledge of God's act of grace in Christ (Rom 1:6; Romans 6; 1 Cor 1:18). Through faith in the promises attached to the Word and the sacraments, the life-narrative of the believer is caught up in and incorporated into Christ's redemptive narrative of death and resurrection (Rom 6:1–14).

THE TRIUNE AND INCARNATIONAL
MANIFESTATION OF REVELATION

Recognizing that the Word of God manifests itself in a variety of ways, Robert Kolb has suggested essentially four distinct forms: Christ, Scripture, the proclamation of the church, and the sacraments.[15] By contrast, Hermann Sasse (basing his insights on Karl Barth[16]) has suggested a threefold manifestation: Christ, Scripture, the proclamation of the church.[17] Although we do not

---

14. Luther's sacramental realism parallels what Robert Preus called biblical realism. Just as the sacraments and their promises are to be taken at face value, the biblical narrative and the promises God has attached to it should be read as factual. See Robert D. Preus, "How Is the Lutheran Church to Interpret and Use the Old and New Testaments?" *Lutheran Synod Quarterly* 14, no. 1 (1973): 31–32. Also see summary and appreciation of Preus's position in Kurt Marquart, "The 'Realist Principle' of Theology," in *Doctrine Is Life: The Essays of Robert D. Preus on Justification and the Lutheran Confessions*, ed. Klemet I. Preus (St. Louis: Concordia Publishing House, 2006), 367–73.

15. Robert Kolb, *The Christian Faith: A Lutheran Exposition* (St. Louis: Concordia Publishing House, 1993), 184–85.

16. Barth, *Church Dogmatics* I/1:98–140.

17. Hermann Sasse, "The Church and the Word of God," in *The Lonely Way:*

condemn Kolb's schematization as in some way false or heretical, Sasse's approach is preferable for a number of reasons.

First, Sasse's approach recommends itself because it accords better with the relationship between God's auditory and visible words as we have expounded them thus far. The underlying assumption of Kolb's approach seems to be that the proclamation of the Word of God within the church can be divided neatly between visible words (sacraments) and auditory words (preaching). As we have seen previously, such a formulation does not take into consideration Luther's observation that every time God gives an audible word He attaches it to a visible word.[18] Thus, just as salvific promises are attached to visible elements in the sacraments (bread, wine, and water), in the oral proclamation of the church the auditory word of preaching is tethered to the events of the history of salvation.

The second reason Sasse's account is preferable is that it more clearly expresses the trinitarian and incarnational nature of the manifestation of God's Word. When God reveals Himself through His Word, He does so according to His own fundamental nature as one who is triune and therefore self-communicating. The center and apex of this self-communication is the Father's begetting of His eternal Word. Such an act of self-communicating is the prerequisite for God's communicative agency in time through the various revelatory events of salvation history, culminating in the incarnation itself.

In human language, every word is a signifier that represents a particular entity. The word "table" is a signifier that represents actual tables in the world. By analogy, God the Father is a speaker who eternally communicates and signifies Himself in the begetting of the Son. The Son is a full and complete manifestation of the Father (Jn 1:1; 14:9; Col 1:15; Heb 1:3) in that He shares fully in the divine essence (*homoousios*). Although the signifier (the Son) is eternally distinct from the signified (the Father), they are not separate (Jn 10:30). Through the dual procession of the Spirit (Jn 15:25; Rom 8:15; Gal 4:6; 1 Pt 1:11), the Father and the Son are eternally united with one another.

Just as the Father in eternity fully communicates His reality to the Son in the unity of the Spirit, in time the Son fully communicates the glory of His divine person (signified) to His humanity (signifier) in the incarnation (*genus majestaticum*). Much as the Father holds nothing back from the Son in His eternal act of begetting, the Son holds nothing back in fully communicating Himself to the humanity of Christ (Col 2:9). In the virgin birth this unity and self-communication occurred through the agency of the Spirit (Mt 1:18–25; Lk 1:26–38). In both eternity and time the Spirit thus unites the signified (the Father and Christ's divinity) and signifier (the Son and Christ's humanity), thereby making them simultaneously distinct and united.

Selected Essays and Letters, Volume 1 (1927–1939), trans. Matthew Harrison et al. (Concordia Publishing House, 2001), 155.

18. *That These Words of Christ, "This Is My Body," Etc., Still Stand Firm Against the Fanatics,* 1527 (AE 37:135–36; WA 23:261).

This same trinitarian pattern of self-communicating unity in difference is what we find in the temporal manifestations of the Word of God in Christ, the Bible, and the church's proclamation. As we have already seen, in manifesting God's historical revelation to the people of God, Christ as the incarnate Word possessed a visible signifier (His humanity) that manifested an invisible signified (His divinity), the unity of which was brought about (Lk 1:26–38) and manifested by an audible revelatory word in the power of the Spirit: "This is my beloved Son, in whom I am well pleased" (Mk 1:11). One can also see this unity in distinction of signified and signifier in the writing of the Scriptures: the signified (salvation history and the person of Christ) is presented through a signifier (the written Scriptures). Likewise, the signifier and signified are united through the Spirit's work of inspiration, made operative both by the divine promise of infallibility to the prophets and apostles and by the command to write. Finally, in the Word and Sacrament ministry of the church the presence of the risen Christ (signified) is manifested in a visible signifier (the means of grace), united by Christ's dominical command and promise to be present in the means of grace in the power of the Spirit.

Sasse's trinitarian *taxis* of the Word has a number of significant implications. Each manifestation of the Word of God flows from another, going back to the historical events of revelation centered in the incarnation. Just as the Father begets the Son, who in turn breathes forth the Spirit, so revelation in creation and history prompts the writing of the Scriptures, which in turn authorizes and serves as a basis for the Word and Sacrament ministry of the church.

Likewise, just as each person of the Trinity possesses the fullness of the divine essence (due to the eternal communicative actions of begetting and procession), each manifestation of the Word of God contains within it the fullness of the presence of the risen Christ. Again, Wingren observes, the confessional Lutheran *capax* must hold sway: "The Word, the Bible, carries within itself Christ's coming as its general aim, to which all tends . . . It is in the simple words, in what is human in the Bible, that God's power is hidden; divine and human must not be separated." Indeed, "even in the passage and even in preaching, *communicatio idiomatum* holds sway."[19] Therefore, just as God fully communicated Himself in history to Christ, Christ Himself promised full inspiration to the prophets and apostles so that their words would not only fully represent the truth He wished to communicate but also mediate His presence.

INERRANCY: LUTHER, THE LUTHERAN CONFESSIONS, AND LUTHERAN SCHOLASTICISM

Belief in the inerrancy (*errore expertes*) and inspiration (*inspiratio Dei*) of Scripture are not a mere theologoumenon for orthodox Lutherans but a matter of creedal and confessional subscription. At the beginning of the Book

---

19. Wingren, *Living Word*, 208.

of Concord the inspiration and truth of Scripture is affirmed in the Nicene Creed's statement that the Holy Spirit "spoke by the prophets" (*qui locutus est per prophetas*).[20] Here the Nicene fathers clearly affirm that the scriptural writings are the speech of the Holy Spirit. It is utterly unthinkable that they intended to affirm with this statement that the Holy Spirit in any way spoke erroneously.

Likewise, the Formula of Concord asserts in its opening paragraphs that the Bible is the inspired and inerrant Word of God. The Concordists confess their faith in the authority of the "Prophetic and Apostolic Scriptures of the Old and New Testaments as the pure, clear fountain of Israel."[21] For those who may question this interpretation, it should be observed that the adjective "pure" (*purissimosque Israelis fontes*) by definition precludes the admixture of the impure. Since the context of the statement is the Concordists' enumeration of the various theological authorities, the word "pure" would indicate an unequivocal affirmation of the authority of all that is within Scripture. Indeed, its use indicates that any sort of error is excluded, insofar as the Concordists put no limitation on this purity of Scripture in all that it teaches and affirms.[22]

In affirming the inerrancy of Scripture, the Concordists confessed the faith of the whole Christian church going back to the first centuries.[23] As we will see in a later section, although there have been a variety of interpretations of the nature of inspiration, the pre-Reformation church agreed with very few exceptions that the Bible was God's inspired and inerrant Word. This is the case even if one agrees with the frequent claim that Matthias Flacius was the first theologian to give an exact and clear articulation to the doctrine of inerrancy and verbal inspiration.[24] In the history of the church many biblical doctrines have been affirmed and taught for centuries in less systematic forms until a crisis prompted by a heresy demanded that they be articulated with greater precision.

In this vein, faced with the Counter-Reformation's two-source theory (that Scripture and unwritten tradition both were authoritative) along with the rise of Socinianism and other forms of early modern rationalism (Hobbes, Spinoza, etc.), the theologians of Lutheran orthodoxy defined the biblical, catholic, and confessional dogma of the inspiration and inerrancy of the Bible with

---

20. Bente, 30.

21. SD RN.1 (Bente, 851).

22. For a relatively good summary of the Lutheran Confessions on the inspiration and authority of Scripture, see Arthur Carl Piepkorn, "The Position of the Church and Her Symbols," *Concordia Theological Monthly* 21, no. 10 (1954): 738–42. For an overview of the views of Scripture held by the reformers and the Protestant scholastics see Robert Kolb, "The Bible in the Reformation and Protestant Orthodoxy," in *The Enduring Authority of the Christian Scriptures*, ed. D. A. Carson (Grand Rapids: Wm. B. Eerdmans, 2016), 89–114.

23. See excellent summary in Robert Preus, "The View of the Bible Held by the Church: The Early Church through Luther," in *Inerrancy*, ed. Norman Geisler (Grand Rapids: Zondervan, 1982), 357–84. Also see John Hannah, ed., *Inerrancy and the Church* (Chicago: Moody Press, 1984).

24. See Rudolf Keller, *Der Schlüssel zur Schrift: Die Lehre vom Wort Gottes bei Matthias Flacius Illyricus* (Hannover: Lutherisches Verlagshaus, 1984).

increasing precision throughout the seventeenth century.[25] One of the best and most concise definitions of inerrancy can be found in the chief dogmatic work of Andreas Quenstedt:

> The original canonical sacred Scripture is of infallible truthfulness and wholly free of error, or, what is the same thing, in the canonical sacred Scripture there is no lie, no falsehood, not even the smallest error either in words or in matter, but everything, together and singly, that is handed on in them is most true, whether it be a matter of dogma or of morals or of history or of chronology or of topography or of nomenclature; no want of knowledge, no thoughtlessness or forgetfulness, no lapse of memory can or ought to be attributed to the secretaries of the Holy Spirit in their setting down of the sacred writings.[26]

In response to formulations like that of Quenstedt, a number of modern theologians have objected that although the Formula of Concord and the theologians of scholastic orthodoxy (particularly the later ones) articulate a doctrine of scriptural inerrancy, this was a break with the position of Luther and the original Lutheran Reformation. In order to support this view many liberal Lutheran theologians point to hyperbolic statements of Luther wherein he identifies Scripture merely with what "preaches and inculcates Christ" (*Christum predigen und treiben*), rather than more broadly with the word of the Bible.[27] Those who make such arguments typically defend a narrative of the history of Lutheran theology that might be described as "Luther against the Lutherans,"[28] reminiscent of Richard Muller's famous "Calvin against the Calvinists."[29]

In response to the claims of discontinuity between Luther and later Lutheranism on the doctrine of inspiration, two main points should be made. First, confessional Lutheran dogmatics assumes Holy Scripture as the norming norm (*norma normans*) and the Lutheran Confessions as the normed norm (*norma normata*).[30] The opinions of private theologians may witness to or explicate principles found in these two dogmatic authorities, but they do not

25. Arthur Carl Piepkorn, "What Does 'Inerrancy' Mean?" in *The Sacred Scriptures and the Lutheran Confessions: Selected Writings of Arthur Carl Piepkorn*, ed. Philip J. Secker and Robert Kolb, vol. 2 (Mansfield, CT: CEC Press, 2007), 26; Preus, *Inspiration of Scripture*, 33.

26. Cited from Piepkorn, "What Does 'Inerrancy' Mean?" 26. Originally taken from Andreas Quenstedt, *Theologia Didatico-Polemica sive Systema Theologicum*, 2 vols. (Wittenberg: Johannes Ludolphus Quenstedt et Elerdi Schumacheri Haeredes, 1685), 1:77.

27. H. H. Kramm, *The Theology of Martin Luther* (Eugene, OR: Wipf & Stock, 2009), 113. Also see a couple of newer examples of this version of Luther's doctrine of Scripture in Miikka Ruokanen, *Doctrina Divinitus Inspirata: Martin Luther's Position in the Ecumenical Problem of Biblical Inspiration* (Helsinki: Luther-Agricola Society, 1985), 49–120; Timothy Wengert, *Reading the Bible with Martin Luther: An Introductory Guide* (Grand Rapids: Baker Academic, 2013), 1–21.

28. Ruokanen, *Doctrina Divinitus Inspirata*, 125–35. "Luther against the Lutherans" would accurately characterize Ruokanen here.

29. Richard Muller, "John Calvin and Later Calvinism: The Identity of the Reformed Tradition," in *The Cambridge Companion to Reformation Theology*, ed. David Bagchi and David C. Steinmetz (Cambridge: Cambridge University Press, 2004), 130–49.

30. Pieper, *Christian Dogmatics* 1:354–58.

serve as a definitive norm. Hence Luther's own private opinion about how and why Scripture is authoritative is not definitive for our understanding of the doctrine of Holy Scripture. This is the case even though the Formula of Concord names him as one specially tasked by God to reform the church, and thus possessing a certain level of authority below the Bible, the ecumenical creeds, and the previous confessions.[31] Ultimately, since Luther's authority is subordinate to these norms, his opinions about the dogma of Scripture cannot trump them.

Second, many Luther scholars over the previous two centuries have ignored passages in the Reformer's writings which affirm the inerrancy and verbal inspiration of the Bible.[32] In contrast to this approach, in the early twentieth century Johann Michael Reu collected a vast number of texts that demonstrate that Luther's position on the authority of Scripture was in harmony with later scholastic orthodoxy.[33] More recently, the Australian Reformed theologian Mark Thompson has defended and vindicated Reu's thesis.[34] If these studies are to be believed, there is no contradiction between Luther, the Lutheran Confessions, and later scholastic orthodoxy on the truthfulness and inspiration of the Bible.[35]

THE LORDSHIP OF CHRIST AS THE BASIS OF THE INERRANCY OF THE BIBLE

The Lutheran Confessions and the theologians of scholastic orthodoxy taught the inerrancy of the Bible only because they believed that this teaching stood in accordance with the clear content of God's revelation. As we have previously

---

31. SD RN.6 (Bente, 853).

32. For example: "The Scriptures have never erred . . . The Scriptures cannot err . . . It is certain that the Scripture would not contradict itself; it only appears so to senseless and obdurate hypocrites." *Sermon for Sunday Jubilate Afternoon*, 1531 (WA 34/1:356). Cited in Millard Erickson, *Christian Theology* (Grand Rapids: Baker Academic, 2009), 252. Other examples can be found in *Defense and Explanation of All the Articles*, 1521 (AE 32:11–12; WA 54:158); *The Misuse of the Mass*, 1521 (AE 36:137; WA 8:485); *Commentary on Psalm 45*, 1534 (AE 12:242; WA 40/2:531); and *Lectures on Genesis*, 1535–45 (AE 1:122; WA 42:92). Many thanks to my friend and former student the Rev. David Jay Webber for directing me to these passages.

33. Johann Michael Reu, *Luther and the Scriptures* (Columbus: The Wartburg Press, 1944). Also see the argument in favor of continuity in Pieper, *Christian Dogmatics* 1:276–97.

34. See Thompson, *Sure Ground on Which to Stand*.

35. Also see these other sources that recognize Luther's teaching of inerrancy: John Warwick Montgomery, "Lessons from Luther on the Inerrancy of Holy Writ," in *God's Inerrant Word*, ed. John Warwick Montgomery (Minneapolis: Bethany Fellowship, 1974), 63–94; Robert Preus, "Luther and Biblical Infallibility," in *Inerrancy and the Church*, ed. John Hannah (Chicago: Moody, 1984), 99–142; A. Skevington Wood, *Captive to the Word: Martin Luther: Doctor of Sacred Scripture* (Grand Rapids: Wm. B. Eerdmans, 1969). B. A. Gerrish represents an interesting hybrid interpretation of Luther, wherein statements that sound as if they affirm inerrancy and verbal inspiration are given the same weight as those which sound Gospel-reductionist. His conclusion is that Luther appears to have two distinct and contradictory doctrines of Scripture. See B. A. Gerrish, "The Word of God and the Words of Scripture: Luther and Calvin on Biblical Authority," in *Protestantism Old and New: Essays on the Reformation Heritage* (New York: T&T Clark International, 1982), 51–68.

observed, Christ Himself and His historical revelation is the foundation of the Christian church: "For no one can lay a foundation other than that which is laid, which is Jesus Christ" (1 Cor 3:11). This is true both of His self-revelation to Israel in His pre-incarnate state and of His revelation to the church during His earthly incarnate life. Nevertheless, Christ exercises His authority through the inerrant and inspired Word of the Bible. The church is "built on the foundation of the apostles and prophets [i.e. their teachings], Christ Jesus himself being the cornerstone" (Eph 2:20).[36]

To this end, during Jesus' earthly ministry He confirmed the authority of the Old Testament: "Do not think that I have come to abolish the Law or the Prophets; I have not come to abolish them but to fulfill them" (Mt 5:17), "Scripture cannot be broken" (Jn 10:35), and "your word is truth" (Jn 17:17). On many other occasions He also implicitly affirmed the authority of the Old Testament (Mt 22:29; 23:35; Lk 24:27).[37]

In commissioning the seventy-two, including the apostles, Jesus said: "The one who hears you hears me" (Lk 10:16; paralleled in Mt 10:40). The authority of the teaching of the sixty who were not apostles was derived from and mediated to them by the infallible teaching authority granted to them by the apostles. Elsewhere we are told repeatedly that the Twelve uniquely received Jesus' direct instruction and authorization: "To you it has been given to know the secrets of the kingdom of God" (Lk 8:10). Furthermore, Jesus promised that in the future the Twelve would uniquely receive divine inspiration to teach the kerygma infallibly to the nations: "But the Helper, the Holy Spirit, whom the Father will send in my name, he will teach you all things and bring to your remembrance all that I have said to you" (Jn 14:26).[38] In affirmation of this point Luther wrote on the subject that "[the] apostles . . . [were] by a sure decree of God . . . sent to us as infallible teachers."[39] Hence, "for that reason, it is not they, but we, since we are without such a decree, who are able to err and waver in faith. . . . after the apostles no one should claim this reputation that he cannot err in the faith."[40]

As David Scaer has argued, the Greek word "apostle" (ἀπόστολος) is very likely a translation of the Hebrew word שָׁלִיחַ. In the context of first-century Judaism, שָׁלִיחַ was a special legal representative with the power of attorney. The actions of a שָׁלִיחַ would be binding even if a person he represented wished to nullify his authority.[41] Such a manner of the communicative agency embodies

---

36. Gerhard, *On the Nature of Theology*, 64.

37. Martin Franzmann, "The New Testament View of Inspiration," *Concordia Theological Monthly* 21, no. 10 (1954): 743–44. Also see John Wenham, "Christ's View of Scripture," in Geisler, *Inerrancy*, 3–38.

38. Franzmann, "New Testament View of Inspiration," 44–45; David Scaer, "Apostolicity, Inspiration, and Canonicity," 46.

39. *Theses Concerning Faith and Law*, 1535 (AE 34:113; WA 39/1:48).

40. *Theses Concerning Faith and Law*, 1535 (AE 34:113; WA 39/1:48).

41. David Scaer, *The Apostolic Scriptures* (St. Louis: Concordia Publishing House, 1971), 38–39. Also see C. K. Barrett, "Shaliach and Apostle," in *Donum Gentilicium: New Testament Studies in Honour of David Daube*, ed. H. Bammel and W. D. Davies (Oxford: Clarendon Press,

what the Reformed philosopher Nicholas Wolterstorff calls "deputized discourse," wherein a person is empowered to speak in the name of another, with the full weight of their authority. The chief example of this would be an ambassador.[42]

Jesus' promise that the prophets and apostles possess infallible teaching authority is not a claim that stands on its own but is validated by His resurrection from the dead. As we observed in the previous chapter, Jesus is the exemplary prophet of God who supremely fulfilled the criteria for true prophecy outlined by Moses in Deuteronomy 18 in multiple ways. The most clear and convincing manner in which Jesus fulfilled these criteria was in His prediction and fulfillment of His own resurrection. In the resurrection God the Father placed a stamp of approval on all that Jesus had said and done through the power of the Holy Spirit (Acts 2:36). This divine stamp of approval included the affirmation of the authority of the Old Testament as well as His authorization of the infallible teaching authority of the apostles. As we observed earlier, in eternity the unity between signifier (Son) and signified (Father) is facilitated by the Spirit. Likewise, in time the Son's claims (signifier) are shown to correspond to the Father's truth (signified) by the Spirit in the resurrection.

Nevertheless, we must emphasize strongly that Christians do not accept the lordship of Christ and His resurrection because of a rationalistic proof. Rather, Christian believers accept the resurrection and its validation of Christ's truth claims because the Holy Spirit works on their hearts and minds through the Gospel (Rom 10:17; Gal 3:2). By the power of the Spirit the recognition of the Word of God as such by the human subject is self-authenticating (αὐτοπιστία).[43] As we have seen, the Holy Spirit objectively mediates the unity between the Father and the Son in eternity and reveals the same unity in time through the events of Christ's life (death and resurrection). Likewise, by working faith in believers, the Holy Spirit gives subjective assurance of the objective unity of the external Word and the reality it manifests. He does this by giving faith to believers so that they recognize the truthful correspondence between Jesus' claims and the Father's truth, as well as the unity between the word of the Bible and the historical reality of revelation which it signifies (*testimonium internum Spiritus Sancti*; Jn 10:27; Rom 8:16; 1 Cor 2:4–5; Gal 3:2; 1 Jn 5:6–12).[44]

Thus, we know the Scriptures are the inerrant Word of God the same way that we know the sacraments are effective signs. Jesus has attached His

---

1978), 88–102.

42. Nicholas Wolterstorff, *Divine Discourse: Philosophical Reflections on the Claim That God Speaks* (Cambridge, UK: Cambridge University Press, 1995), 38–42. Robert Jenson makes a similar argument, although he bizarrely argues that the one deputized can actually misrepresent the intention of the one he represents. Robert Jenson, *On the Inspiration of Scripture* (Delhi, NY: ALPB Books, 2012), 14–32.

43. Preus, *Theology of Post-Reformation Lutheranism* 1:296–99.

44. Baier, *Compendium Theologiae Positivae* 1:132–34; Adolf Hoenecke, *Evangelical Lutheran Dogmatics*, trans. Joel Fredrich et al., 4 vols. (Milwaukee: Northwestern Publishing House, 1999–2009), 1:452–54; Pieper, *Christian Dogmatics* 1:312–15.

word of promises to the prophets and apostles and has bidden us discover His inerrant Word in their writings. The implication is not that every word of the Bible appears to be truthful and without error when examined by human beings. Because humans are both finite and fallen, their noetic capacities are both limited and damaged by sin. Even in a state of grace the human mind may find apparent errors in Scripture. Nevertheless, based on Jesus' promise of infallibility to the prophets and apostles, believers are bidden to trust that the Lord of the Scriptures is faithful to His promises and knows what constitutes truth and error better than they do. It is of course not useless to attempt to overcome apparent falsehoods and discrepancies in the Scriptures through research and argumentation. But just as the validity and power of the sacraments do not depend on believers being able to detect visibly the invisible presence of divine grace (the Holy Spirit, Christ's body and blood), so too the Scriptures are not regarded as inerrant because human reason and investigation can overcome every apparent error and discrepancy in them.

Faith's ultimate object is the invisible God (Heb 11:1), who hides under historical and creaturely masks (*larva Dei*). Indeed, God hides under creaturely masks, the finite external appearance of which conflicts with the glory of His infinite transcendental attributes (*sub contrario*). Nevertheless, the events and creatures God hides under are accessible to historical science and to investigation. Although we must emphasize strongly that historical evidence does not give rise to faith or even ultimately sustain it, the Holy Spirit illuminates the hearts and the minds of believers through faith so as to allow them to recognize and accept the evidence of revelation God provides to them subsequent to their conversion.[45] Doubting Thomas believed because of Jesus' words. But subsequent to his conversion Jesus' risen body with its wounds were still empirically accessible to him (Jn 20:24–29). Similarly, Paul's gospel was established not by plausible words but by the Holy Spirit and His power (1 Cor 2:4–5). Nevertheless, Paul makes rational arguments in favor of his theological positions. When confronted with the Corinthians' denial of the resurrection, the apostle cites eyewitness proof to make his case (1 Corinthians 15).[46]

Likewise, although Christians accept Christ, the resurrection, and the authority of the Scripture not on the basis of historical evidence, there is a significant amount of empirical evidence that validates these realities.[47]

---

45. Robert Preus writes of the seventeenth-century dogmaticians: "The Lutherans . . . held that scientific, historical, archaeological or rational inquiry could never disprove the truthfulness or delimit the authority of Scripture, but that such an investigation was interesting and beneficial as an external criterion by which heathens might be convinced, although only intellectually, of the reliability of Scripture." Cited from Arthur Carl Piepkorn, "Book Review: *The Inspiration of Scripture*," in *Sacred Scriptures and the Lutheran Confessions*, 23. Originally taken from Preus, *The Inspiration of Scripture*, 89.

46. See similar point in Baier, *Compendium Theologiae Positivae* 1:120–23.

47. See Gerald O'Collins, *Believing in the Resurrection: The Meaning and Promise of the Risen Jesus* (New York: Paulist Press, 2012), 126; Gary R. Habermas and Michael Licona, *The Case for the Resurrection of Jesus* (Grand Rapids: Kregel Publishers, 2004), 72–75, 169, 289;

Because Christ and His lordship have authorized the Scriptures and because this authorization is vindicated along with His lordship in the resurrection, it logically follows that there is a secondary empirical basis for arguing in favor of the supreme authority of Scripture.[48]

In the light of this witness of history, Nicolaus Hunnius correctly observed that when compared to other scriptures or bodies of religious teaching that claim an analogous authority, the Bible validates itself by its reliability.[49] Although Hunnius lived in the early seventeenth century and lacked access to the fruits of modern historical research, he was able to cite correctly the fulfillment of Scripture's prophecies as a means by which the triune God reveals Himself to be faithful in concrete and objective history. As we have seen, the resurrection is an especially powerful demonstration of this principle.

So the Christian faith is grounded in historically accessible events to which faith gains access by way of the Spirit's work in objective means of grace. The believer is drawn out of his natural Enthusiasm into a concrete, historical reality *extra nos*. Since the salvation Christians believe in is historical and objective, the possibility of any return to Enthusiasm and its corollary, self-justification, is cut off to them.

By contrast, all other faiths and their scriptures rely not primarily on historical events but on the historically inaccessible and unprovable claims of the subjective religious experiences of their founders. This is the case with those who follow Muhammad, Buddha, Joseph Smith, and even to an extent the pope.[50] Not only are the claims of these false prophets lacking in any objective validation, they are not infrequently blatantly self-serving (e.g., power grabs, demands of monetary payments, sexual favors). By contrast, when understood properly, the Gospel cannot be a power play (in spite of Nietzsche's claim to the contrary)[51] because it reflects the full self-surrender of God in Christ to the believer through an unconditional promise of redemption. Because it lacks any conditions, the Gospel can never be used to try to cajole power, sex, or money from others.

As a natural corollary to their Enthusiasm, the false prophets of the various world religions and sects of pseudo-Christianity also inevitably teach their followers that salvation is available through a set of works. Their own Enthusiasm and self-justification give rise to that of their followers. Through their false teaching their followers are thereby driven back into their own self-incurvature and self-justification. Ultimately Pieper is correct that there are

---

Michael Licona, *The Resurrection of Jesus: A New Historiographical Approach* (Downers Grove, IL: InterVarsity Press, 2010), 349–55; John Warwick Montgomery, *Tracatus Logico-Theologicus* (Eugene, OR: Wipf & Stock, 2013), 135–50.

48. See similar argument in Montgomery, *Where Is History Going?* 179.

49. Nicolaus Hunnius, *Epitome Credendorum*, trans. Paul Gottheil (Nuremburg: U. E. Sebald, 1847), 3–15.

50. See a similar point in Montgomery, *Tracatus Logico-Theologicus*, 62–66, 72–73.

51. Friedrich Nietzsche, *On the Genealogy of Morals*, trans. Douglas Smith (Oxford: Oxford University Press, 2009).

only two religions in the world: one religion of the Gospel and another of the Law.[52] Indeed, this distinction serves as yet another proof of the Gospel's truth. That is to say, if the human default mode after the Fall is works righteousness and self-justification, as is self-evident from even a cursory study of the world religions, then the biblical religion of the Gospel cannot be a projection of the human mind.[53]

THE BOUNDARIES OF INERRANCY

Although the prophets and apostles were granted infallibility in their teaching of the faith, such freedom from error did not imply a limitless knowledge of the truth. As Hermann Sasse observes, divine inspiration did not cause the prophets and apostles to become omniscient.[54] In the same manner, although Jesus revealed much in His state of humiliation, He did not make use of His knowledge of the time of His second coming in the state of humiliation (Mk 13:32). Hence, within the boundaries of His earthly ministry even Christ's knowledge was not limitless but was bounded by His temporary self-suspension of the omniscience fully communicated to His human nature (Jn 21:17; Col 2:3). Similarly, Jesus bound the infallibility of the apostles at different stages and to different purposes. Although the promise of Christ and the truthfulness of God demand that we affirm there are no errors in Scripture, this does not mean that the prophets and apostles within the private recesses of their own minds did not hold errors on certain subjects that did not pertain directly to their witness to the revelation given them by God (e.g., common scientific errors of the day or misinformation about geography). Nevertheless, in order to preserve the written Scriptures from even the slightest error, the Holy Spirit prevented the authors of the Bible from expressing even these minor erroneous beliefs in their composition of the Sacred Scripture.[55]

Recognizing the limited nature of inspiration is important because this insight can help refute a number of possible objections that could be raised to the infallibility of the prophets and apostles. For example, one might object to our earlier interpretation of the infallibility promised by Jesus in a number of key passages by pointing to the fact that the apostles did err during the ministry of Jesus and afterwards. Notably, Peter denied Christ, and the disciples uniformly erred in thinking it was not the proper vocation of Jesus as the Messiah to die and rise. Likewise, in the book of Galatians we find Peter erring in the matter of table fellowship with the Gentiles (Galatians 2).

---

52. Pieper, *Christian Dogmatics* 1:19–21.

53. Montgomery, *Tracatus Logico-Theologicus*, 17–18.

54. Hermann Sasse, "Additional Notes Concerning Holy Scripture," in *Scripture and the Church: Selected Essays of Hermann Sasse*, ed. Jeffrey Kloha and Ronald Feuerhahn (St. Louis: Concordia Seminary, 1995), 167.

55. Scaer, *Apostolic Scriptures*, 47.

In response to these objections we must observe that Jesus' authorization of the apostles as infallible teachers of the church had to do with the exercise of their public ministry. This is clearly indicated by the fact that the context of the passages discussed earlier is Jesus' commissioning the apostles for public ministry. Hence their infallibility did not extend to their private opinions of a variety of subjects, such as politics, the weather, the best fishing techniques, etc.[56]

Neither did the infallibility given to the apostles during Jesus' earthly ministry have anything to do with their private apprehension of certain teachings that were not yet part of the public teaching Jesus wished them to articulate. In Jesus' sending out of the disciples in Luke 10 (paralleled in a seemingly different mission in Matthew 10), He authorized their public infallible witness regarding the limited amount of teaching He had communicated to them up to that point (repentance, forgiveness, ethics, the coming kingdom of God, etc.). The Gospel writers are clear that Christ only later began to expound to the apostles the complete truth about His messianic vocation, including His death and resurrection (Mt 16:21–28; Mk 8:31–33; Lk 9:22–27, etc.). Although the apostles initially rejected or did not understand Jesus' teaching on these points, they did so privately and did not err in their public teaching offices.

Of course, the apostles' understanding of Jesus and His significance did not remain incomplete but became complete after the resurrection and Pentecost. John quotes Jesus as stating that the Spirit would later reveal to them "all things and bring to your remembrance all that I have said to you" (Jn 14:26). Later, having been instructed by Jesus during the forty days between the resurrection and the ascension and being further empowered for ministry by the Spirit at Pentecost, the apostles expounded the kerygma Jesus had entrusted to them in a complete and inerrant form (Acts 2). As evidence of this, observe that John repeatedly highlights the fact that the disciples did not understand the full implications of certain teachings or actions of Jesus until after the resurrection and the public reception of the Spirit (Jn 2:22; 7:39; 12:16; 18:34).[57]

Finally, in Peter's conflict with Paul as recorded in Galatians, though the apostle behaved hypocritically he did not err in regard to any of the articles of the faith. Infallible teaching authority does not make one completely free of sin. Paul states that he confronted Peter and said, "*We know* that a person is not justified by works of the law but through faith in Jesus Christ" (Gal 2:16; emphasis added). In other words, Paul's point is not that Peter was in error regarding the doctrine of justification. Rather, he is stating that Peter was behaving hypocritically by withdrawing from table fellowship with fellow Christians because he feared certain persons loyal to James who had entered

---

56. Scaer, *Apostolic Scriptures*, 47–48.
57. Scaer, *Apostolic Scriptures*, 65–66. According to Robert Preus, certain Lutheran scholastics held that the apostles were genuinely infallible only after Pentecost. We along with Scaer have suggested otherwise. See Preus, *Inspiration of Scripture*, 78.

his community at Antioch (Gal 2:12). Paul's approach assumes that Peter knew and correctly articulated the Gospel, yet was not acting in accordance with this true knowledge.[58]

Although Sasse is correct (as we have argued above) that the inspiration of the authors of Scripture did not amount to omniscience, it seems that he drew some conclusions from this fact, even in later life, that are out of keeping with biblical and confessional teaching. Early in his career Sasse affirmed the truthfulness of Scripture in all theological and moral matters, while allowing that the Bible contained some minor historical and scientific errors in keeping with the authors' humanity and limited vantage point in history.[59] Later Sasse affirmed the inerrancy of the Bible and even stated that he regretted his earlier affirmation that the biblical texts contained errors (*Irrtümer*). Nevertheless, he posited that the biblical authors retained their genuine human limitations in writing the Bible. These limitations fell into three distinct categories: the limitation of human language (i.e., the need of the divine to accommodate limited human language), the limitation of literary and historical conventions of ancient literature, and the limitation of "world picture" (*Weltbild*) with regard to science and cosmology.[60] In the last category Sasse at the very least appears to affirm factual errors in Scripture, but relabeled them as limitations rather than errors.[61]

Sasse's first two categories represent valid limitations on the authors of the Bible. We have already seen how God accommodates Himself to the finitude of human language (Luther's linguistic "wrappings"[62]). Also, it is impossible to deny that although the authors of the Bible were truthful in what they recorded, they did so within the conventions of ancient historical and literary genres, which are somewhat looser in their modes of expression than modern historiography and science. Ultimately these limitations are warranted because they both correspond to the biblical data and posit that although the witness of the scriptural authors was limited, it was always absolutely true. As we saw earlier, this was also true of Christ in His state of humiliation (Mk 13:32).

---

58. Robert Preus summarizes the position of the Lutheran scholastics thus: "But what about Peter? Did he not err when he ate with the Gentiles but ordered others not to do so? Peter erred, but this was a mistake in practice, not in *theoris fidei*. It was not possible for him to err in doctrine. His was a sin of weakness; he simply did not practice what he preached." Preus, *Inspiration of Scripture*, 78.

59. Sasse, "On the Doctrine *De Scriptura Sacra*," in *Scripture and the Church*, 87–96.

60. Sasse, "Additional Notes Concerning Holy Scripture," 167.

61. Sasse, "Additional Notes Concerning Holy Scripture," 165–88. Also see Hermann Sasse, "Concerning the Bible's Inerrancy," in *Scripture and the Church*, 333–38. We acknowledge that our interpretation of Sasse on this point is at variance with many who read him as ultimately coming into harmony with Missourian orthodoxy on this point. For alternative views see Jeffrey Kloha, "Herman Sasse Confesses the Doctrine *De Scriptura Sacra*" in *Scripture and the Church*, 337–424; Kurt Marquart, "Hermann Sasse and the Mystery of Sacred Scripture," in *Hermann Sasse: A Man for Our Times*? ed. John Stephenson and Thomas Winger (St Louis: Concordia Publishing House, 1998), 167–93.

62. *Lectures on Genesis*, 1535–45 (AE 1:15; WA 42:12).

Broadly speaking, such limitations are also in keeping with the definition of inerrancy as it was posited by scholastic orthodoxy, as we will see below.[63]

Problems nevertheless arise when we turn to Sasse's third category, wherein it appears that God did not merely accommodate His Word to the ancient environment but allowed actual errors to enter into the Bible. Sasse seems to wish to maintain this idea for fear of abrogating the genuine humanity of the authors of the Bible.[64] Of course we should note that Sasse's concern for the genuine humanity of the authors of Scripture is a valid one, which we will examine more extensively at a later point. Nevertheless, the humanity of the secondary authors (*auctor secundarius*) of the Bible does not necessarily imply the presence of historical or scientific errors in the text. It is accidental to humanity to err, and not essential. The chief example of this truth would be Jesus, who was fully human and yet never erred.[65] Although, as observed earlier, Christ limited His knowledge during His state of humiliation, just as the authors of Scripture were limited in their knowledge, He was always truthful in all He said. Hence, it does not contradict the nature of humanity for someone to be preserved from error. Indeed, since humans were made to know God and His truth, being preserved from error is a fulfillment of the true vocation of humanity.

Beyond the fact that being prone to err is not essential to humanity, we also know that the Scriptures are completely without error because Christ affirmed the complete truthfulness of the Old Testament as well as the teachings of the apostles. It follows that God did not allow the slightest error, whether scientific or historical, to creep into the biblical text, even if the contrary appears to be the case.

Still, Sasse is correct that the apostles probably believed many common scientific errors of their day. Nevertheless, in ensuring the infallibility of their public ministry the Holy Spirit prevented them from articulating any of these private errors as part of their public witness to the Word of God. Similarly, insofar as they needed to articulate scientific or historical truths as part of the public ministry, through His providence God ensured that they had access to those truths, so that under the inspiration of the Holy Spirit they would always be completely truthful in all things.[66]

Another point about the boundaries of inerrancy as classically defined[67] is that inerrancy extends only to everything Scripture affirms to be true, not to

---

63. See Preus, *Theology of Post-Reformation Lutheranism* 1:339–62. Although the Lutheran scholastics do not take into consideration the limitations of ancient genres of writing, they do affirm repeatedly that the Holy Spirit accommodated Himself to ancient ways of speaking and recoding information, which as a whole tends to be looser than modern historical and scientific modes of speech.

64. Sasse, "*De Scriptura Sacra*," 75–76.

65. See the same point made here: John Stephenson, "Inerrancy," *Logia: A Journal of Lutheran Theology* 2, No. 4 (1993): 7.

66. Scaer, *Apostolic Scriptures*, 47.

67. Muller, *Post-Reformation Reformed Dogmatics* 2:303–9; Preus, *Theology of Post-*

every statement found in Scripture.[68] For example, as Abraham Calov notes, the scriptural authors frequently report the statements of individual speakers or the common opinions of the day, which may not be accurate. Scripture is trustworthy when it asserts that the speaker made these statements or that a particular belief was a common opinion. But taken on their own, such statements may in fact be false.[69]

For example, Jephthah states in Jgs 11:26 that Israel had at his time occupied Canaan for three hundred years. It may or may not be the case that Israel had at that point occupied Palestine for that amount of time, since the speaker is not quoting an oracle of God and the text does not assert that he was divinely inspired. Even if the speaker here is wrong, Scripture is not asserting something erroneous. What Scripture is affirming is not the actual length of time that Israel had occupied the land, but rather that Jephthah made the assertion.

One might draw a similar conclusion about the two accounts of the death of Saul (1 Samuel 31; 2 Samuel 1). Whereas 1 Samuel 31 gives a factual description of how Saul died, the man from Saul's camp in 2 Samuel 1 gives a dishonest account of Saul's death in order to curry favor with David. In both instances the Bible is being truthful. In the former account we are given the actual narrative of Saul's death, whereas the latter is a true report of the fact that a man came to David and gave a false report concerning Saul's death.

There are many other qualifications like this in the classical definition of inerrancy. Following this definition, Robert Preus observes that the inerrancy of the Bible is not contradicted by the following phenomena: round or general numbers (of armies or those who died in a battle, for example); description of nature according to appearance (*secundum apparentiam, secundum veritatem opticam*) rather than actual fact (*secundum veritatem physicam*) (e.g., the sun "stood still" for Joshua); the use of poetical or metaphorical language in general; the use of common expressions of the day that if taken literally could be understood as scientific errors (Joseph's "bowels of mercy"); parallel accounts of certain events from different perspectives, emphasizing different facts (Kings vs. Chronicles, the differences in the Gospels, etc.); the existence of inexact or paraphrased citations of the Old Testament in the New Testament. In the case of all of these phenomena, the inerrancy of the text is not compromised because the author speaks in a truthful albeit not strictly literal or exact manner.[70] In

---

Reformation Lutheranism 1:339–62.

68. This is quite possibly one of the most absurd arguments made by opponents of inerrancy. See Otto Weber, *Foundations of Dogmatics*, trans. Darrell Guder, 2 vols. (Grand Rapids: Wm. B. Eerdmans, 1981), 1:237. Weber posits that individual statements of the Bible cannot be viewed as being inspired in and of themselves, since Ps 14:1 quotes the fool saying that "there is no God."

69. Preus, *Theology of Post-Reformation Lutheranism* 1:358.

70. Robert Preus, "Notes on the Inerrancy of Scripture," *Concordia Theological Monthly* 38 (June 1967): 365–75. One finds a similar set of provisos within various Reformed theologians. See A. A. Hodge and Benjamin Warfield, *Inspiration* (Grand Rapids: Baker, 1979) and Paul Feinberg, "The Meaning of Inerrancy," in Geisler, *Inerrancy*, 298–302.

these cases we should appreciate that the Holy Spirit accommodated Himself to normal and common modes of human speech that are truthful without necessarily always being literal, scientific, or precise.

In the light of these necessary qualifications of what is meant by inerrancy, it is not surprising that the term itself has come under fire by certain theologians. Notably, Arthur Piepkorn in a famous article argues that while the substance of the doctrine of inerrancy should be maintained, the term inerrancy should be abandoned. Although he gives a number of reasons for this, one of his chief criticisms of the term is that it seems to imply that Scripture always speaks the truth in an absolutely literal, precise, and scientific manner. In view of the qualifications of the term proposed by the theologians of scholastic orthodoxy, "inerrancy" can be applied to the Bible and its truthfulness only in a very imprecise and confusing way.[71]

While we must agree with Piepkorn that the term inerrancy is not absolutely necessary for the confession of Christian truth (as Piepkorn notes, it seems to have come into vogue only in the early nineteenth century), we must register our disagreement with him regarding the usefulness of the term. First, the use of the term is important to safeguarding the confessional Lutheran belief in the absolute truthfulness of the Bible. In the history of Christian dogma, certain terms have taken on special significance because they affirm an important truth over against a blatant error.

For example, the term *homoousios* became significant during the Arian crisis. This term's intention was to rule out categorically any Arian interpretation of the relationship between the Father and the Son. The term was important to maintain because any alteration of it would create linguistic wiggle room for Arians to feign orthodoxy.[72] An analogous situation occurs with the term inerrancy. Liberal theologians regularly speak of the Bible as inspired, truthful, and even the Word of God[73] in the same way that the Arians were willing to call Christ "God" in a metaphorical sense.[74] In both cases the true church had to develop special vocabulary to call false doctrine into the open. By insisting unequivocally that a specific term be used, theologians are able to expose the latent heresy hidden under other language more conducive to equivocation. Much like the Arians' rejection of *homoousios* exposed them as not genuinely believing that Christ was God, liberal theologians and clergy reveal their rejection of the complete truthfulness of the Bible by their refusal to use the term inerrancy.

---

71. Piepkorn, "What Does 'Inerrancy' Mean?" 39–47.

72. Roger Olson, *The Story of Christian Theology: Twenty Centuries of Tradition and Reform* (Downers Grove, IL: InterVarsity Press, 1999), 154–56.

73. See Armand Boehme, "The Smokescreen Vocabulary," *Concordia Theological Quarterly* 41, no. 2 (1977): 25–40.

74. For example, see the confession of the Arian missionary Bishop Ulfilas in Peter Heathers and John Matthews, *The Goths of the Fourth Century* (Liverpool: Liverpool University Press, 1991), 143.

Second, although Piepkorn is correct that the term inerrancy may give rise to misinterpretations, this is not a valid reason for rejecting it. Most theological terms need to be clearly and carefully explained and have often given rise to misinterpretations. Again, to use the analogous situation of the Arian crisis, in the period between the first and second ecumenical councils many interpreted *homoousios* as promoting a form of modalism, thereby leading them to reject the term. In response the pro-Nicene party did not abandon the word but rather explained it more clearly (as Athanasius did), while later the Cappadocian fathers integrated it within a series of other more refined theological distinctions, notably the distinction between *ousia* and *hypostasis*.[75] Similarly, articles like those of Robert Preus discussed above do not abandon the term inerrancy in view of misunderstandings but rather give a clearer explanation of its meaning.

OTHER OBJECTIONS TO THE INERRANCY OF SCRIPTURE[76]

Beyond the definitional difficulties that accompany the doctrine of inerrancy, many theologians have rejected it on the grounds that in reading the Bible they themselves cannot work out every discrepancy or conflict with secular science present in the text. For example, Matthew Becker has argued recently that prior to affirming scriptural inerrancy one would theoretically have to examine thoroughly every jot and tittle and discover that the Bible is absolutely true.[77] Becker correctly notes both that this is not possible and that we come to affirm Christ as Lord not by accepting a particular doctrine of inspiration but through the work of the Spirit converting us to the Gospel. Because it is through the efficacious power of the Gospel that we are converted, this Gospel must serve as an ultimate authority for Christian theology. Scripture is authoritative insofar as it witnesses to the Gospel and the doctrines necessary for the Gospel to be true.[78] Hence, for Becker the basis of authority is the Gospel that is contained in the Scriptures and not the Scriptures themselves.[79] Becker here embraces a version of what John Warwick Montgomery famously came to call Gospel reductionism.[80]

As a result, Becker seems oddly to confuse what David Hollaz referred to as Scripture's causative authority (Scripture as the living Word's ability to cause

---

75. Olson, *Story of Christian Theology*, 161–96.

76. Much of the material in this section comes from my earlier review of Matthew Becker's work for the journal *Logia*. See Jack Kilcrease, "Review of Matthew Becker, *Fundamental Theology*," in *Logia Online*, April 8, 2015, accessible at http://www.logia.org/logia-online/book-review-fundamental-theology2015.

77. Matthew Becker, *Fundamental Theology: A Protestant Perspective* (New York: T & T Clark, 2014), 307.

78. Becker, *Fundamental Theology*, 285.

79. Becker, *Fundamental Theology*, 285.

80. John Warwick Montgomery, *Crisis in Lutheran Theology*, 2 vols. (Grand Rapids: Baker Book House, 1967), 1:81–123.

the human subject to give assent to it) and its normative authority (Scripture's authority in and of itself as the inspired Word of God).[81] In other words, we come to acknowledge the Word of God as such because God causes us to recognize the truthfulness of the Word through the power of the Spirit. While it is indeed true that the Spirit's operation through the Gospel causes our belief that the Bible is the inerrant Word of God, this efficacy in and of itself is not the basis or ground of scriptural authority. Once we are illuminated by the Spirit we come to recognize that Scripture is objectively and normatively the Word of God in and of itself due to the reality of its inspiration.[82] To use an analogy: being told that there are jewels and gold in an attic may be the means by which we come into the possession of gold and jewels, but it does not make gold and jewels into gold and jewels. If we were to posit Scripture's authority purely on the basis of its causative authority, as Becker at least appears to do, our belief in the Word of God would be grounded in nothing other than our own belief and experience. This assertion would place us and not Holy Scripture in the supreme position of authority, thereby making us guilty of a form of Enthusiasm.

Beyond these confusions, several other points should be made about Becker's position. First, as noted above, confessional Lutheran dogmatists posit that Scripture is inerrant because Christ has attached a word of promise to the writings of the prophets and apostles. Scripture is not to be posited as inerrant because by our own reason and strength we have discovered that the Bible is without error. Although apologetic arguments in this direction are not without merit, as we have seen above, our faith ultimately is in Christ and His trustworthiness.[83] The Gospel and the facts that underlie it are fully trustworthy because God uses the instrument of faith as a means to recognize the trustworthiness of the risen Christ and His promises. Coming to the recognition of a particular truth on the basis of evidence can be only partial, provisional, and probable (*fides humana*). This recognition is not the kind of supreme certainty that the New Testament attributes to faith (Romans 4, Hebrews 11, *fides divina*). Hence, we can trust the Scriptures as reliable because God in Christ promises that they are reliable, not because we can perceive directly that the text is free of errors.[84]

This affirmation of the centrality of Christ's promise of inerrancy differentiates the historic Lutheran understanding of inerrancy from the nineteenth- and early twentieth-century Princeton school, a key source of

---

81. Heinrich Schmid, *The Doctrinal Theology of the Evangelical Lutheran Church*, trans. Charles Hay and Henry Jacobs (Minneapolis: Augsburg Publishing House, 1961), 104. Also see discussion in Baier, *Compendium Theologiae Positivae* 1:118.

82. Baier, *Compendium Theologiae Positivae* 1:119.

83. See this approach to inerrancy in J. A. O. Preus, *It Is Written* (St. Louis: Concordia Publishing House, 1971).

84. Preus, *Theology of Post-Reformation Lutheranism* 1:302–3. Preus shows that the inner testimony of the Spirit that gives rise to the recognition of Scripture's reliability is actually not different than faith in Christ. This is because faith in Christ is the result of the activity of the Spirit and is facilitated through the Gospel.

later American Fundamentalism. Beginning with the writings of Archibald Alexander,[85] this school claimed that Scripture should be viewed as truthful on the same grounds that in everyday life we accept testimony, especially historical testimony, as reliable. Humans are usually justified in accepting testimony as a matter of course unless we have extremely good grounds to reject it. If we did not, it would be practically impossible to function as a member of human society. This position takes its cue from a philosophical school known as Scottish common-sense realism, popular in early America.[86] Following this same theory of knowledge, Benjamin Warfield opined that on the grounds of its status as reliable historical testimony, Scripture should be affirmed as true and reliable without a doctrine of inerrancy. One should believe in the inspiration and inerrancy of the Bible, of course, but on the grounds that inerrancy and inspiration are two reliable facts along with many others attested by the Bible.[87]

Hence in this school of thought a human epistemological theory and not the resurrected Christ holds pride of place in determining the truthfulness of the Word of God. The ultimate consequence of this view is a form of rationalistic Enthusiasm. Every perceived discrepancy, perceived contradiction, or scientific challenge calls into doubt the status of the Bible as reliable testimony until it can be worked out through empirical evidence. Faith in the Word of God thus becomes provisional and conditional, not complete and absolute as the New Testament account of faith demands (Romans 4, Hebrews 11, etc.).

By contrast, the confessional Lutheran commitment to the inerrancy of Scripture is based on the sacramental nature of Scripture. Just as the reality of grace in the sacraments is hidden in and under the physical elements and is recognizable only due to the word of promise attached to them, God's Word in Scripture is recognizable as such because of the dominical promise of infallibility Christ has attached to the authors and their words. Hence, calling into question the inerrancy of the Bible also means calling into question the validity of the sacraments. If Christ's promise remains good for the sacraments, then it should hold for the inerrancy of the Scriptures. Because Christ has risen from the dead, thereby validating all He has said and done, we must believe Him over our fallen and finite human reason. Indeed, as Luther aptly states in

---

85. See Archibald Alexander, *Evidence of the Authenticity, Inspiration, and Canonical Authority of the Holy Scripture* (Philadelphia: Presbyterian Board of Publication, 1836).

86. See the following works by Thomas Reid: *Essays on the Powers of the Human Mind; to Which Are Prefixed, an Essay on Quantity, and an Analysis of Aristotle's Logic*, 3 vols. (Edinburgh: Bell and Bradfute, 1812); and *An Inquiry into the Human Mind, on the Principles of Common Sense* (Edinburgh: Bell and Bradfute, 1810). Also see the following on the evolution of common-sense realism in the American environment: Theodore Dwight Bozeman, *Protestants in the Age of Science: The Baconian Ideal and Antebellum Religious Thought* (Chapel Hill, NC: University of North Carolina Press, 1977); George Marsden, "Everyone's Own Interpretation? The Bible, Science, and Authority in Mid-Nineteenth-Century America," in *The Bible in America*, ed. Nathan Hatch and Mark Noll (New York: Oxford University Press, 1982), 79–100.

87. Benjamin Warfield, *The Inspiration and Authority of the Bible* (Philadelphia: Presbyterian and Reformed Publishing Company, 1970), 210–12.

the Large Catechism regarding the promise of Christ: "Because we know that God does not lie. I and my neighbor and, in short, all men, may err and deceive, but the Word of God cannot err."[88] If Becker wishes to accept the validity of the sacraments (as one suspects he does) but not the inerrancy of Scripture, then he must insist on arbitrarily rejecting one of Christ's dominical promises while accepting the others.[89]

Finally, as observed earlier with regard to Bultmann, the Gospel cannot be isolated from the scriptural worldview, narrative, and other dogmas of the faith. As we have shown repeatedly, while the Gospel is the central article (*Hauptartikel*) of the faith, it nevertheless does not exhaust the content of the Christian faith. Neither does the Gospel exist in isolation from other revealed truths. By analogy we may say that if the Scriptures are like a wheel, the Gospel is the axle and the other articles of the faith like the spokes. Although an axle is central to the functioning of a wheel, the wheel is in fact non-functional without the spokes.[90]

In the same manner, the Gospel is ultimately a solution to the problem of the sin committed originally by Adam and Eve and transmitted to their descendants. Adam and Eve could sin only because they were creatures who violated the Law of their creator God. Similarly, Christ's atoning work would be incoherent without the doctrines of the Trinity or the incarnation or the background of the whole history of Israel. The difficulty with Becker wishing to make the Gospel the ultimate criterion of all theological authority is that the Gospel does not make sense without the context of the total witness of the Bible and hence its inerrant authority.[91] If I believe the Gospel as true unconditionally, then I must believe the whole Bible as unconditionally true.

Against this it could be argued that only a minimal number of these doctrines and historical facts need to be judged true for the Gospel to be true. Christ could still have died on the cross and been raised even if Exodus was wrong about Moses' face glowing when he came down from Mt. Sinai. Jesus could still basically be the same person portrayed by the New Testament even if the Gospel writers were wrong about a few details of His life. This position was taken by many people in the Erlangen school, notably Paul Althaus.[92] Indeed, several of Becker's statements seem to suggest he would take a similar position. But this proposal is equally problematic. One way or another, every statement of Scripture is connected with the scriptural narrative and worldview, which

---

88. LC IV (Bente, 747).

89. Reu makes a similar point. See Johann Michael Reu, *Lutheran Dogmatics* (Dubuque: Wartburg Theological Seminary, 1951), 459–60.

90. This is a common analogy within many conservative Lutheran circles. Nevertheless, I thank the Rev. David Fleming for first alerting me to it.

91. Becker, *Fundamental Theology*, 285.

92. See Paul Althaus, *Faith and Fact in the Kerygma Today*, trans. David Cairns (Philadelphia: Muhlenberg Press, 1959).

form the context for the Gospel. It is thus impossible to draw the line between which facts and doctrines are absolutely necessary and which are not.

Becker offers other objections to the inerrancy of the Bible. He argues that affirming the inerrancy of the Bible has a flattening effect on the content of Scripture.[93] If every word of Scripture is divinely inspired and inerrant, then even the most innocuous historical facts become as important as the chief article of the Gospel. Among the many points that might be made here, Becker seems to be unaware of the steady drumbeat of "all theology is Christology" from major proponents of inerrancy in twentieth-century Lutheranism, such as David Scaer and Robert Preus.[94] Obviously, what he claims about the flattening effect does not seem to carry through in practice.

Moreover, Becker's concern here represents an obvious category confusion. The category "truthful" is here being confused with the category "important." To illustrate this confusion with a thought-experiment: theoretically, if we posit a husband who was programmed to be utterly unable to tell a lie to his wife, every truthful utterance he made would still not be equally important. For example, the statement "I got gas on the way home from work" would be both equally true and yet considerably less important than his wedding vows.

Becker also argues against the doctrine of inerrancy by complaining that the doctrine has been used to promote what he considers to be anti-scientific views. For example, he derides Francis Pieper's rather eccentric position (at least by the standards of the early twentieth century) that scriptural inerrancy entails the rejection of heliocentrism.[95] According to Becker, on the one hand Pieper is indeed correct that the Bible teaches geocentricism, while on the other he should be faulted for not seeing that this teaching flatly contradicts scientific facts and therefore this disproves the inerrancy of the Bible. Ultimately for Becker, one should simply accept that the Bible is in error with regard to many scientific things. One notable example of Scripture's errors are its references to the "pillars of the earth" (1 Sm 2:8; Jb 9:6).

In response to this, let us first note that Pieper's position was a rather eccentric one even for the theologians of scholastic orthodoxy. As we saw earlier, the Lutheran scholastics accepted a notion of inerrancy compatible with the idea that Scripture often described things as they appear ("the sun is setting") rather than in literal scientific descriptions of the world.[96] This understanding does not undermine inerrancy or the scientific accuracy of scriptural statements any

---

93. Becker, *Fundamental Theology*, 307.
94. See Dean Wenthe et al., eds., *All Theology Is Christology: Essays in Honor of David P. Scaer* (Ft. Wayne: Concordia Theological Seminary Press, 2000); David Scaer, "The Theology of Robert David Preus and His Person: Making a Difference," *Concordia Theological Quarterly* 74, no. 1 (2010): 75–91.
95. Becker, *Fundamental Theology*, 268–69.
96. Preus, *Theology of Post-Reformation Lutheranism* 1:355.

more than contemporary people lie when speaking in the same manner ("the sun is setting"). They are not speaking a falsehood but using a turn of phrase.[97]

Beyond using turns of phrase, the Bible also uses many poetic expressions. One can view references to the "pillars of the earth" as poetic in the same way that the "setting of the sun" is merely a turn of phrase. Much as contemporary poets do not base their language of nature on quantifiable scientific descriptions of the universe, neither did the biblical poets, notably in the Psalms or Job. Indeed, as Peter Leithart has pointed out, language like "pillars of the earth" has the very specific theological/poetic function of describing creation in non-literal terms as a cosmic temple.[98] Ultimately, trying to take poetic descriptions of nature by the biblical authors as scientific propositions of that era is a highly questionable procedure.

However, theology and science are not hermetically sealed off from one another. Theologians should strive to find agreement between contemporary science and the teachings of Scripture. All truth is one (since it comes from God!), and one should expect that when humans investigate nature and other fields of inquiry with right reason, there should ultimately be no conflict with Scripture. We should also note that, contrary to Becker's misrepresentations, Pieper actually shared this sentiment. In the passage in *Christian Dogmatics* in which he rejects heliocentrism, Pieper also expresses hope that Einstein and the theory of relativity would in fact vindicate geocentricism.[99] It did not, of course, but Pieper was not the anti-intellectual, anti-scientific Fundamentalist Becker portrays.

Obviously, although human beings are finite and have damaged noetic capacities due to sin, they are still competent to gain some knowledge of the created world. Still, as the Reformed theologian Keith Mathison observes, our finitude and fallenness make us capable of making mistakes in our interpretations of both scientific data and the Bible.[100] Consequently, just as when Scripture properly understood can expose the errors of science, scientific truth when pitted against a particular interpretation of Scripture may prompt the interpreter to rethink his reading of the text. Perhaps a particular traditional interpretation and not the genuine teaching of Scripture itself may be the barrier to seeing agreement between certain historical or scientific facts and the text. But if there is no way to reconcile certain scientific claims with the text understood on the basis of the literal sense and the analogy of faith, then Scripture must rule supreme. Damaged and finite human reason cannot place a priori limitations on what the Word of God can and cannot say.

---

97. Hoenecke, *Evangelical Lutheran Dogmatics* 1:438.
98. Peter Leithart, *A House for My Name: A Survey of the Old Testament* (Moscow, ID: Canon Press, 2000), 43–45.
99. Pieper, *Christian Dogmatics* 1:473–74.
100. Keith Mathison, *A Reformed Approach to Science and Scripture* (Sanford, FL: Ligonier Ministries, 2013).

In a later section on science and theology Becker protests against this perspective. He asserts that, generally speaking, our knowledge of scientific facts must almost always be correct. If it were not, then God would be attempting to fool us by giving us access to faulty data through our minds and senses.[101] One could of course equally point out that if one accepted the premise, based on science, that Scripture was errant, God would also be guilty of deceiving His people by giving them a record of His revelation which mixed together error and truth without any means of separating them. At another point Becker states that he would like to see mutuality, cooperation, and dialogue between theology and science.[102] However, he ultimately asserts that if science says that Scripture is wrong, Scripture must simply bow to the superior wisdom of science and modify its claims. In this vein Becker tells us that we can no longer believe that death is the result of sin (Romans 5), since the theory of biological evolution presupposes that death is simply another cog in the cosmic machine of life.

Such a perspective is problematic for several reasons. First, it presupposes that raw scientific data simply reveal the inner structures of reality to rational and autonomous human beings in an absolutely transparent manner. Nevertheless, although humans have access to the data of reality, their finitude means that such data are always incomplete. Moreover, such data are always interpreted within a scientific paradigm, or interpretive lens, that organizes the information. Since these lenses are always provisional and not infrequently wrong, humans cannot claim any scientific judgment is infallible.[103]

Hence, if a scientific theory or piece of historical or scientific datum seems to contradict Scripture, there is no particular reason to think Scripture is wrong. Many scientific theories have turned out to be wrong. These incorrect theories and discredited paradigms include many that contradicted Scripture. In these cases the error was in the minds of the interpreters and not in Scripture itself. If we follow Becker's suggestion, we would operate under the assumption that the Word of God is fallible but human reason is not. In the light of history this position is untenable.

Indeed, if Christians of the past had followed Becker and his seeming faith in the near-infallibility of science, they would have been proven wrong in the long term on numerous occasions.[104] One wonders how Becker would answer such a challenge. Should Thomas Aquinas have simply rejected creation *ex nihilo* because Aristotle and the Arab philosophers posited the eternity of the universe?[105] What about scientific racism and eugenics? Should early

101. Becker, *Fundamental Theology*, 440.
102. Becker, *Fundamental Theology*, 446–47.
103. See Thomas Kuhn, *The Structure of Scientific Revolutions* (Chicago: University of Chicago Press, 1996).
104. See similar arguments in Angus J. L. Menuge, "The Cultural and Aesthetic Impact of Lutheranism," in *Where Christ Is Present: A Theology for All Seasons on the 500th Anniversary of the Reformation*, ed. John Warwick Montgomery et al. (Corona, CA: 1517 Legacy, 2015), 220–29.
105. J. B. M. Wissink, ed., *The Eternity of the World in the Thought of Thomas Aquinas and*

twentieth-century Christians simply have rejected the scriptural teaching of a common origin of humanity and accepted what was then considered to be a highly scientific theory of polygenesis and racial gradations?[106] To this latter point Becker would likely say that scientific racism and eugenics were simply junk science, whereas macroevolution and other newer scientific theories are not. Nonetheless, just as contemporary macroevolution is taught at all major universities and forms the basis of many governmental policies, so too were once scientific racism and eugenics. Also, in the light of the paradigmatic anomalies of irreducible complexity, gene entropy, and the lack of transitional species in the fossil record, macroevolution has more problems as a theory regarding the origins of life than Becker allows.[107]

Along similar lines, it often is argued by materialists and atheists that Scripture cannot be truthful on the grounds that it contains supernatural events which, it is alleged, are intrinsically at variance with science and human reason. We have already seen in a previous chapter that this is an absurd argument. Science deals with temporal, finite causes which are observable and quantifiable. Miracles and other supernatural events occur because the supernatural God, who cannot be seen or limited, can transcend the laws of nature as He so chooses. Allowing that miraculous events have occurred in the past does not call into question the rational causal order of the universe. Rather, the entire point of a miracle is that it is an exception to the rule of imminent causation, thereby validating this natural causal order and the ability of the sciences to investigate it.

On another level, though, we should note that the atheist argument for the incompatibility of the Bible and science is ultimately self-contradictory. First, there is a growing body of historical evidence that Christianity and the Bible made the Scientific Revolution possible.[108] Only by believing in a God who created the world out of nothing (*creatio ex nihilo*) according to a rational plan could science work conceptually.[109] Although the Greeks did engage in some science, by the Pax Romana classical science essentially had stalled.[110] And science was possible for the Greeks only because their philosophy often posited a rational or divine principle underlying and organizing the chaotic matter of

His Contemporaries (Leiden: Brill, 1990).

106. See Edwin Black, *War against the Weak: Eugenics and America's Campaign to Create a Master Race* (Washington, DC: Dialogue Press, 2012); Richard Weikart, *From Darwin to Hitler: Evolutionary Ethics, Eugenics and Racism in Germany* (New York: Palgrave Macmillan, 2004).

107. See Michael Behe, *Darwin's Black Box: The Biochemical Challenge to Evolution* (New York: Free Press, 1996); David Berlinski, *The Devil's Delusion: Atheism and Its Scientific Pretensions* (New York: Basic Books, 2009); Philip E. Johnson, *Darwin on Trial* (Downers Grove, IL: InterVarsity Press, 2010).

108. Rodney Stark, *For the Glory of God: How Monotheism Led to Reformations, Science, Witch-Hunts, and the End of Slavery* (Princeton: Princeton University Press, 2004), 121–200.

109. Stark, *For the Glory of God*, 176–77.

110. David Bentley Hart, *Atheist Delusions: The Christian Revolution and Its Fashionable Enemies* (New Haven: Yale University Press, 2009), 67.

the universe (prime mover, demiurge, logos, etc.). Still, since at its deepest level nature remained chaotic, one could argue that science and rationality could go only so far in explaining it. Only a doctrine of creation *ex nihilo* as taught by the Bible, where God's rationality determines nature all the way down to its deepest level, could provide a stable and consistent basis for science.

Ultimately, science presupposes that humans have a capacity for rationality, and that their rationality in part mirrors divine reason (i.e., it is part of the *imago Dei*) as reflected in the created order (Psalm 19; Romans 1).[111] This compatibility is what makes rational scientific investigation possible.[112] As Alister McGrath observes (following Alasdair MacIntyre[113]), in order to remain credible, intellectual disciplines and traditions of thought must give an account of why they are true. The story of creation that the Bible provides gives a rationale for why science should work, thereby supporting science and giving an account of why it is a rational and credible enterprise, something science obviously cannot do on its own.[114]

If such a concept of nature and humans' ability to investigate seems self-evident to the reader, we should note that such assumptions are not held by many cultures, religions, and philosophical schools (Epicureanism, Hinduism, Theravada Buddhism, etc.). Scientific revolutions did not arise in these cultures, because they could not account for why the external world and scientific data were both rational and knowable.

From this argument it also follows that if science is possible because of the existence of a creator God, then this same God who made all things out of nothing certainly can be relied on to have the power to suspend the laws of nature and perform miracles, as the Bible reports. Therefore, as odd as it may seem to many, to have a theoretical basis for science (i.e., an almighty creator God), one must allow for the possibility of miracles. If miracles are at the very least possible, one cannot discount the inerrancy of the Bible because it contains miracles that transcend normal scientific explanation.

Hence, the atheist and materialist argument against the inerrancy of the Bible is inherently contradictory. Indeed, as Alvin Plantinga observes,[115] if atheists and materialists are correct and the Bible is wrong about the existence of a creator God, not only would belief in science lack justification, so would

---

111. Luther: reason is "something divine." *Disputation Concerning Man*, 1536 (AE 34:137; WA 39/1:175).

112. Alister McGrath, *A Scientific Theology*, vol. 1: *Nature* (Edinburgh: T&T Clark, 2003), 197–203.

113. See Alasdair MacInytre, *Whose Justice? Which Rationality?* (South Bend, IN: University of Notre Dame Press, 1988).

114. Alister McGrath, *A Scientific Theology*, vol. 2: *Reality* (Edinburgh: T&T Clark, 2006), 55–121.

115. Alvin Plantinga, "Is Naturalism Irrational?" in *The Analytical Theist: An Alvin Plantinga Reader*, ed. James Sennett (Grand Rapids: Wm. B. Eerdmans, 1998), 72–96.

atheism and materialism themselves. That is to say, if humans are the random products of evolution and not of a rational creator God, then the human mind and its perception automatically must be called into question in a fundamental way. Although evolution may be relied upon to give humans mental pictures of the world that will help them reproduce and spread their DNA, there is no particular reason to think that such ideas will correspond to actual reality. One can imagine the human mind producing all sorts of false beliefs that would promote reproduction and survival but that would not necessarily be true in the sense of corresponding to reality. This uncertainty about whether a mind that has randomly evolved for the purpose of spreading DNA could generate true beliefs about reality would also call into question the validity of atheism and materialism. Hence, atheism and materialism self-destruct from the implications of their own premises. Ultimately, they cannot even give a coherent account of a reality in which human beings could genuinely know that atheism and materialism were true.

FAILED ALTERNATIVES TO INERRANCY
IN MODERN THEOLOGY

As we have seen thus far, Scripture mediates the full presence and truth of the risen Christ. Christ is present and active in the external Word as an effective agent precisely because He is truthful in all He propositionally communicates: "You will know the truth, and the truth will set you free" (Jn 8:32). Hence, in order to be an effective sacramental medium Scripture must be fully inspired and inerrant in all of its content.

The content of Scripture is God's own self-revelation, along with His historical acts of creation and redemption. As we have previously observed, the saving power of the written words of Scripture lies in the fact that they proclaim God's creative and saving acts and the words of Law and promise He has attached to them. If we trust in the Law and promises God has attached to the specific history recorded in the Bible, by implication we must also believe that Scripture has recorded accurately all facts concerning God's activity. If these events did not occur as Scripture recorded them or occurred only partially, then God's promises concerning them would be erroneous and our faith is in vain (1 Cor 15:14). Simply put, to make a promise regarding a non-existent object is absurd.

Since the Enlightenment, many Protestant and Roman Catholic theologians have regarded the doctrine of the full inerrancy of the Scriptures to be unnecessary or even harmful. As we have already seen, this conclusion derives from the prioritization of human reason over Christ's promise of the truthfulness of the Scriptures. Since a rejection of the full inerrancy of the Scriptures has resulted in a theological crisis for many within the modern church, there have been a number of attempts to establish the truth of the Christian religion without an inerrant Bible.

Some theologians would view the events of history as being revelatory in and of themselves: the Bible is revelatory only because it records these events, but it is not itself a form of revelation. According to this view the Bible does not need to be inerrant in all it affirms but merely needs to be an adequate witness to revelation as it has occurred in history. In a previous chapter we have dealt briefly with Wolfhart Pannenberg's advocacy of this position.[116] We could also identify Johannes von Hofmann, Jean Daniélou, and Oscar Cullman as approaching this position,[117] though in contrast to Pannenberg these latter authors give Scripture a greater role in interpreting the events of the history of salvation.

This position ultimately is problematic because it does not take into account that God saves in the present only through the promises He attaches to events of history, and not simply by a recognition that certain historical events are the miraculous or revelatory works of God. Likewise, this position also ignores the fact that for certain events to be revelatory God must place His own interpretation on them through a written or auditory word and preserve this interpretation in an inspired text. Since God is invisible and incomprehensible, His actions are not immediately explicable without His own self-disclosure (Is 40:13–14) or a medium whereby such self-disclosure is conveyed to humanity.[118]

Since these theologians identify revelation primarily with certain historical events while rejecting the notion that Scripture has infallibly preserved this revelation, they also logically must believe that the Bible gives merely probable access to divine revelation. In other words, since all human testimony concerning historical events is merely probable, the truthfulness of the statements of the Bible that revelation has occurred also becomes merely probable. Saying that the biblical documents can contain some errors is to say that their historical claims possess the same degree of probability that all secular history possesses. Even if we have considerable evidence of the central events of the crucifixion and the resurrection of Christ, as we indeed do, admitting that Scripture can err downgrades the certainty of these events to mere probability.

Nevertheless, if faith gives full assurance, as Scripture itself testifies (Romans 4; Heb 10:19–20; Hebrews 11), then the events underlying the promises faith grasps cannot be merely probable but must be absolutely certain. Indeed, the nature of the faith does not allow Christians to confess that Christ "probably"

---

116. Pannenberg et al., *Revelation as History*.

117. See Matthew Becker, *The Self-Giving God and Salvation History: The Trinitarian Theology of Johannes von Hofmann* (New York: T&T Clark International, 2004); Cullman, *Christ and Time*; Cullman, *Salvation in History*; Jean Daniélou, *The Lord of History: Reflections on the Inner Meaning of History*, trans. Nigel Abercrombie (London: H. Regnery, 1958).

118. This is also the problem with William Abraham's theory of inspiration. Abraham claims "inspiration" is merely a human response to the events of salvation history, similar to how a teacher inspires his students, and can therefore exist in degrees. See William Abraham, *The Divine Inspiration of the Scriptures* (Oxford: Oxford University Press, 1981).

died for their sins and "probably" rose for their justification (Rom 4:25). In that case, the assurance of faith would also be probable. But as Luther states repeatedly in the catechisms, these things are not probable; rather, they are "most certainly true." Thus, if one agrees with the premise that faith possesses this joyful assurance, that assurance must be anchored in an object that is itself fully assured. Such an object cannot be a mix of truth and error or a merely probable human witness. Rather, it must be a fully inerrant, inspired Word of God.

Another class of modern theologians, hailing mostly from liberal Protestantism but also the existentialist tradition, tends to focus more on the morals and spiritual/existential truths conveyed by Scripture. To convey certain values or general truths it is not necessary for Scripture to be free from all historical or scientific error. Instead of a record of history, the text is seen in this perspective either as a byproduct of cultural forces in which God was at work or as subjective spiritual experiences thematized and projected outward as imagined or half-remembered history.[119] In either case the scriptural narrative ceases to be fully historical and factual, and instead becomes a parable of either deeply held experiences of God or certain moral values that believers should practice.

Probably the most extreme and explicit version of this stance can be found in Albrecht Ritschl's distinction between "judgments of fact" and "judgments of value."[120] Although Ritschl agreed that facts and values could not be disentangled entirely from one another, he held that theological truth must be seen as much as possible as having to do with personal and spiritual values, independent of the facts of science and history. One example of this approach might be Ritschl's argument that Jesus was not God as a matter of fact but could be judged divine as a matter of value.[121] In large part this approach seems to be an outgrowth of modernity's fact/value dichotomy, which in variance with historic Christian orthodoxy sees all things moral and spiritual as private and subjective preferences.[122]

Since liberal Protestantism largely has accepted this stance, it is no surprise that it has promoted legalism consistently throughout its existence. This result can be observed particularly in American mainline Protestant preaching, which speaks little of divine grace and is focused intensely on social justice and identity

---

119. See summary of this group in George Lindbeck, *The Nature of Doctrine: Religion and Theology in a Post-Liberal Age* (Philadelphia: The Westminster Press, 1984), 16–17. Lindbeck describes this group's approach to doctrine as "experiential-expressive."

120. See discussion in Albrecht Ritschl, "Theology and Metaphysics," in *Three Essays*, trans. Philip Hefner (Philadelphia: Fortress Press, 1972), 149–217.

121. Albrecht Ritschl, *The Christian Doctrine of Justification and Reconciliation: The Positive Development of the Doctrine*, trans. H. R. McIntosh and A. B. Macaulay, vol. 3 (1902; reprint, Clifton, NJ: Reference Book Publishers, 1966), 398.

122. It should be noted that this modern distinction is mediated to Ritschl through the Kantian distinction between theoretical and practical reason. See Immanuel Kant, *Critique of Pure Reason*, trans. Mary Gregor (Cambridge, UK: Cambridge University Press, 1997), 102.

politics. If the Bible is a parable or myth that conveys certain moral values, it is meaningful only if human beings do something to put its moral lessons into practice. That is to say, the Bible is understood as a story that becomes a reality only if humans enact it through their obedience to the Law. By contrast, when Scripture is understood as genuine history, it informs believers what God has already done to save humanity unconditionally and irrevocably. Humans cannot reverse history; they can only trustingly and passively receive what has been established already by divine fiat. Hence, for historic Christian orthodoxy Scripture is a story that is already a reality because God's grace has enacted it.

Beyond the moralism that those who reject scriptural inerrancy tend to drift into, a number of other incoherencies attend with this particular rejection of scriptural inerrancy. The chief one is that fact and values are not disassociated so easily from one another. Even for the thinkers who want to speak of revelation as an experience (Schleiermacher) or a matter of value as opposed to facts (Ritschl) or a mythological medium for an existential encounter (Bultmann), the concrete historical nature of revelation cannot be escaped. Indeed, for Schleiermacher there had to be a historical Jesus who must have communicated His God-consciousness to the apostolic community,[123] just as for Ritschl there must have been a Jesus who founded the Christian community as one of progressive love.[124] Even in the case of Bultmann, there must have been in actual concrete history a Christ-event onto which the apostles were able to project their mythological consciousness.[125] Value therefore cannot be disentangled from fact.

Incidentally, this division between fact and value is also why even somewhat more conservative theories of inspiration that posit Scripture's inerrancy in matters of faith and life but not in all historical and scientific matters (sometimes called infallibility, as opposed to inerrancy[126]) are completely incoherent. Each article of the faith is dependent on certain historical facts being true. If the articles of the faith are infallibly true, then the facts of history and science which underlie them must be infallibly true as well.

Beyond the logical and soteriological difficulties with rejecting scriptural inerrancy are the difficulties such a rejection creates for the public witness of the church. For the church to have clear doctrinal positions, or at minimum make decisions it believes to be in accordance with the will of God, it must eventually posit some infallible authority that can give a final answer. Fallible authority can give only relative and fallible answers that can always be revised and challenged. If this authority is not the inerrant Scriptures, inevitably it will become something else, more often than not the institutional church itself.

---

123. Friedrich Schleiermacher, *The Christian Faith*, trans. H. R. Mackintosh and J. S. Stewart (New York: T&T Clark, 1999), 56–78.

124. Ritschl, *Christian Doctrine of Justification*, 12.

125. Bultmann, *Jesus Christ and Mythology*.

126. Stephen Davis, *The Debate about the Bible: Inerrancy versus Infallibility* (Philadelphia: Westminster Press, 1977), 23.

A perfect example of this development may be found in the American mainline Protestant churches.[127] On the one hand, these churches generally operate with a fairly open-ended approach to doctrine and ethics. Since Scripture is not viewed as inerrant and the historic creeds and confessions are not taken seriously or even enforced, there are no restrictions on any theological opinions a pastor, theologian, or other ecclesiastical authority might want to promote. The difficulties come when these church bodies are pressed to clarify their doctrinal position and make a decision involving Christian ethics.

Unfortunately, without an objective basis for making theological or ethical decisions, all authority degenerates into whatever national church bodies can push through their voting assemblies. For example, when the Evangelical Lutheran Church in America voted to accept homosexual behavior in 2009, the proponents of the moral acceptability of homosexual behavior never articulated a genuinely convincing theological rationale based in Scripture.[128] Instead they tended to rely on vague and general appeals to God's love and acceptance, or social justice. Moreover, advocates of the moral acceptability of homosexual behavior did not genuinely defeat their opponents in theological debates. The leadership of the denomination simply held votes over the course of a decade repeatedly until the desired result was achieved. The voters in such assemblies more often than not are theologically untrained, and therefore lack the ability to understand properly the basis or implication of their decisions.

Hence, when major decisions are made within the mainline Protestant denominations, such decisions frequently lack a satisfying theological rationale or any scriptural basis whatsoever. As a result, the decisions made by these national voting assemblies essentially are viewed by their opponents for what they are, that is, little more than arbitrary exercises of power. Sensing this problem of legitimacy, many persons in leadership positions have attempted to legitimize these decisions by claiming that the Holy Spirit is "doing a new thing"[129] through the denominational voting assembly.[130]

---

127. See similar argument in Jack Kilcrease, "Is *Sola Scriptura* Obsolete? An Examination and Critique of Christian Smith's *The Bible Made Impossible*," *Concordia Theological Quarterly* 82, no. 3–4 (2018): 231–32.

128. See Robert Gagnon, *The Bible and Homosexual Practice: Texts and Hermeneutics* (Nashville: Abingdon Press, 2002); Robert Gagnon, *Homosexuality and the Bible: Two Views* (Minneapolis: Fortress Press, 2009). Gagnon has shown thoroughly that the latitude within the biblical texts that mainline Protestants desire is simply not there.

129. See the following places where mainline Protestants use the phrase in order to justify going against biblical injunctions against homosexuality. Note that Wink even admits that this is in contradiction to Scripture. Marvin Ellison, "Practicing Safer Spirituality: Changing the Subject and Focusing on Justice," in *Out of the Shadows, Into the Light: Christianity and Homosexuality*, ed. Miguel A. De La Torre (Danvers, MA: Chalice Press, 2009), 12; David N. Glesne, *Understanding Homosexuality: Perspectives for the Local Church* (Minneapolis: Kirk House, 2004), 134; Walter Wink, "Homosexuality and the Bible," in *Homosexuality and Christian Faith: Questions of Conscience for the Churches*, ed. Walter Wink (Minneapolis: Augsburg Fortress, 1999), 47.

130. "We are not doing any of this to catch a wave in popular culture or to get more people to come in. We are doing this because we felt motivated by our understanding of Scripture and

Ironically, having rejected a final and inerrant Spirit-breathed authority in the form of the Bible, the mainline denominations posit that the institutional church is divinely guided, not unlike the claims of modern Roman Catholicism. The moment one abandons the infallibility in one source (the Bible), one must necessarily begin to impute it to another source. This is true whether that source be religious experience (Protestant liberalism), a voting assembly's decisions (mainline Protestantism), or an inspired teaching magisterium (Roman Catholicism).

Ultimately what connects these alternatives to the full inerrancy of Scripture is that they attempt to separate the external Word of God from the revelation of which it is the vehicle. As we have seen, the written Word of God is distinct but not separate from the historical revelation that it mediates. Indeed, as an inspired text the Bible is a particular instance of revelation in and of itself. To separate God's Word and promise from the factual truths contained in Scripture (as Quenstedt summarizes it: all historical, geographical, and scientific truths[131]) constitutes a separation of the external Word from revelation itself. That is to say, positing an errant Scripture distances the signifier (external Word) from the signified (God's revelation in history) by claiming that the latter does not fully and truthfully represent the former.

CONCLUSION

Any distancing of the external Word from the thing it signifies opens up a gap between God and His Word within which the Enthusiast can place himself as arbiter of the truth of the Word, just as Satan did in the Garden of Eden. Likewise, positing an errant Bible based on one's own rational assessment of the scriptural text lends itself to a theology of glory. The theologian who judges the Scriptures errant desires to look beyond the outwardly simple and unimpressive words of the Bible (the "cruciform Word") to a glorious Word of God above the humble external form.

Every heresy in the history of the church has been a return to Enthusiasm, that is, a separation of the signifier from the signified, and the external Word from the eternal Word. Arius wished to separate God the Father (signified) from His eternal Word (signifier), Nestorius wished to separate the man Christ (signifier) from the eternal Word (signified), Augustine and the medieval

---

of our own confessional tradition that maybe this *was something that God was doing that was new and it would be important for us to allow this kind of inclusion*" (emphasis added). Bishop Elizabeth Eaton, speech to the ELCA Churchwide Assembly, 2013, accessed September 19, 2013, http://on.aol.com/video/rev--elizabeth-eaton-speaks-about-being-first-female-lutheran-bishop-517899277. The remark that this decision or any other decisions made by mainline Protestants to accept homosexual behavior has nothing to do with catering to personal preferences is beyond absurd.

131. See Quenstedt's aforementioned remarks in Quenstedt, *Theologia Didatico-Polemica* 1:77.

church gave rise to the *res–signum* dualism, and Calvin and Zwingli wished to separate Christ's flesh and the Holy Spirit (signified) from the sacraments (signifier). Finally, in the modern era, both liberalism and neo-orthodoxy have sought to separate the historical revelation of God's Word (signified) from the literal words of Holy Scripture (signifier) by rejecting both inerrancy and verbal inspiration.

Having discussed the inerrancy of Holy Scripture, in the next chapter we will discuss the inspired process through which the Scriptures were composed. Inspiration is the natural corollary of the inerrancy of the Bible: as God's own Word and absolutely truthful, the Bible is necessarily a byproduct of the Spirit's inspiring activity in the hearts and minds of the prophets and apostles.

4

THE WRITTEN WORD OF GOD:
THE INSPIRATION OF SACRED SCRIPTURE

THE NATURE OF INSPIRATION

As we have already seen, in communicating His Word to humanity through the prophets and apostles, God left no gap between the external Word and His eternal will. God graciously communicates the fullness of His truth and being through the word of the Bible. Positing the alternative is to court Enthusiasm. Having examined this reality with regard to the truthfulness of the Word in our discussion of inerrancy, we now turn to the question of the nature of inspiration itself.

The question of the nature of inspiration is related to though distinct from the question of the truthfulness of Scripture. Inspiration is the means and instrument through which God actualized the inerrant text of the Bible. Nevertheless, as we will see below, although theologians of the pre-Enlightenment Christian tradition overwhelmingly agreed that the text of the Bible was both completely truthful and inspired, they disagreed with each other regarding the nature of inspiration.[1] Similarly, as Benjamin Warfield correctly observed, if He had so desired, God very well could have generated a completely truthful text purely by means of His providence without any act of inspiration.[2] Scripture teaches that God supernaturally intervened in the hearts and minds of the prophets and apostles to communicate His truth through the specifically chosen written words of the Bible.

THE REALITY OF INSPIRATION

That God inspired the Scriptures is witnessed to by the traditional *sedes doctrinae* for the inspiration of the Bible: "All Scripture is breathed out by God and profitable for teaching, for reproof, for correction, and for training in righteousness" (2 Tm 3:16). "For no prophecy was ever produced by the will of man, but men spoke from God as they were carried along by the Holy Spirit" (2 Pt 1:21).[3] Although these texts may appear to many readers to be

---

1. See excellent summary in Preus, "View of the Bible," 357–84. Also see Hannah, *Inerrancy and the Church*.
2. Warfield, *Inspiration and Authority of the Bible*, 157–58.
3. Hoenecke, *Evangelical Lutheran Dogmatics* 1:414–15; Pieper, *Christian Dogmatics* 1:217.

fairly straightforward affirmations that the Bible is the inspired Word of God, a number of issues attend their interpretation.

To begin with, 2 Tm 3:16 frequently has been translated, particularly in the KJV, as "All Scripture is inspired." This translation follows the Vulgate version of the text (*omnis scriptura divinitus inspirata*).[4] A more literal rendering of the text would be as the NIV and ESV translate it: "All Scripture is God-breathed/ breathed out" (θεόπνευστος). Although θεόπνευστος is an unusual word in Greek,[5] its meaning is not ambiguous. Warfield shows through an exhaustive investigation that the rendering of θεόπνευστος as "divinely inspired" is witnessed to across many different translations of the Bible from very early on.[6] But the question remains why Paul chose this somewhat unusual expression as a way of speaking about divine inspiration.

The term "God-breathed" hearkens back to descriptions of creation coming about by the work of the Word and the Spirit (Gn 1:2–3; Ps 33:6).[7] It also evokes an image of God breathing the breath of life into Adam (Gn 2:7). Indeed, Jerome made such a connection in his translation of the Vulgate, in that he used the Latin verb *inspiro* in translating both Gn 2:7 and 2 Tm 3:16.[8]

From these associations it is easy to see what Paul intends to teach regarding the inspiration of the Bible. The Scriptures are direct creations of God's Word and Spirit in the same manner as the original creation was. Similarly, God breathes into Scripture in the same way He breathed into Adam. That is to say, much like Adam, Scripture is both a direct creation of God and also a living conduit for the work of the Holy Spirit. Likewise, just as Adam was created in God's image in order to mediate God's reign in creation, so too Scripture as the inerrant Word of God accurately represents God's will (i.e., it is an image of God's will) and mediates Christ's reign (the Second Adam: Romans 5, 1 Corinthians 15) within the church, the firstfruits of the new creation (2 Cor 5:17).

Second Peter 1:21 also uses the imagery of Spirit as breath/wind. Doubtless the usage of this imagery carries with it the background of the Hebrew word רוּחַ, which can mean wind, breath, or spirit.[9] Peter uses the Spirit as breath/wind imagery in a somewhat different manner than Paul, though. Here we are told that when the prophets wrote or spoke, they 'were "carried along" or "moved" (ὑπὸ Πνεύματος Ἁγίου φερόμενοι) by the Holy Spirit. Lenski notes that the metaphor intended here is that inspiration is something like a ship's sails being moved by the wind.[10] In confirmation of this, Norman Geisler adds that the

---

4. George W. Knight III, *The Pastoral Epistles: A Commentary on the Greek Text*. The New International Greek Testament Commentary (Grand Rapids: Wm. B. Eerdmans, 1992), 446.

5. D. A. Carson, *Exegetical Fallacies* (Grand Rapids: Baker Academic, 1996), 33.

6. Warfield, *Inspiration and Authority of the Bible*, 245–96.

7. John McArthur, *Why Believe in the Bible?* (Ventura: Regal Publishers, 2007), 45.

8. Carl F. Henry, *God, Revelation, and Authority*, 6 vols. (Wheaton, IL: Crossway, 1999), 4:129.

9. Veli-Matti Kärkkäinen, *Pneumatology: The Holy Spirit in Ecumenical, International, and Contextual Perspective* (Grand Rapids: Baker Academic, 2002), 23.

10. R. C. H. Lenski, *The Interpretation of the Epistles of St Peter, St. John, and St. Jude*

same word (φέρω) is used in Acts 27:15 to describe a situation where a storm wind moves the sails of Paul's ship.[11]

What this imagery suggests is that the prophets were moved to write and prophesy by God in the manner in which a ship is moved by wind. Without the agency of the vessel being eliminated, a ship at sea is moved in the direction of the wind and not by its own independent volition. Ships' characteristics as ships are not compromised in their being moved by an outside force. A ship can be moved in the way it is moved only because it has sails and other distinctive features. It is moved by the wind in a completely different manner than a life raft or buoy would be.[12]

Thus, although the authors of Scripture were instruments of God, God used them as instruments according to the personal properties they already possessed. Peter and Paul both were moved by the Spirit but still wrote as the distinct individuals they were.[13] Even so, God shaped and determined their agency in the production of the text. The prophets and apostles were precisely the men they were because God formed them as such by His creative providence. But in the end God monergistically moved them as instruments of His Spirit to produce the Scriptures, even down to the very words they chose. Likewise, the ship is moved by the wind, the wind is not moved by the ship.

Another question raised by these verses is to which texts Paul attributes the inspiration. He speaks of "Scripture," a term used in most instances of the New Testament to refer to the Old Testament (Mt 21:42; Jn 5:39–40; 10:35; 13:18, etc.).[14] Indeed, the apostle refers explicitly to the Scriptures Timothy has been taught from his youth (2 Tm 3:15), which obviously does not refer to the New Testament, or at least not to those writings as a whole. Many have objected that Paul's statement attributes inspiration only to the Old Testament and therefore cannot be used as a proof-text for the inspiration of the New Testament.[15] One could make a similar objection about the *sedes* in 2 Peter, in that the apostle never actually specifies what he considers to be prophecy, although from the context it would seem very likely that he is referring primarily to the Old Testament.[16]

(Peabody, MA: Hendrickson Publishers, 1998), 299.

11. Norman Geisler, *When Critics Ask: A Popular Handbook on Bible Difficulties* (Grand Rapids: Baker Books, 1992), 506.

12. Richard Bauckham, *Jude, 2 Peter* (Waco, TX: Word Publishing Group, 1983), 234. Bauckham rejects the notion that Peter is in any manner suggesting a manic or passive concept of inspiration.

13. C. H. Little, *Disputed Doctrines: A Study in Biblical and Dogmatic Theology* (Burlington, IA: Lutheran Literary Board, 1933), 18–19; Pieper, *Christian Dogmatics* 1:228–32.

14. Gerhard, *On the Nature of Theology*, 35–36; Daniel Wallace, *Greek Grammar Beyond the Basics: An Exegetical Syntax of the New Testament* (Grand Rapids: Zondervan, 1996), 314.

15. Oddly, the position taken by Hoenecke on both 2 Tm 3:15 and 2 Pt 1:21. See Hoenecke, *Evangelical Lutheran Dogmatics* 1:414–15.

16. Becker, *Fundamental Theology*, 271. Becker considers the reference to Scripture and prophecy to be ambiguous.

There are number of possible responses to these objections, all of which possess some merit. First, "all Scripture" (πᾶσα γραφὴ) could also be translated as "every Scripture." Lenski insists that not only is "every" a much weaker translation, but the difference between "every" and "all" is meaningless.[17] William Hendriksen has argued that "every" is an acceptable translation and could be taken to mean "everything that counts as Scripture."[18] In other words, even if certain Scriptures (that is, certain New Testament documents) had yet to be written, Paul is nevertheless affirming that when they are written they will be "God-breathed," since everything that counts as Scripture is of an inspired character. Such an argument also works with the *sedes* in 2 Peter, since the apostle simply states that true prophecy comes by God's Spirit, whereas false prophecy (spoken of in 2 Pt 2:1–3, unfortunately segregated from the earlier passage by an artificial chapter break) does not.

Beyond this, let us observe that both Paul and Peter affirm that certain books of the New Testament already exist and that they should be considered to be Scripture. It is thereby also implied that they have at least parts of the New Testament in mind when they speak of the inspiration of Scripture. Paul quotes Luke's Gospel in his first letter to Timothy in 5:17 and refers to it, along with Deuteronomy, as Scripture.[19] Likewise, Bernard Orchard has demonstrated through a thorough examination of verbal parallels that very likely Paul knew and used Matthew's Gospel.[20]

Similarly, in 2 Pt 3:16 Peter refers to Paul's letters as Scripture.[21] Incidentally, many take the fact that Peter calls Paul's letters Scripture as an indication that the book is a late forgery. But Peter also says that Paul's letters contain things which are "hard to understand" (2 Pt 3:15), something a later forger would be unlikely to put into the mouth of an apostle whose authority he was trying to draw upon.

Returning to the issue of what counts as Scripture, in both of these authors, Martin Chemnitz correctly observes, it is very likely that most of the New Testament or at least Paul's Epistles and the Synoptic Gospels were written by the time Paul and Peter composed these letters.[22] If this is the case, then both

---

17. R. C. H. Lenski, *The Interpretation of St. Paul's Epistles to the Colossians, to the Thessalonians, to Timothy, to Titus, and to Philemon* (Peabody, MA: Hendrickson Publishers, 1998), 841.

18. William Hendriksen, *Exposition of the Pastoral Epistles* (Grand Rapids: Baker Book House, 1957), 300.

19. Charles Grannan, *A General Introduction to the Bible*, vol. 3 (St. Louis: Herder, 1921), 33.

20. Bernard Orchard, "The Matthean Tradition before A.D. 150," in Bernard Orchard and Harold Riley, *The Order of the Synoptics: Why Three Synoptic Gospels?* (Macon: Mercer University Press, 1987), 118–20.

21. James Hamilton, *God's Glory in Salvation through Judgment: A Biblical Theology* (Wheaton, IL: Crossway, 2010), 444.

22. Chemnitz, *Examination of the Council of Trent* 1:136.

might implicitly have these books in mind, and not merely the ones explicitly mentioned, in affirming the inspiration of the Scriptures.[23]

Part of this argument hinges on when one dates 2 Timothy and 2 Peter. For those New Testament scholars who accept Paul's authorship of 2 Timothy, it is generally agreed that this is a later letter written sometime in the early 60s (A.D.), just prior to the apostle's death in the Neronian persecution.[24] The same can be said of Peter's second letter, which was written late in the apostle's career[25] when he was already in "Babylon" (i.e., Rome, 1 Pt 5:13).[26]

That most of the New Testament documents were very likely composed by the time of Paul's and Peter's Epistles is suggested by several facts. John Wenham convincingly demonstrates that the patristic witness is uniform in its claim that the Gospels were written sometime between A.D. 40 and the early 60s.[27] Indeed, since as Jews the early Christians saw the enactment of a divinely wrought covenant/testament and its written witness as inexorably linked (one thinks of Moses and the Torah), it seems odd that the Gospel writers would have waited even ten years to begin composing their accounts.[28]

Similarly, it has been shown by liberal theologian and New Testament scholar John A. T. Robinson that most of the New Testament documents very likely date from prior to the First Jewish War and the destruction of the temple. In his *Redating the New Testament* Robinson perceptively observes that although Jesus predicts the destruction of the temple, none of the New Testament documents ever state that this prophecy has been fulfilled.[29] Also supporting this conclusion, N. T. Wright has noted that the Gospel writers certainly did not invent Jesus' temple destruction prophecies after the fact, since none of the Gospels' descriptions of the carnage of A.D. 70 match the accounts of the actual events by Josephus and other writers. Instead, Jesus mainly borrows from the Old Testament poetic and apocalyptic imagery of cosmic collapse.[30]

The fulfillment in A.D. 70 of Jesus' prophecy regarding the destruction of Jerusalem would have been of great polemical value to early Christians (Mark 13; Matthew 24; Luke 21). It would have further vindicated Jesus as a true prophet. Also, as the early Christians were persecuted by and stood in competition with Judaism (Mt 21:33–36; Mk 12:1–12; Lk 20:9–19), the destruction

23. David King and William Webster, *Holy Scripture: The Ground and Pillar of Our Faith*, 3 vols. (Battle Ground, WA: Christian Resources, Inc., 2001), 1:76.

24. D. A. Carson and Douglas Moo, *Introducing the New Testament: A Short Guide to Its History and Message* (Grand Rapids: Zondervan, 2010), 125.

25. Carson and Moo, *Introducing the New Testament*, 145.

26. R. C. H. Lenski, *The Interpretation of St. Mark's Gospel* (Peabody, MA: Hendrickson Publishers, 1998), 8.

27. John Wenham, *Redating Matthew, Mark, and Luke: A Fresh Assault on the Synoptic Problem* (Downers Grove, IL: InterVarsity Press, 1992), 116–72, 183–97.

28. Michael Kruger, *The Question of the Canon: Challenging the Status Quo in the New Testament Debate* (Downers Grove, IL: InterVarsity Press, 2013), 57–67.

29. John A. T. Robinson, *Redating the New Testament* (Eugene, OR: Wipf & Stock Publishers, 2000).

30. Wright, *Christian Origins* 2:353–68.

of the temple would have provided objective validation of God's judgment on their persecutors. Further, the argument of the Epistle to the Hebrews (often dated well after A.D. 70)[31] makes virtually no sense if Christianity is not then in competition with an earlier temple-centered version of Judaism. Would not the destruction of the temple validate the author's central thesis that the rituals of Leviticus were obsolete? As Robinson observes, this is an argument from silence, but it is a deafening silence.[32]

Hence, it is highly unlikely that the New Testament authors would have failed to mention directly the destruction of the temple unless they lived and wrote prior to its occurrence. It is in turn very likely that Paul and Peter knew and had in mind not only the Old Testament but also many of the earlier New Testament documents when they spoke of Scripture and prophecy.

Ultimately, even if these arguments do not prove convincing, the doctrine of inspiration by no means fails. Indeed, properly speaking these *sedes doctrinae* should not be the starting point for the doctrine of inspiration. As we have previously demonstrated, the resurrected Christ and His promises regarding the infallibility of the prophets and apostles is the ultimate basis of scriptural authority. The traditional *sedes* examined above are meaningful explanations of the inspiration of Scripture, but only because the resurrected Christ authorized Paul and Peter as His infallible witnesses. Protestant theology frequently has made these *sedes,* combined with the "inner testimony" of the Spirit, the basis of scriptural authority and inspiration.[33] Nonetheless, apart from the historical authorization of the resurrected Christ, Scripture's own self-attestation combined with the inner testimony of the Spirit are meaningless.[34]

Scripture is certainly self-authenticating (αὐτοπιστία) in that we believe in it as the Word of God because the Holy Spirit enables us to do so. Nevertheless, such an inner testimony of the Spirit is always tethered to faith in the resurrected lordship of Christ, and therefore also to His historical promise that the prophets and apostles are inspired. The inner testimony of the Spirit is not a kind of interior enlightenment that makes the truth of Scripture an abstract axiomatic principle.[35] The Spirit enlightens and frees us so that we can see the

---

31. Harold Attridge, *The Epistle to the Hebrews: A Commentary on the Epistle to the Hebrews* (Philadelphia: Fortress Press, 1989), 6–8. Attridge questions the date of 1 Clement, which cites Hebrews, and then bizarrely concludes that Hebrews could be written as late as A.D. 125.

32. Robinson, *Redating the New Testament,* 205. Also see same point in Scott Hahn, Curtis Mitch, and Dennis Walters, *The Letter to the Hebrews* (San Francisco: Ignatius Press, 2007), 13; and Luke Timothy Johnson, *Hebrews: A Commentary* (Louisville: Westminster/John Knox, 2006), 38–40.

33. Muller, *Post-Reformation Reformed Dogmatics* 2:266–67, 274; Preus, *Theology of Post-Reformation Lutheranism* 1:276, 296–99.

34. Here we take a position similar to Martin Chemnitz rather than to the later Lutheran scholastics. Chemnitz grounded his doctrine of scriptural authority in historic revelation rather than in the inner testimony of the Spirit. See Eugene Klug, "Luther and Chemnitz on Scripture," *The Springfielder* 37, no. 3 (1973): 167.

35. Unfortunately, this seems to be how many Reformed and Lutheran scholastics developed the doctrine of the self-authentication of Scripture. See Heinrich Heppe, *Reformed Dogmatics*

truthfulness of Christ's historical claims and their objective validation through the resurrection. This fact is particularly evident in the agency of the Spirit through the apostles' historical witness to the resurrection in Acts 2.

Beyond these considerations, many have observed that if we treat these texts as the starting point for positing inspiration in isolation from the historical authorization of Christ, we are in danger of making a circular argument ("the Bible is inspired because it says it is inspired"). Such a procedure also raises the question of why the Bible's claim to be inspired should be believed over the Book of Mormon or the Qur'an, both of which also claim to be the Word of God. Hence, 2 Tm 3:16 and 2 Pt 1:21 are better used to explain what inspiration is than as a means of establishing the doctrine of inspiration in and of itself.

Also problematic, alongside the misuse of these texts, is that the inner testimony of the Spirit isolated from faith in Christ and His resurrection degenerates into a mere subjective "religious experience" common to all world religions. This focus on the inner testimony nudges the understanding of the truthfulness and inspiration of Scripture ever more in the direction of Enthusiasm. This movement toward Enthusiasm unfortunately has manifested itself in much of Lutheranism and in Protestantism in general.[36] Indeed, anyone who has encountered Mormon missionaries with their testimony that they have "felt a burning in their bosom" after having "read the Scriptures [Book of Mormon] and prayed" will feel the force of D. F. Strauss's claim that the *testimonium Spiritus sancti internum* is "the Achilles' heel of the Protestant system."[37] Therefore, since the Holy Spirit is the Spirit of the risen Jesus, any inner testimony of the Spirit must direct the believer outside of himself to the historical revelation of Christ and His promise of inspiration to the prophets and apostles.

VERBAL INSPIRATION

As we have already seen, God fully determined the process whereby He communicated His Word through the prophets and apostles. Because of this, the written Word of God found in the Bible is absolutely truthful and without error. Regarding this, Francis Pieper observes that God does not merely inspire the content or ideas in the Bible (*Realinspiration*). Nor did He merely grant an inspired mental state to the authors of the Bible (*Personalinspiration*).[38] Rather,

---

Set Out and Illustrated from the Sources, trans. G. T. Thomson (London: George Allen & Unwin, 1950), 25–26; Schmid, *Doctrinal Theology*, 54–58.

36. See Scaer, "Theology of Robert David Preus," 83–85. Scaer is critical of his mentor Robert Preus and scholastic orthodoxy on this point, since he considers the argument for the inspiration of Scripture based purely on the inner testimony of the Spirit and the Scripture's self-authentication to be circular: "Preus engaged in the circular reasoning of the *autopistia* and *testimonium Spiritus Sancti internum* in demonstrating the Bible's authority" (85).

37. David Friedrich Strauss, *Die Christliche Glaubenslehre*, vol. 1 (Tübingen: C. F. Osiander, 1840), 136. Cited from Weber, *Foundations of Dogmatics* 1:243.

38. See a version of *Personalinspiration* in Hans Martensen, *Christian Dogmatics*

in some mysterious way God shaped the scriptural authors through His act of inspiration so as to determine their very choice of the words (*Verbalinspiration, suggestio verbi*).[39]

Although such a teaching often has been viewed as unnecessary or even vexing to some modern theologians, it is clearly affirmed in biblical tradition itself. In commissioning Moses, God tells the prophet that "I will be with your mouth and teach you what you shall speak" (Ex 4:12). King David speaks of his own inspiration in saying, "The Spirit of the Lord speaks by me; his word is on my tongue" (2 Sm 23:2). God tells Jeremiah He has placed His very words in the prophet's mouth (Jer 1:19). Jesus told the apostles that the one "who hears you, hears me" (Lk 10:16) and that in giving public witness to the kerygma the Holy Spirit will supply the very words necessary to speak (Mt 10:19; Lk 12:11–12). In further support of this understanding, Warfield famously showed that the New Testament authors regularly use the terms "Word of God" and "Scripture" interchangeably.[40]

Although it was not systematically developed at any length, the doctrine of verbal inspiration clearly is found in the teaching of the first generation of the reformers and was not merely a later development of the Lutheran scholastics, as is often alleged.[41] Luther speaks not infrequently of the very grammar of the Bible as the work of the Holy Spirit.[42]

This understanding stands in contrast to the theology of medieval theologians like Thomas Aquinas, who posited that God gave a higher spiritual vision to the authors of Scripture so that they could see His truth, while at the same time allowing them to choose their own words in the process of scriptural composition.[43] Confessional Lutheran theology must reject Aquinas's approach, but this is not because humanity could not know God's truth if it were expressed in somewhat different terms or in different configurations of words. Unlike Kabbalah, we do not regard certain configurations of words as magical or individual words or letters as imbued with secret divine power.[44]

Rather, Aquinas's approach and those like it are not only inaccurate regarding what Scripture teaches directly on the subject of inspiration, they

---

(Edinburgh: T&T Clark, 1898), 402.

39. Pieper, *Christian Dogmatics* 1:217. Also see Franzmann, "New Testament View of Inspiration," 744–48.

40. Warfield, *Inspiration and Authority of the Bible*, 299–350. Also see Little, *Disputed Doctrines*, 24–27; Reu, *Lutheran Dogmatics*, 450.

41. Muller, *Post-Reformation Reformed Dogmatics* 2:245–55.

42. For example, *Commentary on Psalm 45*, 1534 (AE 12:279; WA 40/2:581–84); *Lectures on Galatians*, 1535 (AE 26:92; WA 40/1:169–71). In reference to a particular passage in Paul: "The Holy Spirit does not observe this strict rule of grammar." *Lectures on Galatians*, 1535 (AE 26:139; WA 40/1:244). Cited from Thompson, *Sure Ground on Which to Stand*, 116. See Thompson's full discussion on pages 115–17.

43. *ST* 2a2æ, q. 174, art. 2; BF 45:73–77; *ST* 2a2æ, q. 174, art. 4; BF 45:83. Also see John F. Johnson, "Biblical Authority and Scholastic Theology," in Hannah, *Inerrancy and the Church*, 67–98.

44. See Byron Sherwin, *Kabbalah: An Introduction to Jewish Mysticism* (New York: Rowman & Littlefield, 2006).

also necessarily direct us back to the theology of glory. What Aquinas's view of inspiration suggests is that the words of the Bible are merely human, but they point beyond themselves to concepts and truths which are divine. Instead, Lutherans believe that God interacts with humans only in and through the outward form of creatures. The theology of the cross teaches that the humanity of the crucified Christ is the humble outward creaturely form with which God the Son has fully identified. He does not wish us to find Him above the man Jesus in the form of His hidden glory. One can see this same reality in the sacraments, wherein God has attached His Word of grace to specific and unimpressive visible elements and bids us find His glorious presence hidden within them.

Analogously, if the humble outward form of the words of the Bible are not to be identified directly with the place where God comes to humanity through His direct inspiration, then the external Word necessarily becomes a jumping-off point to a higher and more glorious reality of revelation beyond the text. Hence, verbal inspiration teaches us that God wishes us to find Him in the humble and sometimes unimpressive words of the cruciform Bible itself and not elsewhere.

VERBAL INSPIRATION AND HUMAN AGENCY

The doctrine of verbal inspiration should not be confused with a kind of mania that eliminates human agency.[45] When the Bible and the later Lutheran scholastics speak of verbal inspiration, they do not mean that God took over the minds of the prophets and apostles so that they ceased to function consciously as the men they were.

Nevertheless, it is very common to hear modern scholars and theologians attack the theologians of scholastic orthodoxy for essentially teaching such a doctrine. For example, Matthew Becker suggests that verbal inspiration and inerrancy erase human agency in the production of the Scriptures.[46] Becker claims Johann Gerhard taught that divine inspiration makes the inspired author like a flute played by God.[47] Such a claim lacks validity: Gerhard never uses such an analogy in his treatment of inspiration.

The manic concept of inspiration actually is present not in the Protestant scholastics but in the Ante-Nicene fathers. Indeed, one finds the flute analogy for divine inspiration in the second-century apologist Athenagoras.[48] As men of their time and cultural milieu, these theologians often borrowed this concept of inspiration from earlier Jewish and Hellenistic sources. Within the Palestinian Jewish tradition, the intertestamental Book of Jubilees (second century B.C.) speaks of Moses receiving the Torah as a whole on Mt. Sinai in the form of

---

45. Franzmann, "New Testament View of Inspiration," 746.
46. Becker, *Fundamental Theology*, 305–6.
47. Becker, *Fundamental Theology*, 305.
48. See Leslie William Barnard, *Athenagoras: A Study in Second Century Christian Apologetic* (Paris: Beauchesne, 1972), 76.

heavenly tablets.[49] This concept suggests an extraordinarily crude notion of inspiration as a kind of literal dictation.

Likewise, pagan Hellenistic culture possessed a concept of prophecy that was manic. Inspiration was understood as a state wherein the rationality and self-consciousness of the individual disappeared and was replaced by the divine agent, whatever form that might take.[50] Taking over this conception as part of their cultural assimilation, some Hellenistic Jews (notably Philo of Alexandria) came to think of Moses and the prophets as entering a kind of trance state brought on by the power of the Spirit.[51] Although Hellenistic Jews and the later Ante-Nicene fathers generally did not think the prophets and apostles had behaved in an irrational manner in the state of inspiration,[52] they nevertheless did speak of God taking over their minds.[53]

Although admittedly there are portions of the Bible where those prophesying enter into a trancelike state (1 Sm 10:10–12; 19:24), there is no evidence to suggest that such a state led to the production of the Scriptures themselves. Indeed, writings like the Psalms embody a genuinely human voice that prays, laments, repents, and praises God. At the same time the Psalms repeatedly are referred to by Jesus and the New Testament authors as divine prophecy and therefore the very voice of God (Mk 12:35–37; Jn 10:30–36; Acts 4:25–26; Heb 2:6–8, etc.).

In his account of the history of the doctrine of inspiration within the church, Hermann Sasse mistakenly sees Lutheran and Reformed scholasticism as a continuation of the ancient manic tradition of the Ante-Nicene fathers. He traces their manic conception from the Ante-Nicene fathers through Augustine, and then in an unbroken line of tradition to Protestant scholasticism.[54] By implication he makes the formulation of inspiration and inerrancy taught by the Protestant scholastics a byproduct of an essentially pagan concept of divine communication.

There are a number of difficulties with this account. First, in treating Augustine, Sasse unfortunately seems to confuse his affirmation of the

---

49. Leslie Baynes, *The Heavenly Book Motif in Judeo-Christian Apocalypses 200 BCE–200 CE* (Leiden: Brill, 2011), 110.

50. See Christopher Forbes, *Prophecy and Inspired Speech in Early Christianity and Its Hellenistic Environment* (Tübingen: Mohr Siebeck, 1995), 124–42.

51. For example, Philo writes of prophecy: "No pronouncement of a prophet is ever his own; he is an interpreter prompted by another in all his utterances . . . when knowing not what he does he is filled with inspiration, as the reason withdraws and surrenders the citadel of his soul to a new visitor and tenant, the Divine Spirit which plays upon his vocal organism and dictates words which clearly express its prophetic message." Philo, *De specialibus legibus* 4.49. Cited in Henri Blocher, "God and the Scripture Writers," in *The Enduring Authority of the Christian Scriptures*, ed. D. A. Carson (Grand Rapids: Wm. B. Eerdmans, 2016), 503.

52. Charles Hill, "'The Truth above All Demonstration': Scripture in the Patristic Period to Augustine," in *The Enduring Authority of the Christian Scriptures*, 81–83.

53. Blocher, "God and the Scripture Writers," 503–4; Preus, "View of the Bible," 363.

54. Sasse, "*De Scriptura Sacra*," 55, 66.

inerrancy of the Bible with an acceptance of the ancient manic tradition.[55] As we have already seen, this is a category confusion. Whereas the vast majority of theologians in the pre-Enlightenment era affirmed the inerrancy of the Bible, most did not accept the manic concept of inspiration or even verbal inspiration. Likewise, although Augustine believed in the inerrancy of Scripture, he did not hold the manic conception of inspiration.[56]

Second, Sasse's account overlooks the fact that a profound shift away from the manic concept of inspiration took place in the ancient church as a reaction against the Montanist movement. Living in the mid- to late second century, Montanus claimed to be the Paraclete of John 14 sent to prepare the world for the millennium and the descent of the new Jerusalem. Along with the prophetesses Priscilla and Maximilla, Montanus embodied the manic conception of inspiration found in Greek paganism and Hellenistic Judaism. In the fragments of prophecy that survive from Montanus, he and his companions regularly speak in the first person as the Holy Spirit.[57]

For this reason many of the later Ante-Nicene fathers backed away from the manic conception of inspiration. For example, Origen rejects it in stating: "Moreover, it is not the part of a divine spirit to drive the prophetess [or prophet] into such a state of ecstasy and madness that she [or he] loses control of herself [or himself]."[58] Instead, the Holy Spirit enlightens and elevates the rational capacities of those He inspires so that they can see the truth more clearly:

> Accordingly, we can show from an examination of the sacred Scriptures, that the Jewish prophets, who were enlightened as far as was necessary for their prophetic work by the Spirit of God, were the first to enjoy the benefit of inspiration; and by the contact—if I may so say—of the Holy Spirit they became clearer in mind, and their souls were filled with a brighter light.[59]

Clearly, Origen places a much higher emphasis than the previously-discussed Ante-Nicene fathers on human agency in the production of the Scriptures. He nevertheless still appears to believe that the Holy Spirit is determinative of the verbal content of the text of the Bible.[60]

Following a similar trajectory to Origen's, Aquinas argues in the *Summa Theologiae* that the authors of Scripture possessed degrees of inspiration.[61] In

55. Hermann Sasse, "Augustine's Doctrine of Inspiration," in *Scripture and the Church*, 228–32.

56. Wayne Spear, "Augustine's Doctrine of Biblical Infallibility," in Hannah, *Inerrancy and the Church*, 37–66; Hill, "'The Truth above All Demonstration,'" 59–61; Preus, "View of the Bible," 364–65.

57. See Christine Trevett, *Montanism: Gender, Authority, and the New Prophecy* (Cambridge, UK: Cambridge University Press, 1996).

58. Origen, *Against Celsus* 7.3; ANF 4:612.

59. Origen, *Against Celsus* 7.4; ANF 4:612.

60. See Michael Holmes, "Origen and the Inerrancy of Scripture," *Journal of the Evangelical Theology Society* 24, no. 3 (1981): 221–24.

61. ST 2a2æ, q. 174, art. 3; BF 45:77–82.

the vein of the Greek philosophical tradition, Aquinas considered intelligible knowledge higher than sensible forms of knowledge. The less sensible and the more intelligible the revelation, the closer the inspired prophet or apostle came to a pure reception of God's uncreated and intelligible essence.[62] Within this scheme, Moses (who saw God on Mt. Sinai) and Paul (who went to the third heaven) were considered to be the most illuminated and inspired among the scriptural authors, since their intelligible visions of God came the closest to the fullness of the beatific vision without actually reaching it.[63] Since Aquinas identified inspiration with a sort of spiritual/intellectual vision wherein the authors of the Bible received certain divinely given concepts, he did not find it necessary to suggest that God determined the actual words of the Bible by His act of inspiration.[64] Nonetheless, the Angelic Doctor did believe that God miraculously safeguarded the authors of Scripture from error so that the text of the Bible is inerrant.[65]

The reformers and the later Protestant scholastics rejected aspects of both the Ante-Nicene and medieval views of inspiration and returned to one more in keeping with Scripture. On the one hand, the Protestant scholastics placed greater emphasis on the human agency of the authors than did the Ante-Nicene fathers.[66] The action of writing the Bible was simultaneously wholly God's and wholly that of the prophets and apostles. On the other hand, the Protestant scholastics also insisted that the words of the Bible were those that God Himself had chosen for the conveyance of His truth (verbal inspiration), something that was de-emphasized or not taught explicitly by much of the medieval tradition.[67]

Thus, it can be observed clearly that verbal inspiration as classically defined is not a form of mechanical dictation. Moreover, as Michael Horton has pointed out, those who attack the doctrine of plenary and verbal inspiration as mechanical dictation also implicitly accept a form of ontotheology, that is, the notion that God is merely a being among other beings, not unlike a Greek god.[68] In other words, describing verbal inspiration as mechanical dictation presupposes that causality is something applied to God and creatures in a univocal manner. This assumption makes God and His creatures into beings and causal agents on essentially the same level. From this perspective, if God

62. *ST* 2a2æ, q. 174, art. 2; BF 45:73–77.

63. *ST* 2a2æ, q. 174, art. 4; BF 45:83.

64. *ST* 2a2æ, q. 171, art. 1; BF 45:5–9.

65. "It is heretical to say that any falsehood whatsoever is contained either in the gospels or in any canonical Scripture." Cited in Preus, "View of the Bible," 370. Originally taken from *Exposition on Job* 13, lect. 1. Incidentally, Aquinas's support for biblical inerrancy has won him fans among some modern Evangelicals. See Norman Geisler, *Thomas Aquinas: An Evangelical Appraisal* (Eugene, OR: Wipf & Stock Publishers, 2003), 43–56; Johnson, "Biblical Authority and Scholastic Theology."

66. Muller, *Post-Reformation Reformed Dogmatics* 2:245–47; Preus, *The Inspiration of Scripture*, 66–71; idem, *Theology of Post-Reformation Lutheranism* 1:287–89.

67. Muller, *Post-Reformation Reformed Dogmatics* 2:243–45; Preus, *Inspiration of Scripture*, 39–46; Preus, *Theology of Post-Reformation Lutheranism* 1:281–86.

68. See Heidegger, "Onto-theo-logical Constitution," 42–74.

is wholly responsible for the Scriptures as a causal agent, the causal agency of the creature (which operates on the same level as God's) logically must be eliminated. Otherwise two agents would perform the same task at the same time, which is contradictory.[69]

Likewise, ontotheology in the form of Deism became very closely tied in the seventeenth and eighteen centuries with a view of the causal structure of the universe known as mechanical causation.[70] Belief in mechanical causation has dominated modern science and was part of the paradigm shift that sparked the Scientific Revolution. In this view God is seen as a sort of engineer or mechanic who designed the world as a gigantic machine with parts that work on one another through greater and lesser degrees of physical pressure.

If God's relationship to the world is seen in this way, as many modern theologians implicitly do, it is easy to observe why many have come to see verbal inspiration as a form of mechanical dictation. On the one hand, verbal inspiration might be seen as an arbitrary or even harmful intervention into the machine of nature. On the other hand, since all causation is essentially mechanistic, that is, a matter of applying varying degrees of physical pressure to produce movement, it is difficult to account for how God could act upon the prophets or apostles to cause them to write His direct revelation without crushing their individuality and autonomy, thereby reducing them to the status of robotic dictation machines. From this perspective, if God's own agency in the production of the text increases, the human agent's role must diminish and vice versa.[71]

It is easy to see why modern theology so often has drifted into the equally erroneous alternatives of liberalism and Fundamentalism. In Fundamentalism, at least at the popular level,[72] human agency is erased if the Scriptures are a product of divine agency. In liberalism, if Scripture is a genuinely human book, then God could not have inspired it verbally.

By contrast, the Bible holds that God as the creator is the ground of all causes. He shapes and supervenes on all causes by His creative and sustaining divine power without absorbing them into His being (Heb 1:3). As we have seen earlier, the biblical paradigm conceptualizes God not as the engineer of creation but as the narrator, novelist, or even poet.[73] In Genesis 1 God speaks

---

69. Horton, *Christian Faith*, 162.

70. Sophie Roux and Daniel Garber, eds., *The Mechanization of Natural Philosophy* (New York: Springer, 2013).

71. See a version of this critique in Ferdinand Christian Baur, *History of Christian Dogma*, trans. Peter Hodgson (New York: Oxford University Press, 2015), 290.

72. Not many conservative Protestant theologians actually believe in anything resembling mechanical dictation. See Horton, *Christian Faith*, 162. Michael Horton provides a popular example in W. A. Criswell, *Why I Preach the Bible Is Literally True* (Nashville: Broadman Press, 1969).

73. See various versions of this observation about God's agency in Scripture in the following: Oswald Bayer, "Creation as History," in *The Gift of Grace: The Future of Lutheran Theology*, ed. Niels Hendrik Gregersen (Minneapolis: Augsburg Fortress, 2005), 253; Oswald

creatures into existence as His created speech within the narrative of the seven days. A novelist's or poet's words are separate from himself while being directly determined directly by his intentionality. Analogously, creation is wholly shaped by God's agency, yet acts out of its own internal spontaneity.

This compatibility of divine and human causation has parallels in Augustine's[74] and Luther's discussions of free will and divine grace. Augustine and Luther both speak of creaturely agency as something determined by God's will while at the same time being independent of mechanical determinism. Though God does not coerce our actions, we act out of the nature God has permitted us to possess (as in original sin) or chosen to endow us with by grace (Is 64:8; Jer 18:1–17; Rom 9:20–21). In *The Bondage of the Will* Luther distinguishes divine determination of creaturely agency into the two categories of "necessity of compulsion" and "necessity of immutability."[75] The former refers to God acting on His creation through blunt force, such as when He stopped the motion of the sun (or, actually, the movement of the earth) for Joshua (Jos 10:1–15). The latter refers to creatures acting out of their own determinate nature. As Jesus says: "So, every healthy tree bears good fruit, but the diseased tree bears bad fruit" (Mt 7:17). A tree that bears either good or bad fruit acts according to its own nature and cannot do otherwise. Nevertheless, no external power is compelling it to bear either bad or good fruit.

Likewise, the will under the power of sin necessarily sins because it is corrupted. But no outside force, such as the devil, somehow coerces the will into sinning. The will does what it desires to do freely, without external compulsion. Similarly, in God's action upon His creatures through His Word and the Spirit, He gives new hearts and minds so as to save them by His monergistic act of grace (Dt 30:6; Ps 51:10; Jer 31:33; Ez 36:26). At the same time, creatures of faith act out of their renewed nature freely by doing what they desire to do, namely, trusting and loving God without coercion.

Analogously, by His supernatural act of inspiration God did not coerce the prophets and the apostles into writing what they wrote. Rather, He supernaturally shaped the individual prophets and apostles in their personal agency so as to cause them to be the sorts of persons who would out of the spontaneity of their natures communicate the very words, ideas, and facts God desired them to communicate. Hence, although God's supernatural causal action in inspiration is different from natural human and other historical causal

Bayer, "God as Author of My Life-History," *Lutheran Quarterly* 2 (1988): 437–56; Oswald Bayer, "Poetological Doctrine of the Trinity," *Lutheran Quarterly* 15 (2001): 43–58; Robert Jenson, *Story and Promise: A Brief Theology of the Gospel about Jesus* (Philadelphia: Fortress Press, 1973); Robert Jenson, "How the World Lost Its Story," *First Things* 4 (October 1993): 19–24; Robert Jenson, "Can We Have a Story?" *First Things* 11 (March 2000): 16–17; Balthasar, *Theo-Drama*.

74. See Augustine, *On Grace and Free Will*; NPNFa 5:436–67.

75. *Bondage of the Will*, 1535 (AE 33:64–70; WA 18:634–39). See good discussion in Forde, *Captivation of the Will*, 47–59.

forces, it nevertheless does not compete with or override temporal causes in accomplishing its purpose of communicating God's inerrant truth.

INSPIRATION AS A TRINITARIAN
AND CHRISTOLOGICAL PHENOMENON

As we have seen in the previous section, the act of divine inspiration does not eliminate the human agency of the prophets and the apostles. Although God determines the entire process of the production of Holy Scripture through the power of His inspiring Spirit, He nevertheless does so in, under, and through the human personalities of the individual authors. Although the Bible is the inerrant Word of God, the books of Bible did not fall from heaven. Nor is there anything in Scripture to suggest that its authors used different means of historical research or literary production than other persons within their respective cultures.

The Bible is the Word of God present in and through human words, and thus possesses both a divine and a human nature. For this reason confessional Lutheran theologians have rightly seen the divinity and humanity of the Scriptures as analogous to the two natures in Christ.[76] As the two natures in Christ came together through the supernatural intervention of the Holy Spirit in the virgin birth, so too God caused the authors of Scripture to express the divine Word through human words by means of the supernatural work of His Spirit. As God incorporated Christ's human nature into the *hypostasis* of the Son (*enhypostasis*) from the seed of Abraham and the body of the Virgin Mary, so too the Spirit incorporated the language and personal characteristics of the individual authors into the act of the Spirit-breathed composition of the Bible. As there are two wills in Christ, divine and human, which act in perfect harmony through the unity of the single person of the Son (Dyothelitism), so too the human authors of Scripture were shaped, sanctified, inspired, and enlightened by the power of the Spirit to communicate God's truth always freely in an absolutely perfect and truthful manner through their own human agency. Last, as Christ's human nature was invested with the fullness of divine glory

---

76. See the following examples: *Defense and Explanation of All the Articles*, 1521 (AE 32:11; WA 48:31); Elling Hove, *Christian Doctrine* (Minneapolis: Augsburg Publishing House, 1930), 18–19; Charles Porterfield Krauth, *The Bible a Perfect Book* (Gettysburg, PA: Henry C. Neinstedt, 1857), 10–13; Ulrik Vilhelm Koren, "The Inspiration of Holy Scripture," in *Truth Unchanged, Unchanging: Selected Sermons, Addresses, and Doctrinal Articles,* trans. and ed. Evangelical Lutheran Synod Translation Committee (Lake Mills, IA: Graphic Publishing Company, Inc., 1978), 149–50; Pieper, *Christian Dogmatics* 1:234; George Henry Gerberding, *Lutheran Fundamentals* (Rock Island, IL: Augustana Book Concern, 1925), 63; Conrad Emil Lindberg, *Christian Dogmatics* (Rock Island, IL: Augustana Book Concern, 1928), 388–89; Kolb, *Christian Faith*, 197–98; Sasse, "Concerning the Bible's Inerrancy," 335–36; John Stephenson, *Eschatology,* vol. 13 of Confessional Lutheran Dogmatics (Ft. Wayne: Luther Academy, 1993), 5. Much thanks to my friend and former student David Jay Webber for this list of examples.

(*genus majestaticum*), so too the human words of the Bible contain within their very syllables the coming of the risen Christ in the power of the Holy Spirit.

Nevertheless, the analogy between the incarnation and the inspired Word has not been without criticism in confessional Lutheran circles. In his work on the inspiration of Scripture Robert Preus raises a number of objections in the light of his dialogue with the Lutheran scholastics. First Preus assets that the analogy is unknown in the Age of Orthodoxy.[77] Although Preus is correct that the analogy was uncommon in the theologians of scholastic orthodoxy, Francis Pieper[78] notes that Quenstedt in his dogmatics describes the condescension of God to His people in the act of inspiration as being reminiscent of the incarnation.[79] Beyond this, the analogy can be found in the earlier work of Luther himself: "The Holy Scripture is God's Word, written and, so to speak, lettered and put into the form of letters (*gebuchstabet und in Buchstaben gebildet*), just as Christ, the eternal Word of God, is clothed in humanity. And men regard and treat the written Word of God in this world just as they do Christ. It is a worm and no book compared with other books."[80]

Preus makes the second objection that the theologians of scholastic orthodoxy considered the incarnation unique and without analogy.[81] Although it is correct to say that the incarnation is unique (i.e., one of a kind), the theologians of Lutheran orthodoxy certainly did use analogies for it, a point that Preus himself admits.[82] If this is the case, then by their own admission the incarnation must clearly possess some analogies, and drawing analogies between Scripture and the incarnation cannot be prohibited. Along similar lines, the premise of many of Preus's criticisms seems to be that since there are differences between the act of inspiration and the incarnation, all analogies are unwarranted. Nevertheless, analogies are by definition not one-to-one correspondences, and merely noting differences between the two does not invalidate analogical similarities.

Third, Preus objects that due to the anhypostatic nature of Christ's humanity, the analogy with the divine and human elements in inspiration fails completely. Since Christ's humanity is without personality within itself (*anhypostasis*), according to the analogy the human personalities of the authors of Scripture would be abrogated.[83]

However, in view of what we have argued above, this conclusion does not follow. The fact that Christ's humanity lacks a distinct personality apart from the Logos does not abrogate the fact that it possesses all the distinctive components

---

77. Preus, *Inspiration of Scripture*, 201.
78. Pieper, *Christian Dogmatics* 1:234.
79. Pieper cites Johannes Andreas Quenstedt, *Theologia Didactico-Polemica sive Systema Theologicum*, vol. 1 (Leipzig, 1715), 109.
80. *Defense and Explanation of All the Articles*, 1521 (AE 32:11; WA 48:31).
81. Preus, *Inspiration of Scripture*, 202.
82. Preus, *Inspiration of Scripture*, 201.
83. Preus, *Inspiration of Scripture*, 202.

of normal human nature. The key to this doctrine of Christ's anhypostatic humanity is that these components of human nature in Christ find their center of identity in the person of the Logos. Seen in this light, Christ's anhypostatic humanity is in reality a very fitting analogy for the event of inspiration. In inspiration the individuality and agency of the author's humanity are not abrogated. Rather, because of the revelatory event of inspiration they become instruments of God's Spirit and Word. In this sense the words and agency of the inspired author cease to find their center of identity inside the autonomous intentionality of the author. Instead, they find their center of identity in the eternal Word and Spirit of God supervening on the author's agency in the production of the inspired text.

Finally, Preus objects that in describing the Bible as the inspired Word of God, it is difficult to distinguish the divine and human elements in Scripture, which again suggests a problematic analogy with the incarnation. At least in the abstract, the incarnation can be described in terms of a union of distinct divine and human natures with attending attributes.[84]

Although it is correct to state that one cannot go through the Bible and distinguish what is purely human from what is purely divine, it is nevertheless possible to abstract from the event of inspiration what is divinely derived and what is humanly derived. The words of the Bible are created human words. These words were placed on the pages of the Bible by human agents. Likewise, the divine Spirit and the Word that acted upon the human authors to write the Word of God are clearly the divine element in Scripture. If one objects that because of the doctrine of verbal inspiration the combinations and configurations of words are in themselves divine, it could be countered that in the virgin birth the humanity of Christ also was directly created and shaped by a miracle worked by the Spirit of God.

In positing a view of the inspiration of Scripture as analogous to the incarnation, confessional Lutheran dogmatists give a fully Chalcedonian account of the coming of God's eternal Word into human speech. The Ebionitism of Protestant liberalism/historical criticism is avoided, along with the Docetism of the Ante-Nicene and modern Fundamentalist approaches. In this regard, John Stephenson helpfully observes:

> The Lutheran upholder of verbal inspiration sees no reason to downplay the full reality of the human writers of the Scripture, with all their distinctive individual characteristics; indeed, such a procedure would amount to an unbecoming rebuff to the incarnation of God. Since our models are the Chalcedonian understanding of the incarnate Person and the eucharistic presence of the sacred body and blood not alongside of or instead of, but precisely "in, with, and under" the bread and wine, we shall have no taste for a Docetic-Monophysite "transubstantiated Scripture." The inspiration of the Spirit is discerned "in, with, and under" the pen of the sacred writer, whose own labors must under no circumstances be minimized . . . Yet the analog of the incarnate Person must be taken utterly

---

84. Preus, *Inspiration of Scripture*, 202–4.

seriously. The genuine creatureliness of our Lord's humanity is not surrendered, but rather only appreciated aright, by recognition of his sinlessness (Heb 4:15). The miraculous preservation from error of the sacred writers is a precise parallel of the sinlessness of Jesus. *Errare est humanum* is not a Lutheran sentiment, and must be understood in the light of the distinctions propounded in FC II. Theological scholarship can prove the errorlessness of Holy Writ just as little as historical investigation can demonstrate the sinlessness of Jesus. Both affirmations are, in the strict sense, articles of faith, propositions believed because the Bible says so.[85]

Beyond this, just as the incarnation is the work of the whole Trinity, so too is the inspiration of the Bible.[86] In accordance with the First Article of the Creed, God the Father as the creator shaped the authors of the Bible to be the men they were. In inspiring Paul, God did not somehow override his Hellenistic and Jewish education or his personal characteristics. Paul writes and argues as a Greek-speaking Jew with a Palestinian rabbinic education. But Paul's individual characteristics and knowledge base must not be seen as his own individual contribution to the production of Scripture alongside God's divinely inspired truth. Rather, because the Father is the creator He created Paul and gave him the experiences necessary to be a proper instrument through which the Holy Spirit could write the divine Scriptures.[87]

The inspiration of the Bible is a work of the Son, who has always been the agent of revelation. Of course, revelation in history happened in "many and various ways" (Heb 1:1).[88] Nevertheless, as we observed in an earlier chapter, the eternal Son/Word of God was the agent of revelation in all history. In the presence of the prophets it was Christ who supernaturally spoke, gave visions and dreams, and performed the miraculous events of the history of salvation. These preliminary revelations in the Old Testament culminated in the full manifestation of the eternal Word of God in the incarnation, death, and resurrection of the Son. In the incarnation God did not merely address creatures through creaturely media (created voice, visions and dreams, historical events, etc.) but actually became a creature Himself. In all these events the prophets and apostles providentially were given access to revelation, so that through the power of the Spirit they would be able to gain knowledge of and write down the source material God wished them to convey in Scripture (*suggestio rerum*).[89]

Finally, through the words and promises of the pre-incarnate and incarnate Christ the prophets and apostles received the Holy Spirit so as to be "moved" (2 Pt 1:21, *impulsus ad scribendum*) to write down the very words (*Verbalinspiration, suggestio verbi*) God desired.[90] In that prophets and apostles were not Enthusiasts, the Word of God did not come to them as an

---

85. Stephenson, "Inerrancy," 7. Many thanks to my friend and former student the Rev. David Jay Webber for directing me to this quote.

86. See Preus, *Inspiration of Scripture*, 28–29.

87. See similar argument in Warfield, *Inspiration and Authority of the Bible*, 156–58.

88. Gerhard, *On the Nature of Theology and Scripture*, 41.

89. See a good discussion in Reu, *Lutheran Dogmatics*, 448–49.

90. Reu, *Lutheran Dogmatics*, 450–52.

inner experience or as a form of enlightenment. Rather, through the revelation of Christ in history the prophets and apostles were given the material they needed to write the content of the Bible. Although the Spirit spoke through the prophets, He did so only in relationship to previous historical revelations and the words God attached to them. As Luther states:

> For God wished to appear even to Moses through the burning bush and spoken Word; and no prophet, neither Elijah nor Elisha, received the Spirit without the Ten Commandments [or spoken Word]. 12] Neither was John the Baptist conceived without the preceding word of Gabriel, nor did he leap in his mother's womb without the voice of Mary. And Peter says, 2 Pet. 1:21: *The prophecy came not by the will of man; but holy men of God spake as they were moved by the Holy Ghost.* Without the outward Word, however, they were not holy, much less would the Holy Ghost have moved them to speak when they still were unholy [or profane]; for they were holy, says he, since the Holy Ghost spake through them.[91]

Hence the Spirit preserved God's revelation in the minds of the prophets and apostles in an absolutely perfect manner, gave them the impulse to write it down, and mysteriously worked within them to cause them to select the very words God wished them to use.

In the light of this way of conceptualizing inspiration, we may observe that many of the false views of inspiration and scriptural authority we have previously examined have gone wrong precisely because they failed to see that the whole trinitarian agency of God comes to bear in the divine act of inspiration. Historical criticism has seen Scripture as nothing more than a natural byproduct of fallen human culture. It therefore ignores and categorically rules out the supernatural work of the Son and the Spirit, thereby interpreting the Bible purely from the perspective of the possibilities the Father has established for creation after the Fall. Historical criticism does not recognize the fact that Scripture is a witness to the Son and the Spirit's enactment of the new creation and its miraculous possibilities which transcend the old world burdened with sin and death (Rom 8:20).

Likewise, Barth and many in neo-orthodoxy focused so exclusively on Scripture's witness to the Son that they failed to appreciate the work of the Spirit in preserving and inerrantly inspiring a true witness of the Scriptures to the Son's work. Finally, both theological liberalism (Catholic and Protestant) and the ancient manic tradition isolated the work of the Spirit from that of the Father and the Son in inspiration. From the perspective of the manic tradition, the Spirit overrides the faculties of the prophet or apostle, thereby ignoring the fact that these same faculties are a work of the Father-creator and the medium whereby these men received the historical revelation of the Son. In the view of theological liberalism the Spirit's untethered nature makes it free to blow hither and thither, wherever the false wind of contemporary culture takes it. Most recently, mainline Protestants have untethered the work of the Spirit from that

---

91. SA III.ix (Bente, 496).

of the Father-creator by excusing sexual license and redefining marriage. They also have untethered the work of the Spirit from that of the Son by promoting religious universalism and pluralism.

As reflective of the trinitarian and incarnational agency of God, Scripture is not only a unity of the divine and the human but also of objectivity and subjectivity. Beginning with the Enlightenment's subject–object dualism (originating in Descartes's *Meditations on First Philosophy* of 1641),[92] subjectivity in modern thought has come to be seen as a problem to be overcome by a humanly constructed epistemological bridge into objectivity. This is true whether this bridge be clear and distinct ideas (Descartes) or empirical experience purified through distinction between primary and secondary qualities (Locke).[93]

Nevertheless, contrary to all this, subjectivity is not something to be overcome in the quest for knowledge; indeed, it is the precondition for the knowledge of objective truth. A "pure objectivity" without any admixture of perspective and subjectivity presupposes that the knower is not a particular subject, and as such the knower becomes nothing. For example, if I am watching a play in a theater and the main character is wearing a red jacket, I can identify this as an objective fact. Nonetheless, I identify the presence of the red jacket as an objective fact only from the particular place in which I am sitting in the audience. If I lacked a vantage point I would not occupy any space, nor would I be an independent subject. I would in fact not even exist.

Conversely, pure subjectivity is also nothingness, since a subject is a subject only in relationship to something else. I am a subject precisely because I am not something else, and the "something else" is necessarily some objective reality outside of me which intrudes on my subjectivity. It thus becomes clear that objectivity and subjectivity are perichoretically united with one another, and without their unity true knowledge is impossible.

In contrast to the Enlightenment's subject–object dualism, Scripture teaches that all reality is rooted in the triune God, who unites subjectivity and objectivity in His personal existence. On the one hand, God is omniscient and therefore possesses an absolutely objective knowledge of Himself and all His creatures. At the same time, God's knowledge of Himself and His creation comes in and through His personal and subjective existence as eternally actualized in the persons of the Trinity. God therefore knows what He knows absolutely objectively, but from the analogical "perspective" of the individual persons of Father, Son, and Holy Spirit. Moreover, God's knowledge, particularly of Himself, is relational in that it is actualized through the perichoretic mutual indwelling of the persons within one another. Although the persons of the

92. René Descartes, *Meditations on First Philosophy,* trans. Donald Cress (Indianapolis: Hackett Publishing Company, 1993).

93. John Locke, *Essay Concerning Human Understanding* (Indianapolis: Hackett Publishing Company, 1996).

Trinity know one another through mutual indwelling, they do not lose their personal and distinct subjectivity as persons.

Beyond the life of the Trinity, one can see the unity of objectivity and subjectivity in the incarnation. Here the universal and absolutely objective God takes into Himself a particular subjective human existence in time. Again, the subjective and objective are not antithetical to one another but perichoretically indwell one another through the *communicatio idiomatum* of the incarnation. Just as the persons of the Trinity perichoretically know and dwell in one another without abrogating their distinct personal realities, the two natures communicate their properties to one another without obliterating their distinctness as divine and human.

Therefore, the man Jesus participates in the fullness of divine glory (*genus majestaticum*, Col 2:9) and even the archetypal theology of God's eternal self-knowledge (*theologia archetypa*, Col 2:3).[94] Likewise, in and through His unity with the human nature the person of the Son in His absolute objectivity and omniscience participates in the historical situatedness and particularity of the human nature. As a result of the *communicatio idiomatum* in Christ, creatures in their subjectivity, finitude, and historical situatedness are given access to the full objectivity of God's reality and truth.

The form taken by Scripture as the inspired Word of God thus comes into focus. As we have already seen, in moving the scriptural authors to write, the Holy Spirit incorporated (one might say by *enhypostasis*) the individuality of each scriptural author and his particular situation in time and space into the composition of the divinely inspired books. In the incarnation the human nature of Christ possesses its own individual characteristics while at the same time lacking its own center of identity (*anhypostasis*). Rather, Christ's humanity is incorporated into and possesses its center of identity in the eternal person of the Word (*enhypostasis*). By analogy, the individual characteristics of each scriptural author are not negated by the revelation of the Holy Scriptures but are incorporated into the act of inspiration and composition. Nevertheless, since the words of the Bible are the very words of God, the written words of the scriptural authors find their ultimate center of identity not in the personality, intentionality, and circumstances of the individual author but rather in the *hypostasis* of God's revelation.

Hence, as a byproduct of God's trinitarian and incarnational agency the Bible gives the Word of God in and through a variety of creaturely witnesses. Indeed, in the Bible there is a "cloud of witnesses" (Heb 12:1). Like the Trinity and the incarnation, Scripture witnesses to a single harmonious truth manifested in and through difference. The Bible is absolutely objective and inerrant. It witnesses to what genuinely occurred in time and space, but it does so from the perspective of the individual authors in their individual

---

94. Muller, *Post-Reformation Reformed Dogmatics* 1:252; Preus, *Theology of Post-Reformation Lutheranism* 1:170–72.

communities and historical situations, thus conveying to its readers a symphony or even a polyphony of truth.[95]

For example, Genesis, Isaiah, and Daniel all witness to the same Christ, but they do so in different ways according to the individuality and subjectivity of the authors. Genesis describes Christ as "the Seed," Isaiah as "the Suffering Servant," and Daniel as "the Son of Man." While these witnesses all proclaim the inerrant and objective truth about the one Christ, they nevertheless do so from their distinct historical settings and vantage points which conditioned the nature of their witness to the one Christ.

The authors of Scripture also write in a variety of genres: parables, poetry, prophetic speech, histories, and apocalyptic visions. These differing genres of Scripture also give access to God's truth through a polyphony of media. Genesis, the Psalms, and Job all witness to the reality of creation, but in different genres and from different perspectives. Genesis gives a more historical-literal description of the nature and origins of creation, whereas Job and the Psalms more often speak in a poetical fashion.

The perspectival nature of inspiration and revelation also accounts for why we possess many books in the Bible that cover the same events but from different points of view. This phenomenon within Scripture encompasses the historical and theological distinctions among the four Gospels, the distinctions between the Synoptic Gospels and John and between the Deuteronomic history and Chronicles, and the literary feature of doublets in individual biblical texts. Through differing perspectives as well as literary and historical choices, we are given a multitude of entry points to the one divine Word and truth of God actualized in human history.

CONCLUSION

Now that we have addressed the inspiration and inerrancy of Scripture, we will turn to the question of the canon of Holy Scripture. Whereas the Spirit-wrought content of Scripture is self-authenticating, the historical form the Word of God has taken must be discerned. To this task of "testing the Spirits" (Jn 4:1) we will move next in our discussion of the canon of Holy Scripture.

---

95. See Hans Urs von Balthasar, *Truth Is Symphonic: Aspects of Christian Pluralism*, trans. Graham Harrison (San Francisco: Ignatius Press, 1987).

5

THE WRITTEN WORD OF GOD:
THE CANON OF HOLY SCRIPTURE

THE QUESTION OF THE CANON

Although Scripture itself repeatedly testifies to the inspired and infallible witness of the prophets and the apostles, this testimony does not entirely settle the question of the discernment of true and false prophecy. The question remains: which writings count as those of a true prophet or apostle? This issue of the discernment of true prophecy thus brings us directly to the thorny question of the canon of Scripture.

On the one hand, Scripture speaks of God's Word as being self-authenticating. The testament of the Gospel is written by the Spirit on the hearts of believers, in a self-authenticating knowledge of God (Jeremiah 31, 2 Corinthians 3, etc.). The truth that it is the Holy Spirit alone who bestows true knowledge of the Word of God, in repentance and faith, is a necessary consequence of the truth that the human will is in bondage to sin. The human heart left to its own rational and autonomous activity will always reject God because it desires to be God (1 Cor 2:14).[1] Humans are bound creatures. They stand either under the influence of one spirit that binds them to the falsehoods of Satan (Eph 2:2) or under the Holy Spirit who binds them to God's truth (1 Cor 2:15–16).

On the other hand, both testaments also tell believers to test prophecy. Although Christians are enlightened by the Spirit and know the truth because of God's monergistic action, they nevertheless can be deceived and fall away from the truth, succumbing to false prophecy like Adam and Eve. Because of the *simul* of Christian existence, not everything that finds a place in our hearts is pure and from God. Just as there is a subjective principle of the inner testimony of the Spirit, there are objective principles to employ in "testing the spirits" through the means granted to us by God (Deuteronomy 18; 1 Cor 12:3; 1 Jn 4:1–2). Scripture itself gives objective criteria for testing and discerning who speaks from God and who does not. God grants believers the ability to discern what counts as part of the canon of Scripture and what does not. Hence, the discernment of the canon is not a rationalistic and autonomous enterprise but one performed by faith under the authority of the Word of God.

---

1. Martin Luther, *Disputation against Scholastic Theology*, 1517 (AE 31:10; WA 1:221).

Nevertheless, if Scripture serves as a means of discerning Scripture, do we not fall back into a circular argument that "the Bible is inspired because the Bible says that it is inspired"? In response a number of things should be considered. First, in many cases human knowledge of particular realities comes through those realities themselves. For example, we can see the sun only because of the light of the sun. The sun's light is not known by means of other lights. We can of course see evidence of the sun by the light it casts on other entities, but the sun in and of itself is known only through its own power to give off light. Analogously, the Spirit gives us the ability to recognize the Word and its validity. The Spirit does so by inculcating the truthfulness of the historical revelation to which the word of the Bible witnesses. Such historical revelation establishes the authority of the Bible and also establishes certain valid internal criteria for the truthfulness of revelation. As we have already seen, these include the Mosaic criteria of true prophecy and ultimately Christ's own authorization of the apostolic testimony. The Bible thus simultaneously establishes and fulfills these criteria of authenticity.

Second, it follows that although the authority of Scripture is known through its own internal criteria of self-authentication, the Bible ultimately is founded on historical revelation that objectively exists prior to it and that authorizes its composition. As argued at some length in a previous chapter, the historical revelation which establishes Scripture most foundationally is the resurrection of Christ. Christ's resurrection validates His authority. With this authority Christ authorized the inspired witness of the prophets and apostles. Analogously, light from the sun gives us access to the sun. The sun is light in itself, but the light the sun gives off is distinct from the sun and makes the sun knowable. Scripture (light) is thus not the same as the historical revelation (the sun) that authorizes it. Nevertheless, Scripture is in and of itself a form of revelation and is the only means whereby one gains access to the historical revelation that authorizes it. Put another way: in discerning the authority of the canon of Scripture, the ontological order of revelation (i.e., revelatory events authorize the production of revelatory texts) is distinct and indeed the inversion of the epistemic order (i.e., revelatory texts give access to the revelatory events that authorize them).

Hence, when we turn to the written form of the Word of God, certain texts possess a foundational authority granted to them by historical revelation as a means of discerning valid and true revelation. Put succinctly, as I will argue below, for the Old Testament, Moses and the historical revelation he mediated not only validated his own individual ministry but also established foundational criteria for all future prophecy. Likewise, in the New Testament Christ's authority is foundational to the canon of Sacred Scripture as it is received by the Christian church.

Here we follow basically the same line of reasoning as Matthias Flacius in his *Clavis Scripturae Sacre* (1567). Flacius states that God authenticates Scripture and its canonical form with two syllogisms: everything God says is true and needs no proof; and everything the Old Testament says about the Messiah is true. From this second syllogism it also follows that everything Christ and the apostles say is true, since they have fulfilled Old Testament prophecy.[2] Flacius's approach is helpful because it is consistent with Scripture's own internal criteria of truthfulness founded in historical revelation. As we have seen, the Word of God is self-authenticating. Nevertheless, in terms of discerning whether our hearts and minds have been captured by the Word of God or that of a false spirit, the Old and New Testaments find their objective authorization in their witness to the true fulfillment of prophecy, and ultimately in Christ's own authority as one who has risen from the dead.

WHAT IS THE CANON OF SCRIPTURE?

Before we develop our biblical and confessional basis for positing the canon of Holy Scripture, it is important to define what we mean when we speak of the canon. This task is not straightforward, since a number of definitions have been put forward in recent years. These definitions are by no means theologically neutral, so it is important to establish a clear understanding of what we mean by canon if we wish to proceed in a theologically responsible manner.

Over the previous decades it has become increasingly common in canonical studies to distinguish between the categories of "canon" and "scripture." Whereas scripture refers to a text being used by a community in a manner that recognizes it as divinely authoritative, canon refers to a text officially recognized by a community as divinely inspired.[3]

For confessional Lutheran dogmatics this distinction can be helpful in many respects. Most helpful is the fact that this distinction counters the Roman Catholic tendency to conflate the existence of a canon with the reality of the Scripture as the Word of God itself. Popular Catholic apologists frequently use this conflation as a means of arguing against the Reformation principle of *sola scriptura*. The claim is often made that since the councils of Carthage and Hippo decided the canon of Scripture only in the late fourth century, there were no Scriptures prior to their decisions. The premise here is that Scripture became Scripture only because the institutional church decided on the specific content of the canon.[4]

From this premise it is also argued that since there was no canon and therefore no Scriptures, the institutional church's authority necessarily must be thought of as existing prior to the Scriptures and therefore as superior to them.

---

2. Matthias Flacius Illyricus, *How to Understand the Sacred Scriptures: From* Clavis Scripturae Sacre, trans. Wade Johnston (Saginaw, MI: Magdeburg Press, 2011), 70–72.

3. See the classic article by Albert Sundberg, "Towards a Revised History of the New Testament Canon," *Studia Evangelica* 4, no. 1 (1968): 452–61.

4. See an argument of this nature in Peter Kreeft, *Catholic Christianity: A Complete Catechism of Catholic Beliefs Based on the Catholic Catechism* (San Francisco: Ignatius Press, 2001), 100.

After all, if there was no Bible in the first centuries of the church for people to appeal to and yet people authoritatively taught Christianity, the implication is that theologians must have relied purely on the authority of the church and its tradition. In the minds of Roman Catholics, therefore, Lutherans and Protestants in general contradict themselves when they pit Scripture against the authority of the Roman Catholic Church, since if they accept the authority of Scripture (established by the Roman Church), they must also accept all the other things that church has authoritatively decreed (Marian doctrines, sacrifice of the Mass, papal infallibility, etc.).

The distinction between Scripture and canon has much to offer in response to arguments like this. First, as we have already seen, the authority of Scripture does not derive from the institutional church's act of canonization but from the command and promise of the risen Christ. Indeed, as Martin Chemnitz observes, the church does not make texts inspired by their official act of recognition.[5] When the church makes an accurate decision regarding what counts as Scripture (canonization), the validity of the decision derives from the qualities inherent to the texts themselves, namely, their reality as inspired prophetic and apostolic writing. Just as jewels and gold do not become jewels and gold by being gathered up into a basket, the church's decisions about canon do not make Scripture into Scripture.

Second, although the many official decisions regarding the canon came about in the late fourth century, Christians regarded the Bible as inspired and authoritative long before this.[6] As a number of Protestant apologists also have noted helpfully, Israel had very little difficulty recognizing the Old Testament without the infallible authority of the Roman Catholic Church.[7] Roman Catholics must acknowledge not only these points but also the fact that according to their own understanding neither the Council of Hippo nor that of Carthage was an infallible council of the church. Rather, they were merely local synods, and in fact the list of canonical books they decided upon differed from that of the Council of Trent (1545–63),[8] the first infallible council (according to present Catholic theology) to decide the question of the canon.[9]

If the logic of the Catholic position is followed, the Roman Catholic Church had no authoritative Scriptures until after the Reformation was well underway. Nevertheless, Roman Catholic theologians cited the Bible as authoritative long before Trent, and so one must inevitably come to the conclusion that the authority of the Bible, even in Catholic theology, pre-exists the institutional church's decisions and therefore is not founded on the authority of the institutional church. Hence, as should be clear, it is possible to have Scripture

---

5. Chemnitz, *Examination of the Council of Trent* 1:175–76.
6. Kruger, *Question of the Canon*, 155–203.
7. Keith Mathison, *The Shape of Sola Scriptura* (Moscow, ID: Canon Press, 2001), 315–17.
8. James White, *Sola Scriptura: Exploring the Bible's Accuracy, Authority, and Authenticity* (Minneapolis: Bethany House, 2001), 116.
9. Mathison, *Shape of Sola Scriptura*, 317–18.

(authoritative texts) without an official canon decided upon by an ecclesiastical body.

Roman Catholic apologists could argue that although the Scriptures possess an inherent authority based on their inspiration, it is impossible to know that Scripture is an infallible authority without the infallible authority of the church to discern the canon of the Bible. Since human beings are normally fallible, they might say, it is impossible for them to be able to recognize an infallible authority (i.e., the Bible) apart from the discernment provided by another infallible authority (the institutional Roman Church).

This argument has several problems. If it is necessary to have an infallible authority to recognize an infallible authority (i.e., the Roman Church to recognize the Bible), then logically we must posit yet another infallible authority to help us recognize the infallible authority of the Roman Catholic Church. Likewise, above the infallible authority that validated the institutional church there would have to be yet another infallible authority to validate its infallible authority. Logically, this would lead to an infinite regress of infallible authorities.[10]

Not only do Roman Catholics not follow this infinite regress in practice, their position ultimately implies that fallible people of faith are capable of recognizing infallible authorities. Although not every baptized Roman Catholic is deemed infallible, they are supposed to recognize the infallible authority of the Roman Catholic Church.[11] The presupposition then is that fallible believers can recognize infallible authority. This assumption then provokes the question of why equally fallible Lutherans are not capable of discerning the infallible authority of the Bible without the authority of the institutional church.

Ultimately, discerning the canon of Scripture must be an act of discovering where in history God has chosen to manifest His will by the means of His appointed revelatory channels. Although God certainly does work through His Word and Spirit to help the church recognize the canon in its official decisions, the institutional church's decisions regarding what counts as Scripture are valid only if they rely on the objective historical facts about what has come down from the prophets and apostles and what has not.[12] Accepting the alternative would be to court Enthusiasm, wherein apart from God's Word and promise attached to the prophets and apostles, specially enlightened ecclesiastical authorities would appeal to the Spirit's decisions within their hearts regarding what counts as the Bible. By making the untethered Spirit the exclusive means of discerning the canon, Roman Catholics relying on an infallible church and Evangelical Protestants relying almost exclusively on the inner testimony of the Spirit are equally guilty of this sort of Enthusiasm.

---

10. James White, *The Roman Catholic Controversy: Catholics and Protestants—Do the Differences Still Matter?* (Minneapolis: Bethany House, 1996), 234.

11. Mark Powell, *Papal Infallibility: A Protestant Evaluation of an Ecumenical Issue* (Grand Rapids: Wm. B. Eerdmans, 2009), 14–15.

12. Scaer, "Apostolicity, Inspiration, and Canonicity," 48.

With many of these initial considerations in mind, Richard Kruger has offered a helpful threefold definition of the canon, which we will follow in our discussion below. First there is the ontological canon, that is, those writings that God has inspired to be written. In the sense of this definition of the canon, each of the books of the New Testament was established as canon the moment it was completed. These books formed a body of texts that God inspired and recognized as His Word from the moment of their composition.[13] Again, God has established the canon; the church merely discerns it. Second, one can define the canon of Scripture as the informal communal recognition of the books of the Bible as God's Word. With regard to the Old Testament as a whole, this recognition seems to have happened at least by the early Second Temple period. The recognition of the New Testament as a whole seems to have occurred during the mid- to late second century, although as we will see there is evidence that this might have occurred even earlier. Finally, one can define the canon as the official list of inspired books made by a council or assembly within the church, something that began to happen only in the late fourth century.[14]

In proceeding in our discernment of the canon, we will be concerned primarily with Kruger's first definition of the canon, namely, the ontological canon. But we will also utilize evidence from the church's historical process of discernment reflected in the second and third definitions of the canon. Although the process of canonization does not cause the books of the Bible to become authoritative and inspired, the manner in which certain books came to be recognized as inspired may serve as historical evidence for the ontological canon.

To return to our earlier analogy of the sun being like the Word of God: although the sun is recognizable by the light it gives off in and of itself, that same light illuminates all other visible objects on earth. In turn, the recognition of the fact that these objects are illuminated indirectly points to the reality of the sun beyond them. Likewise, we can garner evidence of the historical reception and recognition of the biblical texts as a means of demonstrating their divine origins.

THE CANON OF THE OLD TESTAMENT

The first prophet from whom we have a written record is Moses, who mediated the Sinaitic covenant to Israel. All of Israel received and agreed to his covenant (Exodus 24, etc.), and thereby attested that Moses was God's authoritative prophet. Moses' authority was validated not only by the fact that God used him as a means of confirming promises once made to the patriarchs but by miraculous interventions on God's part. Moses' authority was challenged and repeatedly reconfirmed throughout the later books of the Pentateuch.

---

13. Warfield, *Inspiration and Authority of the Bible*, 415; Kruger, *Question of the Canon*, 42. Kruger cites the same passage in Warfield and makes the same point.
14. Kruger, *Question of the Canon*, 43.

This confirmation is particularly clear in the Book of Numbers where Moses' opponents are judged, thereby vindicating his call as a true prophet of God. As a result, the pattern of revelation followed by testing (discussed in an earlier chapter) finds an exemplary embodiment in the Mosaic revelation.

Moreover, Moses' final speech to Israel both authorized and provided the basis for testing all future prophecy in Israel (Deuteronomy 18). As we have already discussed, authentic prophets had two characteristics: first, they were to prophesy in the name of God (i.e., stand in continuity with all previous revelations of Yhwh). Second, the word they had spoken (predictive prophecy, a word commanding a miracle or the creation of faith, etc.) must be seen to have come to fulfillment.

For this reason and a number of others, the genuine Mosaic authorship of the Pentateuch is important. First, as we saw earlier, the validity of all subsequent prophecy and therefore also the canon of the Old Testament is dependent on Mosaic authorization. Such a criterion is crucial to discerning the boundaries of the Old Testament canon. Without the authorization of Moses, the decisions Israel and the later church made regarding the Old Testament canon would be completely arbitrary and would lack any objective validity.

Second, Jesus testified to Moses' authorship of the Pentateuch and used it as a means of validating His own mission and authority (Mt 8:4; 19:7–8; Mk 7:10; 12:26; Lk 24:27, 44; Jn 5:46–47; 7:19). Indeed, the Pentateuch itself (Ex 17:14; 24:4–7; 34:27; Nm 33:2; Dt 31:9, 22, 24) and much of the rest of the Old Testament (Jos 1:7–8; 8:32–34; Jgs 3:4; 1 Kgs 2:3; 2 Kgs 14:6; 21:8; 2 Chr 25:4; Ezr 6:18; Neh 8:1; 13:1; Dn 9:11–13) imply or state directly that Moses was the author of the first five books of the Bible. To call into question these statements is to call into question the truthfulness of Christ, the inerrancy of Scripture, and thus also the validity of the Christian religion.[15]

Some liberal theologians might argue that we cannot rely on Jesus' authority in the matter of the authorship of the Pentateuch because in His state of humiliation He was subject to the same false opinions about the origins of the Old Testament as His contemporaries were. As John Warwick Montgomery has noted, this is a false line of reasoning. Although Christ limited His knowledge during His state of humiliation, as we have seen, He was very much aware of where the boundaries of His knowledge lay. The best example of this is the fact that Christ acknowledged He was unaware of when the last judgment would occur (Mk 13:32).[16] Had He suspended His divine knowledge of who wrote the Pentateuch during His state of humiliation, He would have acknowledged that.

Although He temporally limited His knowledge, Christ never propagated false information out of ignorance or accommodated Himself to the false opinions of His day. If we posit that Christ did in fact propagate false

---

15. See summary of the biblical data for Mosaic authorship of the Pentateuch in Edward Young, *Introduction to the Old Testament* (Grand Rapids: Wm. B. Eerdmans, 1989), 42–46.

16. Montgomery, *Tracatus Logico-Theologicus*, 117–18.

information out of ignorance or cultural accommodation, we must necessarily conclude that it is impossible to discern what is false culturally-based opinion and what is divine truth in His teachings. The ultimate result of Christ's ministry then would not be the revelation of divine truth but a body of teachings that were partially divine and true, and partially false and human. The same point could be made regarding the claims made by the rest of the scriptural authors regarding the Mosaic authorship of the Pentateuch.

Incidentally, these same arguments apply to the contested origins of Isaiah and Daniel. There are of course many good historical and linguistic arguments to be made in favor of the authenticity and unity of both books.[17] Nevertheless, Jesus' attestation of their authenticity is valid for the same reasons as is His attestation of the Mosaic authorship of the Pentateuch discussed above.

Beyond these considerations based on theological coherence, there are a number of historical reasons to consider it credible that Moses was the main author of the first five books of the Bible. The first reason is the weakness of the chief alternative to Mosaic authorship, the highly flawed documentary hypothesis. According to this theory, four anonymous writers, referred to as J, E, P, and D, actually authored the Pentateuch over several centuries, sometime between the ninth and third centuries B.C.[18] In spite of its wide acceptance this theory contains a number of internal contradictions and in fact is based largely on groundless speculation.

The first difficulty with the documentary hypothesis is the fact that we have no direct archaeological evidence any of the documents that were supposedly blended together to make the Pentateuch ever existed. Indeed, there is no existing evidence that people in ancient Israel composed scriptural works by gradually cutting and pasting together older documents to create new ones over hundreds of years.

Such evolutionary theories of literary development were considered self-evidently rational by nineteenth-century scholars.[19] Nevertheless, in the hundred-plus years since then, many scholars outside of biblical studies have moved away from these sorts of models of literary development. For example, in the nineteenth century, Homeric studies, particularly in the Analyst school, assumed that the Iliad and the Odyssey were the result of evolutionary cutting and pasting. Nonetheless, modern scholarship increasingly has come to acknowledge that these two works were written by a single author (possibly named Homer), albeit one who collected an evolving oral poetry.[20]

---

17. See arguments in Seth Erlandsson, *The Scroll of Isaiah* (Handen: XP Media, 2014); Andrew Steinmann, *Daniel* (St. Louis: Concordia Publishing House, 2008), 1–20.

18. See the classical formulation of the documentary hypothesis in Julius Wellhausen, *Prolegomena to the History of Israel*, trans. J. Sutherland Black (Edinburgh: Adam and Charles Black, 1885).

19. Gleason Archer, *A Survey of the Old Testament, Introduction* (Chicago: Moody Press 1985), 111.

20. See a description of nineteenth-century evolutionary theories in John Edwin Sandys, *A History of Classical Scholarship: The Eighteenth Century in Germany and the Nineteenth Century*

The second difficulty with this hypothesis is the absurdity of positing the existence of multiple sources based on the different uses of the divine names throughout the Pentateuch, or on narrative repetition and doublets. Proponents claim the source E used the name Elohim almost exclusively, while source J used Yʜwʜ almost exclusively. But as Umberto Cassuto has demonstrated, the divine names of Yʜwʜ and Elohim are used intermittently throughout the Old Testament and in later Jewish literature to denote God's personal covenantal presence and His transcendent majesty, respectively.[21] Also, other ancient Near Eastern texts use multiple names for a given deity, yet this is never taken to denote that the document in question is a blending together of previous sources.[22] As Gleason Archer notes, one also finds the phenomenon of multiple names for the deity in the Qur'an, which (although edited by later Muslim scholars) is widely believed to have come down from a single oral source, Muhammad.[23] Ultimately, if liberal scholars do not wish to claim that the use of multiple names for a single deity indicates multiple sources in these other writings, they cannot justify their claim about the Pentateuch.

With regard to the appearance of repetition and doublets, R. N. Whybray has called into question the usefulness of appealing to such features as a sign of multiple authorship. In his book *The Making of the Pentateuch* Whybray argues convincingly that the appeal of the documentary hypothesis to such phenomena as evidence of the blending together of multiple sources is essentially self-contradictory. One of the key assumptions of the documentary hypothesis is that the repetition of certain stories (doublets) and repetitive language (parallelism) throughout the Pentateuch is a clear indication that the author is not a single person but rather a series of sources strung together. According to the theory, individual authors would have avoided repetition and would have carefully written a single account of events with all necessary details they wished to convey.[24]

As Whybray shows, this is a flawed argument because it assumes that the final editors of the Pentateuch did not seek to avoid doublets and repetition, and that the authors whose sources they utilized necessarily would have.[25] This argument not only is contradictory but presupposed that ancient authors

in Europe and the United States of America (Cambridge, UK: Cambridge University Press, 2011), 48–143. Also see Albert Lord, *The Singer of Tales* (Cambridge, MA: Harvard University Press, 1960); George Dimock, *The Unity of the Odyssey* (Amherst: University of Massachusetts Press, 1989).

21. Umberto Cassuto, *The Documentary Hypothesis and the Composition of the Pentateuch*, trans. Israel Abrahams (Jerusalem: Shalem Press, 2008), 29–30.

22. John Walton, *Ancient Near Eastern Thought and the Old Testament: Introducing the Conceptual World of the Hebrew Bible* (Grand Rapids: Baker Academic, 2006), 92. Walton notes that Marduk had fifty names.

23. Archer, *Survey of the Old Testament*, 125.

24. R. N. Whybray *The Making of the Pentateuch: A Methodological Study* (Sheffield: Sheffield Academic Press, 1987), 80–83, 130–31.

25. Whybray, *Making of the Pentateuch*, 19.

wrote history in as dispassionate and unliterary a manner as modern ones do. Similarly, the documentary hypothesis does not take into consideration the literary value of repetition (i.e., Semitic poetical parallelism) and multiple accounts.[26]

Beyond these obvious difficulties with the documentary hypothesis, there is much positive evidence for Moses' composition of the core of the original text. As discussed in an earlier chapter, P. J. Wiseman famously demonstrates that the Hebrew word תּוֹלְדוֹת (meaning "generations," as in "these are the generations of") appears at regular intervals throughout the book of Genesis as a means of bracketing historical material. The use of this term as a literary device parallels the form of ancient family records written on ceramic tablets. These tablets contained accounts of individual members of a clan or the history of a clan over a particular period of time. Ultimately Wiseman convincingly argues that the use of תּוֹלְדוֹת serves as colophon, namely, a subscription of the owner or composer of the tablet. This observation suggests that Genesis is a compilation of shorter tablets composed or owned by the patriarchs.[27]

It is interesting to note that the use of the תּוֹלְדוֹת as a literary device persists at regular intervals throughout the book of Genesis but stops at the book of Exodus. From this pattern it may be inferred that the use of earlier sources (indicated by the תּוֹלְדוֹת) ceases at the point when the author of the Pentateuch entered history personally and became a firsthand witness to the events. In this scenario Moses would have compiled and edited the tablets handed down to him from the patriarchs and composed the rest of the Pentateuch from his own personal recollections.

Another significant evidence for Moses' composition of the Pentateuch is the literary structure of Deuteronomy. Both K. A. Kitchen and Meredith Kline have shown that the book of Deuteronomy and the other covenant formulas in the Pentateuch mirror almost exactly those of Hittite suzerainty treaties widely used in the ancient Near East during the later second millennium B.C.[28] Since such treaty formulas were not used after the eleventh century B.C., the authorship of the Pentateuch clearly must be placed before that date. Especially in its historical prologue Deuteronomy presupposes the reader is familiar with all the contents of the previous four books, which therefore cannot be isolated from this fifth book. These facts, combined with implications of the use of the literary form of the תּוֹלְדוֹת discussed earlier, suggest very strongly that the occasion for the composition of the Pentateuch was the exodus. Thus, it seems

---

26. Whybray, *Making of the Pentateuch*, 81. Also see a similar argument in Gioacchino Michael Cascione, *Repetition in the Bible* (Tucson: Redeemer Press, 2016).

27. See Wiseman, *Ancient Records*. In support of Wiseman see Harrison, *Introduction to the Old Testament*, 542–50.

28. K. A. Kitchen, *On the Reliability of the Old Testament* (Grand Rapids: Wm. B. Eerdmans, 2006), 283–94; Meredith Kline, *Treaty of the Great King: The Covenant Structure of Deuteronomy, Studies and Commentary* (Eugene, OR: Wipf & Stock, 2012).

more than likely that the author of the core of the material in the first five books of the Bible was Moses himself.

Many other internal indications suggest both the historical reliability and Mosaic origin of the Pentateuch. These indications include the attestation of the names of the patriarchs in early second millennium B.C. sources, the depiction in the patriarchal narratives of marriage customs peculiar to that same time period,[29] the presence of authentic Egyptian words in portions of the Pentateuch that deal with Egypt,[30] the familiarity of the author of the Pentateuch with Egyptian flora and fauna, seasonal structure, and other customs,[31] and the fact that Leviticus has more primitive cultic vocabulary than that of the book of Ezekiel.[32] On the last point it should be noted that according to the documentary hypothesis Leviticus was written at a time very close to or later than Ezekiel.

Of course, to counteract these arguments liberal critics frequently cite supposed anachronisms in the Pentateuch, which they argue suggest a composition at a much later period. Some of these supposed anachronisms have been addressed through the advance of our knowledge of the historical period that the Pentateuch covers. For example, Kitchen shows that camels were domesticated much earlier than once thought, and hence the claim that the patriarchs could not have owned them is false.[33] Other supposed anachronisms are probably the result of the fact that the Pentateuch, like all other ancient Near Eastern literature, accrued annotations, updated geographical references, and updated grammar and vocabulary during its long period of transmission within ancient Israel.[34]

In the light of all of this, John Sailhamer has convincingly argued, this editing and annotating of the Mosaic core of the Pentateuch very likely went on until the end of the Old Testament period.[35] This fact in no way compromises the inspired character of the Pentateuch, since the point of such updating was to maintain the original sense of the inspired text so it would be understandable to a newer audience. Indeed, Jesus and the rest of the inspired authors of the New Testament clearly affirmed the Pentateuch to be the Word of God as it existed in their day. This means even if the annotative editing continued throughout the Old Testament period, it in no way compromised the revelatory character of the inspired text.

Similarly, such updating and annotating in no way compromised Mosaic authorship of the Pentateuch. Scholarly defenders of Mosaic authorship always

---

29. Archer, *Survey of the Old Testament*, 179; Kitchen, *Reliability of the Old Testament*, 324–28.

30. Archer, *Survey of the Old Testament*, 115–18; James Hoffmeier, *The Archaeology of the Bible* (Oxford: Lion Hudson, 2008), 46–53.

31. Archer, *Survey of the Old Testament*, 118–19; Hoffmeier, *Archaeology of the Bible*, 48.

32. John Kleinig, *Leviticus* (St. Louis: Concordia Publishing House, 2003), 17.

33. Kitchen, *Reliability of the Old Testament*, 338–39.

34. Kitchen, *Reliability of the Old Testament*, 304–6.

35. See the overall argument in John Sailhamer, *The Meaning of the Pentateuch: Revelation, Composition, and Interpretation* (Downers Grove, IL: InterVarsity Press, 2009).

have been careful to emphasize that affirming Moses is the author of the Pentateuch does not necessarily entail positing that the prophet wrote every single word of it.[36] After all, it seems unlikely that Moses wrote about his own death.

The subsequent books of the Old Testament and their prophetic authors drew on Moses' authority formalized in the prophetic criteria of Deuteronomy 18. All prophets that Israel came to recognize as authoritative by the time of the post-exilic period conformed to this pattern. All true prophets of the Old Testament prophesy in accordance with the analogy of faith established by the Pentateuch. Likewise, when the prophets spoke of things that would happen in the distant future, they also would prophesy concerning more immediate events so that their authority could be tested and confirmed in the hearing of Israel.

The fact that the fulfillment and validity of the prophetic office was witnessed in a corporate and public manner by Israel can in some measure serve as a response to the objection that a number of Old Testament works are anonymous. Some might complain that without knowing who the authors of certain Old Testament works were, it is difficult to know whether or not they conform to the pattern of testing established by Moses in Deuteronomy 18. In response to this it could be argued that even if the names of the people who wrote texts like Judges, 1 and 2 Kings, or 1 and 2 Chronicles have not come down to us, the prophets who composed these works were well known to ancient Israel and conformed to the Mosaic criteria. As a result of the corporate witness of Israel, the people of God came to view these texts as the Word of God and therefore a proper part of the canon.

It might also be the case that certain anonymous books in the Old Testament were composed by an already well-known prophet. For example, the block of history found in 1 Samuel through 2 Kings has much in common stylistically with the book of Jeremiah, and therefore very well could have been composed by Jeremiah himself or possibly Baruch, his authorized scribe.[37]

Yet another solution to the problem of literary anonymity might be that the Old Testament canon was validated by a well-known prophetic witness. For example, Ezra seems to have placed his stamp of canonicity on the Pentateuch (Ezra 8), and it may be that he publicly commended the other Old Testament books that came down to him. Indeed, there appears to have been a half-garbled memory of this in the rather bizarre legend believed by many church fathers that the books of the Old Testament were burned in the destruction of Jerusalem and that Ezra miraculously transcribed them by the prophetic Spirit of God.[38]

---

36. Horace Hummel, *The Word Becoming Flesh: An Introduction to the Origin, Purpose, and Meaning of the Old Testament* (St. Louis: Concordia Publishing House, 1979), 60–61; Young, *Introduction to the Old Testament*, 42, 45–46.

37. Richard Elliot Friedman, *Who Wrote the Bible?* (San Francisco: HarperOne, 1987), 145–48.

38. Gerhard, *On the Nature of Theology and Scripture*, 115–19. Gerhard summarizes these traditions and correctly rejects them as fanciful.

Indeed, in view of the imperatives of ancient scribal culture to establish canons of religious and literary material as part of the process of organizing a religious/political community, Karel Van der Toorn has argued it is credible that Ezra officially canonized the Pentateuch for the post-exilic community. He posits that much of the rest of the Old Testament was added throughout the early Second Temple period.[39] While Van der Toorn is obviously correct that at least some of the later post-exilic prophets and writings were likely added during a later period insofar as they post-date Ezra, the question remains: if one is willing to admit that Ezra canonized the Pentateuch, then why not the later portions of the Old Testament? After all, in very recent memory these works had proven themselves inspired by unambiguously fulfilling the Mosaic criteria for prophecy (i.e., they prophesied the destruction of Jerusalem and exile, which had come true). Why would they not be automatically recognized as valid prophecy and be used as authoritative?

Moreover, the fact that in the later Second Temple period the Sadducees accepted only the authority of the Pentateuch[40] cannot be taken as evidence of an earlier and less expansive canon being the norm. Indeed, many scholars describe the Sadducees as conservatives,[41] but the evidence points in the opposite direction.

First, the Zadokite priesthood that ruled Judah after the exile based its legitimacy on God's instructions to Ezekiel that the Aaronic clan of Zadok should hold the office of high priest from that point forward (Ez 48:11).[42] This need to legitimate the Zadokite priesthood suggests that in the early post-exilic period the official leadership of Israel at minimum acknowledged as canon Ezekiel and the Deuteronomistic history (1 Samuel through 2 Kings,[43] wherein David establishes Zadok as high priest and the idea of the temple itself). A canon that accepted the legitimacy of only the Pentateuch and these two other books would be strange, since it arbitrarily would tear the latter two books out of the wider blocks of tradition within which they are embedded, and also out of the overall flow of Old Testament history. Thus, it is more likely that the Zadokites accepted a much wider canon of the Old Testament, if not more or less the Old Testament as a whole. Second, since for centuries prior to the Maccabean crisis the Zadokites were able to sustain their rule in an ideologically credible way, it seems likely that the rest of post-exilic Israel accepted the canonicity of the Old Testament as well.

---

39. Karel Van der Toorn, *Scribal Culture and the Making of the Hebrew Bible* (Cambridge, MA: Harvard University Press, 2009), 248–51.

40. E. P. Sanders, *Judaism: Practice and Belief 63 BCE–66 CE* (Valley Forge, PA: Trinity Press International, 1992), 13.

41. John Drane, *Introducing the New Testament* (Oxford: Lion Hudson, 2010), 36.

42. Sanders, *Judaism*, 15.

43. Note that in ancient times 1 Samuel and 2 Kings were viewed as a single work. Francesca Aran Murphy, *1–2 Samuel* (Grand Rapids: Brazos Press, 2010), xvii.

Beyond this, the later Sadducees were made up largely of the supporters of the Hasmonean temple aristocracy[44] and therefore would have had significant ideological incentive to reject the claims of canonicity for the Old Testament beyond the Pentateuch. The Pentateuch itself requires only that the high priest be from an Aaronite clan (Numbers 18), which the Hasmoneans were, rather than a member of the house of Zadok as Ezekiel had mandated. Also, since the Old Testament outside of the Pentateuch insists that the Israelite king must be of the house of David, the logical implication is that Hasmoneans would be ineligible for kingship, an office they had claimed prior to the advent of the Romans. Total delegitimization of Hasmonean rule thus probably would have been incentive enough for the Sadducees to reject most of the Old Testament.

Ultimately, even if we are not able to resolve the issues regarding anonymous works of the Old Testament through these arguments, all that is necessary for the church to know is Christ's evaluation of the Old Testament as a whole. As we have previously demonstrated, Christ Himself conforms to the Mosaic criteria of prophecy. By dying and rising, Christ fulfilled the whole of the Old Testament and proved that all He said and did was approved by God. So we know that all the works of the Old Testament are the inspired and inerrant Word of God because Jesus has stamped His approval on them as canonical and inspired.

Moreover, despite the disagreements between various sectarian groups within Judaism in the Second Temple period regarding the content of the canon, we can be certain of what Jesus understood to be the canon of the Old Testament. By the time of Christ, the Pharisees affirmed the canonicity of the Old Testament in more or less the form that modern Jews and Protestants understand it. There is significant evidence of this fact in the writings of Josephus (who himself was a Pharisee)[45] and later Rabbinic literature.[46] Since in His debates with the Pharisees Jesus presupposed a common understanding with them of what constitutes the Scriptures and affirmed these to be the Word of God, the church's decisions about the canon of the Old Testament should correspond to the understanding of the Pharisees rather than that of any of the other parties in Judaism.[47] Since the Pharisaic canon did not include the Apocrypha the church cannot view these books as being the inspired Word of God, since Jesus obviously did not either.[48]

---

44. Sanders, *Judaism*, 28.

45. Josephus, *Contra Apionem* 1.8, in *The Works of Josephus*, ed. and trans. William Whiston (Peabody, MA: Hendrickson Publishers, 1995), 776; Duane L. Christensen, "Josephus and the Twenty-Two-Book Canon of Sacred Scripture," *Journal of the Evangelical Theology Society* 29, no. 1 (1986): 37–46; Gerhard, *On the Nature of Theology and Scripture*, 79–80.

46. F. F. Bruce, *The Canon of Scripture* (Downers Grove, IL: InterVarsity Press, 1988), 32–38.

47. Gerhard, *On the Nature of Theology and Scripture*, 85.

48. Bruce, *Canon of Scripture*, 41–42; Montgomery, *Tracatus Logico-Theologicus*, 141. See further arguments in favor of the majority of Second Temple Jews affirming the validity of the Old Testament (minus the Apocrypha) as a whole in Roger Beckwith, *The Old Testament Canon of the New Testament Church and Its Background in Early Judaism* (1986; reprint, Eugene, OR: Wipf & Stock, 2008).

THE CANON OF THE NEW TESTAMENT

As we have previously seen, Christ promised that the apostles would be His inspired and infallible witnesses to the nations. Much as the Old Testament prophets could appeal to Mosaic authorization, so too the New Testament canon is authorized by Jesus' promise that the apostles would possess infallible teaching authority. In this sense, although apostolic testimony is just as infallible as the prophetic authority of the Old Testament, it validated itself by different means. Whereas Old Testament authority validated itself by events in the future (that is, by the fulfillment of prophecy), apostolic authority looked back to Christ's authority and its validation through His resurrection from the dead. Indeed, all prophecy is centered in Christ: Old Testament prophecy found its ultimate validation in the future coming of Christ, whereas New Testament apostolic testimony pointed back to a Christ who had already come.

Christ's authorization of the apostles' ministry extends to all the books they produced as well as to the books they commissioned to be produced by their immediate followers. The specific promise of Christ concerning the apostles is significant because it serves as an objective measure of the canon. Certain books are to be viewed as inspired and others are not, based on these criteria. Again, canonicity and inspiration attach to the books of the Bible not because the church has selected them arbitrarily. Rather, canonicity depends on the promise and command of Jesus concerning the apostles and those they authorized.

The Authorship and Canonicity of the Four Gospels
At the core of the apostolic testimony found in the New Testament are the four Gospels. The Gospels are central to the apostolic testimony, not only because they give a direct witness to the reality of God's salvation manifest in Jesus but also because, as Moses authorized subsequent prophecy in Israel in Deuteronomy, Jesus in the Gospels authorizes the infallibility of apostolic witness.

The Gospels were written by at least two apostles (John and Matthew) and two persons authorized by the apostles (Mark by Peter, Luke by Paul). They therefore bear the stamp of the risen Christ's authority. Although liberal scholars have questioned the reliability of the four Gospels and their authorship, there are many good arguments in favor of both their reliability and their traditional authorship.

First, it is often alleged that the Gospels were written anonymously, and that after being circulated without titles for decades they arbitrarily received their current titles at some point in the early second century. This claim is absurd for a number of reasons. There is no manuscript evidence for this position: every copy of the Gospels we possess from the early church bears the traditional titles.[49]

---

49. H. H. Drake Williams, *Jesus, Tried and True: Why the Four Gospels Provide the Best*

Beyond this, as Martin Hengel observes, most writings in antiquity had titles and attributed authors. Those that did not have them quickly gained both. When the author or title was invented after the fact, texts often would circulate under a variety of titles and authors.[50]

These facts make it highly unlikely that the Gospels were originally anonymous. Christianity was widely disseminated throughout the Roman Empire by the end of the first century, yet as far as we know there were never any alternative titles of attribution for the Gospels. If titles had been added later, undoubtedly there would have been a variety of local traditions regarding their origin. Instead, we have a uniform attribution of the Gospels throughout early Christianity, suggesting that these titles of attribution are original to the text.[51]

Second, the New Testament documents themselves are blunt about the fact that the early church was filled with debates regarding authority. There was rivalry among the followers of different apostles (1 Cor 1:12; Galatians 1–2) as well as the warnings of Jesus and the New Testament authors about false prophets (Mt 7:15; 2 Pt 2:1–22). Thus, the claim that the Gospels were written and circulated anonymously makes little sense. If the early church had such significant debates about authority, it is hardly credible that these believers would have accepted and used in public church services anonymous gospels which lacked any specific claims to be connected to an apostle or other authoritative witness.[52] The liberal critics make this claim even more absurd by suggesting that the church did this for decades before adding names to the texts.

Third, the claim that the names of the authors of Gospels were added only later raises the question: if later Christians had their choice of authors to which to attribute the Gospels, why did they not choose more authoritative authors? Why bother attributing the Gospel of Mark to a mere follower of Peter when it was possible to attribute it to Peter himself? Why a Gospel of Luke and not a Gospel of Paul? Why choose a second-tier apostle in the person of Matthew? Indeed, later pseudonymous gospels certainly did attempt to bolster their authority by claiming to be written by more prominent apostles.[53] By contrast, the canonical Gospels are far more modest in their claims. Of course this argument does not apply to the Gospel of John, but as we will see below, there is much evidence to suggest John was the author of the Gospel that bears his name. Ultimately the fact that the Gospels for the most part are attributed to minor figures in the early church is a strong indication of the authenticity of their titles and traditional authorship.

Picture of Jesus (Eugene, OR: Wipf & Stock, 2013), 59–60.

50. Martin Hengel, *The Four Gospels and the One Gospel of Jesus Christ: An Investigation of the Collection and Origin of the Canonical Gospels*, trans. John Bowden (Harrisburg, PA: Trinity Press International, 2000), 48.

51. Hengel, *Four Gospels*, 54.

52. Hengel makes a similar though not identical point. See Hengel, *Four Gospels*, 116–27.

53. Hengel, *Four Gospels*, 45.

Fourth, the patristic evidence also must be taken into consideration. Many of the patristic theologians lived in communities established by the apostles or their immediate followers and thus would have access to direct lines of tradition. Indeed, according to Charles E. Hill in his book *Who Chose the Gospels?* there is convincing evidence that the traditions these men received regarding the authorship and even structure of the canon of the four Gospels go back to apostolic times.

To prove this, Hill starts with manuscript evidence and the later Ante-Nicene fathers. From there he works his way back to the end of the apostolic era. Hill shows that the majority of early manuscripts and fragments of the Gospels are in fact of the four canonical Gospels rather than of any non-canonical gospels. This is true even in the Roman-era garbage dumps of Egypt, a region known for being a hotbed of heresy in the early church.[54] Even there, fragments of the canonical Gospels outnumber the non-canonical gospels three to one.[55] Likewise, even from the earliest times, when the Gospels were bound together in a common codex they were always bound with other canonical Gospels and never with non-canonical ones.[56] Moreover, the Ante-Nicene fathers and early canonical lists like the late second-century Muratorian fragment uniformly endorse or strongly imply their endorsement of the canon of the four canonical Gospels and their traditional titles and origin stories.[57] The early church also seems to have agreed uniformly about the order in which the Gospels were written (Matthew first, John last).

Overall this evidence suggests that there was an early, very strong, and geographically diffuse consensus in the early church that the four canonical Gospels were indeed Scripture and that they were handed down from the apostles. All this prompts Hill to ask the fairly obvious question: what can account for this consensus over an enormous geographical area? Indeed, this uniformity in tradition is remarkable because it extends not only to the account of the authorship of the Gospels but also to the order in which they were written.[58] In order to answer this question Hill follows the evidence to fragments taken from Bishop Papias of Hierapolis's book *Exposition of the Lord's Oracles*.

Papias's book probably was written sometime between A.D. 110 and 130. It is preserved only in fragments found in Eusebius's *The Ecclesiastical History* (circa A.D. 340).[59] In one fragment Eusebius cites, Papias explicitly states that he received the traditions he is expounding orally from either immediate followers of the apostles or persons who were actual disciples of Jesus, namely, a man named Aristion and "John the Elder." In another fragment Papias tells us that

54. C. E. Hill, *Who Chose the Gospels? Probing the Great Gospel Conspiracy* (New York: Oxford University Press, 2010), 23–24.
55. Hill, *Who Chose the Gospels?* 18.
56. Hill, *Who Chose the Gospels?* 117.
57. Hill, *Who Chose the Gospels?* 69–102.
58. Hill, *Who Chose the Gospels?* 211–13.
59. Hill, *Who Chose the Gospels?* 208.

"the Elder" (that is, John) told him that Mark wrote down the recollections of Peter and that Matthew originally wrote his Gospel in Hebrew (in actuality, probably Aramaic).[60]

Even though Papias's fragment directly gives the origins only of Mark and Matthew,[61] it is interesting to note that Eusebius also gives the origin stories for the Gospels of Luke and John in another passage where he recounts the same origin stories provided by Papias for Mark and Matthew.[62] Oddly, he does not tell his readers directly where this information came from. Hill suggests these traditions also come from Papias's book. Eusebius simply takes it for granted that his readers would recognize that the information about Gospel origins came from the same source.[63] Since Eusebius gives no alternative sources for his information regarding the origins of Luke and John, this seems to be a reasonable inference.

Adding to this evidence, later authors who had direct access to Papias's work, such as Irenaeus, appear to cite the same tradition about all four canonical Gospels as Eusebius does. This is the case regarding not only the authorship and circumstances within which they were written but also the order of their composition (Matthew first, John last).[64]

As we saw earlier, at least regarding the origins of Matthew and Mark, Papias credits traditions received from the Elder John, "the disciple of the Lord." That this "Elder" was in fact John the apostle seems likely, since all the authors within the Ante-Nicene period that cite Papias understand John the Elder to be John the apostle. In particular, Irenaeus identifies the Elder as the apostle John and tells us that John and Papias were both associates of his teacher, Polycarp.[65]

Of course, many might note the fact that Eusebius himself in commenting on the fragment claims that John the apostle and John the Elder are two distinct persons. According to Eusebius, John the apostle is one of the Twelve, whereas the Elder[66] is seen implicitly as one of the seventy-two (Lk 10:1).[67] One of the problems with this claim is that no one prior to Eusebius ever spoke of a person distinct from John the apostle named John the Elder.[68] Indeed, as we saw above, Irenaeus, who had a living connection with both Papias and John, held that the

---

60. Eusebius, *The Ecclesiastical History* 3.39, in *Eusebius—The Church History: A New Translation with Commentary*, trans. and ed. Paul Maier (Grand Rapids: Kregel Publications, 1999), 127–30.

61. Hill, *Who Chose the Gospels?* 210–11.

62. Eusebius, *Ecclesiastical History* 3.24; Maier, *Eusebius*, 113–15.

63. Hill, *Who Chose the Gospels?* 219.

64. Hill, *Who Chose the Gospels?* 221.

65. "And these things are borne witness to in writing by Papias, the hearer of John, and a companion of Polycarp . . ." Irenaeus, *Against the Heresies* 5.33.4; ANF 1:563.

66. Eusebius, *Ecclesiastical History* 3.39; Maier, *Eusebius*, 127.

67. Craig S. Keener, *The Gospel of John: A Commentary*, 2 vols. (Peabody, MA: Hendrickson Publishers, 2003), 1:97. Keener correctly observes that ancient authors often conflate two persons with the same name. Nevertheless, they just as accidentally create two persons out of one individual.

68. Simon Kistemaker, *Revelation* (Grand Rapids: Baker Academic, 2001), 20–21.

apostle is the Elder spoken of by Papias. Since Eusebius lived two centuries later it is very difficult to prioritize his testimony over that of Irenaeus.

Although Hill does not mention Eusebius's possible motivations for making the distinction between the Elder and the apostle, it seems more than likely that he wished to use the distinction as a way to distance St. John from the authorship of the Book of Revelation. In the same passage Eusebius attributes to John the Elder the Book of Revelation,[69] a book about which he earlier implicitly expresses doubts.[70] His doubts stem largely from his rejection of millennialism (something he criticizes Papias for supporting[71]), which he thinks the Book of Revelation will necessarily promote if read incorrectly. Hence, although Eusebius does not completely reject Revelation, he seems to have strong motivation to demote its importance by questioning its authorship.

Nevertheless, in the light of the identification of the apostle with the Elder throughout the early church, it seems very unlikely that Papias speaks of a distinct disciple of Jesus named John the Elder. Indeed, as Hill notes, it would take a massive conspiracy to promote such a misidentification with such uniformity over such a vast geographical area. Such a conspiracy strains credulity.[72]

Beyond the traditions concerning Mark and Matthew that Papias explicitly attributes to the Elder (i.e., John the apostle), Hill conjectures that the aforementioned traditions concerning Luke and John also come from John.[73] The information Papias attributes to John about Matthew and Mark always appears in tandem with the traditions about Luke and John in later sources (Irenaeus, the Muratorian fragment, Eusebius, etc.).[74] Similarly, the traditions regarding the origins of the Gospels share a series of other extremely significant and telling characteristics:

(a) A concern to maintain that each of the Gospels had its origin in the preaching of one or more of the apostles of Jesus.
(b) A further idea that the apostles, who were first of all preachers and teachers of the gospel of Jesus Christ, did not simply take it upon themselves to write but they, or their associates, wrote at the request of others.
(c) A prevalent use of some form of the words 'remember' (cf. John 14.26) or 'remembrances' to describe these Gospels as first-hand reports of the Lord's disciples who knew him personally. We have seen how Justin [Martyr] would later use this concept, designating the Gospels as 'Memoirs of the Apostles,' and even how the *Epistle of the Apostles* [an apocryphal writing] emphasized, like John's Gospel and I John do, the sensory experience of Jesus by those who bore their witness of him.

69. Eusebius, *Ecclesiastical History* 3.39; Maier, *Eusebius*, 127.
70. Eusebius, *Ecclesiastical History* 3.25; Maier, *Eusebius*, 115.
71. Eusebius, *Ecclesiastical History* 3.39; Maier, *Eusebius*, 129.
72. Hill, *Who Chose the Gospels?* 216.
73. Hill, *Who Chose the Gospels?* 217.
74. Hill, *Who Chose the Gospels?* 217.

(d) A concern with the 'order' or 'literary arrangement' of the contents of the Gospels, with the undertones of a desire to defend from criticism. This concern is repeated in the *Muratorian Fragment* . . .

(e) An attempt to find an 'endorsement' for each Gospel from another accepted, apostolic source.[75]

Ultimately the implication of all this is that the traditions concerning the authorship and canon of the four Gospels come from a common source. For this source's traditions concerning the four Gospels to receive such wide and uniform acceptance, it would have had to be supremely authoritative; namely, it would have had to be apostolic. All these factors together point to the conclusion that John the apostle verified the authorship of the four Gospels and established their canon.

Finally, beyond the external evidence of the traditional authorship, there is evidence within the Gospels themselves. Richard Bauckham has shown that the Gospels bear literary features that suggest the authors were themselves eyewitnesses or had access to eyewitness testimony. One feature of the Gospels that points to their status as eyewitness testimony is their use of names. Bauckham demonstrates that statistics gleaned from ancient records, histories, and inscriptional evidence reveal that there was a series of common Jewish names in first-century Palestine. The occurrences of names reported in the Gospels correlate nearly perfectly with the evidence for naming practices in Palestine. This fact is significant because Jewish people in other parts of the Roman Empire named their children differently than Palestinian Jews. If the Gospel writers had not been eyewitnesses or at least had not employed eyewitnesses, the names they reported in the Gospels would have been very different. Indeed, had they simply made up the names out of a "novelistic interest" (Bultmann), they would have chosen names largely reflecting their own cultural and geographical environment. Bauckham further suggests that the Gospel writers mention specific persons by name because they would be known to their communities as eyewitnesses.[76]

Another groundbreaking argument Bauckham makes involves his identification of a literary feature he calls "*inclusio* of eyewitness."[77] Bauckham demonstrates that many Hellenistic biographies, particularly those of great philosophers, employ this literary device. For those unfamiliar with it, an *inclusio* is a literary device based on a concentric principle. It serves as a means of bracketing literary material in a written work. For example, at the beginning of Mark's Gospel the "ripping" of the heavens at Jesus' baptism (Mk 1:10) parallels the "ripping" of the curtain of the temple that is mentioned at the crucifixion (Mk 15:38).[78] The result is the

75. Hill, *Who Chose the Gospels?* 220.
76. Bauckham, *Jesus and the Eyewitnesses*, 39–92.
77. Bauckham, *Jesus and the Eyewitnesses*, 114–55.
78. Stephen Motyer, "The Rending of the Veil: A Markan Pentecost," *New Testament Studies* 33, no. 1 (1987): 155–57.

bracketing of the ministry of Jesus between two instances of "ripping." In the case of early Hellenistic biographies the *inclusio* of the eyewitness served as a means of identifying the main historical source for the biography. Often the philosopher's disciple who served as the main source of the information utilized by the biographer is mentioned at the beginning of the work and at the end.[79]

Bauckham argues that the Gospels themselves employ this literary device. This pattern points not only to the Gospels being eyewitness accounts but also to their traditional authorship. Although Matthew lacks an *inclusio* of this sort,[80] in Mark's Gospel Peter is mentioned at the beginning and end, thereby strongly suggesting the use of the *inclusio* of eyewitness form.[81] This fact neatly correlates with Irenaeus and Papias's tradition that Peter was Mark's main source for his Gospel.[82] Luke employs this same Petrine *inclusio* (suggesting he is acknowledging his use of Mark's Gospel), while employing an even wider *inclusio* of Jesus' female followers.[83] The use of this device suggests that these women were a major source of Luke's information (though not the ultimate source of his authorization, who was Paul: Col 4:14; 1 Tm 5:18), and this fact may explain the prominent role women play in his Gospel.

John's Gospel also contains a Petrine *inclusio*, with a wider one for the Beloved Disciple. Correlating well with Hill's findings that John established the canon of the four Gospels, this literary structure suggests that John recognizes and affirms the validity of Peter's testimony embedded in the Synoptic Gospels while at the same time wishing to add his own testimony to it.

At the beginning of the Gospel the Beloved Disciple is seen following after Jesus subsequent to John the Baptist's testimony, and he "abided" (ἔμειναν) with Him for the day (Jn 1:38–39). Only after this is Peter mentioned (Jn 1:40–42). At the end of the Gospel Jesus reinstates the fallen Peter with the famous "feed my sheep" counsel (Jn 21:15–17). Then Jesus discovers that as He and Peter are walking along, the Beloved Disciple is following after them (Jn 21:20). His action of following Jesus and Peter directly mirrors his activity at the beginning of the Gospel. Likewise, just as the Beloved Disciple "abides" with Jesus for the day at the beginning of the Gospel, at the end of the Gospel Jesus askes Peter, "What is it to you if he [the Beloved Disciple] remains [abides, μένειν] until I come?" (Jn 21:22).[84]

Unfortunately, Bauckham does not consider this Beloved Disciple to be John the apostle but rather the aforementioned John the Elder. Bauckham

---

79. Bauckham, *Jesus and the Eyewitnesses*, 132–54.
80. Bauckham, *Jesus and the Eyewitnesses*, 131–32.
81. Bauckham, *Jesus and the Eyewitnesses*, 124–27.
82. Kruger, *Question of the Canon*, 183.
83. Bauckham, *Jesus and the Eyewitnesses*, 129–31.
84. Bauckham, *Jesus and the Eyewitnesses*, 128–29.

makes a number of arguments against the disciple John being the author. But he still posits that the author of the Gospel is an eyewitness based on the internal structure of the Gospel.[85]

Several observations should be made in response to Bauckham's rejection of John the apostle's authorship. First, if one is willing to admit that the author of John is an eyewitness, the character of that eyewitness does not suggest a second- or third-tier disciple. Rather, it suggests someone who was one of the Twelve. Indeed, the Gospel itself states that the author was a member of Jesus' inner circle and even leaned on His chest at the Last Supper (Jn 13:23). This corresponds best with John the apostle.

Second, the author is an eyewitness and everyone in the early church believed him to be the apostle John. Incidentally, this includes Eusebius, the person who seemingly invented John the Elder as a distinct historical figure. If everyone made this identification, why would it not be simpler to affirm the apostle John was the author? In this vein, it should be observed that Irenaeus, a follower of one of John's students, Polycarp, testifies that the apostle is indeed the Beloved Disciple and the author of the Gospel.[86] If John did not write the Gospel that bears his name, we would have to charge John's disciple Polycarp with an outright lie. For a faithful bishop who was eventually martyred, a lie of this magnitude seems highly unlikely.

Third, there is other internal evidence for John's authorship that is worth noting. John A. T. Robinson's posthumously published *The Priority of John* uncovers a surprising collection of facts in support of John's authorship and the historical accuracy of the Gospel in general. Robinson largely agrees with our earlier argument about the reliability of Irenaeus's tradition concerning John's authorship as mediated through Polycarp.[87] He also demonstrates that the author of the Gospel possessed an extensive knowledge of the customs of first-century Judaism, the geography of Palestine, and the details and chronology of Jesus' life.[88] It seems very unlikely that this knowledge would have been accessible to an author living far from Palestine in the post–A.D. 70 era, simply making up most of the Gospel out of his own imagination. This evidence thus greatly undermines typical liberal theories of authorship. Although Robinson's contextual proofs are by no means definitive on their own, when they are combined with Bauckham's findings of signs of eyewitness testimony, the reliability of the tradition of Irenaeus, and the uniform witness of the early church, it seem almost certain that John the apostle is indeed the author of the Gospel that bears his name.

---

85. Bauckham, *Jesus and the Eyewitnesses*, 358–471.
86. Irenaeus, *Against the Heresies* 3.1.1; ANF 1:415.
87. John A. T. Robinson, *The Priority of John* (London: Meyer-Stone Books, 1985), 100–122.
88. Robinson, *Priority of John*, 45–93, 123–58.

The Authorship and Canonicity of the New Testament Epistles

The affirmation of canonicity based on apostolic authorship faces other challenges with the Epistles. Although the texts of these documents more often than not explicitly affirm that they were written by an apostle, modern liberal scholarship in many cases has discounted the author's explicit self-identification. We will briefly address below the arguments of the critics with regard to the Johannine, Pauline, and Petrine Epistles.

Regarding first the question of the authenticity of the Johannine Epistles, there are many reasons to consider them the authentic work of the apostle John. Although the author does not give his name directly, the style and theological vocabulary closely approximates that of the Gospel of John.[89] Thus, it is not very difficult to accept the notion that the author of the Johannine Epistles is the same as that of the Gospel, which, as we have already seen, was most certainly written by John the apostle. Indeed, as in the Gospel, the author of at least the first Epistle claims to be an eyewitness to the life of Christ (1 Jn 1:1–5). In 2 and 3 John the author calls himself the Elder, which correlates well with the tradition of Papias and Irenaeus that John was called the Elder. Moreover, since the title Elder was used interchangeably with Bishop in much of the early church,[90] John's self-designation as the Elder also correlates well with the tradition that in his old age the apostle served as a bishop for the churches in western Asia Minor.[91]

Similar evidence validates John's authorship of the Book of Revelation. John sends the book out to the seven churches in the manner of a bishop exercising counsel and oversight. It is also worth noting that the author simply calls himself John. Since this was a common Jewish name, the author must have expected that the churches of Asia Minor would be able to identify immediately who he was.[92] Incidentally, this apparent expectation also could serve as a convincing basis to rule out the existence of a separate figure named John the Elder. If another John was operative in the same region at the same time, why would the author of the Book of Revelation not wish to clarify his identity? Moreover, we have Irenaeus's tradition, received directly from Polycarp and the church of Ephesus, that the apostle was the author.[93] Last, the Book of Revelation uses much of the same unique theological vocabulary as John's Gospels and Epistles. For example, Revelation calls Christ the Word of God and the Lamb of God (Rv 5:12; 19:13), much like the Gospel and the Epistles.[94]

---

89. Andreas J. Köstenberger, *A Theology of John's Gospel and Letters* (Grand Rapids: Zondervan, 2009), 133–35.

90. Stuart Hall, *Doctrine and Practice in the Early Church* (Eugene, OR: Wipf & Stock, 2011), 31.

91. Eusebius, *Ecclesiastical History* 3.23–24; Maier, *Eusebius*, 110–15.

92. David Chilton, *The Days of Vengeance: An Exposition of the Book of Revelation* (Ft. Worth: Dominion Press, 1990), 15.

93. Irenaeus, *Against the Heresies* 4.20.11; ANF 1:491.

94. Paul Coxon, *Exploring the New Exodus in John: A Biblical Theological Investigation of John Chapters 5–10* (Eugene, OR: Resource Publications, 2014), 38–39; S. S. Smalley, "John's

Paul's Epistles offer other challenges. Although even liberal scholars hold that seven of these works were written by Paul (Romans, 1 and 2 Corinthians, Galatians, 1 Thessalonians, Philippians, and Philemon), others are considered either highly questionable in their authorship (Ephesians and Colossians) or outright forgeries by later generations (2 Thessalonians, Titus, 1 and 2 Timothy).[95]

There is much evidence to commend the authenticity of 2 Thessalonians. Stylistically, the differences between the first and second letters to the Thessalonians are quite insignificant.[96] It also could be argued that the subject matter of the Epistle logically follows from Paul's previous correspondence to the Thessalonians. In the first letter Paul emphasized the suddenness of the second coming of Christ (1 Thes 5:2), which seems to have caused a panic in the community (2 Thes 2:2; 3:6–15). The second letter seeks to soothe the fears of the community by adding that prior to the end of all things there will be definite signs, notably the revelation of the "man of lawlessness" (2 Thes 2:3–5).[97]

With regard to Ephesians, Colossians, and the Pastoral Epistles, one of the main arguments against Paul's authorship is the alleged difference in style and vocabulary between these works and the seven authentic Pauline letters.[98] This argument is faulty for a number of reasons. First, the style of any given author develops over time, and hence differences are inevitable in documents written over a long period of time (e.g., the late A.D. 40s to the early A.D. 60s). If one adds to this the fact that the subject matter of these Epistles (particularly the Pastorals) is quite different from that of Romans or Galatians, differences in vocabulary become all the more explicable.

Second, most documents in the ancient world were dictated to a scribe who was authorized to modify or improve the style and vocabulary of the one dictating the document. Hence, differences in language and style may be attributed simply to different scribes being involved in the production of the different letters.[99] Incidentally, this is probably also the best explanation of the

---

Revelation and John's Community," *Bulletin of the John Rylands Library* 69, no. 2 (1987): 549–71.

95. James D. G. Dunn and John Rogerson, eds., *Eerdmans Commentary on the Bible* (Grand Rapids: Wm. B. Eerdmans, 2003), 1274. There is a minority opinion affirming their authenticity, even among critics who possess a lower view of Scripture. See the following defenses of the authenticity of all the Pauline letters in Joachim Jeremias, *Die Briefe an Timotheus und Titus* (Göttingen: Vandenhoeck & Ruprecht, 1953), 3–8; Luke Timothy Johnson, *Letters to Paul's Delegates: 1 Timothy, 2 Timothy, Titus* (Valley Forge, PA: Trinity Press International, 1996), 2–32; Donald Guthrie, *The Pastoral Epistles: An Introduction and Commentary* (Grand Rapids: Wm. B. Eerdmans, 1990), 18–62; Knight, *Pastoral Epistles*, 13–52.

96. Andreas J. Köstenberger, L. Scott Kellum, and Charles Quarles, *The Cradle, the Cross, and the Crown: An Introduction to the New Testament* (Nashville: B & H Academic, 2009), 435.

97. For the alternative view that 2 Thessalonians was written first, see Bo Reicke, *Examining Paul's Letters: The History of the Pauline Correspondence* (Edinburgh: T&T Clark, 2001).

98. Donald Guthrie, *New Testament Introduction* (Downers Grove, IL: InterVarsity Press, 1990), 619.

99. Dennis Jowers, "Observations on the Authenticity of the Pastoral Epistles," *Western Reformed Seminary Journal* 12, no. 2 (2005): 10.

differences between 1 and 2 Peter. Peter's first letter was written through the scribal help of Silvanus, which accounts for the more polished style. The second letter, with its rougher style, probably was written through the hand of a less skilled scribe, or perhaps even by the apostle himself.

Among other challenges to their apostolic authenticity, it is often alleged that the Pastoral Epistles promote more sophisticated models of church governance than those found in the other letters of Paul.[100] This detail is taken as an indication of the Pastoral Epistles being both late and inauthentic. In response to this, Luke Timothy Johnson has argued that the structure of ecclesiastical governance that Paul suggests seems to be adapted largely from the Hellenistic synagogue.[101] Hence they are neither elaborate nor innovative. It is clear as well from Paul's other letters and the Book of Acts that the church was already well organized and had distinct offices in its first decades (Acts 6; 1 Cor 12:28–30).

With regard to the Pastoral Epistles' blueprint for church governance, liberal scholars often claim that the letters bear the stamp of a later era in which the church needed to devise ways of governing itself as a result of disappointment in the delay of the parousia.[102] This is also a weak argument. Not only is the theory that early Christians were disappointed by the delay of the parousia largely a scholarly construct (indeed, there is little evidence of this), but apocalyptically minded groups (notably, the Jewish Essenes living at Qumran) often have sophisticated organizational structures.[103]

In terms of external evidence there are good indications that in the early second century both Polycarp[104] and Ignatius of Antioch[105] were familiar with and utilized the Pastoral Epistles, although they did not quote them directly. Irenaeus very clearly knows the Pastoral Epistles,[106] as does the Muratorian fragment, which explicitly recognizes all thirteen Pauline Epistles as authentic.[107] Thus, persons who lived relatively close to the period of the composition of the letters viewed them as being authentic. These figures had access to lines of historical tradition that modern liberal scholars do not possess.

---

100. Guthrie, *New Testament Introduction*, 615.

101. Luke Timothy Johnson, *The First and Second Letters to Timothy: A New Translation with Introduction and Commentary* (New York: Doubleday, 2001), 222–24.

102. Pheme Perkins, *Reading the New Testament* (New York: Paulist Press, 1988), 281–83.

103. See discussion of the structure of the Essene community rule in Sarianna Metso, *The Textual Development of the Qumran Community Rule* (Leiden: Brill, 1997).

104. Michael Holmes, "Polycarp's *Letter to the Philippians* and the Writings That Later Formed the New Testament," in *The Reception of the New Testament in the Apostolic Fathers*, ed. Andrew Gregory and Christopher Tuckett (Oxford: Oxford University Press, 2005), 226.

105. Paul Foster, "Ignatius of Antioch and the Writings That Later Formed the New Testament," in Gregory and Tuckett, *Reception of the New Testament*, 185.

106. Benjamin White, "How to Read a Book: Irenaeus and the Pastoral Epistles Reconsidered," *Vigiliae Christianae* 65 (2011): 125–49.

107. Benjamin Fiore, *The Pastoral Epistles: First Timothy, Second Timothy, Titus* (Collegeville: Liturgical Press, 2006), 8.

In response some scholars might cite the fact that the heretic Marcion's scriptural canon of the mid-second century did not contain the Pastoral Epistles. From this fact it is inferred that there were at least some collections of Paul's letters in the second century that did not recognize Paul's authorship of the Pastoral Epistles.[108] Nevertheless, Marcion, who rejected the Old Testament and who had been censored by ecclesiastical authorities, probably would not favor the Pastoral Epistles since they commend both the authority of the Old Testament and respect for ecclesiastical authorities. In fact, within his own canon Marcion creatively edited Paul's letters and Luke's Gospel to remove any references to the Old Testament.[109] Hence, in view of the fact that Marcion was accustomed to removing theological authorities he found objectionable, it is not unlikely that in creating his own canon he would have removed the Pastoral Epistles from the collections of the Pauline letters he inherited.

Finally, with regard to the Petrine witness we note that the authorship of Peter's first letter was never questioned in the early church.[110] And in contrast to the Pauline Epistles, liberal scholars recognize no writings by Peter with which they can negatively compare the style of the Petrine Epistles. They often argue that the style of 1 Peter is far beyond anything a simple fisherman would be capable of writing, but as we have seen, this argument does not hold up. Peter says explicitly that he writes through Silvanus, who would have elevated the style of the Epistle as scribes in the ancient world were empowered to do.

Turning to 2 Peter, the authorship of which is also disputed, the author states in one passage that Paul's letters are at times difficult to understand (2 Pt 3:16)—not something a later forger would have put in the apostle's mouth. Nigel Turner also has described the style of the letter as "Jewish Greek," a style consistent with what a simple Jewish fisherman would have used.[111]

Did the Apostles Establish the Canon?

As should be clear from this discussion, the claims to apostolic origins made by the New Testament documents are extremely credible and grounded in objective historical fact. From this it is assured that they possess the infallibility Christ promised the apostolic witness and therefore legitimately belong to the canon. But it is also possible to go beyond the argument for mere apostolic authorship of each individual. Below we will argue that a case can be made that at least certain blocks of canonical materials, if not the whole canonical list itself, were recognized and authorized during the apostolic period. If valid, this

108. J. J. Clabeaux, *A Lost Edition of the Letters of Paul: A Reassessment of the Text of the Pauline Corpus Attested by Marcion* (Washington, DC: Catholic Biblical Association, 1989).

109. Joseph Lienhard, *The Bible, the Church, and Authority: The Canon of the Christian Bible in History and Theology* (Collegeville, MN: Liturgical Press, 1995), 34.

110. Donald Hagner, *The New Testament: A Historical and Theological Introduction* (Grand Rapids: Baker Academic, 2012), 688.

111. Nigel Turner, *A Grammar of New Testament Greek*, 4 vols. (Edinburgh: T&T Clark 1980), 4:142–43.

argument would suggest that the canonical decisions of the fourth century were correct not simply because they accurately ascertained the apostolic source of each writing. Rather, their canonical lists grew organically out of the implied or explicit decisions the apostles themselves made about their own writings and their apostolic co-witnesses in the faith.

As we have already seen, the goal of the writing of Sacred Scripture is the mission of the church to proclaim Christ through Word and sacraments. Christ's command and promise to the apostles that they would be His witnesses before the nations (Acts 1:8) entails the authorization of New Testament canon. In this capacity the apostles divided the mission field amongst themselves. This is particularly clear from the official divisions of missions that Paul recounts at the beginning of Galatians (Gal 2:7). In the light of this division, Earle Ellis has argued that different blocks of written material within the New Testament canon correspond to these differing missions: Jacobean (Jewish): James, Matthew, Jude; Pauline: Paul's letters, Luke/Acts, Hebrews; Johannine: John's Gospel, John's letters, Revelation; Petrine: 1 and 2 Peter, Mark.[112] Ellis's suggestion makes a great deal of sense. If the apostles agreed upon and validated one another's missions, a logical outgrowth of this mutual affirmation would be validation of one another's written testimony in the service of these missions.

In making this argument we will follow a line of reasoning first pursued by the great Lutheran confessional theologian Martin Chemnitz. In his *Examination of the Council of Trent* (1565–1573) Chemnitz makes an argument in favor of direct apostolic authorization of the canon in an implicit attempt to counteract the Tridentine fathers' claim that the authority of the Scriptures was dependent on the church's authority. Of course, we have already seen that the Roman Catholic theory of scriptural authority falsely conflates the category of canon with that of Scripture. We also have observed that taken on their own terms the books of the New Testament can credibly claim apostolic authorship.[113] Nevertheless, Chemnitz's argument is worth considering. In showing that the canon of the New Testament can be established directly from the judgments of the apostles themselves, confessional Lutherans are able to put up yet another apologetic bulwark for the biblical faith of the Reformation.

Beginning with John's Gospel and other writings, we have a very firm witness. As we have already seen, the combination of the Petrine *inclusio* in John's Gospel and Papias's Gospel origins tradition supports the conclusion that John affirmed not only the canonical authority of his writings (Gospel of John, 1–3 John, Revelation) but also the authority and apostolicity of the Synoptic Gospels.

---

112. Earle Ellis, *The Making of the New Testament Documents* (Leiden: Brill, 2002), 28–49.

113. "In the New Testament John saw the writings of the three evangelists and approved them. Paul marked his epistles with a peculiar sign; Peter saw them and commended them to the Church. John added both his testimony and that of the church to his writings. For it is not just any authority that is required, but that of the apostles, in order that a writing in the New Testament may be proved to be canonical, or divinely inspired." Chemnitz, *Examination of the Council of Trent* 1:177.

Beyond this, Chemnitz suggested that John was the only apostle to live until the end of the first century in order that he might affirm the canon of the whole New Testament and bequeath it to the post-apostolic church.[114] Indeed, Louis Brighton has argued that Jesus' question to Peter, "What if he [John] is to remain until I come?" (Jn 21:22), meant that John would remain alive to witness to the coming of Christ through the canonical New Testament.[115]

As we have seen, this interpretation of Chemnitz and Brighton is perhaps not as far-fetched as many might initially find it. Not only do we have credible evidence showing that John established the canon of the four Gospels, but in the late second century the books Irenaeus considered canonical (which correspond more or less to our New Testament)[116] could very well reflect a list commended by John. After all, Irenaeus is emphatic that he is merely a conduit for the apostolic tradition mediated to him by the church of Ephesus, whose ultimate source is John the apostle.[117]

Turning to Paul, the apostle repeatedly affirms his call and authorization by Christ, usually at the beginning of his letters. Indeed, at one point Paul directly affirms his divine inspiration (1 Cor 7:40). Beyond the authority and inspiration of his own letters, Paul also affirms Luke's Gospel as Scripture (1 Tm 5:18), and as we saw earlier there is some evidence that Paul knew and used Matthew's Gospel as Scripture.[118] Last, Douglas Judisch has argued that Paul affirms Mark as an authorized conduit of apostolic tradition in Col 4:10. Here the apostle counsels his readers to "receive" (δέξασθε) Mark implicitly as an authorized apostolic representative.[119]

Finally, Peter affirms the authority of Paul's Epistles as Scripture (2 Pt 3:16). We also have seen that Papias gives us a reliable tradition that Peter authorized Mark to write his Gospel, which is corroborated by Bauckham's argument that Mark seemingly attributes to Peter the role of his chief source through the *inclusio* of eyewitness testimony.

In addition, David Scaer has argued convincingly that Peter affirms the inspiration of the Gospel of Matthew.[120] In his second letter Peter recounts his experience of the transfiguration (2 Pt 1:17–18). After this he states, "We have the prophetic word more fully confirmed" (2 Pt 1:19), and then goes on to affirm that all Scripture is inspired by God. Since the words he uses here to describe the transfiguration are almost the same as those in the Gospel of Matthew, Scaer

---

114. Chemnitz, *Examination of the Council of Trent* 1:178.
115. Louis Brighton, *Revelation* (St. Louis: Concordia Publishing House, 1998), 21–22.
116. Robert Grant, *The Formation of the New Testament* (New York: Harper & Row, 1965), 154–56.
117. Irenaeus, *Against the Heresies* 3.3.4; ANF 1:416.
118. Orchard, "Matthean Tradition before A.D. 150," 118–20.
119. Douglas Judisch, *An Evaluation of Claims to the Charismatic Gifts* (Grand Rapids: Baker Book House, 1978), 19.
120. David Scaer, "2 Peter and the Canon," in *Mysteria Dei: Essays in Honor of Kurt Marquart*, ed. Paul McCain and John Stephenson (Ft. Wayne, IN: Concordia Theological Seminary Press, 2000), 269–86.

argues that the "prophetic word" Peter refers to includes the Gospel of Matthew. Scaer claims that Peter is paraphrasing Matthew as a true apostolic witness, thereby corroborating the event to which he himself was an eyewitness.[121]

Scaer also correctly points out that the communities to which Peter is writing in the early to mid–A.D. 60s already possess much of the biblical canon, which they undoubtedly would have regarded as the "prophetic word" (1:19) as well. From the apostle's statements in the letter it is clear that his audience at minimum had access to the Old Testament (LXX), 1 and 2 Peter, a collection of Paul's letters, and (possibly) Matthew's Gospel.[122]

If these arguments regarding the apostles' affirmation of canonicity hold, then the results are as follows: John affirmed the authority of the Synoptic Gospels, his own Gospel and Epistles, and the Book of Revelation. Paul either directly or indirectly affirmed the authority of the Synoptic Gospels, Acts, and his own letters. Peter affirmed the authority of the Gospels of Mark and Matthew, his own letters, and Paul's letters.

The canonical list that results from these apostolic affirmations corresponds roughly to all the books deemed canonical at Carthage and Hippo and in Athanasius's Festal Letter in the late fourth century.[123] The only books included in these later canonical lists, but seemingly not directly affirmed by the statements of the apostles themselves, are Hebrews, James, and Jude.[124] These along with 2 Peter, 2 and 3 John, and Revelation constitute what the ancient church and the Lutheran reformers called the *antilegomena*, or those books "spoken against" in the early church's tradition. In the last section of this chapter we will turn to a discussion of the validity of the historic Lutheran distinction between the *homologoumena* (those books not spoken against) and *antilegomena* (those books spoken against).

Homologoumena and *Antilegomena*

Historically, Lutherans have made a distinction within the canonical books of the New Testament between the *homologoumena* and *antilegomena*. As noted above, the distinction refers to the division between the books of the New Testament that were affirmed unanimously by the witness of the early church as being written by the apostles, and those that were not thus affirmed. Among the first class (*homologoumena*) are reckoned the Gospels, Acts, Paul's letters, 1 Peter, and 1 John. Among the second class (*antilegomena*) are reckoned Hebrews, James, 2 Peter, 2 and 3 John, Jude, and Revelation.[125]

---

121. Scaer, "2 Peter and the Canon," 274–79.
122. Scaer, "2 Peter and the Canon," 274.
123. Bruce Metzger, *The Canon of the New Testament: Its Origin, Development, and Significance* (Oxford: Clarendon Press, 1987), 312–15.
124. Hebrews clearly was written by someone in the Pauline circle (Heb 13:23), and most of Jude is contained in 2 Peter. Hence, one could claim indirect apostolic authorization in both cases, leaving only James's Epistle as unauthorized.
125. Lee Martin McDonald, *The Biblical Canon: Its Origin, Transmission, and Authority*

It is important to recognize that for Lutherans the *antilegomena* does not relate to the undisputed books of the New Testament in the manner that the Apocrypha relates to the Old Testament proper. Whereas the Apocrypha is not considered the Word of God because it was not authorized as such by Christ, the *antilegomena* may be apostolic in origin, but that origin is disputed.

The distinction between primary and secondary canonicity came to the Lutheran reformers from the ancient church as mediated to them through Renaissance scholarship's retrieval of early Christian orthodoxy under the scholarly principle of *ad fontes*. Indeed, during the Middle Ages the distinction between primary and secondary canonicity was largely lost or ignored.[126]

Within the theology of the ancient church, the clearest delineation of the distinction between the *homologoumena* and the *antilegomena* can be found in the third book of Eusebius's *Ecclesiastical History*. Here Eusebius deals with the canonicity of the New Testament. In order to clarify the canonical status of various books he makes a threefold division: those books that are undisputed (the *homologoumena* as outlined above), disputed books (the *antilegomena* as outlined above, with the exception of Revelation, the status of which he seems uncertain about), and those books that all parties within the catholic and orthodox church reject (the gospel of Peter, etc.).[127]

Lutherans would agree to a great extent with this division, although many including Luther placed the Apocrypha in a category below that of the disputed books (since it was uniformly agreed among the Wittenberg reformers that the Apocrypha was not the Word of God), but also above the category of the rejected and heretical books. For Luther the Apocrypha was to be viewed as edifying, even if it is not the inspired Word of God.[128]

As we have seen, the ancient church largely settled the issue of the canon through a series of local synods at the end of the fourth century (Hippo, Carthage, etc.). These various synods used three main criteria to decide the canonicity of the New Testament: apostolicity (was it written by an apostle or one authorized by an apostle?), church usage (is it read publicly in the divine service?), and agreement with the apostolic faith (does it form a harmonious theological whole with the other books of the New Testament?).[129] If these criteria were not met, the book could not be deemed canonical.

In the light of what we have argued about the nature of faith's recognition of the Word of God, these criteria make a great deal of sense. On the one hand, faith recognizes the objective promise of Christ that He would speak through the apostles and those whom they have authorized (first criterion). On the

---

(Grand Rapids: Baker Academic, 2011), 308–10.

126. J. A. O. Preus, "The New Testament in the Lutheran Dogmaticians," *The Springfielder* 25, no. 1 (1961): 8.

127. Eusebius, *Ecclesiastical History* 3.25; Maier, *Eusebius*, 115.

128. *Prefaces to the Apocrypha*, 1529, 1533–34 (AE 35:337–54; WADB 12:5–7, 49–55, 109–11, 145–49, 291, 315–17, 417–19, 493).

129. See summary in Metzger, *Canon of the New Testament*, 251–54.

other hand, subjectively, by its proclamation the Word of God creates belief in its self-authenticating validity through the work of the Spirit in the hearts and minds of believers within the church (second criterion). As a result, the Spirit's work gives rise to a true confession of the faith in harmony with that of the apostles (third criterion).

In his introductions to the New Testament books in the early 1520s (revised in the 1530s), Luther revived the ancient division between the *homologoumena* and the *antilegomena*, albeit in a somewhat eccentric, evangelically oriented form. It is often asserted by liberal Lutheran theologians that Luther rejected any kind of objective criteria for discerning the New Testament in favor of a principle of "what preaches and inculcates Christ" (*Christum predigen und treiben*).[130] But this is inaccurate. It would be more accurate to say that in seeking to discern the canon Luther accepted the first two criteria (apostolicity and church usage), and with regard to the third criterion focused almost exclusively on the question of the Christocentricity of the given text. One might even say that he added an "evangelical principle" as a criterion of canonicity.

As we have already seen, Luther taught that due to Christ's promise and the work of the Spirit, the apostles' teaching was necessarily without error.[131] But the question still remained: how does one discern that a work is the writing of an apostle? In his introductions Luther often expresses his doubts regarding the canonicity of books of the *antilegomena* on the basis of what he considered to be the questionable authorship of certain books.[132] Nevertheless, he seems often to think that the best way to detect genuine apostolic authorship is the text's Gospel-centricity. Although this approach may initially seem highly subjective, Luther considers this means of discernment to be grounded in the objective promise of Christ that the disciples' witness would be bounded by the Gospel.[133] Luther points to the fact that Jesus said to the apostles, "You will be *my witnesses...*" (Acts 1:8; emphasis added). Therefore, if a writing is apostolic it should center on Christ and His Gospel promise.[134]

How Luther deals with the Book of James perfectly illustrates this approach. Contrary to the claim of many Roman Catholic apologists,[135] he did

---

130. For example the aforementioned sources: Ruokanen, *Doctrina Divinitus Inspirata*, 49–120; Wengert, *Reading the Bible*, 1–21.

131. "[The] apostles ... [were] by a sure decree of God ... sent to us as infallible teachers." Hence, "for that reason, it is not they, but we, since we are without such a decree, who are able to err and waver in faith.... After the apostles no one should claim this reputation that he cannot err in the faith." *Theses Concerning Faith and Law*, 1535 (AE 34:113; WA 39/1:48).

132. *Preface to the Epistles of St. James and St. Jude*, 1522 (AE 35:395–96; WADB 7:384–87); *Preface to the Revelation of St. John*, 1530 (AE 35:398–99; WADB 7:404).

133. See Mark A. Pierson, "Chemnitz's Pearls vs. Luther's Rose: A Comparison of Canonical Criteria in the Two Martins," in *Theologia et Apologia: Essays in Reformation Theology and Its Defense Presented to Rod Rosenbladt*, ed. Adam S. Francisco, Korey S. Maas, and Steven P. Mueller (Eugene, OR: Wipf & Stock, 2007), 182–83.

134. *Preface to the Revelation of St. John*, 1530 (AE 35:399; WADB 7:404).

135. Karl Keating, *Catholicism and Fundamentalism: The Attack on "Romanism" by "Bible Christians"* (San Francisco: Ignatius Press, 1988), 132.

not arbitrarily reject James because the apostle contradicted *sola fide*. Rather, Luther first points to the fact that the book and its authorship were disputed in the early church.[136] He then argues that because the book states that Abraham was justified by works (Jas 2:21), James disagrees with Moses and Paul, who explicitly say that Abraham was justified by faith alone (Gn 15:6; Rom 4:3; Gal 3:6).[137] Luther then reasons that if a true prophet (Moses) and apostle (Paul) agree on the evangelical truth that Abraham was justified by faith, it must follow that a book of questionable origins that says the opposite cannot be the writing of a true apostle.[138] Luther used similar arguments in the case of the Book of Revelation, in which he claimed he could not find the Gospel.[139]

Luther's teaching here is problematic. On the one hand, the Reformer is correct that the Holy Spirit is always tethered to the incarnate Son, and consequently is always Gospel-centered in His teaching. On the other hand, how a particular biblical text inculcates Christ is not always immediately apparent, even for those enlightened by the Spirit. Simply because it was not immediately clear to Luther how James and Revelation inculcate the Gospel does not mean they do not do so. Indeed, both David Scaer[140] and Charles Gieschen[141] have in great and convincing detail demonstrated that both James and Revelation are thoroughly evangelical and Christ-centered. Luther's evangelical principle thus ultimately works better as a hermeneutical rule (that is, all statements in the Bible must relate back to the Gospel) than as a means of determining canonicity.

Later Lutheranism generally did not follow Luther in his critical use of the evangelical principle, and instead focused on the less subjective standard of apostolicity and early church attestation of that apostolicity.[142] Indeed, this is what we find when we turn to Chemnitz's treatment of the *homologoumena* and *antilegomena* in his *Examination of the Council of Trent*. First, Chemnitz focuses on the ancient church's standard of apostolicity and does not employ Luther's method of evangelical criticism.[143] We must emphasize that Chemnitz still believed the Gospel was the center of Scripture, but there is no hint that he employed grace-centeredness as a critical criterion for canonicity as Luther did.

Second, Chemnitz was somewhat harsher in his application of the distinction between the *homologoumena* and *antilegomena* than was Luther.[144]

---

136. *Preface to the Epistles of St. James and St. Jude*, 1522 (AE 35:395; WADB 7:384).

137. *Preface to the Epistles of St. James and St. Jude*, 1522 (AE 35:396; WADB 7:387).

138. *Preface to the Epistles of St. James and St. Jude*, 1522 (AE 35:396; WADB 7:387). Luther added in his edition of the 1530s that James was a good teacher of the moral law and therefore valuable.

139. *Preface to the Revelation of St. John* (35:399; WADB 7:404).

140. David Scaer, *James, Apostle of Faith: A Primary Christological Epistle for a Persecuted Church* (Eugene, OR: Wipf & Stock, 2004).

141. Charles Gieschen, "The Relevance of the *Homologoumena* and *Antilegomena* Distinction for the New Testament Canon Today: Revelation as a Test Case," *Concordia Theological Quarterly* 79, no. 3–4 (2015): 279–300.

142. Chemnitz, *Examination of the Council of Trent* 1:171.

143. Chemnitz, *Examination of the Council of Trent* 1:171–72.

144. Chemnitz, *Examination of the Council of Trent* 1:187.

Whereas in his New Testament introductions Luther still has much positive to say about the *antilegomena* as a witness to divine truth, Chemnitz considered *antilegomena* to merit nearly total rejection. Since these books lack a unanimous testimony of their apostolic origins, he considered them shaky ground upon which to establish the articles of the faith and thus suitable to attest true doctrine only secondarily.[145] Still, Chemnitz's rejection was rarely mirrored by his practice. We note the Formula of Concord, which Chemnitz co-authored, is filled with citations from *antilegomena* without distinction of authority.[146]

Chemnitz's approach generally was followed by Lutheran theologians of his own generation and the one immediately following the writing of the Formula of Concord.[147] Nonetheless, starting with Johann Gerhard the distinction between *homologoumena* and *antilegomena* was gradually eroded and in practice finally abandoned by the early eighteenth century.[148] This approach was gradually abandoned probably in part because of the arguments of the apologists of the Counter-Reformation, who charged Luther and by proxy his followers of abandoning parts of Scripture (i.e., works and faith in the Book of James) less than congenial to their theological position.

While Gerhard acknowledges the distinction between the *homologoumena* and *antilegomena*, he nevertheless does not consider it to be entirely important.[149] According to Gerhard, what ultimately matters is not so much the authorship of the book in question as whether or not it was inspired by the Holy Spirit:

> There have been noted certain books of the New Testament called apocryphal, but almost for no other reason than that there was doubt concerning them—not whether they were written by the inspiration of the Holy Ghost, but whether they were published by the apostles by whom they had been signed. But because there was no doubt concerning the more important of their authors, namely, the Holy Ghost (but only concerning their writers or ministering authors), and because despite this doubtful authority of these books certain outstanding ancients of the church had raised them to a high level, they have obtained equal authority with the canonical books in the opinion of many people. Indeed, in order that a certain book be regarded as canonical, it is not necessarily required that there be agreement concerning the secondary author or writer. It is sufficient if there be agreement concerning the primary author or the dictator, who is the Holy Ghost; for the books of Judges, Ruth, and Esther are canonical, the authors of which, however, are unknown.[150]

---

145. Preus, "New Testament in the Lutheran Dogmaticians," 15.
146. Preus, "New Testament in the Lutheran Dogmaticians," 16.
147. Preus, "New Testament in the Lutheran Dogmaticians," 16–18.
148. Preus, "New Testament in the Lutheran Dogmaticians," 18–23. See Gerhard, *On the Nature of Theology and Scripture*, 225–29.
149. Preus, "New Testament in the Lutheran Dogmaticians," 20.
150. Cited from Preus, "New Testament in the Lutheran Dogmaticians," 19. See Gerhard, *On the Nature of Theology and Scripture*, 228.

In other words, for Gerhard the secondary nature of the *antilegomena* has to do not with authority and canonicity but rather with the doubts certain persons within the early church had regarding their "secondary authorship" (*auctor secundarius*). The primary author (*auctor primarius*) of the books of the *antilegomena* (namely, the Holy Spirit) is for Gerhard apparently not at all in doubt due to the readily recognizable apostolicity of the teaching.[151] Of course this approach raises the question why a book that merely agrees with apostolic teaching should be considered inspired and therefore canonical. Under this criterion, could not the Augsburg Confession be included in the canon?

As a result of the influence of Gerhard's approach, throughout the seventeenth century the distinction between the *antilegomena* and the *homologoumena* came to be regarded by many Lutherans as almost insignificant.[152] Readers of his dogmatics will recognize that Gerhard not only relaxes the distinction between the *antilegomena* and the *homologoumena* but also often cites the Apocrypha as if it were canonical Scripture.

Although the Lutheran Confessions (unlike the Reformed)[153] do not specifically give a canonical list, certain approaches to the question of the canon seem to be more consistent with confessional principles than others. Hence, aspects of both Chemnitz's and Gerhard's approaches fit best with the theological premises regarding Scripture that we have already established. Throughout our discussion we have consistently emphasized the centrality of Christ's promise of inspiration to the prophets and apostles. Belief in inspiration is therefore derivative of our faith in Christ and His historical reality, mediated to us by the power of the Spirit as active in the Word and Sacrament ministry of the church.[154] For this reason we should not abandon the distinction between the *antilegomena* and the *homologoumena*. The canon of Scripture must be grounded in the actual authorship (or at least authorization) of a prophet or apostle, because Christ has attached His promise of inspiration to them alone.

Our approach to discerning the canon is thus quite different from that of the Reformed and Roman Catholic traditions, both of which tend to distance the work of the Spirit from the external Word, albeit in different ways. In the Reformed tradition the canon is established mainly on the basis of the subjective reality of the inner testimony of the Spirit.[155] Catholicism holds that the Spirit-

---

151. Preus, "New Testament in the Lutheran Dogmaticians," 19.

152. Preus, "New Testament in the Lutheran Dogmaticians," 18–23. See Gerhard, *On the Nature of Theology and Scripture*, 225–82.

153. Jack B. Rogers and Donald K. McKim, *The Authority and Interpretation of the Bible: An Historical Approach* (Eugene, OR: Wipf & Stock, 1999), 204.

154. John Warwick Montgomery writes: "Note that we do not argue that the Bible must be divine revelation because it is inerrant; we argue, rather, that it must be a divine revelation because Jesus, who proves himself to be God, declares that it is such—and he regarded it as inerrant." Montgomery, *Tracatus Logico-Theologicus*, 146.

155. John Calvin, *Institutes of the Christian Religion* 1.7.1 and 1.7.4, in *Calvin: The Institutes of the Christian Religion*, trans. and ed. John T. McNeill and Ford Lewis Battles, 2 vols.

guided (Roman Catholic) Church can establish the canon by fiat. Both assume that the Spirit makes the canon discernible not through the objective historical promise of Christ but through the interior work of the Spirit. Both represent Enthusiasm, albeit in different forms: one individualist (Reformed) and the other authoritarian (Catholicism). In contrast to all this, the historic Lutheran approach insists upon the unity of the Word and the Spirit, that is, the objective principle (apostolicity and the historical promise of Christ) with the subjective principle (the inner testimony of the Spirit).

For this reason, to the extent that certain texts are of mixed attestation or face other credible challenges to their apostolic origin, we cannot treat them as possessing the status of primary canonicity. Of course this does not mean that our judgment on this issue must remain static. Indeed, over time our judgment may change in the light of the evidence. As we saw in the previous section, a number of books were spoken against in the early church for ulterior motives (e.g., Eusebius's questioning of Revelation), and not because their authorship was doubted on especially good grounds. Moreover, we have credible reasons to think most of the *antilegomena* is authentically apostolic in its origin (notably 2 and 3 John, 2 Peter, and Revelation).

Indeed, based on our previous arguments regarding apostolic authorship, perhaps a more reasonable *antilegomena* would consist only of Hebrews, James, and Jude. Perhaps we could cut this list down even further. Since most of the content of Jude is in 2 Peter[156] and Heb 13:23 suggests that the author was in the Pauline circle and therefore received his authorization to write from Paul, one could even possibly argue that the *antilegomena* consists only of James.

Nevertheless, even if the authorship of the *antilegomena* is historically ambiguous, as Gerhard properly notes, it does not mean that the divinity of the content itself is ambiguous. That is to say, even if the *antilegomena* possesses mixed attestation regarding authorship, we may still recognize its content as being the Word of God in the light of its agreement with the apostolic content of the *homologoumena*. As we saw in an earlier chapter, when the church preaches in accordance with the teachings of the prophets and apostles, that too is a proper form of the Word of God. So the *antilegomena* may be understood at minimum as the proclaimed Word of God even if there is some ambiguity as to whether or not it is the directly inspired Word of God.

Ultimately, though, the *antilegomena* must remain distinct from the *homologoumena*. To establish doctrine we must look to the fountain of truth (that is, the inspired books of the Bible themselves) and only secondarily to the stream (subsequent preaching of the church). As in a stream of water, the stream of doctrine may become mixed together with muck while the fountain remains pure and clear. For this reason we also stand in moderate

---

(Philadelphia: The Westminster Press, 1967), 1:74–75, 78–80; Heppe, *Reformed Dogmatics*, 25–26.

156. See Terrance Callan, "Use of the Letter of Jude by the Second Letter of Peter," *Biblica* 85, no. 1 (2004): 42–64.

agreement with Chemnitz. While not totally rejecting the canonicity of the *antilegomena*, we affirm the interpretative primacy of the *sedes doctrinae* found in the *homologoumena*.[157] This rule is a logical outgrowth of the primacy of the apostles and their infallible witness over that of the post-apostolic church. Hence, just as the New Testament clarifies the meaning of the Old, the *homologoumena* should be seen as possessing the ability to clarify the content of the *antilegomena*.

CONCLUSION

Jesus is the Lord of the church, and all authority derives from His authorization. Because Lutherans hold that Jesus exercises His authority through the Spirit by means of specific channels (i.e., the prophets and apostles), discerning the canon is a matter of discovering where the Lord has placed His word of promise. Recognizing the canon is therefore not a matter of Enthusiastic discernment, as in the Roman Catholic and Reformed traditions, but a matter of historical investigation in order to "test the spirits" (1 Jn 4:1) in Christian freedom. In the next chapter we will extend the task of testing the spirits to the question of the validity of the interpretation of Scripture within the Christian church.

---

157. Chemnitz, *Examination of the Council of Trent* 1:189.

6

THE WORD OF GOD AND HERMENEUTICS

SCRIPTURAL HERMENEUTICS
AND THE *COMMUNICATIO IDIOMATUM*

Having explored the inerrancy, inspiration, and canonicity of Scripture, we now turn to its interpretation. As we have previously seen, Holy Scripture exists for the purpose of proclaiming the Gospel within the church. For this to occur the written form of the Word of God must be interpreted and expounded in the midst of the people of God.

Hermeneutics, or the art of interpretation, necessarily presupposes a certain distance between a given text and its readers. Indeed, it is often claimed that the word hermeneutics derives from Hermes, the messenger of the gods in Greek mythology.[1] Just as Hermes bridged the gap between the gods and humans in delivering his messages, so too the interpreter seeks to bridge the gap between contemporary readers of the text and the author's original intention. Likewise, as Hermes allowed his hearers to participate in the knowledge of the divine, similarly Christians are given a participatory knowledge of God and His Word through the Spirit-guided exegesis of the church.

In examining the interpretation of the Bible we must recognize that because Scripture is the inerrant Word of God manifest and sacramentally present in historical time, the distance between readers of the Bible and the text is twofold. First, there is a distance between God's truth and sinful human nature (1 Cor 2:14). Because of this distance only God in Christ working through the power of the Holy Spirit can remove the veil from the hearts of believers and make His truth manifest through the text (2 Cor 3:14–16).[2] Since it is by grace alone that humans are saved from sin and its consequences, likewise the saving truth of the Gospel can be known only by the illuminating power of the Spirit present in the Gospel.

Second, because Scripture is a byproduct of a genuine history within which God judges and saves His people, there is an inherent historical distance between contemporary believers and the original historical context of the text. The hermeneutical study of the text of the Bible therefore serves as a means of

---

1. Kevin Vanhoozer, *Is There Meaning in the Text? The Bible, the Reader, and the Morality of Literary Knowledge* (Grand Rapids: Zondervan, 1998), 27.
2. Flacius, *How to Understand the Sacred Scriptures*, 12.

bridging the gap between the original audience and contemporary believers by translating the meaning of the text into the hearers' idiom.

In the light of these premises, Christian interpretation of Scripture must be understood as essentially trinitarian, incarnational, and sacramental. First, it must be understood that from all eternity God is His own exegete.[3] Humans are exegetes of God's Word only in a secondary and derivative sense: "All things have been handed over to me by my Father, and no one knows the Son except the Father, and no one knows the Father except the Son and anyone to whom the Son chooses to reveal him" (Mt 11:27). The Father's begetting His Word is an eternal act of self-communication. It consists of the Father communicating and therefore translating the idiom of His being (the divine substance) into another (the *hypostasis* of the Word/Son). Just as hermeneutics presupposes a gap between the original speaker and a contemporary audience, so too there is an analogical "distance" between the Father and His eternal Word.[4] This distance consists in the fact that the Father is not the Son and the Son is not the Father. This distance is bridged by the "hearing" (Luther) of the Holy Spirit (Jn 16:13).[5] It should be noted that the Spirit does not perform this act of eternal exegesis by abrogating the distance between the Father and the Son but by facilitating a unitary "hearing" between Them.

Likewise, much like the Father communicates and interprets Himself eternally through the begetting of the Word in the unitary hearing of the Spirit, so too in time the Spirit translates God's eternal Word into the idiom of humanity through the incarnation. In His prophetic ministry the Son is the supreme exegete of the Father. Much as in eternity the Father and the Son know and "interpret" one another through the unity of the Spirit without abrogating Their difference and distance, so too in time the Spirit unites the divine and human natures in Christ in a way that communicates to the human nature the fullness of divine glory (*genus majestaticum*) without abrogating its distinct human reality.

Finally, the risen Jesus in the power of the Spirit comes to believers in and through Word and Sacrament. Because He possesses and exercises the fullness of divine glory, the man Jesus and His Spirit are limited by neither the distance of history nor the gap between eternity and time. The glorified and incarnate Christ thus can bridge the distance between believers and Himself, making the Word understandable to them through the translating power of the Spirit.

Just as the Spirit does not abrogate the difference between the Father and the Son or between Christ's divine and human natures, so too in His act of making the Word explicable to believers in the event of exegesis the Spirit incorporates the rational human capacities already present in the believing

---

3. Hans Urs von Balthasar, "God Is His Own Exegete," *Communio* 13, no. 4 (1986): 280–87.
4. See Balthasar, *Theo-Drama* 5:91–95.
5. Hinlicky, *Luther and the Beloved Community*, 130–35. The section of the sermon he refers to can be found in WA 46:433.

subject. Among others these include historical and linguistic knowledge of the interpreter as well as his ability to apply this knowledge. These capacities do not operate independently of divine grace, though. Rather, God the Holy Spirit incorporates them into the act of His self-exegesis operative in, under, and through the reading of the external Word.

As a result, in the event of exegesis the interpreter's creaturely understanding in a sense becomes an *anhypostasis* within the *hypostasis* of the self-exegesis of the Word of God Himself. As the *anhypostasis* of Christ's human nature finds its center of identity in the *hypostasis* of the eternal Word without abrogating its reality as human, similarly the understanding of the interpreter remains distinctly human while finding its center of understanding in the external Word.[6]

Hence, Christian interpretation of Scripture is inherently incarnational, which highlights that exegesis necessarily involves an exchange of realities between the divine and the human. As noted earlier, the aim of all exegesis is the preaching of the Gospel within the church. Insofar as exegesis aims to bring about and aid proclamation, its ultimate aim (*scopus*)[7] is the happy exchange (*commercium admirabile, der fröhliche Wechsel*)[8] between Christ and sinners: Christ's righteousness for the sin of believers. The exegesis and proclamation of the Word is thus itself an act of exchange.

In eternity the Father and the Son exchange realities between Themselves through Their mutual exegesis. The Father communicates the divine substance to the Son, and in turn the Son eternally returns Himself to the Father through the doxological exegesis of the Spirit (Jn 17:4; Phil 2:11). In the incarnation the eternal Word incorporates within His already existing *hypostasis* the full reality of humanity. This act facilitates an exchange between the divine Word and the human idiom (*communicatio idiomatum*) through the power of the Spirit. The full solidarity Christ possesses with humanity as a result of the incarnation culminates on the cross, in His exchange with humanity of sin and death for life and righteousness. Christ's objective exchange of realities with sinners is appropriated subjectively by faith in the proclaimed Word of the Gospel.

In a similar manner, through the power of the Spirit the interpreter is illuminated and thereby given the ability to translate and speak God's Word in the contemporary idiom. In the act of interpretation a communication of idioms (*communicatio idiomatum*) takes place. On the one hand the Holy Spirit communicates God's Word to the interpreter through the text of the Bible. On the other hand, through proper interpretation the Word of God incorporates into Himself the contemporary idiom of the interpreter's speech. This occurs without the Word of God ceasing to be the Word of God. In a similar manner, when the Father begets the Son He communicates the same divine substance

6. Bayer, *Theology the Lutheran Way*, 53.
7. Flacius, *How to Understand the Sacred Scriptures*, 31.
8. *On the Freedom of Freedom of a Christian*, 1520 (AE 31:351; WA 7:54).

while translating Him into the distinct idiom of a differing *hypostasis*. The Word of God thus entrusts Himself to the interpreter's Spirit-guided handling and thereby allows Himself to be incorporated within His already existing reality (*enhypostasis-anhypostasis*). There is an exchange of realities: the Divine Word communicates Himself to the human word and takes upon Himself the human characteristics of the speaker's speech.

ORATIO, MEDITATIO, TENTATIO

This trinitarian, incarnational, and sacramental account of the *commercium admirabile* of interpretation finds expression in Luther's teaching through the threefold rule of *oratio* (prayer), *meditatio* (meditation), and *tentatio* (suffering/trial/temptation). The Reformer found the basis of this rule in Psalm 119, although there is some evidence that monastic practices of reading Scripture also played a role in the rule's formulation.[9] Later Lutheran masters of scriptural interpretation such as Matthias Flacius, Johann Gerhard, and Johann Conrad Dannhauer also recommended following the rule in their treatment of the art of exegesis.[10] This threefold rule is therefore central to classical Lutheran hermeneutics, and unfortunately it has been ignored by many Lutheran theologians in the post-Enlightenment era.

In interpreting the text of the Bible, prayer, meditation, and testing/suffering/temptation represent a cyclical process wherein God continuously works through His Word and Spirit to break down humanity's inborn self-incurvature and Enthusiasm. In prayer the believer calls upon the guidance of the Holy Spirit to draw him away from his own wisdom and conceit (Prv 3:5). As we have already seen, without the Spirit those damaged by original sin cannot accept the things of God (1 Cor 2:14).[11]

Likewise, meditation on the Word encompasses the whole study of its grammatical and historical dimensions as well as the theologian's continuous deepening of receptivity through reflecting on what he has gleaned from his study of the Word using these tools. Such tools along with an internalization of and rumination on the content of the Word make it one's own and cause the interpreter to translate the Word into his own idiom.[12] Again, through meditation the Spirit works to direct the believer away from his own internal seat of authority to the content of the Word outside of him (*extra nos*).

---

9. *Preface to the Wittenberg Edition of Luther's German Writings*, 1539 (AE 34:283–88; WA 50:657–61). Also see a good description in Bayer, *Martin Luther's Theology*, 32–37; idem, *Theology the Lutheran Way*, 33–64; Kleinig, "Oratio, Meditatio, Tentatio," 255–68; Pieper, *Christian Dogmatics* 1:186–90; Nicol, *Meditation bei Luther*, 91–101.

10. Johann Conrad Dannhauer, *Stylus vindex aeternae spiritus S. a patre filioque processionis* (Strassburg: Sumptibus Josiae Staedelii, 1663), 268; Flacius, *How to Understand the Sacred Scriptures*, 9, 12; Gerhard, *On the Legitimate Interpretation of Holy Scripture*, 120–25.

11. Bayer, *Theology the Lutheran Way*, 43–50.

12. Bayer, *Theology the Lutheran Way*, 50–59.

Last, suffering/trial/temptation breaks down the interpreter's pretenses and conceit regarding what he has received through the power of the Spirit and the Word. Trial and suffering test whether the interpreter's translation of the Word into the idiom of contemporary speech is from God or from another source.[13] If opposition to the theologian's interpretation proves that his recitation of the Word has been unfaithful, he is humbled and necessarily driven back to the power of the Word and the Spirit for illumination and correction. If the theologian's interpretive recitation of the Word proves true, he will also suffer opposition because the sinful and fallen world cannot accept or understand the Word of God (Mt 10:16–25). In this case he also will be driven to call upon the Spirit in prayer and meditate on the Word to strengthen him against the opposition of the sinful world. As a result the process of prayer, meditation, and suffering begins again and continues throughout the theologian's life. Through the cycle of Spirit-guided interpreting and testing, the theologian is perpetually pulled away from himself (*se rapiuntur*) and his own sinful understanding and reoriented toward the Word and Spirit external to him.

Several observations about this cycle are in order. First, the threefold rule stands as the natural corollary of Luther's understanding of divine activity and human passivity as mediated through the Word. Put succinctly, the threefold rule represents the Spirit-driven practice of passivity and receptivity before the Word of God (*vita passiva*). When the Word comes, it enhypostatizes the hearer so that he is drawn out of his own interiority into a life of faith oriented toward the Word external to him (*verbum externum extra nos*). The Law empties the sinner of any pretense of the possibility of interior authority (Enthusiasm). The Gospel draws the sinner outside of himself to new and eternal life through the Word. Hence, prayer, meditation, and suffering are the Spirit-induced practice of bearing the Word's continuous judgment on one's own interior judgment which is then replaced by faith's orientation to God's external address.

Second, the threefold rule is incarnational and Christomorphic: it conforms the faithful interpreter to the image of Christ (Rom 8:29). The believing interpreter suffers the coming of the Spirit (*oratio*) and the Word (*meditatio*) in a manner analogous to how Christ became incarnate through the power of the Word and the Spirit (Lk 1:35, 38). As the incarnation is an act of self-communication, the human understanding of the interpreter is the result of the self-communication of the Word in the power of the Spirit. As Christ became incarnate as true man through the operation of the Word and the Spirit, the believer gives a recitation of the Word of God in his own interpretative speech guided by and embodying the self-communication of the Word and the Spirit. The result is the *communicatio idiomatum* and *commercium admirabile* of interpretation mentioned earlier.

Finally, the interpreter of the Word must proclaim its content and suffer testing and opposition as Christ did in His state of humiliation. Just as Christ

---

13. Bayer, *Theology the Lutheran Way*, 59–64.

was vindicated in His suffering, God in His grace vindicates those who faithfully interpret and proclaim His Word.

THE INTERNAL AND EXTERNAL CLARITY OF SCRIPTURE

As we have already seen in our discussion of the threefold rule (*oratio, meditatio, tentatio*), God speaks clearly to His creatures through His Word by translating it into the idiom of their speech. Such clarity is wrought by the power of the Spirit invoked in prayer (*oratio*) and in the study of all the historical-grammatical dimensions of the external Word (*meditatio*). As the author of Scripture, God Himself makes Scripture clear. The Reformation principle of *sola gratia* thus should be applied to the interpretive process as well, insofar as the content of Scripture is ultimately what brings people to faith.

Standing in coherence with the threefold rule, Luther teaches in *The Bondage of the Will* that Scripture is clear (*claritas scripturae*) in two distinct yet interlocking ways: internal clarity and external clarity. The internal clarity of Scripture is the manner in which God makes the Bible clear to His creatures through the work of the Holy Spirit operative in the Gospel.[14] The external clarity of Scripture consists in the grammatical-historical clarity of the Bible discernible through the study of its language and historical background.[15]

Such a teaching is the logical corollary of Luther's claim in the same work regarding the two horizons within which human agency is operative: things above us (spiritual things) and things below us (temporal things).[16] With regard to spiritual things, Luther teaches we are bounded creatures who cannot understand Scripture unless the Spirit clarifies it through the Gospel. But with regard to earthly things, such as understanding language and history, we are free and rational. Therefore, we can discern and debate the grammatical-historical meaning of specific passages.

In his description of the inner clarity, Luther works from Paul's teaching in 2 Cor 3:16–18 that those without faith (in this case, non-Christian Jews) read the Scriptures with a veil over their hearts. They are spiritually blind and do not genuinely understand the goal (*scopus*) of Scripture, which is Christ. When they come to faith the Spirit removes the veil and believers see the glory of God in Christ's face.[17] When people have faith in Christ they understand the central meaning of Scripture, and the content of Scripture (especially the articles of the faith) falls into its proper place. As Norman Nagel observes: "Scripture has

---

14. *Bondage of the Will*, 1525 (AE 33:26–28; WA 18:608–9). See the same notion in the Lutheran symbols in Ralph Bohlmann, *Principles of Biblical Interpretation in the Lutheran Confessions* (St. Louis: Concordia Publishing House, 1983), 59–64.

15. *Bondage of the Will*, 1525 (AE 33:24–26; WA 18:606–8).

16. *Bondage of the Will*, 1525 (AE 33:70; WA 18:639).

17. *Bondage of the Will*, 1525 (AE 33:26; WA 18:607). Gerhard, *On the Legitimate Interpretation of Holy Scripture*, 118–19.

spoken Christ to us, and therefore, when Scripture speaks, we receive and accept whatever it says, *for whatever it says is heard in relationship to Christ.*"[18]

When Spirit-wrought faith is absent and Christ is not properly understood, the other articles of the faith fall into darkness, or at least disorder. For example, the ancient Arians, the Jehovah's Witnesses, and the Mormons all contend in one way or another that Christ is a mere creature. Believing that Christ as a mere creature can work salvation, they also hold the parallel view that human creatures can work out their own salvation. One can readily draw the conclusion that when who Christ is and what He has done for humanity is misrepresented, the other articles of the faith inevitably will be distorted.

Hence, the inner clarity is not a kind of interior enlightenment that gives believers a higher consciousness of what Scripture teaches. Rather, the Spirit opens the ears of believers to hear every tune in the great symphony of Scripture as relating back to the master key of Christ. The inner clarity is available only in the outward written form of the Bible. Just as the divine nature is present and operative in and through the human nature of Christ (*genus majestaticum*), so too the inner clarity is present in, under, and through the written content of the Bible. The text of Scripture itself is a sacramental medium by which the Spirit does His work of orienting the believer to the centrality of Christ and the Gospel.

The hallmarks of the Spirit's work as He inculcates Christ are that He pulls the sinner away from his interior conceit through judgment and reorients him to faith in the external Word of the cross. Jesus taught the apostles in His farewell address that the Spirit would do two things when He came: first, He would convict the world of sin (Jn 16:8). Second, He would glorify Christ (Jn 16:14). Ultimately this meant that the Spirit would proclaim the centrality of the cross and its full condemning (Law) and saving (Gospel) implications. On the one hand, in the cross the totality of human nature is condemned by the wrath of God (Rom 8:3). There is no small piece of human nature left over which is uncorrupted by sin (Gn 6:5). If there were anything uncorrupted left over in human nature, the convicting office of the Spirit would in some sense be restricted, and only part of Christ's humanity would have had to die under the wrath of God. Instead, when we look to the cross, to which the Spirit is tethered, we see the totality of human nature condemned and God's wisdom and glory hidden *sub contrario* (1 Cor 1:18–25).

For this reason, when American Evangelicals and Roman Catholics both contend that the human will is not bound by sin and that there is some aptitude for good left over in human nature, they read the Scriptures contrary to the Spirit-wrought harmony of Christ. Likewise, when the Reformed claim that human reason is competent (and therefore implicitly not subject to the Spirit's judgment) even after the Fall to decide what God's actual intentions are with

---

18. Norman Nagel, "The Authority of Scripture," *Concordia Theological Monthly* 27, no. 9 (1956): 693; emphasis added.

regard to the sacraments and predestination, such a position also must be rejected as being out of harmony with Scripture's inner clarity.

As Luther contends in *The Bondage of the Will*, everything that exalts the powers of the human subject steals glory from Christ as the sole source of salvation. This is why these readings of the Bible necessarily must fail. Every claim of free will over against divine grace transfers glory away from the triune God.[19] Every claim that Christ is really not the savior of the whole world (Jn 3:16) but only of the elect also takes away from His glory. Every attempt to rationalize away Christ's clear promise to be present in the sacraments exalts the power of human reason over the promise of Christ and His ability to fulfill it.

For this reason all the articles of the faith must be understood in the light of the chief article (*Hauptartikel*) of the Gospel. Christ and His Gospel serve not only an important hermeneutical function in clarifying and harmonizing the symphonic unity of Scripture, but also provide an important explanatory model for why the confessional Lutheran understanding of Scripture is correct and other traditions are wrong. It is not enough for confessional Lutherans to say that they just happen to be reading Scripture correctly while everyone else is mistaken. They must give an account of why their interpretation is correct and others are wrong by explicating their central principles and assumptions. Vital to this is the centrality of Christ and the Gospel to the Scriptures.

With regard to the external clarity of the Bible, the words of Scripture are clear because God is the good creator of our language, and through it He conveys even to our fallen reason knowledge of the external world, as well as of His being and will. Since He is the one who eternally corresponds to Himself in His Word (Jn 14:9; Col 1:15), we may trust that God has created human language in such a manner that it can correspond realistically to the world and carry the freight of truth. Regarding the study of the Bible, Luther notes that while it is true that God has hidden many things from us, those things He has decided to reveal to us are by no means opaque (Ps 119:105).[20] To have made the content of the Bible opaque in fact would be counterproductive, since the point of divine revelation is to reveal things. Hence, the Lord speaks to His hearing creatures in language that is clear to the extent that we know and understand the grammar and vocabulary of the original languages of Scripture.[21]

Nevertheless, as Luther correctly notes, we do not have an absolutely perfect knowledge of the grammar and language of Scripture. So according to the external clarity not every text in the Bible is absolutely clear, even to the trained exegete. Still, every passage that deals with the articles of the faith (most importantly the chief article, Christ and the Gospel) is grammatically clear.[22] Moreover, the articles of the faith serve as a means of illuminating the passages

---

19. *Bondage of the Will*, 1525 (AE 33:226; WA 18:742–43). Again, see the same notion in the Confessions in Bohlmann, *Biblical Interpretation in the Lutheran Confessions*, 77–88.

20. *Bondage of the Will*, 1525 (AE 33:25; WA 18:606–7).

21. *Bondage of the Will*, 1525 (AE 33:25-26; WA 18:607).

22. *Bondage of the Will*, 1525 (AE 33:27-28; WA 18:608–9).

that are murkier due to the obscurity of the language. Indeed, as we will see in some detail later, the articles of the faith provide a framework for how Scripture as a whole is to be understood (*analogia fidei, typus doctrinae, regula fidei*).[23]

Furthermore, certain murkier passages are of primarily historical interest (Gn 6:4: what does Nephilim mean?) or esoteric interest (what does Gog and Magog mean?). In either case, salvation does not depend on knowing the answers to these questions, and the Christian church can tolerate a number of different opinions on these issues as long as they stand in harmony with the articles of the faith. In many cases such questions probably should be left for God to explain to believers in heaven.

Like the inner clarity, the external clarity also provides an explanatory model for why confessional Lutheran interpretation of Scripture is correct and others are wrong.[24] Not only did Luther note that the Roman Catholic Church denigrated Christ through its promotion of works righteousness and the cult of the saints (inner clarity),[25] many of Rome's key doctrinal positions were based on mistranslations of the Vulgate. Marriage was viewed as a sacrament because Jerome had translated Eph 5:32 ("This mystery [marriage] is profound") as "This sacrament [marriage] is profound" (*Sacramentum hoc magnum est*).[26] In the Ninety-five Theses (1517) Luther notes that Jesus actually commands us to "repent" (Mk 1:15) and not "do penance," as the Vulgate translated it.[27] Finally, with regard to the doctrine of justification, the Vulgate mistranslated the Greek word δικαιόω (meaning "to judge righteous") as the Latin *justificare* ("to make righteous").[28]

Luther's Reformed opponents had a similar problem. In his eucharistic writings the Reformer repeatedly pointed to the fact that there was no historical-grammatical ambiguity regarding the words "This is My Body."[29] The actual disagreement between Luther and the southern reformers thus was not the grammatical-historical meaning of the words but whether human reason had the right and ability to discover a higher truth behind the literal words of the Bible.

---

23. Ap. XXVII (Bente, 441). Bohlmann, *Biblical Interpretation in the Lutheran Confessions*, 89–98; Heinrich Schmid, *The Doctrinal Theology of the Evangelical Lutheran Church*, trans. Charles Hay and Henry Jacobs (Minneapolis: Augsburg Publishing House, 1961), 70.

24. Richard Bucher, *The Ecumenical Luther: The Development and Use of His Doctrinal Hermeneutic* (St. Louis: Concordia Publishing House, 2003). Bucher sees the dual "canonical" (external clarity) and "Christological" (inner clarity) principles as being the lodestar of Luther's doctrinal hermeneutics.

25. SA II.ii (Bente, 469).

26. Hilmar Pabel and Mark Vessey, *Holy Scripture Speaks: The Production and Reception of Erasmus' Paraphrases on the New Testament* (Toronto: University of Toronto Press, 2002), 177.

27. *Explanations of the Ninety-five Theses*, 1518 (AE 31:84; WA 1:530).

28. McGrath, *Iustitia Dei*, 13–15.

29. See description in Jaroslav Pelikan, *Luther the Expositor: Introduction to the Reformer's Exegetical Writings* (St. Louis: Concordia Publishing House, 1959), 137–56.

INTERPRETATION AND THE GOSPEL
AUTHORITY OF THE CHURCH

In the light of this account of the external and internal clarity, the centrality of the teaching authority of the public ministry of the church becomes apparent. As we have already seen, Christ's authorization of Scripture was embedded in His commission of the Word and Sacrament ministry of the church (Matthew 28; Acts 1). As Luther suggests in the Large Catechism, *oratio* would not be possible had we not been given God's name in baptism to call upon.[30] Likewise, *meditatio* would be impossible without the written Word handed down (*paradosis*) by the church. Abstracting the Bible from the context of the public ministry of the church thus ultimately ends up distorting the proper interpretation of Scripture.[31]

This distorting effect on the interpretation of Scripture has taken a number of forms through the history of Christianity. To oversimplify things a bit, in Catholicism the pope engages in private interpretation of Scripture by asserting with his claim of infallibility that he is not publicly responsible to the royal priesthood. Conversely, Evangelical Protestants often have claimed their right as members of the priesthood of all believers to interpret Scripture as they like, while acknowledging no responsibility to listen to or engage the public Word and Sacrament ministry of the church. Nevertheless, as the apostle Peter said, "No prophecy of Scripture comes from someone's own interpretation" (2 Pt 1:20).

God clarifies the meaning of Scripture through the public preaching and teaching office according to both its external and internal clarity. On the one hand, properly trained teachers and ministers of the Word can give access to the external clarity of Scripture through their knowledge of the biblical languages and proper interpretive technique. Indeed, Gerhard goes so far as to argue that God has allowed linguistic and grammatical difficulties to be present in His written Word as a means of drawing believers to the office of the ministry in order to have them explained.[32]

Likewise, as we have seen, the goal of Scripture is to deliver Christ and His Gospel to believers. For this reason the Gospel is central to understanding the aim (*scopus*) of every passage of Scripture. Although one can come to this understanding from reading the Bible itself, Scripture always was intended to be read as a document embedded in and ordered toward the public ministry of the church. Hence the sacraments and the Gospel promise attached to them can orient our reading of Scripture properly.

The apostle John testifies that the Spirit speaks the truth of eternal life and forgiveness in Christ (Jn 5:11–12) through the testimony of the apostles (1 Jn

---

30. LC III.1 (Bente, 707).
31. Gerhard, *On the Legitimate Interpretation of Holy Scripture*, 14–15.
32. Gerhard, *On the Legitimate Interpretation of Holy Scripture*, 34.

1:1–3). Nevertheless, the testimony the Holy Spirit gives is not isolated but speaks in unison with the water (baptism) and the blood (the Lord's Supper): "For there are three that testify: the Spirit and the water and the blood; and these three agree" (1 Jn 5:7–8). Ultimately, then, what the Spirit says through the prophets and apostles must agree with what He says through baptism and the Lord's Supper, and vice versa. So the Word of the Gospel present in the sacraments can serve as a lodestar for discerning the inner clarity of Scripture. Scripture must be interpreted in harmony with the unconditional Word of promise that the Spirit gives through the visible words of the sacraments. Interpretations of the Bible that do not agree with what the Spirit says through the water and blood cannot be correct.

Thus, it may be observed that the relationship of the sacraments to the Bible is analogically similar to the relationship the Son and the Spirit have to the Father. Just as the *hypostasis* of the Father, Son, and Holy Spirit contain the same divine *ousia*, the Bible, the Lord's Supper, and baptism all contain the same Gospel message. As there is a Son and a Spirit, so too there is a sacrament of the Son (the Lord's Supper) and one of the Spirit (baptism). As the Father is the source of the Son and the Spirit in eternity and in their respective missions within time, so too the Bible authorizes baptism and the Lord's Supper. Finally, as the Son and the Spirit are the exegetes of the Father in eternity and in the history of salvation, they also serve as exegetes to the believer through the Word and Sacrament ministry of the church. In baptism the Spirit gives the divine name to the believer so that he might call upon the triune God in faith and repentance. This act in turn leads him to the Son, whose sacrificed body and blood are offered to him in the Lord's Supper for the forgiveness of sins. As a person of faith who has received the unilateral promise of the Gospel through the public ministry of the church, the believer is given a clear perspective from which to read and understand the Bible. Because he has comprehended the goal of creation and redemption in the unilateral promise of the Gospel made visible in the sacraments, he is capable of seeing the inner harmony of the works of the triune God described in the Bible as centering on the Gospel.

Therefore, as the Augsburg Confession asserts, the public ministry of the church has a real and genuine authority and its teaching of the faith should be heeded by believers.[33] It is a myth that Luther taught that all believers have the right to interpret the Bible according to their own consciences. What Luther taught is that in the light of the New Testament's admonition to test all teachers (Rom 16:17; 1 Cor 2:15; 1 Thes 5:21), the royal priesthood has the right and responsibility to hold ministers of the Word accountable to the teachings of the Bible.[34] Ministers and others called to teaching offices within the church have authority to interpret Scripture publicly, but the authority of such interpretation is based on its coherence with the criteria that are accessible to the royal

---

33. CA XXVIII (Bente, 83–95).

34. *To the Christian Nobility of the German Nation Concerning the Reform of the Christian Estate*, 1520 (AE 44:123–217; WA 6:404–69).

priesthood: the Gospel and the historical-grammatical meaning of the text. If the interpretation of the church does not cohere with this twofold criterion, then the royal priesthood must reject it.

The Roman Catholic Church's teaching that it is infallible simply removes ecclesiastical authorities from responsibility to the priesthood of all believers and the Bible. The basis of their teaching authority is an invisible charisma that the royal priesthood cannot test. On the same grounds, one can also criticize the claim of American Evangelicals that everyone has the right to interpret Scripture according to his conscience. To claim this is to place such interpretation outside the realm of responsibility to the grammatical-historical meaning of the text and the Gospel testimony of the sacraments, both of which the believer gains access to through the activities of the office of the ministry.

It must be stressed that the church's public authority to interpret Scripture is not a legal but an evangelical authority. By "legal" we mean that, unlike the Roman Catholic Church, the Lutheran church does not view itself as a government above other governments, which is empowered to enforce its decisions coercively. Rather, the preaching of the Law and the Gospel in order to produce Christian freedom defines the identity and mission of the church: "For freedom Christ has set us free" (Gal 5:1). Although the church certainly proclaims, interprets, and applies God's Law, the various uses of the Law serve the evangelical freedom they are meant to actualize in the lives of believers.

In the activity of interpreting Scripture, then, the relationship between members of the royal priesthood and those called to public preaching and teaching offices is also defined by the Law and Gospel mission of the church. If each member of the royal priesthood has the right to interpret the Scriptures according to his own conscience without any guidance from the public teaching authority, then he is not accountable to the Law publicly proclaimed in the church (e.g., God's condemnation of false doctrine). Likewise, if those who hold public office cannot be challenged by the royal priesthood in their preaching and teaching (i.e., the Roman doctrine of infallibility), then neither are they subject to the Law. That is to say, the voice of the Law as exercised through the royal priesthood cannot call them to account before the Word of God.

The pastoral office exercises a Gospel-centered authority by creating faith that gives Christian freedom. False doctrine not only violates God's Law but ultimately attacks the Gospel and Christian freedom as well. Since all true doctrine is aimed at promoting the Gospel, by definition false doctrine is something enslaving that takes away evangelical freedom. When Paul teaches Christians to resist false doctrine he thus writes: "Stand firm therefore, and do not submit again to a yoke of slavery" (Gal 5:1).

The pastors and others called to public teaching offices in the church therefore have the right to condemn everything that is not coherent with the freedom of the Gospel. This responsibility is the ultimate aim of the Office of the Keys as well. In turn, the royal priesthood receives this Christian freedom from the Word and Sacrament ministry of the church and has the right to resist all enslaving false doctrine when it is taught by public authorities in the church (1 Cor 2:15). Though believers have the right to hold public teaching authorities accountable, they do not have the right simply to reject any doctrine that does not accord with their private judgment. They have the right to resist being subjected to the bondage promoted by false doctrine, which by definition is that which seeks to rob them of their Christian freedom.

THE LOCI-METHOD

As we have already seen, Luther taught in *The Bondage of the Will* that the passages pertaining to the articles of the faith are grammatically clear enough to supply the Christian church with a solid basis for its confession of the faith.[35] To engage these grammatically clear passages systematically, most pre-Enlightenment Lutheran theologians relied on what is often referred to as the loci-method.

This method was first employed by Melanchthon in the various editions of his systematic theology, *Loci Communes Theologici*. Melanchthon appears to have been influenced by the methods of Renaissance rhetorical criticism mediated to him by the fifteenth-century humanists Rudolph Agricola and Erasmus.[36] In the period of scholastic orthodoxy the loci-method was employed not only by Lutherans but Reformed theologians as well.[37]

In order to establish the dogmatic content of Scripture, Melanchthon posited that one should gather together all the grammatically clear passages (*sedes doctrinae* or "seats of doctrine") on a given dogmatic topic (for example, on baptism), compare their content, and allow them to interpret one another mutually. The result was the formation of individual treatises pertaining to specific doctrines known as *loci communes theologici*, or "theological commonplaces."[38] Although these "commonplaces" (or simply "topics") were gathered into textbooks of theology to form a dogmatic system of sorts, each individual treatise was developed independently of the others. Moreover, contrary to the assumptions of many, the arrangement of the dogmatic subjects usually was chosen arbitrarily and implied little to nothing about the individual theologian's doctrinal emphasis. In the first edition of his dogmatic textbook (1521), Melanchthon arranged his loci around the structure of Paul's Epistle to the Romans, while others chose an arrangement of topics corresponding to the Apostles' Creed.[39]

---

35. *Bondage of the Will*, 1525 (AE 33:28; WA 18:608–9).

36. Richard Muller, *The Unaccommodated Calvin: Studies in the Foundation of a Theological Tradition* (New York: Oxford University Press, 2000), 110.

37. Muller, *Post-Reformation Reformed Dogmatics* 1:177–81; Preus, *Theology of Post-Reformation Lutheranism* 1:35, 44–49.

38. See Robert Kolb, "The Ordering of the *Loci Communes Theologici*: The Structuring of the Melanchthonian Dogmatic Tradition," *Concordia Journal* 23, no. 4 (1997): 317–37.

39. Muller, *Post-Reformation Reformed Dogmatics* 1:178–79.

Many modern historians of dogma have characterized this gathering together of the various *sedes doctrinae* as a form of pedantic "proof-texting."[40] But this is not an accurate assessment. Melanchthon as well as the later Lutheran scholastics produced a vast array of exegetical works wherein they thoroughly examined the *sedes doctrinae* within the context of the rest of the Bible. Their interpretation of individual passages in their dogmatic textbooks thus does not represent merely an uncritical quoting of a series of verses taken out of context. Rather, this group of theologians' dogmatic works must be read in the context of their larger body of work, which included lengthy and serious engagements with the various books of the Bible as a whole.[41]

For this reason it would be wrong to suggest that the loci-method serves only to isolate the *sedes doctrinae* from the larger context of Scripture. It would also be wrong to suggest that the loci-method allowed the theologians of scholastic orthodoxy to deal only with the *sedes doctrinae*, thereby forming a "Bible within the Bible" and effectively abdicating their responsibility to wrestle with the wider meaning of the Scripture.[42] Rather, the clear passages are a better vantage point from which to survey the greater landscape of Scripture.

Because the loci-method does not abstract the individual *sedes doctrinae* from their places within the individual books of the Bible, the interpreter must also take into account the place of these passages in the canon of Scripture. Since Christ is the final and complete revelation of God (Heb 1:1–2), the New Testament and its *sedes doctrinae* have interpretive priority over the Old Testament.[43] Likewise, as we suggested in the previous chapter, in dealing with the hermeneutic relationship between the *homologoumena* and *antilegomena*, a modified version of Chemnitz and Gerhard's procedure is probably the most adequate. Although the *antilegomena* and its *sedes doctrinae* are not to be rejected, they should nonetheless be subordinated to the *sedes* found in the *homologoumena*. If a passage in the *antilegomena* is perceived to be in tension with the *sedes* found in the *homologoumena* (Heb 6:4–7 being one of the chief examples), then the former must be read in a fashion harmonious with the latter.

---

40. Louis Berkhof, *Principles of Biblical Interpretation* (Grand Rapids: Baker Book House, 1950), 29.

41. See numerous examples of this in Richard Muller, "Biblical Interpretation in the 16th and 17th Centuries," in *Historical Handbook of Major Biblical Interpreters*, ed. Donald K. McKim (Downers Grove, IL: InterVarsity Press, 1998), 123–52.

42. Scaer, "Theology of Robert David Preus," 80–81.

43. Johann Anselm Steiger, "The Development of the Reformation Legacy: Hermeneutics and the Interpretation of Scripture in the Age of Orthodoxy," in *Hebrew Bible/Old Testament: The History of Its Interpretation. II: From the Renaissance to the Enlightenment*, ed. Christianus Brekelmans, Magne Sæbø, and Menahem Haran (Göttingen: Vandenhoeck & Ruprecht, 2008), 718. The interpretative priority of the New Testament over the Old Testament is a point of difference between the Lutheran and Reformed scholastics. Steiger notes this is particularly true with regard to typology.

The loci-method possesses several distinct advantages. First, as Robert Preus notes, insofar as the loci-method relies strictly on the *sensus literalis*, it allows Scripture to speak on every doctrinal subject distinctly without being forced into the straightjacket of false systematizations. Within each commonplace, different dogmas can be developed on the basis of the texts that pertain to them in an independent fashion. This approach serves as a bulwark against a false harmonization between two different dogmas that may appear from a human perspective to be in tension with one another. For example, Preus notes that if the doctrine of universal grace stands in tension with the doctrine of election, the theologian must follow the *sedes doctrinae* and allow the perceived tension between the two scriptural doctrines to stand.[44]

A second advantage of the loci-method is that it provides a safeguard against the tendency of theologians and interpreters to read their own biases into the text of the Bible. By allowing the simple grammatical-historical meaning of one text to interpret another text, the incorrect interpretation of one verse may be checked by what is said in another. The individual is forced to contend with the question of whether any of the verses on a given subject in Scripture actually support his interpretation of a particular doctrine.

This last point possesses great apologetic possibilities. For example, most Protestants insist that the sacraments are either merely signs of the presence of disembodied grace or purely symbolic. The major difficulty with this belief is that there is no passage of the New Testament that teaches this. To counteract this criticism, proponents of these doctrinal stances often attempt to read individual passages of the Bible in a manner consistent with this understanding. For example, one often hears that Paul's statement that we die and rise with Christ in baptism (Romans 6) must be understood as a metaphorical way of talking about how repentance and faith are symbolized publicly in baptism.[45] Beyond the fact that Paul does not actually say this, placing the passage in interpretive dialogue with the other *sedes* that pertain to baptism demonstrates that this is not an appropriate way to interpret Romans 6. When one compares Romans 6 with all the other verses referencing baptism, it become clear that no *sedes* on baptism in the New Testament actually says that baptism symbolizes repentance and faith. Every verse speaks in such a manner so as to inculcate the fact that baptism communicates a genuine forgiveness and regeneration. The desire to read a metaphorical interpretation into a single passage thus is checked by the fact that one cannot find interpretive support for this supposition in any of the other passages.

---

44. Robert D. Preus, "The Hermeneutics of the Formula of Concord," in *Doctrine Is Life: The Essays of Robert D. Preus on Scripture*, ed. Klemet I. Preus (St. Louis: Concordia Publishing House, 2006), 230–31.

45. Wayne Grudem, *Systematic Theology: An Introduction to Biblical Doctrine* (Grand Rapids: Zondervan, 1994), 966–87.

THE ANALOGY OF FAITH

The articles of the faith established by a careful reading of the *sedes doctrinae* form a harmonious and organic whole. This is unsurprising: although God used a variety of secondary authors as His instruments to write the Scriptures, He Himself is the singular primary author. And God and His truth do not contradict each other.[46] Therefore, it is important that individual passages of Scripture, especially the murkier ones, be interpreted in the light of the overall coherence of the creedal and confessional faith gleaned from the *sedes doctrinae*.[47] Historically this method of interpretation has been referred to as the analogy of faith (*analogia fidei*, sometimes also termed *typus doctrinae, regula fidei*).[48] Regarding this mode of interpretation Martin Chemnitz writes: "Neither may the Holy Scripture be bent, twisted, or perverted . . . but rather it should be accepted in its plain sense as it is given in the clear, lucid letter, and as one passage of Scripture interprets another according to the analogy of faith."[49]

Nevertheless, it must be understood that the articles of the faith are not abstract concepts taken from some disembodied realm. Rather, the organic unity of the faith can be seen most clearly in the unified story the Bible tells regarding the activities of the Father, Son, and Holy Spirit in historical time. Indeed, the baptismal creeds of the ancient church, in particular the Apostles' Creed, are essentially a recitation of the story of the triune God's activities in creation and history. Our creedal confession of faith then is a commitment to the truth about what God has done in history and what He does in the present through Word and Sacrament on the basis of that historical past. When someone interprets Scripture on the basis of the *analogia fidei*, he thus interprets it from the overall perspective of this creedal narrative.[50]

The narrative dimension of the *analogia fidei* becomes especially clear when we examine the first theologian to give a lengthy description of the concept, Irenaeus of Lyons. Irenaeus used the *analogia fidei* as a means of counteracting the twisting of the Scripture by the Gnostic heretics. When describing what he calls the rule of faith (*regula fidei*), Irenaeus gives a narrative description of the manifestation of the triune God that is virtually identical with the Apostles' Creed.[51] It describes the actions of the three distinct persons of the Trinity as a

---

46. Raymond Surburg, "The Presuppositions of the Historical-Grammatical Method as Employed by Historic Lutheranism," *The Springfielder* 38, no. 4 (1974): 282–83.

47. See description in Preus, "How Is the Lutheran Church to Interpret and Use the Old and New Testaments?" Also see in the same collection "Hermeneutics of the Formula of Concord," 232–35. Schmid, *Doctrinal Theology of the Evangelical Lutheran Church*, 76.

48. Flacius, *How to Understand the Sacred Scriptures*, 16.

49. Martin Chemnitz, *Church Order for Braunschweig-Wolfenbüttel: How Doctrine, Ceremonies, and Other Church-Related Matters Shall (by God's Grace) Be Conducted Henceforth*, trans. Jacob Corzine and Matthew Carver (St. Louis: Concordia Publishing House, 2015), 12–13.

50. Robert Jenson, *Creed and Canon* (Louisville: Westminster/John Knox, 2010), 45, 49–50.

51. Irenaeus, *Against the Heresies* 1.10.1; ANF 1:330–31.

single coherent story of salvation. Such a narrative centers on Christ and His redemptive recapitulation and redemption of humanity.[52]

This creedal-narrative interpretation of Scripture was central to Irenaeus's critique of the Gnostics. The bishop described the various pieces of the Bible as resembling tiles that make up a mosaic. Although these bits and pieces of tile may be intended by their producer to be made into a specific image (Irenaeus uses the example of the picture of a king), it is very possible for some imposter artist to come along and arrange them into some alternative image, perhaps a fox or a dog.[53] Irenaeus recognized that anyone could twist the Scriptures as they so choose by taking bits and pieces of the text and rearranging them. To understand the true meaning of the individual parts of Scripture, one must have the master blueprint (present in the creedal-triune narrative rule of interpretation) to put together the disparate pieces of Scripture.

Although the Gnostics wrote their own heretical scriptures (the gospel of Thomas, etc.), they also corruptly interpreted the Bible.[54] For Irenaeus their reading of Scripture was fundamentally wrong because it interpreted individual verses and books of the Bible from the perspective of an overarching story that was alien to the creedal narrative of the church. The overarching story the Gnostics told was of an evil and inferior creator God overcome by the gnosis of a good and superior redeemer God.[55] In other words, whereas Irenaeus interpreted Scripture from the perspective of the internal coherence of creation and redemption as the work of the single triune God, the Gnostics told a story of the incoherence of the evil creator (the Father) and the good savior (the Son).[56]

Although Irenaeus was fundamentally correct in seeing creation, redemption, and consummation as a single coherent, redemptive advent of the triune God, he did not give proper weight to the tensions in this advent due to divine hiddenness. As Luther notes, God is revealed in His masks (*larva Dei*) while remaining hidden above them. From a human perspective, the activities of the Father in His mask of creation and the Spirit in His mask of the means of grace often seem in tension with the work of the Son in the covering of His incarnate humanity. From the perspective of fallen humanity, creation appears to be a realm of wrath that crushes creatures in a seemingly haphazard fashion (i.e., Job, Ecclesiastes, the psalms of lamentation, etc.). Likewise, although the basis of the means of grace is the universal love of the Son, from a human perspective the work of the Spirit through these means seems arbitrary and

---

52. Paul Hinlicky, *Divine Complexity: The Rise of Creedal Christianity* (Minneapolis: Fortress Press, 2011), 153.

53. Irenaeus, *Against the Heresies* 1.8.1; ANF 1:326.

54. Bernhard Lohse, *A Short History of Christian Doctrine*, trans. F. Ernest Stoeffler (Philadelphia: Fortress Press, 1985), 32.

55. Kurt Rudolph, *Gnosis: The Nature and History of Gnosticism*, trans. Robert McLachlan Wilson (San Francisco: HarperSanFrancisco, 1987), 74–84.

56. Jenson, *Creed and Canon*, 27–32.

uneven. All people are equally sinful, yet only a certain number come to faith by the electing power of grace operative in Word and Sacrament.[57]

Hence, under the veil of divine hiddenness and the perverse interpretations of fallen human reason, there appears to be a tension between the activities of the Father and the Spirit, and the universal and unconditional love revealed in the Son. Nevertheless, by faith worked through the Spirit, the believer trusts that the divine love manifest in Christ has revealed the hidden coherence of the triune Being in a preliminary sense in the means of grace. Likewise, at the eschaton the full unity of the works of the one God will be revealed fully:

> For (as explained above) we could never attain to the knowledge of the grace and favor of the Father except through the Lord Christ, *who is a mirror of the paternal heart*, outside of whom we see nothing but an angry and terrible Judge. But of Christ we *could know nothing either*, unless it had been revealed by the Holy Ghost.[58]

Since the Son and His Gospel are an exegesis to us of who God truly is in spite of the veil of divine hiddenness and wrath, the inner clarity of Scripture makes the analogy of faith possible as a means of interpretation.[59]

In discussing the basis of the *regula fidei*, Irenaeus spoke of it primarily in terms of an oral tradition that had been handed down continuously from the apostles to the churches they had founded.[60] Contrary what some might like to claim, this does not mean that Irenaeus regarded the *regula fidei* as supplementary to Scripture in the manner of the Council of Trent's two-source theory of Scripture and tradition. For Irenaeus the *regula fidei* did not have a different content from the Bible. Rather, the *regula fidei* was the church's condensation and summary of the apostolic tradition that was also fully present in a written form in the Bible.[61]

As we will discuss in the next chapter, the Lutheran reformers and scholastics held a very high view of the role of churchly tradition as a means of witness to the truths of Scripture. Nevertheless, they also believed they had found direct mandates for interpretation according to the analogy of faith in the Scriptures themselves. Many pointed to Rom 12:6, which urges believers who have the gift of prophecy to exercise it "in proportion to [the] faith." Lutherans often understood this to mean that in public teaching one should use the rule of faith as an interpretive guide.[62] Another verse Lutherans have used historically

57. *Bondage of the Will*, 1525 (AE 33:291–92; WA 18:785).

58. LC II.3 (Bente, 695); emphasis added.

59. See Wolfhart Pannenberg, *Systematic Theology*, 3 vols., trans. Geoffrey Bromiley (Grand Rapids: Wm B. Eerdmans, 1991–98), 1:339–41. We agree with Pannenberg's interpretation of Luther on this point.

60. Irenaeus, *Against the Heresies* 3.2.2; ANF 1:415.

61. Heiko Oberman, "*Quo Vadis, Petre?* Tradition from Irenaeus to *Humani Generis*," in *The Dawn of the Reformation: Essays in Late Medieval and Early Reformation Thought* (Grand Rapids: Wm. B. Eerdmans, 1992), 273.

62. *Lectures on Genesis*, 1535–45 (AE 2:151; WA 42:367–68); Gerhard, *On the Nature of Theology and Scripture*, 484; Adolf Hoenecke, *Evangelical Lutheran Dogmatics* 1:495–96.

in support of the *analogia fidei* is 2 Tm 1:13: "[Timothy] Follow the pattern of the sound words that you have heard from me [Paul], in the faith and love that are in Christ Jesus." In these verses Paul describes the body of Christian teaching (faith and love) and urges Timothy to use this body of teaching as a rubric for his public proclamation of the Scriptures (2 Tm 3:16).[63]

Of these two *sedes*, Rom 12:6 has been by far the more controversial. In particular, the Wisconsin Synod theologian J. P. Koehler, a member of the circle known as the Wauwatosa Gospel, challenged the idea that Paul is referring to "the faith" in the sense of the articles of the faith (*fides quae*), and claimed rather that the apostle is speaking of the gift of faith by which one believes (*fides qua*). Although space does not permit an exploration here of Koehler's grammatical arguments, they are not without merit.[64]

Let us observe, though, that even if Koehler is correct, the *fides qua* is always rooted in and measured by *fides quae*. So even if Paul is merely mandating an exercise of the gift of faith in preaching, such faith necessarily will have to be exercised in public instruction according to the standard of the *regula fidei*. Thus, although the criticism of the traditional reading of the text may have some validity, Paul is still indirectly urging believers to speak in accordance with the overall structure of the faith handed down to them by the apostles.

Moreover, Scripture itself urges its interpretation according to the analogy of faith in a subtler manner. As we have already seen, the authors of the Bible saw themselves as writing the next chapter in what was a continuous and single narrative of the manifestation of the one God. Moses demanded that prophets speak in God's name, meaning they would have had to stand in continuity with the revelatory history to which God had attached His name. So the prophets and apostles viewed their own prophecy as making sense only in the light of the corporate confession of faith of the people of God. Indeed, Deuteronomy even mandates a creedal formula that summarizes God's history with Israel in this manner (Dt 26:5–9). Similarly, the New Testament authors not infrequently give narrative creedal formulas, many of which might have been early hymns or possibly baptismal creeds (Jn 1:1–18; Rom 1:2–4; Gal 4:4–5; 1 Cor 8:6; 15:1–11; Phil 2:5–11; Col 1:15–20; 1 Tm 3:16; 1 Pt 3:18–9).[65] Such creedal formulas give summaries of the deep theological structures of Scripture. They thus provide a general framework for understanding the Bible, and therefore may serve as an interpretive lens from which it may be read.

---

63. Robert Preus, "The Unity of Scripture," *Concordia Theological Quarterly* 54, no. 1 (1990): 1; Johann Jacob Rambach, *Institutions Hermeneutica Sacra* (Jena, 1723), 87–106, 315.

64. J. P. Koehler, "The Analogy of Faith," in *The Wauwatosa Theology*, 3 vols., ed. Curtis Jahn (Milwaukee: Northwestern Publishing House, 1997), 1:221–68.

65. J. N. D. Kelly, *Early Christian Creeds* (London: Continuum, 2006), 13–29.

THE *SENSUS LITERALIS*[66]

Historically, confessional Lutherans have held that the interpreter of Scripture should rely on the literal sense (*sensus literalis*).[67] The *sensus literalis* provides the single and unequivocal meaning to the text of the Bible (*sensus literalis unus est*). It is important to recognize that with this term we are by no means referring to literalism, or perhaps better, "letterism." Indeed, Lutheran reformers and scholastics were well aware that the Bible is composed of a number of different genres and speaks in metaphor, analogy, and hyperbole,[68] and used the term as it was defined by the medieval church.[69] Reflecting this definition, Thomas Aquinas claimed that the literal sense referred to the meaning God intended when He communicated the content of the Bible through the inspired authors.[70] God's intention encompasses both His address to the original audience and the place of this address within the wider history of salvation.

The literal sense is therefore not, as modern interpreters have often thought, the meaning of the text as we might want to construe it based on the limited horizons of the original author's historical context.[71] As we have already seen, God is the primary author of the Bible and therefore reveals Himself in a single unified narrative throughout Scripture. At the same time, the authors of Scripture genuinely participated in the production of the Scriptures through their human agency guided and shaped by the Spirit. The Reformation's preference for the literal sense thus reflects its incarnational notion of inspiration as discussed in an earlier chapter. The literal meaning of the text of the Bible is found at the intersection of the historical context of the individual human authors and the wider divinely-wrought meaning of God's own history of self-revelation recorded throughout the Bible. As incarnational, the classical understanding of the *sensus literalis* takes seriously both divine and human agency in the production of the text of the Bible.

By contrast, it could be argued that the allegorization of Scripture by the Hellenistic Jewish and Ante-Nicene interpreters was possible only partially, because their manic theory of inspiration marginalized the human agent and his historical circumstances in the production of the text. They could thus look past the human and historical aspect of the external Word to the purely

---

66. I have covered this material in a similar although not identical manner in Jack Kilcrease, "The Life and Theological Contribution of Matthias Flacius Illyricus," in Flacius, *How to Understand the Sacred Scriptures*, 28–34.

67. Bohlmann, *Biblical Interpretation in the Lutheran Confessions*, 77–88.

68. Preus, *Theology of Post-Reformation Lutheranism* 1:317–18.

69. See Hans Frei, *The Eclipse of the Biblical Narrative: A Study in Eighteenth and Nineteenth Century Hermeneutics* (New Haven: Yale University Press, 1974), 18–37.

70. *ST* Ia.1.1; BF 1:38.

71. Frei, *Eclipse of the Biblical Narrative*, 66–104. Frei here describes the emergence of this sort of thinking.

spiritual and divine meaning of the text lying beyond it, discernible through allegory. Instead of incarnational, such a notion of inspiration and hermeneutics is essentially docetic.[72]

Conversely, modern liberal historical critics assume the text of the Bible is a mere human production, or possibly only an indirectly divine one. Consequently, historical critics interpret the Bible as a simple byproduct of the human author who was more or less limited by his historical circumstances. If the ancient church's allegorization of the text was docetic, modern historical criticism operates with a Nestorian or even Ebionite view of the Bible.[73]

The *sensus literalis* was essential to the emergence of the Lutheran Reformation and its theology. As J. Samuel Preus has demonstrated,[74] Luther's theological shift toward Reformation theology began with a movement away from the medieval quadriga, or the fourfold sense of Scripture, to an almost exclusive reliance on the literal sense.[75] Luther's insistence on the *sensus literalis* was not unprecedented. In making this shift he simply followed earlier medieval interpreters such as the Franciscan Nicholas of Lyra and Bishop Paul of Burgos.[76] Luther's reliance on the *sensus literalis* was unique only because it became one of the means by which he eventually came to realize the Bible centers on God's fulfillment of His promises in historical time.

Thus, according to Preus, during the period in which he was writing his first Psalms commentaries (1513–1515) Luther came to see that the Old Testament should be interpreted from the perspective of the promise about salvation coming in the future. This stood at odds with typical medieval approaches to the Old Testament, which saw the text as a vast series of allegories for the moral and doctrinal teachings of the medieval church.[77] By contrast, Luther saw in the Old Testament a narrative about people awaiting the fulfillment of promises regarding the Messiah, in the same way he and other modern Christians awaited the second coming.[78]

Not only did the *sensus literalis* open up the promissory dimensions of the history of salvation to Luther, it opened up the sacramental dimensions of the Word. According to Oswald Bayer, the genuine Reformation breakthrough was the Reformer's realization, sometime around 1518–19, that the words "I absolve

---

72. See confessional Lutheran evaluations of allegory in Gerhard, *On the Legitimate Interpretation of Holy Scripture*, 74–80; Norman Nagel, "Allegory," *The Springfielder* 35, no. 1 (1971): 41–54.

73. David Scaer, "The Historical Critical Method: A Short History Appraisal," in *The Springfielder* 36, no. 4 (1973): 294–309.

74. James Samuel Preus, *From Shadow to Promise: Old Testament Interpretation from Augustine to the Young Luther* (Cambridge, MA: Belknap Press of Harvard University Press, 1969).

75. Preus, *From Shadow to Promise*, 182.

76. See discussion in Steven Ozment, *The Age of Reform, 1250–1550: An Intellectual and Religious History of Medieval and Reformation Europe* (New Haven: Yale University Press, 1980), 67–72.

77. Preus, *From Shadow to Promise*, 226–27.

78. Preus, *From Shadow to Promise*, 212–25.

you" (*ego te absolve*) were a direct sacramental medium wherein the risen Jesus forgave sinners.[79] If the reception of justification in Christ through faith was identical with the appreciation of the literal word of promise, then Christ Himself must be present in that Word, giving Himself to sinners. Consequently, unlike the allegorical reading of Scripture and the corresponding *res–signum* dualism of its sacramental theology, God's literal demands and literal promises did not point the sinner to some higher spiritual reality beyond themselves. Rather, the Word of God gave the reality it described in the concrete historical-grammatical words of the Bible. It is thus easy to see why the *sensus literalis* continued to be a mainstay of Luther's theology even into his later years, as his comments in the Genesis commentary (1535–45) demonstrate.[80]

In contrast to Luther's sacramental concept of the Word and its corollary of justification by faith, for Roman Catholics salvation, not unlike in the Greek philosophical tradition, is a movement from the sensible world to the intelligible world of God (*visio beatifica*). To achieve this movement, one believes the dogmas of the Roman Catholic Church and keeps its moral teachings by the power of grace. The medieval quadriga parallels Roman Catholic soteriology and the divine-human relationship. The fourfold sense of Scripture[81] understands the Bible as having a literal (historical-grammatical),[82] tropological (morally instructive),[83] allegorical (metaphorically or symbolically descriptive of church dogma or morals),[84] and anagogical sense (typological of eschatological and heavenly realities).[85] Each level of meaning in the text represents a movement from the sensible and material to the intelligible and spiritual.

Broadly speaking, in medieval and later Roman Catholic theology the individual is given grace and thereby is able to move closer and closer to God in a kind of ascension through merit.[86] The "wayfarer" (*viator*) does this by leaving earthly things behind through contemplating the divine (faith) and accumulating merit (love).[87] Paralleling this scheme of salvation, for medieval interpretation the text has an earthly jumping-off point (literal sense). It also has

---

79. Bayer, *Martin Luther's Theology*, 52–53; idem, *Promissio: Geschichte der reformatorischen Wende in Luthers Theologie* (Göttingen: Vandenhoeck & Ruprecht, 1971), 240–41.

80. *Lectures on Genesis*, 1535–45 (AE 2:150–64; WA 42:367–77); *Lectures on Genesis*, 1535–45 (AE 3:27; WA 42:567–68).

81. See brief description in Jaroslav Pelikan, *The Christian Tradition: A History of the Development of Doctrine*, 5 vols. (Chicago: University of Chicago Press, 1971–1989), 3:40–41. See Aquinas's summary in *ST* 1a.q.1, art. 10; BF 1:37–39.

82. See discussion in Henri De Lubac, *Medieval Exegesis: The Four Senses of Scripture*, 3 vols., trans. Mark Sebanc and E. M. Macierowski (Grand Rapids: Wm. B. Eerdmans, 1998–2009), 2:41–82; Pelikan, *Christian Tradition* 3:100.

83. De Lubac, *Medieval Exegesis* 2:127–78.

84. De Lubac , *Medieval Exegesis* 2:83–126; Pelikan, *Christian Tradition* 3:39–40.

85. De Lubac, *Medieval Exegesis* 2:179–226.

86. McGrath, *Iustitia Dei*, 100–109.

87. See discussion of Thomas Aquinas's view of the virtues faith and love in *ST* 2a2æ.q.4, art. 1; BF 31:114, 116; *ST* 2a2ae.q.26, art. 13; BF 34:154–59.

a means of ascending to the heavenly realm through true knowledge of God's transcendental reality (allegorical sense) and accumulating merit through good behavior (moral sense).[88] Through this process one finally reaches heavenly existence (the anagogical sense). In this conception God does not graciously make Himself fully available to sinners in the external Word; rather, through the Word He gives temporal echoes of His heavenly reality so humans may use them as vehicles of ascension.

Ultimately Luther and the Lutheran symbols focus on the literal-historical meaning of the text as a direct medium whereby God makes Himself graciously available to sinners. Instead of envisioning salvation as an ascension from the visible world of sense to the invisible heavenly world, Luther and the Lutheran Confessions envision salvation in terms of a God who condemns and promises in the midst of a concrete history of salvation centering in Jesus Christ.[89] Because Jesus Christ is the fullness of the heavenly and spiritual reality of God present in human flesh (*genus majestaticum*), there is no need to move beyond the sensible word to a hidden spiritual one through allegory. Because of the Lutheran *capax*, spiritual reality of God is present in, under, and with the tangible text of the Bible.

TYPOLOGY AND RECTILINEAR PROPHECY

As we have already seen, the Bible is a book that centers on God's historical promise in Christ. For this reason Scripture is a book of both predictive prophecy and typological shadow. The prophets genuinely spoke ahead of time regarding Christ, just as much as the apostles truthfully testified of Him as one who had fulfilled the Law and the prophets. Moreover, if God is all-powerful and the primary author of Scripture, then the reality of rectilinear prophecy or typology logically follows.

It is important to recognize that predictive prophecy in Scripture can function in several ways. Some rectilinear prophecies possess a straightforward one-to-one correspondence. Jesus is the Seed of the Woman (Gn 3:15), the Son of Man (Daniel 7), and the Suffering Servant (Isaiah 53). In other instances there is a preliminary fulfillment of the prophecy in an incomplete manner, with a final and complete fulfillment in Christ.

The classic example of this second kind of prophecy is God's promise to David in 2 Samuel 7. Through the prophet Nathan, God promises David that his offspring would be the Son of God and build the temple. Solomon of course did possess a filial relationship with God in the sense of being one who inherited and exercised God's rule within Israel (1 Chr 29:23). Solomon also built the

88. McGrath, *Iustitia Dei*, 109.

89. Bohlmann, *Biblical Interpretation in the Lutheran Confessions*, 65–75; Holsten Fagerberg, *A New Look at the Lutheran Confessions, 1529–1537*, trans. Gene Lund (St. Louis: Concordia Publishing House, 1972), 42.

physical temple in Jerusalem. Nevertheless, this was an imperfect fulfillment, and in Christ there was a perfect fulfillment of the prophecy. Jesus was David's "son" (descendant) and God's eternal and natural Son (Rom 1:1–2), and He built the eschatological temple of the church (Eph 2:20–21).[90]

This example suggests that there is some validity to Nicholas of Lyra's notion of the double fulfillment of prophecy (*duplex sensus literalis*),[91] a notion unfortunately rejected by Luther.[92] Such a concept does not contradict the unity of meaning to be found in the literal sense (*sensus literalis unus est*), since it pertains not to levels of meaning (one thing standing for another, as in allegory[93]) but to degrees of fulfillment of rectilinear prophecy. That is, the text does not possess several meanings that are inherently different from one another, as in the medieval quadriga; rather, the text portrays a single movement from promise to fulfillment, albeit in multiple stages, one preliminary and the other complete.

This point also brings us to the importance of typology in Scripture. By typology we refer to an analogical similarity, whereby one event in salvation history prefigures a future one. Since the Bible is a book of promise and inspired by a single divine author, it logically follows that the works of God analogically resemble one another. As a novelist has a style that comes across in all his works, so too the divine Narrator of salvation history has a particular style which results in an analogical resemblance between events. And as a novelist uses foreshadowing to prepare his audience for future events in his story, so too the divine Novelist uses typological prefigurations.

This analogical resemblance serves as an important marker for the subsequent fulfillment of God's promises. The fact that New Testament realities are foreshadowed by Old Testament realities highlights the faithfulness and continuity of God's Gospel promises throughout the history of salvation. The New Testament authors consistently recognize this fact (Col 2:17; Heb 10:1). Such shadows also serve an important purpose in giving context to and educating the people of God about the meaning of His final revelation in Christ. For example, Christ's sacrifice would have made little sense had it not been foreshadowed for thousands of years by Old Testament sacrifice. Likewise, Christ and His mission would make little sense without the types of Adam, Abel, Shem, Melchizedek, Moses, David, and Jonah.

---

90. Luther's attempt to read the passage as pertaining directly only to Christ is not entirely convincing. See *On the Last Words of David*, 1543 (AE 15:279–86; WA 54:37–44).

91. Corrine Patton, "Creation, Fall, and Salvation: Lyra's Commentary on Genesis 1–3," in *Nicholas of Lyra: The Senses of Scripture*, ed. Philip D. W. Krey and Lesley Janette Smith (Leiden: Brill, 2000), 39.

92. Gerhard Ebeling, "The New Hermeneutic and the Early Luther," *Theology Today* 21 (1964), 40–41; Erik Herrmann, "Luther's Absorption of Medieval Biblical Interpretation," in *The Oxford Handbook of Martin Luther's Theology*, ed. Robert Kolb, Irene Dingel, and L'Ubomir Batka (New York: Oxford University Press, 2014), 76.

93. Gerhard, *On the Legitimate Interpretation of Holy Scripture*, 76.

It should be emphasized that typology does not abrogate the literal sense of the text. Indeed, both Luther[94] and Gerhard[95] observe that typological interpretation is not different than the literal sense of Scripture. As we saw earlier, the *sensus literalis* in the premodern era indicated the concrete historical meaning of the text as envisioned in the overall framework of salvation history, and not, as is often thought, merely the literal meaning of the words seen from the limited circumstances of their original historical context.

In his Genesis commentary, for example, Luther sees the literal meaning of the story of Jacob's ladder as a typological prefiguration of Christ, based on Jesus' statement in Jn 1:51.[96] Luther's point is that if this story is seen from the wider perspective of salvation history, the historical and literal reference of the text—something that actually happened to Jacob—would not exclude an ultimate typological reference to the coming of Christ. If God is the primary author of the Bible and the history of salvation, then it is logical to think His action in the encounter with Jacob was intended from the beginning to serve as an image and shadow of what He would do in Christ.

This notion of typology being part of the literal sense is what seems to lie behind later Lutheran commentators and theologians (such as Salomon Glassius, Johann Jacob Rambach, and Johann Baier) talking of a double meaning in Scripture, one literal and the other mystical or spiritual (*sensus literalis et mysticus/spiritualis*).[97] Again, the intention is not to promote a meaning on a higher level that is discernible beyond the external Word, as in allegory, but rather to distinguish between the meaning of an event as considered in itself and the meaning of an event considered from the perspective of its place in the much wider context of the whole history of salvation.

LAW AND GOSPEL: HERMENEUTICAL PRINCIPLES?

It has often been asserted that the distinction between Law and Gospel represents a uniquely Lutheran hermeneutic for understanding Scripture. Edward Schroeder, a liberal partisan in The Lutheran Church—Missouri Synod civil war of the 1970s, famously stated that the "Law–Gospel hermeneutic" allowed the theologian to discern what is Gospel and what is not Gospel in Scripture. Here Schroeder sought to promote a version of Gospel reductionism,

---

94. *Lectures on Genesis*, 1535–45 (AE 5:223; WA 43:582).

95. Gerhard, *On the Legitimate Interpretation of Holy Scripture*, 76.

96. *Lectures on Genesis*, 1535–45 (AE 5:223; WA 43:582). See Jeffrey Silcock, "Jacob's Ladder—A Bridge between Heaven and Earth: Reading Genesis 28:10–22 against the Grain of Modernity," *Lutheran Theological Journal* 46, no. 3 (2012): 180.

97. Salomon Glassius, *Philologia Sacra* (Leipzig: Gleditsch, 1743), 347–49; Baier, *Compendium Theologiae Positivae* 1:178; Benjamin Mayes, "The Mystical Sense of Scripture According to Johann Jacob Rambach," *Concordia Theological Quarterly* 72, no. 1 (2008): 45–70.

wherein believers were free to limit the articles of the faith to those that could be connected with justification.[98]

On one level, it is indeed correct to say that everything in Scripture is connected to Law and Gospel. As Melanchthon notes in Article IV of the Apology, the content of the Bible does automatically place the reader under either demand or promise:

> *All Scripture ought to be distributed into these two principal topics*, the Law and the promises. For in some places it presents the Law, and in others the promise concerning Christ, namely, either when [in the Old Testament] it promises that Christ will come, and offers, for His sake, the remission of sins, justification, and life eternal, or when, in the Gospel [in the New Testament], Christ Himself, since He has appeared, promises the remission of sins, justification, and life eternal. Moreover, in this discussion, by Law we designate the Ten Commandments, wherever they are read in the Scriptures. Of the ceremonies and judicial laws of Moses we say nothing at present.[99]

Still, in this passage Melanchthon intends that all the biblical material be read in the light of the centrality of the Gospel. Unlike Schroeder, he does not suggest that the believer can use the Law–Gospel principle as a means of surgically removing biblical material from the corpus of revelation.

Moreover, in an ultimate sense, Law and Gospel cannot be understood properly as a hermeneutic in the sense that the interpreter can definitively organize all material in the Bible into either a Law category or a Gospel category. This is because the various texts in Scripture and articles of the faith possess the potential to function as either Law or Gospel, depending on their relationship to the listener. For example, the article of the second coming of Christ functions as Gospel to believers, who eagerly await it as redemptive, and as Law to unbelievers, who fear the judgment of Christ. Luther makes the same point about the First Commandment in the Large Catechism. On the one hand, the First Commandment is Law insofar as it affirms that God alone is the true God and punishes all who reject Him in favor of idolatry. On the other hand, it affirms that God has graciously become our God, and therefore the believer is promised that he does not need any alternative gods.[100]

For this reason David Scaer observes that Law and Gospel are not doctrines like other doctrines of the faith. Rather, these categories describe how the Holy Spirit, active in the Word of the preacher, applies the content of Scripture and

---

98. Edward Schroeder, "Law–Gospel Reductionism in the History of The Lutheran Church—Missouri Synod," *Concordia Theological Monthly* 43, no. 4 (1972): 232–47. Also see discussion in Scott Murray, *Law, Life, and the Living God: The Third Use of the Law in Modern American Lutheranism* (St. Louis: Concordia Publishing House, 2002), 103–7.

99. Ap. IV (Bente, 121; emphasis added); Bohlmann, *Biblical Interpretation in the Lutheran Confessions*, 99–112. Also see parallel comments in Johann Gerhard, *On the Gospel and Repentance*, trans. Richard Dinda (St. Louis: Concordia Publishing House, 2016), 57.

100. LC I.1 (Bente, 587); LC I.1 (Bente, 589).

the doctrines of the faith to the listening congregation. Law and Gospel are thus better described as a kind of phenomenology of the Word than a hermeneutic.[101]

THE CHALLENGE OF TEXTUAL CRITICISM

In the light of recent attacks by popular figures like Bart Ehrman, textual criticism increasingly has come to be seen as a challenge to scriptural authority.[102] As Robert Preus observes, the Lutheran scholastics spoke of the authority of the original texts of the Bible (*autographa*) in relationship to later copies and translations. In doing this they sought to bolster the claims of the original Hebrew and Greek texts over against the supposed authority of the Vulgate, which had been canonized at the Council of Trent.[103]

Nevertheless, although they were aware of small differences between extant manuscripts, the theologians of scholastic orthodoxy generally assumed that the Textus Receptus and the Masoretic text of the Old Testament were largely identical with the original text (*autographa*).[104] In the subsequent centuries many newly discovered manuscripts show that although the Textus Receptus is certainly an adequate text insofar as it preserved true doctrine, it was by no means the most reliable text.[105] As a result of the discoveries of the Dead Sea Scrolls the Masoretic Text has stood up better to textual criticism,[106] not least because ancient Jews had much stricter rules regarding the copying of manuscripts than did early Christians.[107]

While these discoveries do not call into question the doctrines of inerrancy and verbal inspiration, they certainly do challenge their practical viability. In other words, if there are textual variants, how can we be certain that the words before our eyes are the very words of God? Indeed, many might ask: what does it matter that God has verbally inspired the Bible, if those inspired words are uncertain?

---

101. David Scaer, "The Law–Gospel Debate in the Missouri Synod Continued," *The Springfielder* 40, no. 2 (1976): 107–18. Also see Raymond Surburg, "An Evaluation of the Law–Gospel Principle as a Hermeneutical Method," *The Springfielder* 36, no. 4 (1973): 280–93.

102. Bart Ehrman, *Misquoting Jesus: The Story Behind Who Changed the Bible and Why* (San Francisco: HarperOne, 2007); idem, *The Orthodox Corruption of Scripture: The Effect of Early Christological Controversies on the Text of the New Testament* (Oxford: Oxford University Press, 2011).

103. Preus, *Inspiration of Scripture*, 48–49.

104. Jeffrey Kloha, "Theological and Hermeneutical Reflections on the Ongoing Revisions of the *Novum Testamentum Graece*," in *Listening to the Word of God: Exegetical Approaches*, ed. Achim Behrens and Jorg Christian Salzmann (Göttingen: Edition Ruprecht, 2016), 188.

105. Bruce Metzger, *The Text of the New Testament: Its Transmission, Corruption, and Restoration* (Oxford: Oxford University Press,1992), 124–48.

106. Robert Solomon, *The Enduring Word: The Authority and Reliability of the Bible* (Singapore: Genesis Books, 2011), 69.

107. Larry Stone, *The Story of the Bible: The Fascinating History of Its Writing, Translation, and Effect on Civilization* (Nashville: Thomas Nelson, 2013), 24–26.

One response to these questions has been an attempt to support the continuing validity of the Textus Receptus. Some strains of the King James Only movement[108] have taken this approach in spite of the rather significant evidence to the contrary. Part of the rationale for defending the Textus Receptus seems to be the peculiar twist on the Protestant scholastic doctrine of inspiration found in the nineteenth-century Princeton school, which as noted in an earlier chapter was very influential on twentieth-century American Fundamentalism.

Starting with A. A. Hodge and Benjamin Warfield, it was posited that inspiration pertained only to the original copy of the text (*autographa*) and not to the subsequent copies.[109] The obvious implication is either that when someone opens his Bible he does not have a genuinely inspired text before him, or if he does it is only because the text is identical word for word with the original. Implicitly, contemporary champions of the Textus Receptus seem to have drawn the latter conclusion from the Princetonian thesis, and therefore find it necessary to posit that the majority text is the only valid one.[110] If this were not the case, the church of the Reformation, which utilized the Textus Receptus, would not have had access to genuinely inspired text.

Francis Pieper's response to this particular challenge was far saner and quite faithful to the trajectory of the theology of Lutheran scholasticism. Unlike certain strains of modern Fundamentalism, Pieper does not in any way deny the findings of textual criticism. After all, unlike higher criticism, textual criticism deals with real texts instead of hypothetical or make-believe ones. In spite of the variants, the theologian must assume that knowing God's Word through extant texts is possible. Jesus commanded the apostles to continue in His Word (Jn 8:31–32; 17:20), which would not be possible without adequate copies of the scriptural texts. Consequently, although we do not possess the *autographa* of the original biblical texts, we can be certain that their essential content has not been altered.[111]

Also, Pieper notes that although there are textual variants, none to date has ever called into question or altered a Christian doctrine.[112] Even a hundred years after Pieper wrote these words, Jeffrey Kloha shows that this remains true.[113] We can also note that the vast majority of textual variants do not alter the meaning of the text but merely change the wording.[114] Consequently the apostolic and prophetic content remains even if the wording is somewhat different. Again,

---

108. James White, *The King James Only Controversy: Can You Trust the Modern Translations?* (Minneapolis: Bethany House, 1995), 1–4.

109. See A. A. Hodge and Benjamin Warfield, "Inspiration," *The Presbyterian Review* 6, no. 2 (1881): 225–60.

110. Lawrence Rast and Grant Knepper, "Collecting Autographs: Missouri's Assumption of Princeton's Doctrine of the *Autographa*," in Wenthe et al., *All Theology Is Christology*, 357–59.

111. Francis Pieper, *Christian Dogmatics*, 3 vols. (St. Louis: Concordia Publishing House, 1951), 1:237–39.

112. Pieper, *Christian Dogmatics* 1:237–39.

113. Kloha, "Ongoing Revisions of the *Novum Testamentum Graece*," 189.

114. Solomon, *Enduring Word*, 91–93.

as we saw in an earlier chapter, the point of the doctrine of verbal inspiration is not to identify certain magical configurations of words, as in Kabballah, but to prompt us to look for God and His truth in the concrete words of the Bible and not beyond them.

Pieper's important points of clarification of course do not answer the question of whether we can genuinely regard the text before us as being inspired if we are not absolutely certain that every word is exactly as the prophets and apostles wrote them. Pieper answers this question indirectly in response to the claims of Henry Eyster Jacobs that only the Hebrew and Greek manuscripts were genuinely inspired. Although the original texts as far as they can be reconstructed certainly serve as the *norma normans* of the faithfulness of subsequent copies and translations of the text, insofar as they are faithful, copies and translations are no less the inspired Word of God than the originals.[115] Copies and translations of the *autographa* participate in the property of inspiration either directly by reproducing the exact words of the original text or indirectly by reproducing the same content. If the content remains the same though the wording is different, the text still possesses the promise of inspiration that the risen Christ attached to the teaching of the prophets and apostles. Thus, not only do these texts participate in the inspiration of the original manuscript, they also serve as a medium whereby the Holy Spirit works on the hearts and minds of believers to create faith. Ordinary believers can encounter the Word of God directly when they open their Bibles.

Finally, Jeffrey Kloha has noted that there are some instances where the science of textual criticism has been unable to resolve a discrepancy between two or more equally plausible readings of a verse. He proposes that until textual science can resolve the discrepancy, the distinction between the *homologoumena* and the *antilegomena* should be extended to individual verses in the New Testament, and by implication to those in the Old Testament as well. Verses that lack variants would be classified as *homologoumena*. Verses with more than one plausible reading are not non-apostolic or non-prophetic per se (Apocrypha), but they are disputed. These would fall into the category of *antilegomena* and therefore cannot be used to be prove doctrine until the issues regarding them are resolved.[116]

This proposal has some merits, though in the light of our understanding the role of the *antilegomena* more along the lines of Gerhard than of Chemnitz, we would modify it somewhat. First, if the two or more equally plausible readings possess the same content and the wording is merely different, there is little point in calling them into question as a means of proving doctrine. In these cases the prophetic and apostolic content of the verses obviously has been preserved even if the original wording is ambiguous. Next, if a plausible though not certain variant reading teaches a doctrine already firmly established in the undisputed

---

115. Pieper, *Christian Dogmatics* 1:346; Rast and Knepper, "Collecting Autographs," 364.
116. Kloha, "Ongoing Revisions of the *Novum Testamentum Graece*," 196–98.

sedes doctrinae of the *homologoumena*, then like the rest of the *antilegomena* it may be used as a secondary proof of a doctrine. Nevertheless, it must not be used as a primary proof of a doctrine since it is not of firmly prophetic or apostolic origin.

THE CHALLENGE OF HISTORICAL CRITICISM

Starting with the writings of Spinoza's *Theologico-Political Treatise* (1670) and Hobbes's *Leviathan* (1651) in the seventeenth century, the historical critical method has represented a significant challenge to Christian orthodoxy.[117] Historical criticism destroys the traditional reading of the Bible by using what it claims are neutral scientific methods. However, the historical critical method is not simply a neutral and scientific approach to Scripture but an approach based on a series of unproven philosophical assumptions.

Both Spinoza and Hobbes took over the ancient Epicurean tradition that had been revived during the Renaissance and applied its theory of religion to the origins of the biblical texts.[118] According to Epicurus, the world is essentially reducible to atoms, the void, and motion. There is no divine design to the world. All perceived design in the world is due to the pressure of the blind laws of nature. Although there are gods, they are in another realm and have no connection to the temporal world. The gods never speak to anyone; thus, priests and prophets who claim to speak for them are using this ruse as a way to control and manipulate others.[119]

Following the trajectory set by Hobbes and Spinoza, modern biblical scholars have operated under both the assumption of methodological atheism and the correlative assumption that religion itself can be decoded a priori as mere manipulation. The texts of the Bible therefore can be divided up into smaller *Ur*-texts that are discernible based largely on whose power interests they serve in the reconstructed historical *Sitz im Leben*. For example, since we know that God does not supernaturally intervene in the affairs of humans, the story of Aaron's budding staff in Numbers 17 must have been written down by later Levites as a way of maintaining their political power in Israel. Since other texts do not display such a concern for the authority of the Aaronic clans or the Levites' place in Israelite society, they must have been written by other authors with other power interests, such as the imagined party of the Deuteronomists.[120]

---

117. Thomas Hobbes, *The Leviathan: or, The Matter, Forme, and Power of a Commonwealth, Ecclesiastical and Civil* (Cambridge, UK: Cambridge University Press, 1904); Baruch Spinoza, *Theologico-Political Treatise* (Cambridge, UK: Cambridge University Press, 2007).

118. See Roy Harrisville and Walter Sundberg, *The Bible in Modern Culture: Baruch Spinoza to Brevard Childs* (Grand Rapids: Wm. B. Eerdmans, 2002), 30–43. Also see J. Samuel Preus, *Spinoza and the Irrelevance of Biblical Authority* (Cambridge, UK: Cambridge University Press, 2009).

119. Bertram Russell, *A History of Western Philosophy* (New York: Touchstone, 1967), 240–52.

120. See this approach expressed in Wellhausen, *Prolegomena to the History of Israel*.

The ultimate subtext of this way of reading Scripture is human self-justification. Viewing the Bible as a form of covert heteronomous legalism of the ancient authors, liberal critics of the Bible seek to free themselves from its grip by embracing a form of antinomianism. Nevertheless, this kind of freedom is of course not real freedom. The only real freedom is in Christ. By accepting that the Bible is truthful and centers on Christ, believers gain the true freedom that modern liberal biblical scholars seek through the destruction of biblical authority.

Both Hobbes and Spinoza embedded their advocacy of historical criticism and metaphysical naturalism within political treatises. Their goal in doing so was to promote a worldview within which God does not supernaturally intervene in creation in the form of revelation or miracles. If God did so, religion would possess a social and political authority, since teachings found in that revelation would be publicly and morally binding. This authority would disrupt the absolute authority of the secular state both writers were attempting to establish in order to end the violence of the wars of religion.[121]

In view of this original goal of historical criticism, we should note that the totalitarian regimes of the modern era consistently have attacked supernatural religion. Similarly, in modern America the mainline Protestant denominations, which promote a notion of salvation tied to the progress of secular order, like social democracy, have been the most open to the historical critical method. Believing that salvation lies in the secular state's improvement of human society, mainline Protestants find historical criticism to be a necessary ideological superstructure to make certain that their true god, the secular state, possesses maximal power to manipulate the world of naturalistic causes in order to improve it (Rv 13:4).

There are numerous difficulties with the historical critical method and its assumptions. First, practitioners of historical criticism often claim that they are simply neutrally following where the evidence of history leads them. But reading texts in this manner is in fact a product of a particular anti-supernaturalist worldview that has been demonstrably neither neutral nor objective. It is based not on empirical evidence—no one has ever found these speculative *Ur*-sources of the biblical texts, and indeed a single author can use various styles)—but on conjecture worked out on the basis of metaphysical naturalism, or of unproven theories of social and historical development. Christians, who operate within the biblical-creedal worldview, should find no need to make these assumptions and therefore can justifiably believe in the claims the Bible makes about itself and history.

Second, much empirical evidence (particularly from biblical archaeology) supports the biblical accounts, even if not every detail of these accounts can

---

121. See a similar but not identical argument in Scott Hahn and Benjamin Wiker, *Politicizing the Bible: The Roots of Historical Criticism and the Secularization of Scripture 1300–1700* (St. Louis: Herder & Herder, 2013).

be verified.[122] When Hobbes and Spinoza wrote, such facts were not known; consequently, the historical critical method's foundational assumptions do not rest on empirical evidence. These facts frequently are ignored by practitioners of historical criticism. If it can be shown that the Bible faithfully reports history insofar as we can verify it, why not believe its other claims about its authorship or the overall origins of its texts?

Third, the inerrancy and reliability of the Bible do not rest on empirical evidence, even if this evidence can help make such claims intellectually defensible. Rather, Scripture must be understood to be reliable because the resurrected Jesus promises us that it is. If Christians do believe they have found an error in Scripture, they should search for the best explanation that is in accordance with the truthfulness of the Bible. In cases where an explanation may not be attainable, they should wait for God's own explanation in heaven (*lumen gloriae*). Such an approach makes sense in view of the fallenness of human reason and the natural limitations of human knowledge.

Last, the methods of modern biblical studies must be distinguished from historical criticism as a worldview. In an earlier chapter we ourselves in part used modern historical methods to argue in favor of the traditional authorship of various books of the Bible. As Kurt Marquart observed, no method of historical investigation is off limits for confessional Lutherans as long as it is used in accordance with the basic assumptions of the Christian worldview.[123]

In keeping with the assumptions of the Christian worldview, the biblical scholar must not approach the Bible as he would any other book but must assume that it is inerrant, divinely inspired, and centered on Christ. In this respect, inerrancy is not merely an ontological claim about the truthfulness of the text but a hermeneutical assumption that must serve as one of the proper starting points for any confessional Lutheran exegesis of a biblical text.

---

122. Werner Keller, *The Bible as History* (New York: Bantam, 1983); Kitchen, *Reliability of the Old Testament*.

123. Kurt Marquart, *Anatomy of an Explosion: Missouri in Lutheran Perspective* (Ft. Wayne: Concordia Theological Seminary Press, 1977), 113.

7

SCRIPTURE, TRADITION, AND CONFESSION

THE QUESTION OF SCRIPTURE AND TRADITION

As we have seen, the Word of God is sacramental. The risen Christ continually works through the external Word in the midst of the church to communicate His truth and create faith. He uses believers, especially those called to public offices in the church, as means of translating the idiom of the inspired Word of God into the contemporary idiom. He thereby effects a *communicatio idiomatum* aimed at bringing about another exchange of realities, namely, the *fröhliche Wechsel* of subjective justification. Because the Word of God is living, it possesses a genuine history within the life of the visible church. The teachers of the visible church participate in this living history in their public exposition of the Word of God through the power of the Holy Spirit.

In the light of this history, we are confronted with the question of the relation between Scripture and tradition. By Scripture we mean of course the prophetic and apostolic books that God the Holy Spirit has inspired. By tradition we refer to the Spirit-guided public teaching of the church in the form of confessions and creeds, as well as preaching, teaching, prayers, and liturgy. Whereas the former is the inspired Word of God itself, the latter phenomena are the fruit of the efficacious nature of the Word in the history of the church. Tradition is the Word of God only to the extent that it is an accurate recitation and translation of the content of the Scriptures into the contemporary idiom. As we will see below, the Lutheran Reformation consistently taught that although the aforementioned forms of tradition certainly were to be honored as genuine authorities, ultimately they were responsible (*norma normata*) to the supreme authority of the Bible (*norma normans*).[1]

The question of Scripture and tradition is a particularly thorny issue, insofar as there has been a tendency in the Western church to swing wildly back and forth between two extremes. On the one hand, the Roman Catholic Church historically has relied on unwritten tradition and the infallibility of the institutional church as a source of apostolic authority. Although Catholics would deny that this makes tradition and the institutional church independent from Scripture, many observers would argue that in practice it does just that. At the other end of the spectrum, Protestant Evangelicals have made the claim that it

---

1. See a good summary in Carl Braaten, *The Principles of Lutheran Theology* (Philadelphia: Fortress Press, 1985), 8–11.

is possible to jump past centuries of church history to read the Bible in isolation from tradition and the public teaching authority of the church.

Because of its belief in the living and sacramental nature of the Word of God, confessional Lutheranism wisely has served as a *via media* between the Scylla of Roman Catholicism and the Charybdis of generic low-church Protestantism.[2] In order to better locate our position in Christian history, below we will delineate a fourfold typology of the relationship between Scripture and tradition drawn largely (but slightly modified) from the work of the Dutch church historian Heiko Oberman. The four theories of the relationship between Scripture and tradition are Tradition I, Tradition II, Tradition III, and Tradition 0.

TRADITION I IN THE ANCIENT CHURCH

In his essay "*Quo Vadis, Petre?* Tradition from Irenaeus to *Humani Generis*,"[3] Oberman identifies three main interpretations of the relationship between Scripture and tradition throughout church history. Alister McGrath has supplemented this model with a fourth category, Tradition 0, which we will also discuss below.[4] Oberman's model is of course not the only one,[5] but it has been used widely and in general terms accurately encompasses the material we are going to discuss.

The first category Oberman discusses is Tradition I. Our author attributes this view mainly to the early church fathers and the Magisterial Reformers of the sixteenth century. Oberman defines Tradition I as the belief that although Scripture is the supreme authority within the church, subsequent church tradition is good insofar as it correctly explains and confesses the content of Scripture in the variety of contexts that have arisen in the post-apostolic history of the church.

In this discussion we must recognize that questions surrounding the nature and relationship of Scripture and tradition began to take shape largely in the late second century. The emergence of these questions was inevitable on one level. By the mid- to late second century the church became increasingly aware of the new distance that had emerged between itself and the apostolic generation. As we have already seen, even in the early second century, figures like Bishop

---

2. See Jaroslav Pelikan, *Obedient Rebels: Catholic Substance and Protestant Principle in Luther's Reformation* (London: SCM Press, 1964); Quentin Stewart, *Lutheran Patristic Catholicity: The Vincentian Canon and the Consensus Patrum in Lutheran Orthodoxy* (Zürich: LIT Verlag, 2015).

3. Oberman, "*Quo Vadis, Petre?*" 269–96.

4. Alister McGrath, *Reformation Thought: An Introduction* (Oxford: Basil Blackwell, 1993), 107–8.

5. For example, see an alternative model in Yves Congar, *Tradition and Traditions: A Historical and Theological Essay*, trans. Michael Naseby and Thomas Rainborough (New York: Macmillan, 1966).

Papias possessed a living connection with the apostles.[6] He consequently saw
little difference between what the church taught and what was written down
in the New Testament. Indeed, both were simply the voice of the apostles
themselves.[7] Lacking the living voice of the apostles, subsequent generations
began to have to distinguish between what church leaders taught and what was
written in the Bible.

Another issue that led the Fathers of the second century to examine
the issue of Scripture and tradition was the emergence of the Gnostic
heresy.[8] The Gnostics claimed to be the true heirs of the apostolic tradition.
They occasionally forged their own Scriptures, but more often they wrote
commentaries on actual apostolic Scriptures and corruptly expounded them.[9]
In order to bolster the authority of these corrupt interpretations, the Gnostics
claimed that they possessed a secret oral tradition handed down to them by
the apostles through lines of succession.[10] Whereas the content of the New
Testament documents and the public teaching tradition of the church contained
part of the apostolic kerygma, the Gnostics themselves possessed the secret
master key with their unwritten supplemental tradition.

In responding to the Gnostics, Irenaeus in some respects simply inverted
their arguments.[11] The Gnostics had claimed to be able to disclose the secret
meaning of the Scriptures on the basis of their secret apostolic succession
and a secret tradition. Irenaeus claimed to have a knowledge of the correct
understanding of the Scripture based on his very public apostolic succession.[12]
As a student of Bishop Polycarp, who himself had sat at the feet of the apostle
John, Irenaeus claimed that he had direct access to the church's public teaching
tradition and therefore the true understanding of the Bible.[13]

Although many Roman Catholics would like to claim that Irenaeus is here
anticipating the later Tridentine two-source theory (Tradition II),[14] this is not
the case. As we have already observed, for Irenaeus the *regula fidei* possesses
the same content as the apostolic Scriptures.[15] Tradition for Irenaeus does

6. J. N. D. Kelly, *Early Christian Doctrines* (San Francisco: HarperCollins, 1978), 37.

7. Eusebius, *Ecclesiastical History* 3.39; Maier, *Eusebius*, 127–30.

8. Kelly, *Early Christian Doctrines*, 36.

9. Lohse, *Short History of Christian Doctrine*, 32.

10. Kelly, *Early Christian Doctrines*, 37; Williston Walker et al., *A History of the Christian Church*, 4th ed. (New York: Simon & Schuster, 1985), 74–75.

11. Alberto Ferreiro, *Simon Magus in Patristic, Medieval, and Early Modern Traditions* (Leiden: Brill, 2005), 43.

12. Irenaeus, *Against the Heresies* 3.2–3; ANF 1:415–17.

13. Irenaeus, *Against the Heresies* 5.33.4; ANF 1:563.

14. See example in Joseph Gallegos, "What Did the Church Fathers Teach about Scripture, Tradition, and Church Authority?" in *Not by Scripture Alone: A Catholic Critique of the Protestant Doctrine of Sola Scriptura*, ed. Robert Sungenis (Santa Barbara: Queenship Publishing, 1997), 389–486.

15. R. P. C. Hanson, *Tradition in the Early Church* (London: SCM Press, 1962), 102–10. This fact is even attested by Roman Catholic scholars. See Jean Daniélou, *Gospel Message and Hellenistic Culture*, trans. John Austin Baker (Philadelphia: The Westminster Press, 1973), 152–53.

not supplement Scripture in the manner asserted by the Council of Trent. The Bible is both completely clear and the foundation of the Christian faith.[16] The public teaching tradition of the church handed down from the apostles is merely a condensation and public confession of the content of Scripture.[17] Moreover, possessing the office of bishop and standing in succession with the apostles, Irenaeus does not claim any special spiritual powers to interpret the faith infallibly. Indeed, he often does speak of his possession of the "charisma of truth" (*charisma veritatis certum*). Nevertheless, what Irenaeus means by this charisma is merely a general guidance by the Holy Spirit, not infallibility, and the reception of the teaching tradition of the church from his historical connection to Christ through the apostles.[18]

In a similar manner, Tertullian in his *Prescription against Heretics* claims that the Scriptures are authoritative because of their agreement with the public teaching tradition of the church (*regula fidei*) going back to the apostles (*apostolorum traditio apostolica traditio*).[19] While from the Reformation perspective this construal of the relationship between Scripture and tradition puts the cart before the horse, it is nevertheless important to recognize that in this statement Tertullian also shows his basic agreement with Irenaeus's view that Scripture possesses the same content as the oral apostolic tradition. Indeed, Tertullian gives a description of the orally transmitted *regula fidei* identical with that of Irenaeus and the later Apostles' Creed.[20] Tradition is therefore not supplemental to Scripture in any way.

Although we do not have the space to detail every figure in the ancient church, the key point is that for the majority of the Ante-Nicene fathers there is no doctrine that was not contained in the Scriptures. When the Ante-Nicene fathers speak of tradition, they almost invariably mean the same apostolic teaching found in the New Testament handed down in an oral form, something to which they would have had greater access at that point; or simply the church's public confession of what the Scriptures teach. The most important implication here is that there is no sense in which unwritten tradition supplements Scripture or contains more apostolic truths than what one finds in the Scriptures, as would later be asserted by the Council of Trent. For the early patristic authors the Tridentine view would have been anathema insofar as it was identified with the Gnostic heresy they so vociferously opposed. [21]

The one exception to this rejection of the supplementary view of tradition may be found in figures like Clement of Alexandria, who speaks in his *Stromata*

---

16. Irenaeus, *Against the Heresies* 2.27.1; ANF 1:398.

17. Kelly, *Early Christian Doctrines*, 38–39; Oberman, "*Quo Vadis, Petre?*" 272; Irenaeus, *Against the Heresies* 1.10.1; ANF 1:330–31.

18. Irenaeus, *Against the Heresies* 4.26.2; ANF 1:497. See Ellen Flesseman-van Leer, *Tradition and Scripture in the Early Church* (Assen: Van Gorcum & Co., 1953), 120–22.

19. Tertullian, *Prescription against Heretics* 19–20; ANF 3:251–52.

20. Tertullian, *Prescription against Heretics* 13; ANF 3:249; Kelly, *Early Christian Doctrines*, 39.

21. Flesseman-van Leer, *Tradition and Scripture*, 191.

of a *disciplina arcani* ("Discipline of the Secret" or "Discipline of the Arcane").[22] This *disciplina arcani* seems to constitute a secret mystagogic teaching tradition of the church supplemental to Scripture. Indeed, in *The Arians of the Fourth Century* John Henry Newman makes a great deal out of the *disciplina arcani* as an implicit parallel to the Tridentine theory of a supplemental unwritten apostolic tradition.[23] Nevertheless, what Clement means by the *disciplina arcani* is not entirely clear. In the *Stromata* he makes statements commending the *disciplina arcani* along with others that seem to suggest the sufficiency of Scripture.[24]

There is also some evidence that the *disciplina arcani* was simply parts of the Scripture that the early church thought was appropriate for the baptized alone to know. For example, Hippolytus reports that unbaptized catechumens were dismissed before the liturgy of the sacrament and therefore were not permitted to hear the Words of Institution.[25] Moreover, even if Clement is referring to an unwritten tradition of the church supplemental to Scripture, as Jaroslav Pelikan once observed, it is at times tempting though ultimately not fully tenable to see Clement and his student Origen as the far left wing of the ancient catholic church, or the far right wing of Gnosticism.[26]

TRADITION II

Oberman designates a second model of Scripture and tradition which he calls Tradition II, sometimes referred to as the two-source theory. Oberman defines Tradition II as the idea that tradition supplements Scripture with additional revelational and doctrinal content. One finds this idea in its purest form in the fourth session of the Council of Trent, which claims that the apostles wrote down some of their teachings, while others they passed down orally through the institutional church.[27] Not only can Scripture not be read on its own terms (formal sufficiency), it does not contain all the divinely mandated truth Christ revealed to the apostles (material sufficiency). Still, the exact content of this unwritten tradition is extremely ambiguous. The Council of Trent does not designate what doctrines are in the unwritten tradition, and the Roman Catholic Church has never provided a definitive list.

---

22. "And the *gnosis* itself is that which has descended by transmission to a few, having been imparted unwritten by the apostles." Clement of Alexandria, *The Stromata* 6.7; ANF 2:494; Kelly, *Early Christian Doctrines*, 43.

23. John Henry Newman, *The Arians of the Fourth Century* (South Bend, IN: Notre Dame University Press, 2001), 51–57.

24. Clement of Alexandria, *The Stromata* 7.16; ANF 2:550–54.

25. Hippolytus, *On the Apostolic Tradition* 18.1, 19.1; in Hippolytus, *On the Apostolic Tradition*, trans. Alistair Stewart-Sykes (Crestwood, NY: St. Vladimir's Seminary Press, 2001), 104.

26. Pelikan, *The Christian Tradition* 1:96.

27. See H. J. Schroeder, trans., *The Canons and Decrees of the Council of Trent* (Rockford, IL: TAN Books, 1978), 17–20.

The origins of Tradition II are not entirely clear and therefore are hotly debated. Oberman holds that it emerged at the end of the patristic period with the writings of figures like Basil of Caesarea.[28] In his book *On the Holy Spirit* Basil appeals to the authority of an unwritten apostolic tradition handed down to him.[29] Nevertheless, he considers this tradition to be made up largely of liturgical customs bequeathed to the church by the apostles, and thus it is difficult to identify this unwritten tradition as a second source of divine revelation. Moreover, as we will see below, in defending *sola scriptura* against the Council of Trent, Martin Chemnitz positively cites Basil and commends this form of tradition as one of the seven that may be considered valid.[30]

Other authors like Brian Tierney have argued that the notion of two sources of revelation emerges unambiguously only at the beginning of the fourteenth century in the writings of William of Ockham.[31] George Tavard has argued similarly that for the first thousand years of the church, what he terms the "classical view" of Scripture and tradition prevailed. Tavard identifies this classical view with the notion that whatever Scripture teaches, the church teaches and vice versa.[32] The possibility of a dualism between Scripture and tradition (and hence also the possibility of a two-source theory) emerged only in the thirteenth century when Henry of Ghent fatefully asked whether it was possible for the church to teach something that was contrary to Scripture, and concluded that indeed it was.[33] According to Tavard, this recognition opened up a gap between Scripture and the public teaching of the church, thereby making possible both the Reformation, where Scripture served as a critical tool for testing tradition, and the Council of Trent, where tradition was viewed as supplementing Scripture.[34]

There are numerous problems with Tradition II. First, there is no evidence whatsoever that the apostles did not write down all their teachings in the New Testament documents. As we have already seen, the church fathers closest to the apostles do indeed talk of an oral tradition handed down from apostles, but it possesses the same content as the Scriptures. Moreover, none of the earliest theologians of the patristic period appear to be aware of later Roman Catholic doctrines such as purgatory, the assumption and immaculate conception of Mary, the mass as a sacrifice of the living and the dead, or the penitential system. Since these are not scriptural doctrines, Roman Catholics often have claimed that these teachings were handed down to the church through the unwritten

28. Oberman, *"Quo Vadis, Petre?"* 277.

29. Basil, *On the Holy Spirit* 66; NPNFb 8:40–43.

30. Chemnitz, *Examination of the Council of Trent* 1:267–71.

31. Brian Tierney, *Origins of Papal Infallibility, 1150–1350: A Study on the Concepts of Infallibility, Sovereignty, and Tradition in the Middle Ages* (Leiden: Brill, 1972), 218–21.

32. George Tavard, *Holy Writ or Holy Church: The Crisis of the Protestant Reformation* (New York, Harper, 1960), 3–21.

33. Tavard, *Holy Writ or Holy Church*, 23–25.

34. Tavard, *Holy Writ or Holy Church*, 172–209.

apostolic tradition.[35] Nevertheless, since none of the early patristic authors who would have had firsthand access to the apostolic oral tradition mentions these doctrines, it is overwhelmingly likely that these teachings were not handed down orally from the apostles but simply invented in the course of church history. Indeed, modern scholars even can demonstrate the point at which doctrines like the assumption of Mary were invented (the fifth century A.D.) and spread through a series of forged documents.[36] The fact that this doctrine is first witnessed to by forgeries is even acknowledged by many conservative Catholic apologists.[37]

Indeed, at best Roman apologists could argue that a few of these doctrines (purgatory, the sacrificial character of the mass, the penitential system) are either hinted at or existed in an extremely rudimentary form in a select number of later Ante-Nicene fathers (most often in the North African Latin fathers).[38] Nevertheless, the fact that several Roman Catholic doctrines existed in an embryonic form would by no means commend them as genuinely being part of the apostolic deposit of the faith. Their existence in a rudimentary form does not commend as apostolic the fully-developed version taught by the present Roman Catholic Church. Moreover, if these teachings were apostolic, why would they not be universally accepted and explicitly commended even by the earliest Fathers? Even worse, since these doctrines are rooted in legalism, they directly contradict the chief article of the Gospel and therefore cannot be compatible with the revelation we find in Scripture.

Another major difficulty with Tradition II is that it undermines the possibility of doctrinal criticism. The New Testament authors repeatedly tell ordinary Christians to flee from heresy and to test all teachers (Rom 16:17; 1 Cor 2:15; 1 Thes 5:21; 1 Jn 4:1). For proponents of Tradition II, the tradition of the visible church is to be identified directly, in various ways, with divine revelation. Unwritten traditions become authoritative on the basis of the institutional church's own testimony as the custodian of said traditions. Therefore, what the institutional church teaches officially on the basis of these traditions is authoritative and beyond the testing of ordinary believers. This practice not only illegitimately adds on to God's revelation in Scripture, but it also greatly

---

35. See a popular example in Mark Shea, *By What Authority? An Evangelical Discovers Catholic Tradition* (Huntington, IN: Our Sunday Visitor Publishing, 1996), 174–75.

36. Walter Burghardt, "Assumption of Mary," in *Encyclopedia of Early Christianity*, 2 vols., ed. Everett Ferguson (New York: Garland Publishing, 1997), 1:134–45.

37. Ludwig Ott, *Fundamentals of Catholic Dogma* (Rockford, IL: TAN Books, 1974), 209–10. The liberal Catholic historian Eamon Duffy states that there is no historical evidence whatsoever for the assumption of Mary. See Eamon Duffy, *What Catholics Believe about Mary* (London: Catholic Truth Society, 1989), 17.

38. See the following studies: Abigail Firey, *A New History of Penance* (Leiden: Brill, 2008); Everett Ferguson, "Sacrifice," in *Encyclopedia of Early Christianity*, 2 vols., ed. Everett Ferguson (New York: Garland Publishing, 1997), 2:1017; Robert Meens, *Penance in Medieval Europe, 600–1200* (Cambridge, UK: Cambridge University Press, 2014); Jacque Le Goff, *The Birth of Purgatory* (Chicago: University of Chicago Press, 1986).

limits the ability of Christians to test church doctrine, something the New Testament itself commends. Criticism of the institutional church's teaching on the basis of unwritten tradition becomes an attack on revelation itself, and consequently it is automatically illegitimate.

Beyond these considerations, unwritten tradition is extremely easy to manipulate and can hardly serve as a critical principle of the institutional church. If one likens the original apostolic revelation to a fountain and subsequent tradition as a stream, it is not difficult to imagine how the purity of the fountain can become diluted by all kinds of muck when it becomes a stream. But even if the stream (tradition) did become full of muck, people would still be able to get pure water from the fountain (Scripture). Indeed, the corruptibility of the oral form of tradition is due not only to the failure of human memory but to the willingness of fallen humanity to twist or add to the Word of God if given the opportunity (Dt 4:2; Rv 22:19).

Moreover, the recognition that the public witness of the visible church can fail goes hand in hand with the Lutheran insistence on the *simul* of Christian existence. Christians fall into many sins, including the sin of doctrinal error. They must continuously test their own teaching, thoughts, and feelings against the Word. Thus, the uncritical reception of church tradition does not take into account the fallenness even of believers. Revelation needs a fixed form in a text so that it might be able to stand over against the church and call it to repentance and faith.

By making revelation dependent on the memory and authority of the institutional church, Tradition II effectively exempts it from the condemning judgment of the Law. Indeed, appeals to unwritten tradition also drive one's focus away from the external Word into one's own interior memory, or into that of ecclesiastical authorities.[39] Therefore, such a position inevitably encourages Enthusiasm, which Luther famously argued was the world's oldest sin.[40]

As we have seen, Enthusiasm and legalism go hand in hand. Legalists are inevitably Enthusiasts, because they need to generate meritorious works in order to justify themselves. Indeed, the works Scripture prescribes often are viewed as too hard or too mundane. Even more problematic, they carry with them no promise of justification (Lk 17:7–10; Rom 3:20). Similarly, since the external Word glorifies Christ and condemns everything in human nature, the only court within which the legalist can be found not guilty is his own interior conceit. The legalist must therefore become an Enthusiast in order to make legalism work.

It is therefore no surprise that the doctrines Catholics seemingly base on unwritten church tradition promote or are a byproduct of works righteousness. Purgatory, the penitential system, and the sacrificial character of the mass are means of promoting salvation by works. Even the Marian doctrines assume a

---

39. See Barth's similar remarks in Barth, *Church Dogmatics* I/1:104–11.
40. SA III.viii (Bente, 495–96).

theology in which a graced human subject (Mary) through her personal virtue becomes the means by which the incarnation and atonement for sin can occur. In other words, even in the Marian doctrines there is an assumption that God cannot carry out redemptive acts without some sort of worthiness on the human side of the equation.[41]

There also is an instructive parallel in post-biblical Judaism and Islam to Catholicism's tendency to generate and rely upon unwritten tradition as a supplemental source of revelation. Modern Orthodox Jews, much like the Pharisees before them, rely on the Oral Torah supposedly passed down from Moses to the rabbis through lines of succession.[42] Similarly, Islam teaches that the sayings of Muhammad (*sunnah*) are authoritative as a supplemental source of revelation alongside the Qur'an.[43] As with Catholicism, the goal is to supplement the scriptural source of revelation.

What these religious systems have in common is their belief in works righteousness. Indeed, supplemental forms of non-scriptural revelation are necessary for works righteousness to function plausibly. If like Jews, Catholics, and Muslims a person believes God ultimately will count him as righteous on the basis of his own works, it is only logical to think there is no room for Christian freedom in indifferent matters. Since righteousness is performative, every action is potentially either a demerit or meritorious in the quest for holiness. Unfortunately, neither the Bible nor the Qur'an covers the minutiae of every possible action an individual might take, and so questions arise in the course of the history of these religions about how a person is to justify himself by his works if he does not know in every situation what he is supposed to do. As a result, within these religions, bodies of tradition naturally arise which intend to fill in the legal gaps.

Nevertheless, for these traditions to guarantee as God-pleasing the works performed on the basis of these bodies of teaching, these traditions logically must be viewed increasingly not merely as inferences drawn from the original scriptural revelation, but in fact as part of the original revelation itself. Hence, we see the Pharisees' opinions on how to apply Torah in the Second Temple period being attributed to Moses, Catholic church customs and doctrines that arose largely in the Middle Ages being attributed to the apostles, and Muslims insisting that legal opinions generated by later Islamic scholars were in fact unwritten statements of Muhammad himself.

---

41. See this argument in Hermann Sasse, "Liturgy and Confession: A Brotherly Warning Against the 'High Church' Danger," in *The Lonely Way* 2:299–316. Also see Barth, *Church Dogmatics* I/2:143–46.

42. Nathan T. Lopes Cardozo, *The Oral and Written Torah: A Comprehensive Introduction* (New York: Rowman & Littlefield, 1998).

43. Alī Nāṣirī, *An Introduction to Hadith: History and Sources*, trans. Mansoor Limba (London, MIU Press, 2013), 37–46.

TRADITION III AND HYPERENTHUSIASM

In modern Roman Catholic thought, the already existing weaknesses of Tradition II are exacerbated by what Oberman refers to as Tradition III. According to this model, doctrinal development itself and not merely the visible church's unwritten traditions is identified with the voice of the Holy Spirit. Here the marginally regulative role of Scripture still present in Tradition II is destroyed almost completely. Scripture is now demoted almost to the level of insignificance, and thus possesses little ability to check the unending development of official church teaching. Although Roman Catholics theoretically would deny it, Scripture becomes merely a single moment in the larger history of the Holy Spirit's continuous revelation to the magisterium of the institutional church. If Tradition II encourages a somewhat adulterated Enthusiasm, Tradition III represents Enthusiasm in a very nearly pure form.[44]

Historically, it appears that Tradition III arose for two significant reasons. First, it was the next logical step in the growth of Tradition II's legalism and Enthusiasm as described in the last section. Imputing apostolic authority to extrabiblical traditions that have arisen as a means of clarifying the original revelation creates the further problem that the bodies of interpretation themselves become larger and more complicated than the original revelation they are supposed to clarify. By the twelfth century the canons of various councils, their creeds, their liturgy, and the writings of the church fathers were capable of filling many monastic libraries.[45] It should be borne in mind that in the medieval church the Bible was still the central text, and therefore these traditions, whether considered directly apostolic or not, were intended either to clarify or to be read alongside the Bible.[46] Still, it could be argued that these traditions ultimately became more complicated and vast than the Bible itself.

For this reason canon lawyers began to develop techniques of harmonizing various contradictory bits of church legislation.[47] A similar phenomenon can be found in the sphere of theology. Peter Abelard demonstrated in his *Sic et Non* that the fathers of the church had said contradictory things that were not easily reconciled.[48] Abelard and other scholastic theologians borrowed harmonization techniques from the canon law as a means of reconciling disparate authorities.[49]

---

44. Oberman, "*Quo Vadis Petre*?" 290–96.

45. John Bonaventure O'Connor, *Monasticism and Civilization* (New York: P. J. Kenedy & Sons, 1921), 131–45.

46. See Beryl Smalley, *The Study of the Bible in the Middle Ages*, 2d ed. (1952; reprint, South Bend, IN: Notre Dame University Press, 1989); Frans Van Liere, *An Introduction to the Medieval Bible* (Cambridge, UK: Cambridge University Press, 2014).

47. Paul Tillich, *The History of Christian Thought: From Its Judaic and Hellenistic Origins to Existentialism* (Chicago: University of Chicago Press, 1972), 169.

48. Peter Abelard, *Sic et Non: A Critical Edition,* ed. B. B. Boyer and R. McKeon (Chicago: University of Chicago Press, 1978).

49. Tillich, *History of Christian Thought*, 169–71.

William Abraham has suggested that such a situation also logically gave rise to the notion of papal teaching authority and infallibility.[50] Although the specific occasion for the invention of the doctrine of papal infallibility was the Franciscan controversy over the absolute poverty of Christ,[51] Abraham's explanation as a description of the overall logical trajectory of the medieval Latin tradition makes a great deal of sense. It could be argued that even if the Franciscan controversy over poverty had not occurred, the medieval church still would have invented something approximating papal infallibility as the natural outgrowth of the inadequacies of Tradition II.

The shortcomings of Tradition II logically call for an inspired magisterial teacher such as the pope or a council to decide which parts of the tradition are valid and which are not. One cannot accept the whole mass of tradition the visible church presents as apostolic, since it is not entirely harmonious. One needs a critical principle to negotiate what is legitimately apostolic tradition and what is not.

Similarly, a legalist needs a living voice to prescribe new works as new situations arise. Because new situations inevitably will arise over time, it is important for a legalist to have a person who can speak with the authority of God about what works will be meritorious of salvation and which will not. There can be no ambiguity in this, because one cannot risk performing the wrong actions in the minutiae of everyday life. The legalist quest for self-justification thus leads logically to the generation of more Enthusiastic teaching authorities. A very similar phenomenon can be seen in the structure of authority in contemporary Mormonism, where the Latter-Day Saints Prophet-President provides a continuous stream of prophecy as historical circumstances change.[52]

The theory of papal authority and works righteousness thus are natural corollaries. Luther makes this point in the Smalcald Articles when he observes that reliance on manmade meritorious works such as the sacrifice of the mass as means of salvation are dependent on the existence of a papacy willing to prescribe them. The implication is that works righteousness and the papacy are mutually legitimating.[53]

---

50. Personal conversation. See discussion of the papacy in William Abraham, *Canon and Criterion in Christian Theology: From the Fathers to Feminism* (Oxford: Oxford University Press, 1998), 64–81. In this section Abraham focuses on the papacy's additional rationale for the desire to supersede the authority of the ecumenical councils on the issue of the dual procession of the Holy Spirit.

51. Tierney, *Origins of Papal Infallibility*, 115–30. Tierney makes a nice summary comment on the innovative nature of the theory of papal infallibility: "There is no convincing evidence that papal infallibility formed any part of the theological or canonical tradition of the church before the thirteenth century; the doctrine was invented in the first place by a few dissident Franciscans because it suited their convenience to invent it; eventually, but only after much initial reluctance, it was accepted by the papacy because it suited the convenience of the popes to accept it." Tierney, *Origins of Papal Infallibility*, 281.

52. See Bruce McConkie, *Mormon Doctrine* (Salt Lake City: Bookcraft, 1966), 591–92.

53. SA II.ii (Bente, 463–69).

Conversely, if one rejects works righteousness, the need for a papacy ceases. The Gospel creates a situation in which there is no reason to have a pope.[54] The Gospel gives the benefits of Christ freely through its effective communication in Word and Sacrament. Christ promises to communicate His benefits freely, and the pope giving his seal of approval, whether through validation of priestly charisma or magisterial teaching authority, adds nothing to the power of Christ's words. One does not need a person to prescribe the conditions of something for which there are no conditions. Likewise, one does not need to clarify something that is self-interpreting either by its internal clarity (the Gospel does what it says, namely, justifies) or external clarity (the words of the Bible that communicate the Gospel are grammatically clear and simple).

The second reason for the development of Tradition III was the genuine effectiveness of Reformation apologetics. When Martin Chemnitz in *Examination of the Council of Trent* and Johann Gerhard in *Confessio Catholica* demonstrated that no one in the early church had ever heard of these supplemental traditions, Roman Catholics ultimately went back to the drawing board. As Susan Rosa has shown, by the late sixteenth and early seventeenth centuries Roman Catholic apologists stopped attempting to defend individual doctrines, which, it might be surmised, was rather difficult in the light of the new historical and exegetical knowledge provided by Renaissance and Reformation scholarship. Rather, the Council of Trent's apologists emphasized the Spirit-guided unity and intellectual certainty that the institutional Roman Church provided.[55] Since the institution was Spirit-guided, what the church placed its stamp of infallibility on logically must always be true, even if such pronouncements were perceived to change over time.

In the view of the many apologists of Tradition III, the original apostolic teaching represents a kind of seed of truth which matures into a full-grown tree of doctrine under the watering and care of the Spirit-guided institutional church. The theory of doctrinal development posited by Tradition III provided Roman Catholics with what they considered to be a plausible explanation for why much of what the contemporary Catholic Church teaches cannot be found in the original kerygma. This notion seems to have been articulated first by Petavius in the early seventeenth century,[56] and later was developed into a more sophisticated form by Cardinal Newman in the nineteenth century.[57]

The main logical problem with this position is that it represents a kind of special pleading for the Roman Catholic tradition. Though the Roman Church endorses things that are missing empirically from the teaching of the

---

54. SA II.iv (Bente, 471–73). Luther observes that if the pope does not have the divine right to prescribe works meritorious of salvation, the papacy is useless.

55. Susan Rosa, "Seventeenth-Century Catholic Polemic and the Rise of Cultural Rationalism," *Journal of the History of Ideas* 57, no. 1 (1996): 87–107.

56. Petavius, *De Theologicis Dogmatibus*, 4 vols. (Paris, 1644).

57. John Henry Newman, *Essay on the Development of Christian Doctrine* (South Bend, IN: Notre Dame University Press, 1989).

Scriptures and even from the tradition of the early church, Christians should simply accept the Roman magisterium's unverifiable claim that the pope and councils are guided divinely and are adding to the faith only because the Holy Spirit has prompted them to do so. Indeed, such a concept looks very much like a simple admission on the part of the Roman Church that, as the Reformers and the Eastern Orthodox Church have always contended, they corrupted the faith once delivered to the saints (Jude 1:3) and simply relabeled such corruption as "developments." As observed in an earlier chapter, a similar phenomenon is found in American mainline Protestant churches' tendency to attribute their deviations from Scripture to the "new work" of the Holy Spirit.

As a counter to many of these criticisms, Catholics often focused on the question of intellectual certainty. They argued that Lutherans and the other traditions coming out of the Reformation cannot have certainty regarding the articles of the faith, since without an inspired magisterium they must admit the possibility of their own fallibility. In other words, since Lutherans admit that the visible church may err, how, ask Catholics, can they be definitively certain that they are correct?[58] A new generation may find that Lutherans have read their Bibles incorrectly and overturn everything the Augsburg Confession says.[59] Indeed, it is often argued that the multitude of Protestant denominations demonstrates the intellectual uncertainty that *sola scriptura* creates.[60] Ultimately the price of such certainty is accepting everything the Roman magisterium teaches and has "developed," no matter how exegetically or historically implausible. As a result, Catholics often feel justified in simply ignoring the profound exegetical and historical difficulties with their own theological position, and instead focus on the argument that the only alternative to the absolute authority of the Roman magisterium is theological uncertainty and exegetical anarchy.

There are several problems with this argument. First, as we have already seen, there are objective criteria by which Scripture is to be interpreted (external and internal clarity, the analogy of faith, etc.). For those who do not follow these routes to clarity, Scripture is nothing but darkness.

Second, the Catholic argument lacks coherence. When the Roman magisterium speaks in order to clarify the faith, it does so by producing documents that are supposedly infallible. Of course, this process of clarification elicits the question of why one set of infallible documents (papal decrees, conciliar canons, etc.) should be clearer and therefore provide more certainty

---

58. See this approximate argument in John Henry Newman, *An Essay in Aid of a Grammar of Assent* (London: Longmans, Green, and Co., 1870); John Henry Newman, "Private Judgment," in *Essays Critical and Historical*, vol. 2 (London: Basil, Montagu, Pickering, 1877), 336–74.

59. Joseph Ratzinger, *Principles of Catholic Theology: Building Stones for a Fundamental Theology*, trans. Mary Frances McCarthy (San Francisco: Ignatius Press, 1987), 222–23.

60. Robert Fastiggi, "What Did the Protestant Reformers Teach about *Sola Scriptura*?" in *Not by Scripture Alone*, 366.

than another set of infallible documents (the Bible).[61] After all, much as Protestants debate the Bible, Catholics still fight over the meaning of many of their own conciliar documents, notably Vatican II. The only difference is that the massive theological differences present among Catholics (and even between two successive popes, Benedict XVI and Francis I) are masked by their participation in a common institutional church.

Third, the Catholic argument that an infallible magisterium creates absolute intellectual certainty works only if one assumes that ordinary believers share the infallibility of the institutional church. Since ordinary believers in the Catholic tradition are not infallible, in interpreting the infallible teachings of the church they are in no better a position than fallible Lutherans interpreting the infallible teachings of the Bible.[62] If Roman Catholics are willing to admit that fallible people can interpret infallible teaching of the magisterium in a responsible and accurate manner, which logically they must, then it follows that they must also allow that Lutherans can do the same with the infallible teachings of the Bible.[63]

This contradiction is no more manifest than when Catholics argue for the papacy on the basis of Matthew 16.[64] Setting aside the poor exegesis[65] and the lack of early church support for the Catholic reading of the text,[66] appealing to these verses creates a series of logical problems for the papacy and its claims to interpretive authority. If one can appeal to Scripture in order to establish the authority of the pope, then it follows that Scripture is sufficiently clear without the pope's interpretive authority. Otherwise, how would an appeal to an ambiguous and uncertain authority (Scripture) establish an unambiguous and certain authority (the papacy)? If the Scriptures are clear and unambiguous enough to establish the papacy and its promise of intellectual certainty, why would one need the papacy to interpret Scripture in the first place?[67]

Conversely, one could claim that the Scriptures are not sufficiently clear, and so even the correct interpretation of Matthew 16 depends on the interpretation of the pope. But this places Catholics in a position where they must make

---

61. Powell, *Papal Infallibility*, 14.

62. Powell, *Papal Infallibility*, 14–15.

63. See John Warwick Montgomery, "You Are Looking for a Church Home—or Perhaps You Aren't," in *Where Christ Is Present*, 5.

64. Dave Armstrong, *Biblical Proofs of an Infallible Church and Papacy* (Lulu, 2015), 149; Richard McBrien, *Catholicism*, 2 vols. (Minneapolis: Winston Press, 1980), 2:830, 832.

65. Tr. 1–5 (Bente, 505–7). Also see R. C. H. Lenski, *The Interpretation of Matthew's Gospel* (Peabody, MA: Hendrickson Publishers, 1998), 604–9; William Webster, *The Church of Rome at the Bar of History* (Edinburgh: The Banner of Truth Trust, 1995), 34–55; James White, *Answers to Catholic Claims* (Southbridge, MA: Crowne Publications, 1990), 104–8.

66. Tr. 5–9 (Bente, 507–9). Also see Manlio Simonetti, ed., *Ancient Christian Commentaries on Scripture, New Testament, Ib: Matthew 14–28* (Downers Grove, IL: InterVarsity Press, 2002), 45–46; Webster, *Church of Rome*, 56–71.

67. Abraham, *Canon and Criterion in Christian Theology*, 359–60; Montgomery, "You Are Looking for a Church Home," 5. Also see compelling arguments in Hans Küng, *Infallibility: An Inquiry* (New York: Doubleday, 1983).

a circular argument: the papacy is established by Matthew 16, because the papacy says that Matthew 16 establishes it. Either way, an appeal to this passage necessarily must destroy the entire rationale for an inspired magisterium on the grounds of the purely contradictory and circular nature of the argument it produces.

REVIVAL OF TRADITION I IN
THE LUTHERAN REFORMATION[68]

Oberman sees the Tradition I of the ancient church being revived during the time of the Reformation. Both Lutheran and Reformed theologians of the sixteenth and seventeenth centuries were concerned with the catholicity of the Gospel.[69] In large part this concern grew out of the charges of novelty and arrogance their Roman Catholic opponents made.[70] Luther's opponents famously had asked him at the Diet of Worms: "Are you alone wise?"[71] By studying the writings of the church fathers, the reformers sought to establish it was the medieval church and not the Reformation that promoted novel doctrines and interpretations of the Bible.[72]

In terms of a concern for the catholicity of the Reformation, Luther's approach was considerably more muted than others. In his early writings Luther often appealed to the church fathers, particularly St. Augustine,[73] along with later medieval figures like Bernard of Clairvaux.[74] After his encounter with Zwingli and the other southern reformers, he increasingly began to sour on appeals to earlier church tradition. The southern reformers compiled statements of the church fathers that they argued validated a symbolic or spiritualistic interpretation of the Lord's Supper. Luther countered this claim by emphasizing the grammatical-historical clarity of the Words of Institution, and increasingly became suspicious of arguments that sought to bolster the external clarity of the Word with appeals to the consensus of the early church.[75] Nevertheless, Luther

---

68. Much of the material in this section appears in a similar though not identical form in "Johann Gerhard's Reception of Thomas Aquinas' *Analogia Entis*," in *Aquinas among the Protestants*, ed. Carl Manfred Svensson and David VanDrunen (Hoboken, NJ: Wiley-Blackwell, 2017), 109–28.

69. See Rupert Davies, *The Problem of Authority in the Continental Reformers: A Study in Luther, Zwingli, and Calvin* (London: Epworth Press, 1946). Also see Anthony Lane, *John Calvin: Student of the Church Fathers* (Grand Rapids: Baker Book House, 2000).

70. Stewart, *Lutheran Patristic Catholicity*, 37–54.

71. Roland Bainton, *Here I Stand: A Life of Martin Luther* (1950; reprint, Nashville: Abingdon Press, 1978), 190.

72. Headley, *Luther's View of Church History*, 156–223.

73. Bernhard Lohse, *Martin Luther's Theology: Its Historical and Systematic Development*, trans. and ed. Roy A. Harrisville (Minneapolis: Fortress Press, 1999), 23.

74. Franz Posset, *Pater Bernhardus: Martin Luther and Bernard of Clairvaux* (Kalamazoo: Cistercian Publications, 2000).

75. See Kent Heimbigner, "The Evolution of Luther's Reception of the Early Church Fathers in Eucharistic Controversy: A Consideration of Selected Works, 1518–1529," *Logia* 7, no. 1 (1998): 3–12.

retained his respect for the catholicity of the church, particularly with regard to the authority of the ancient ecumenical councils. This respect can be observed in later writings like *On the Councils and the Church* (1539).[76]

By contrast, Melanchthon was considerably more interested in the use of the writings of the ancient church as an apologetic tool. In his personal and confessional writings he seeks to show continuity between the Wittenberg Reformation and the early church. As Peter Fraenkel has demonstrated, Melanchthon possessed a highly sophisticated notion of the church's catholicity going all the way back to Eden.[77] In the Fall the church had completely apostatized, in that Adam and Eve constituted the whole church, and God had restored it through the preaching of Law and Gospel. By entrusting Adam with the promise of a Savior in Gn 3:15, God reformed and revived the church. Melanchthon thus saw a catholic unity between God's sermon of Genesis 3 and the proclamation of the Gospel in the contemporary church. Indeed, he saw the current proclamation of the church and its body of doctrine as nothing but a more refined explication of the content of the *protoevangelium*.[78]

It is also important to note that Melanchthon claimed that by giving the *protoevangelium* God had brought about a reformation. This claim suggested that Luther's own reforming project was by no means unprecedented, but rather part of a larger pattern in the life of the church catholic. By the proclamation of the promise of the Savior, God had overturned the false doctrine through which Satan had led our first parents astray, much as Luther had demonstrated that the false teaching of the medieval church had led much of Christendom astray.[79] Indeed, Melanchthon held that throughout human history the true church remained a remnant within a sea of apostasy (1 Kgs 19:18). Despite this dire situation, a true remnant of the faithful always persists; but the price of this persistence is that the true church must be conformed to the image of its master, Christ, and bear the cross.[80] The existence of this remnant of the true church within the visible church made periodic reformations in the life of the people of God possible, even after long periods of mass apostasy.[81]

Hence, the catholicity of the church was to be discerned not in the judgments of the pope or even in the consensus of the church fathers, but in its proclamation of the Gospel through both time and space. Such an approach allowed Melanchthon to be critical of many of the church fathers, especially Origen and Jerome, while still affirming in them what was evangelical and catholic.[82] Likewise, Melanchthon also had little difficulty in ranking earlier Christian theologians according to how well their theology centered on the

76. *On the Councils and the Church*, 1539 (AE 41:3–178; WA 50:488–653).
77. Fraenkel, *Testimonia Patrum*, 61.
78. Fraenkel, *Testimonia Patrum*, 61–62.
79. Fraenkel, *Testimonia Patrum*, 61.
80. Fraenkel, *Testimonia Patrum*, 100–118.
81. Fraenkel, *Testimonia Patrum*, 69.
82. Fraenkel, *Testimonia Patrum*, 86–93.

chief article of the Gospel.[83] According to such criteria, Augustine fared the best[84] while the medieval scholastics fared the worst.[85]

Let us note two points with regard to Melanchthon's appropriation of tradition in contrast to that of the ancient and medieval church. First, although Oberman is correct that Melanchthon's use of churchly tradition falls within the same trajectory of the ancient church's version of Tradition I, there is nevertheless a critical edge to Melanchthon's appropriation of tradition that is missing in the Ante-Nicene fathers. Whereas the early church tended to believe there was a relatively smooth correspondence between the Scriptures and the public teaching of the church, Melanchthon is much more comfortable with the notion of the visible church's perpetual apostasy and need for reformation. Here the effective power of the Scripture both makes the catholicity of the church possible (i.e., God never ceases creating faith through the Word) and at the same time serves as a critical principle. We may also infer that for Melanchthon the church needs a critical principle to call it to perpetual repentance because of the *simul* of Christian existence.

Second, it might be argued that in a certain sense Melanchthon and the other Lutheran reformers faced the same dilemma that challenged the early canon lawyers and scholastic theologians after the twelfth century. Namely, due to the mass of traditionary teaching that had been built up in Christendom, there was a need for a critical principle to discern what is apostolic and what is not. As suggested above (following William Abraham), this dilemma may have precipitated the development of the theory of papal teaching authority. In other words, for Catholics the papacy discerns the catholicity of the church and its teaching by reserving the power to decide what is catholic and what is not. To be catholic is to be in accordance with the judgment of the bishop of Rome, and thus the term "Roman Catholic" makes a great deal of sense.

Similarly, Melanchthon certainly agreed with his Roman Catholic opponents that the church possesses a continuity over time in its teaching. Nevertheless, it is the Scriptures as interpreted from the perspective of the Gospel and not the pope's judgment that serve as a critical measure of what is catholic. Lutherans often have called themselves evangelical catholics, since it is the Gospel and not the Roman pontiff that serves as the means of discerning the catholicity of the church and its teaching.[86]

Melanchthon's apologetic technique of using the church fathers and the decisions of early Christian councils as a means to witness to the catholicity of the Wittenberg Reformation was picked up and expanded by his student Martin Chemnitz. Chemnitz's greatest achievement in regard to his use of the church fathers can be found in his massive and highly influential apologetic

---

83. Fraenkel, *Testimonia Patrum*, 125–34.
84. Fraenkel, *Testimonia Patrum*, 93–96.
85. Fraenkel, *Testimonia Patrum*, 100–107.
86. See David Scaer, "Evangelical and Catholic: A Slogan in Search of a Definition," *Concordia Theological Quarterly* 65, no. 4 (2001): 323–44.

work *Examination of the Council of Trent* (1565–73). Regarding the question of catholicity, the *Examination* follows the common Melanchthonian apologetic technique of demonstrating by way of extensive patristic citations that it is the Lutheran church and not the Roman Church that is really catholic in the fullest sense of the term.

Throughout the work Chemnitz juxtaposes statements from the Council of Trent and its defenders with both Scripture and early church fathers. Chemnitz is able very skillfully to show the contradiction between the Tridentine position and the teaching of the ancient church, as well as the agreement between the latter and the Lutheran stance.[87] Chemnitz and his fellow authors of the Formula of Concord worked out a similar apologetic program in an appendix entitled the Catalog of Testimonies.[88] In the early seventeenth century Johann Gerhard deployed the same technique on an even more massive scale with his famous *Confessio Catholica* (1633–37).[89]

One of the most significant sections of the first volume of the *Examination* deals with the definition of tradition. Chemnitz suggests that the term refers to eight distinct phenomena. Seven of these categories of tradition are theologically valid. Among the valid forms of tradition are included: (1) the oral preaching of Christ and the apostles; (2) the written form of the apostolic tradition, that is, the New Testament; (3) the oral version of the apostolic tradition handed down to the churches; (4) the church's tradition of faithful exposition of the Scriptures in its public ministry; (5) doctrines inferred from the teaching of Scripture but not explicitly stated therein; (6) the consensus of the ancient church regarding the teaching of Scripture; (7) rites and liturgical customs handed down by the apostles or other persons in the ancient church.[90]

Chemnitz condemns only the eighth category of tradition, namely, the Council of Trent's supplemental unwritten tradition. This category of tradition is not valid because it teaches things contrary to Scripture, and was obviously generated long after the apostolic era and therefore invented. In Chemnitz's treatment, ultimately church tradition is valid to the extent that it is based on the explicit content of or at least draws necessary conclusions from explicit statements of Scripture.[91]

For Chemnitz, not only does tradition appropriately witness to the content of Scripture, it also serves as a means to establish the appropriate limits of the interpretation of Scripture. In one passage Chemnitz goes so far as to argue that

---

87. See Fraenkel, *Testimonia Patrum*, 267–68; Arthur Olsen, "Martin Chemnitz and the Council of Trent," *Dialog* 2 (1963): 60–67; Stewart, *Lutheran Patristic Catholicity*, 55–124.

88. See Thomas Manteufel, trans., "The Catalog of Testimonies," in *Sources and Contexts of the Book of Concord*, ed. Robert Kolb and James Nestingen (Minneapolis: Augsburg Fortress, 2001), 220–44.

89. Johann Gerhard, *Confessio Catholica*, 2 vols. (Jena, 1634–37); Stewart, *Lutheran Patristic Catholicity*, 134–42.

90. Chemnitz, *Examination of the Council of Trent* 1:217–71.

91. Chemnitz, *Examination of the Council of Trent* 1:272–307.

if there is no precedent for a particular interpretation of the Bible, it is a good indication that the interpretation is incorrect:

> No one should rely on his own wisdom in the interpretation of the Scripture, not even in the clear passages, for it is clearly written in 2 Peter 1:20: "The Scripture is not a matter of one's private interpretation." And whoever twists the Holy Scripture so that it is understood according to his preconceived opinions does this to his own destruction (2 Peter 3:16). The best reader of Scripture according to Hillary [of Poitiers, A.D. 300–368] is one who does not carry the understanding of what is said to the Scripture but who carries it away from the Scripture. We also gratefully and reverently use the labors of the fathers who by their commentaries have profitably clarified many passages of the Scripture. And we confess that we are greatly confirmed by the testimonies of the ancient church in the true and sound understanding of the Scripture. *Nor do we approve of it if someone invents for himself a meaning which conflicts with all antiquity, and for which there are no testimonies of the church.*[92]

A number of points should be made about this passage. First, Chemnitz does not suggest that the power and clarity of Scripture lie dormant unless they are activated by the church. Neither is he making a theological argument for "truth by consensus" in the manner of contemporary Anglican figures like Richard Hooker.[93] Rather, his emphasis is on the fact that the interpretation of the Bible is a public act of the church catholic. As we saw in the previous chapter, the Augustana teaches that the church has a genuine public authority in giving an exposition of Scripture in its preaching and teaching.[94] The key difference between the confessional Lutheran and Roman Catholic understandings of this public teaching authority is that for the former, the teachers of the church are responsible to both the royal priesthood and the text of the Bible, whereas for the latter, despite their protests to the contrary, they are not.

Still, Chemnitz holds that God has not forsaken His church but is present and effective within it through the media of Word and Sacrament. Chemnitz's underlying assumption is that God creates faith monergistically and therefore does not have to rely on the free will of human beings to read Scripture correctly, thereby preserving the church. If one believes that the risen Christ is present with His church, creating faith and preserving a true confession of faith, then it is logical to assume that there has always been a true interpretation of the Bible present in the church, to which believers can look. Interpretations of the Bible that give no heed to what the church has said in its tradition of public preaching and teaching thus cannot be correct. To assume that everyone between the closing of the canon and one's own time has been mistaken is to

---

92. Cited in Adam Francisco, "Authority: The Holy Scriptures," in *Where Christ Is Present*, 72. Originally taken from Chemnitz, *Examination of the Council of Trent* 1:208–9. Emphasis added.

93. See Richard Hooker, *Of the Laws of Ecclesiastical Polity* (Cambridge, UK: Cambridge University Press, 1989).

94. CA XXVIII (Bente, 83–95).

ignore the fact that God the Holy Spirit has always been creating faith through the means of grace.

Hence, the *tentatio* of the interpretative process involves testing one's reading of a text not only against the positive criteria of the internal and external clarity of Scripture, but also negatively against the precedent in the history of exegesis. Although confessional Lutherans do not read Scripture under the authority of the church (as does Roman Catholicism), Chemnitz certainly does seem to suggest that an individual will get the Bible wrong if he does not read it with and alongside the church.

Such a formulation may leave many readers confused: Chemnitz simultaneously wishes to maintain that Scripture is the supreme authority while also suggesting that church tradition places limits on one's reading of Scripture. If tradition can place limitations on one's reading of Scripture, does it not follow that tradition can overrule what one finds in Scripture? To answer this question we turn to an analogy found in the concept of paradigm put forward by the philosopher of science Thomas Kuhn.

Kuhn maintains that the scientific community interprets the data of experience through a communal lens he calls a paradigm.[95] One example of such a lens in the history of science is the collective assumption of either heliocentrism or geocentricism.[96] Scientists are educated in these lenses as a precondition for scientific research.[97] Having such a lens is necessary as a grid or framework within which to organize the raw data of experience and make sense of scientific findings. Nevertheless, a paradigm is good only insofar as it is able to find a place for and explain all the data. If there are too many anomalies in the paradigm, a scientific revolution occurs and the paradigm is discarded.[98]

Analogously, Christians read Scripture through the lens of the public teaching tradition of the church. Teachers of the Word and their ancestors in the faith produce maps and guides for ordinary Christians to read the Bible profitably and accept its message. They do this not only through preaching and teaching but through the production of creeds and confessions. For Lutheran Christians, the ecumenical creeds and the Lutheran symbols serve as an authoritative lens through which we properly read the Bible.[99]

Nevertheless, although these creeds and confessions are genuine authorities, they are subordinate norms (*norma normata*) to the final and supreme norm of Scripture (*norma normans*). If these norms cannot explain and organize the data of Scripture they must be rejected or reformulated. For example, due to the

---

95. Kuhn, *Structure of Scientific Revolutions*, 10–11.
96. Kuhn, *Structure of Scientific Revolutions*, 10.
97. Kuhn, *Structure of Scientific Revolutions*, 10–11.
98. Kuhn, *Structure of Scientific Revolutions*, 52.
99. Johann Gerhard, *On the Church*, trans. Richard Dinda (St. Louis: Concordia Publishing House, 2010), 523; Pieper, *Christian Dogmatics* 1:354–58; James Voelz, *What Does It Mean? Principles of Biblical Interpretation in the Post-Modern World* (St. Louis: Concordia Publishing House, 1997), 347–61.

failure of medieval theology to explain the findings of Renaissance scholarship on the Bible, Luther and his colleagues modified and in many cases outright abandoned much of the paradigm of the Roman Church.[100]

TRADITION 0

Tradition I represents a rejection not only of Traditions II and III but also of a fourth model, Tradition 0,[101] or as some call it, *sola scriptura*. It appears that Tradition 0 originated with the Anabaptist movement of the sixteenth century,[102] and it has been the popular understanding of *sola scriptura* among British and North American low-church Evangelicals.[103] Advocates of Tradition 0 posit that adherence to the Scripture principle of the Reformation entails a total rejection of all church tradition. Hence, according to Tradition 0, Scripture is not merely the ultimate authority (as in Tradition I) but in fact the only authority.

As we observed earlier, the Lutheran Reformation's high view of tradition correlates well with its belief in the efficacy of the means of grace and the bondage of the will. In other words, because the Word and sacraments have always been present throughout church history, it logically follows that there has always been a remnant of the church that confesses the true faith. Along with this remnant, then, there must always have been a true tradition within the church. Contemporary Christians thus can look to this true confession of the faith as a guide to their reading of Scripture. Ultimately the church's confession of the truth of the Gospel depends not on human free will but on the efficacy of Word and Sacrament. To doubt the existence of a true tradition of the faith within the church is in fact to deny the divine power of the means of grace.

By contrast, Tradition 0 seems to correlate very strongly with popular[104] (though not classical[105]) Arminianism. In such a theology, God's grace and a true reading of Scripture is dependent on the decision of humans in their free will. As observed above, for the Lutheran it is impossible that everyone in church history has misread the Bible, since God is faithful to His church (Mt 16:18). By contrast, within the popular Arminian framework where the preservation of the church depends on human decision, it is possible the church has ceased to exist for long periods of time.

Whereas Luther could point to the fact that God had for fifteen hundred years justified and sanctified Christians through infant baptism and therefore

---

100. See description in Lowell Green, *How Melanchthon Helped Luther Discover the Gospel* (Greenwood, SC: Attic Press, 1980).

101. McGrath, *Reformation Thought*, 107–8; Mathison, *Shape of Sola Scriptura*, 152–53.

102. McGrath, *Reformation Thought*, 144–46.

103. See Nathan Hatch, *The Democratization of American Christianity* (New Haven: Yale University Press, 1989).

104. Charles Finney, *Finney's Systematic Theology* (1851; reprint, Minneapolis: Bethany House, 1994).

105. See Roger Olson, *Arminian Theology: Myths and Realities* (Downers Grove, IL: InterVarsity Press, 2006).

the practice could not be wrong,[106] his Anabaptist opponents, who in many cases were outright Pelagians, believed that the church had virtually evaporated by the time of Constantine and had been reconstituted by them only in the sixteenth century. It was thus plausible that infant baptism was contrary to the faith, since it was possible that the entire faith had been corrupted through freely chosen human neglect.[107]

Beyond its implicit Pelagianism, the main difficulty with *sola scriptura* or Tradition 0 is that it is impossible. The Word of God has a definite history within the church, just as all ideas have a history. Although Scripture is the ultimate authority, we also must recognize that every explication by the post-apostolic church of what the Bible teaches is part of a historic theological tradition. The fact that one's reading of the Bible stands within a tradition does not make such a reading unfaithful. A given tradition of interpretation may or may not be an accurate representation of what the Bible teaches. Nevertheless, any interpretation stands within a particular tradition.[108]

Tradition 0 is problematic because it lacks the self-awareness to distinguish between the Bible and a given church community's historically formed understanding of the Bible. If an individual recognizes that he stands in a tradition as a normed norm, then he can test and subordinate that tradition to what he finds in the un-normed norm of the Bible. If he does not acknowledge this dependency on the tradition of interpretation, it is much harder to distinguish between his own historically and contextually formed confession of the faith and the supreme authority of the Bible.

Tradition 0 thus inevitably drifts into a covert form of Tradition II. Without a conscious recognition of the hermeneutical presuppositions with which the ecclesial community approaches the Bible and their historical origins, certain nonbiblical traditions (for example, the insistence on the metaphorical nature of the Words of Institution, the transference of the Sabbath to Sunday, the sinner's prayer, and the ban on alcohol) are treated as if they are self-evidently scriptural.

Returning to the scientific paradigm analogy, Tradition 0's understanding of scriptural authority is not unlike the pre-Copernican scientific worldview, in which people simply identified geocentricism with the self-evident order of things with little reflection on where such a belief came from or whether it correlated to reality. The ironic result is that this supposedly radical commitment to Scripture actually undermines its ultimate authority through the introduction of unacknowledged nonbiblical traditions into the canons of authority.

---

106. *Concerning Rebaptism*, 1528 (AE 40:225–62; WA 26:137–74).

107. See summary in George H. Williams, *The Radical Reformation* (Kirksville, MO: Truman State University Press, 2000), 431–59.

108. Kevin Vanhoozer, *The Drama of Doctrine: A Canonical-Linguistic Approach to Christian Theology* (Louisville: Westminster/John Knox, 2005), 113.

In contrast, advocates of Tradition I recognize a distinction between their present church's confession and the supreme authority of the Bible. Therefore, although the Lutheran Confessions are an accurate representation of what Scripture teaches (*quia*, not *quatenus*), in every generation there must be a comparison of the teaching of Scripture and the Confessions in order to confirm that the latter accurately correspond to the former. This distinction between our present confession of faith and Scripture itself makes it possible to engage in appropriate doctrinal criticism when this is necessary.

THE TRUE CONFESSION OF THE FAITH AND THE PRESENCE OF THE RISEN CHRIST

Ultimately the problem of Traditions II, III, and 0 is that they are forms of Enthusiasm. Their particular form of Enthusiasm is an outgrowth of the larger Christological failure of both Roman Catholic and Reformed theology. Both the Roman Catholic and Reformed traditions reject the Lutheran *capax* and *genus majestaticum*. For both Catholics and the Reformed, the risen Christ is confined to heaven and cannot be with His church by His own divine power. Hence, for Catholics, Christ may become present in the mass only because the institutional church as a medium of His Spirit is empowered to perform the miracle of transubstantiation. Within this Christological tradition, the only alternative to this understanding is the possibility that Christ remains in heaven and becomes present to His church only metaphorically, or spiritually, as most Protestants believe.[109]

The end result of this way of thinking is that the church and its encounter with Christ through the Word and sacraments will be mediated through the presence of the Spirit either in the heart of the pope or in the heart of individual believers. The byproduct is the Enthusiasm of Traditions II, III, and 0. Traditions II and III result in an authoritarian Enthusiasm, where for the truth of Scripture to become manifest everyone must subordinate himself to the law of the inner spiritual experience of the pope and the church hierarchy. By contrast, generic Protestantism typically has degenerated into Tradition 0's anarchic Enthusiasm, wherein everyone is his own inner pope. Lacking any objective means of grace, generic Protestantism seeks signs of the Spirit's presence within the individual, whether by a spiritual experience or extraordinary moral holiness.

Likewise, since the Spirit is the agent of Scripture's clarity, the result of this situation is that both Catholics and Protestants therefore prioritize private interpretation of Scripture. They both thereby seek to silence the voice of the Law, which judges everything within the human heart. In the case of Catholics, the pope exalts his private judgment over the judgment of the Law mediated through the royal priesthood and the Bible. Likewise, in Protestantism the

---

109. See similar argument in Robert Jenson, *The Unbaptized God: The Basic Flaw in Ecumenical Theology* (Minneapolis: Fortress Press, 1992), 119–31.

individual believer exalts his private conscience over the judgment of the Law present in the external Word and the public teaching authority of the church.

We must also note that the ultimate aim of this avoidance of the full judgment of the Law is self-justification. For the Catholic, the pope as the supreme Enthusiast guarantees the divine law and the ability of the individual to stand righteous through his grace-induced performative righteousness. Conversely, the generic Protestant theoretically believes in justification by faith, but lacking objective means of grace nonetheless focuses on the signs of the presence of the Spirit in his own heart as a means to confirm his own salvation (*syllogismus practicus*). In both cases the authority of Scripture and the assurance of salvation are construed in legal and Enthusiastic terms. For the Catholic, righteousness is guaranteed by the inner law of the pope; for the Protestant it is assured through the inner law of the individual.

By contrast, the confessional Lutheran holds that the risen Christ is not bound by time or space but is fully present in His Word and in the sacraments. The preaching of the Law destroys the possibility of Enthusiasm, since it judges everything within the Christian. This is true whether the individual is a representative of the public teaching authority of the church or a layperson. Being emptied of his own internal authority through the Law, the Christian is prepared for the Gospel external to him. Through the promise of the Gospel the Christian lives outside himself in Christ manifest and objectified in Word and Sacrament (Col 3:3).

The Gospel is God's own self-donation. This is necessarily the case, because in order to make a truly unconditional promise one must surrender his very self to the person to whom it was made. For the Gospel to be fully credible as an unconditional promise, Christ must surrender His very self to Christians in Word and Sacrament (Mt 18:20; 28:20). The means of grace are thus objective and external means of the manifestation of the risen Christ.

The risen Christ is the true expositor of Scripture (Lk 24:27). The external clarity of the Bible is visible, objective, and tangible to believers in the grammatical-historical meaning of the words of the prophets and apostles authorized by Christ. Likewise, the presence of the risen Christ in the sacraments makes visible and tangible the internal clarity of Scripture, thereby illuminating the Christian about the true goal (*scopus*) of Scripture. The Spirit speaks one Word of the Gospel through Bible, water, and the blood (Jn 5:7–9), so what the water and the blood say must be what the Bible says and vice versa. The self-donation of Christ in the means of grace thus frees the Christian from Enthusiasm and legalism, since the believer recognizes Christ's full self-surrender in the Gospel. As a result of his faith in the Gospel, the believer no longer needs to protect himself from God's judgment by means of self-justification. He is thus freed to see the true meaning of Scripture (2 Cor 3:16).

The risen Christ holds His whole church accountable to the teaching of Scripture as illuminated by the external and objective means of grace. It is not the church's teaching authority alone that holds the laity accountable because of its special supernatural endowment with the Spirit (Catholicism). Neither is it the laity alone who hold teachers of the faith accountable because of their rights as members of the royal priesthood (Protestantism). Rather, empowered by the presence of the risen Christ Himself manifest in the concrete means of grace, both the public teaching authority of the church and the royal priesthood hold one another accountable to the Scriptures as understood from the perspective of the Gospel.

Christ effects in the hearers of the Gospel a proper confession of faith, thereby generating a true tradition of the church over time. Confessing the truth found in Scripture, the church is conformed to the cruciform image of its Lord (Rom 8:29) and must necessarily suffer the *tentatio* of opposition from the present evil age. It is important for the believer to use tradition as a guide, because the history of the church is the story of the perpetual manifestation of the brightness of God's truth in the face of the darkness of the present age.

According to His permissive will, God allows the sinful world to rage against His church so that the brightness of the truth of Scripture may be manifested. The manifestation of God's truth in opposition to the sinful world at certain points in church history can serve as a witness to future generations of Christians of the proper interpretation of Scripture as well as the pitfalls of heresy. Paul demonstrates this purpose when he tells the Corinthians: "I hear that there are divisions [KJV: heresies] among you. And I believe it in part, for there *must be factions among you in order that those who are genuine among you may be recognized*" (1 Cor 11:18; emphasis added).[110]

Although God does not cause heresy and division, He nevertheless uses them within His church as a means to manifest with ever greater precision true confessions of the faith. Athanasius and the Cappadocians were given an occasion to confess the doctrine of the Trinity more precisely than many of the theologians of the Ante-Nicene church because of Arianism. Augustine and the Second Council of Orange were able to explain the relationship between God's grace and human choice with more specificity than their predecessors because they were faced with the challenge of Pelagianism. Finally, Luther was given the opportunity to explain all the articles of the faith in relationship to the central message of the Gospel because of late medieval superstition and works righteousness. These men and their confessions of faith were subject to trial and temptation but ultimately were vindicated. Thus is the movement of the Word of God made flesh recapitulated in the cruciform movement of the Word in the history of the church's battle with heresy.

---

110. This insight was gleaned from Dr. Walter Sundberg, who pointed to this verse. See his dissertation on issues of doctrinal development: "The Development of Dogma as an Ecumenical Problem: Catholic–Protestant Conflict over the Authority and Historicity of Dogmatic Statements" (Ph.D. diss., Princeton Theological Seminary, 1981).

In reading Scripture, Christians thus must look to the true tradition of the church as manifest through the labors of earlier generations of Christians, and find where God has given occasion to manifest His scriptural truth in a more brilliant manner in the face of the ugliness of heresy. We do not need to rethink our theology from the bottom up in every generation. Rather, in reading Scripture we should look to our ancestors in the faith and seek to humble ourselves before the guidance of the true tradition of the church.

BIBLIOGRAPHY

PRIMARY SOURCES

Abelard, Peter. *Sic et Non: A Critical Edition.* Edited by B. B. Boyer and R. McKeon Chicago: University of Chicago Press, 1978.

Alexander, Archibald. *Evidence of the Authenticity, Inspiration, and Canonical Authority of the Holy Scripture.* Philadelphia: Presbyterian Board of Publication, 1836.

Aristotle. *The Metaphysics.* Translated by Joe Sachs. Santa Fe: Green Lion Press, 2002.

———. *Poetics.* Translated by Joe Sachs. Newburyport: Focus Publishing, 2006.

Athanasius. *Against the Arians.* In *Nicene and Post-Nicene Fathers,* edited by Philip Schaff and William Wace, Second Series, vol. 4, 303–447. Peabody, MA: Hendrickson Publishers, 2004.

Augustine. *On Grace and Free Will.* In *Nicene and Post-Nicene Fathers,* edited by Philip Schaff, First Series, vol. 5, 436–67. Peabody, MA: Hendrickson Publishers, 2004.

———. *On the Trinity.* In *Nicene and Post-Nicene Fathers,* edited by Philip Schaff, First Series, vol. 3, 17–228. Peabody, MA: Hendrickson Publishers, 2004.

———. *Tractates in the Gospel of John.* In *Nicene and Post-Nicene Fathers,* edited by Philip Schaff, First Series, vol. 7, 7–452. Peabody, MA: Hendrickson Publishers, 2004.

Baier, Johann. *Compendium Theologiae Positivae.* Edited by C. F. W. Walther. 3 vols. Grand Rapids: Emmanuel Press, 2005–6.

Basil. *On the Holy Spirit.* In *Nicene and Post-Nicene Fathers,* edited by Philip Schaff and William Wace, Second Series, vol. 4, 1–50. Peabody, MA: Hendrickson Publishers, 2004.

Calvin, John. *Calvin: The Institutes of the Christian Religion.* Translated and edited by John T. McNeill and Ford Lewis Battles. 2 vols. Philadelphia: The Westminster Press, 1967.

Chemnitz, Martin. *Church Order for Braunschweig-Wolfenbüttel: How Doctrine, Ceremonies, and Other Church-Related Matters Shall (by God's Grace) Be Conducted Henceforth.* Translated by Jacob Corzine and Matthew Carver. St. Louis: Concordia Publishing House, 2015.

———. *Examination of the Council of Trent.* Translated by Fred Kramer. 4 vols. St. Louis: Concordia Publishing House, 1971–86.

———. *Loci Theologici.* Translated by J. A. O. Preus. 2 vols. St. Louis: Concordia Publishing House, 1989.

———. *The Two Natures in Christ.* Translated by J. A. O. Preus. St. Louis: Concordia Publishing House, 1971.

Chemnitz, Martin, Polycarp Leyser, and Johann Gerhard. *The Harmony of the Four Evangelists,* vol. 1. Translated by Richard Dinda. Malone, TX: Repristination Press, 2009.

Clement of Alexandria. *The Stromata.* In *Ante-Nicene Fathers,* edited by Alexander Roberts and James Donaldson, 10 vols., 2:299–568. Peabody, MA: Hendrickson Publishers, 2004.

Concordia Triglotta: The Symbolical Books of the Evangelical Lutheran Church, German-Latin-English. Translated and edited by F. Bente, W. H. T. Dau, and The Lutheran Church—Missouri Synod. St. Louis: Concordia Publishing House, 1921.

Dannhauer, Johann Conrad. *Stylus vindex aeternae spiritus S. a patre filioque processionis.* Strassburg: Sumptibus Josiae Staedelii, 1663.

Descartes, René. *Meditations on First Philosophy.* Translated by Donald Cress. Indianapolis: Hackett Publishing Company, 1993.

Eusebius. *Eusebius—The Church History: A New Translation with Commentary.* Translated and edited by Paul Maier. Grand Rapids: Kregel Publishers, 1999.

Finney, Charles. *Finney's Systematic Theology.* 1851. Reprint. Minneapolis: Bethany House, 1994.

Flacius Illyricus, Matthias. *How to Understand the Sacred Scriptures: From* Clavis Scripturae Sacrae. Translated by Wade Johnston. Saginaw, MI: Magdeburg Press, 2011.

Geivett, R. Douglas, and Gary Habermas, eds. *In Defense of Miracles: A Comprehensive Case for God's Action in History.* Downers Grove, IL: InterVarsity Press, 1997.

Gerhard, Johann. *Confessio Catholica.* 2 vols. Jena, 1634–37.

———. *On the Church.* Translated by Richard Dinda. St. Louis: Concordia Publishing House, 2010.

———. *On Creation and Providence.* Translated by Richard Dinda. St. Louis: Concordia Publishing House, 2013.

———. *On the Gospel and Repentance.* Translated by Richard Dinda. St. Louis: Concordia Publishing House, 2016.

———. *On the Law.* Translated by Richard Dinda. St. Louis: Concordia Publishing House, 2015.

———. *On the Legitimate Interpretation of Holy Scripture.* Translated by Richard Dinda. Malone, TX: Repristination Press, 2015.

———. *On the Nature of Theology and Scripture.* Translated by Richard Dinda. St. Louis: Concordia Publishing House, 2006.

———. *On the Person and Office of Christ.* Translated by Richard Dinda. St. Louis: Concordia Publishing House, 2009.

———. *On Sin and Free Choice.* Translated by Richard Dinda. St. Louis: Concordia Publishing House, 2014.

Glassius, Salomon. *Philologia Sacra.* Leipzig: Gleditsch, 1743.

Hamann, Johann Georg. "Metacritique on the Purism of Reason (1784)." In *Hamann: Writings on Philosophy and Language,* edited by Kenneth Haynes, 205–18. Cambridge, UK: Cambridge University Press, 2009.

Hegel, G. W. F. *Faith and Knowledge, or the Reflective Philosophy of Subjectivity in the Complete Range of Its Forms as Kantian, Jacobian, and Fichtean Philosophy.* Translated by Walter Cerf and H. S. Harris. Albany: State University of New York Press, 1977.

Hesiod. *Theogony.* Translated by Richard Caldwell. Indianapolis: Hackett Publishing, 1987.

Hippolytus. *On the Apostolic Tradition.* Translated by Alistair Stewart-Sykes. Crestwood, NY: St. Vladimir's Seminary Press, 2001.

Hobbes, Thomas. *The Leviathan: or, The Matter, Forme, and Power of a Commonwealth, Ecclesiastical and Civil.* Cambridge, UK: Cambridge University Press, 1904.

Hodge, Archibald, and Benjamin Warfield. "Inspiration." *The Presbyterian Review* 6, no. 2 (1881): 225–60.

Hodge, Archibald Alexander, Benjamin Breckinridge Warfield, and Roger R. Nicole. *Inspiration*. Grand Rapids: Baker Book House, 1979.

Homer. *The Odyssey*. Translated by Robert Fagles. New York: Penguin Classics, 1999.

Hooker, Richard. *Of the Laws of Ecclesiastical Polity*. Cambridge, UK: Cambridge University Press, 1989.

Hunnius, Nicolaus. *Epitome Credendorum*. Translated by Paul Gottheil. Nuremburg: U. E. Sebald, 1847.

Irenaeus. *Against the Heresies*. In *Ante-Nicene Fathers*, edited by Alexander Roberts and James Donaldson, 10 vols., 1:309–567. Peabody, MA: Hendrickson Publishers, 2004.

Josephus. *Contra Apionem*. In *The Works of Josephus*, edited and translated by William Whiston. Peabody, MA: Hendrickson Publishers, 1995.

Kant, Immanuel. *Critique of Pure Reason*. Translated by Mary Gregor. Cambridge, UK: Cambridge University Press, 1997.

Locke, John. *Essay Concerning Human Understanding*. Indianapolis: Hackett Publishing Company, 1996.

Luther, Martin. *D. Martin Luthers Werke. Deutsche Bibel*. 12 vols. Weimar: Hermann Böhlaus Nachfolger, 1906–61.

———. *D. Martin Luthers Werke. Kritische Gesamtausgabe*. 120 vols. Weimar: Hermann Böhlau and H. Böhlaus Nachfolger, 1883–2009.

———. *D. Martin Luthers Werke. Tischreden*. 6 vols. Weimar: Hermann Böhlaus Nachfolger, 1912–21.

———. *Luther's Works*. American Edition. 82 vols. Edited by Jaroslav Jan Pelikan, Hilton C. Oswald, Helmut T. Lehmann, and Christopher Boyd Brown. St. Louis: Concordia Publishing House; Philadelphia: Fortress Press, 1955–86.

———. *Only the Decalogue Is Eternal: Martin Luther's Complete Antinomian Theses and Disputations*. Edited and translated by Holger Sonntag. Minneapolis: Lutheran Press, 2008.

Manteufel, Thomas, trans. "The Catalog of Testimonies." In *Sources and Contexts of the Book of Concord*, edited by Robert Kolb and James Nestingen, 220–44. Minneapolis: Augsburg Fortress, 2001.

Melanchthon, Philipp. *Loci Communes 1543*. Translated by J. A. O. Preus. St. Louis: Concordia Publishing House, 1992.

Nietzsche, Friedrich. *On the Genealogy of Morals*. Translated by Douglas Smith. Oxford: Oxford University Press, 2009.

Origen. *Against Celsus*. In *Ante-Nicene Fathers*, edited by Alexander Roberts and James Donaldson, 10 vols., 4:239–384. Peabody, MA: Hendrickson Publishers, 2004.

Petavius. *De Theologicis Dogmatibus*. 4 vols. Paris, 1644.

Philo. *On the Special Laws (De specialibus legibus), Book 4. On the Virtues. On Rewards and Punishments*. Translated by F. H. Colson. Loeb Classical Library 341. Cambridge, MA: Harvard University Press, 1939.

Plato. *Plato: The Complete Works*. Edited by John Cooper. Indianapolis: Hackett Publishing, 1997.

Proclus. *The Six Books of Proclus, the Platonic Successor, on the Theology of Plato*. Translated by Thomas Taylor. London: A. J. Valpy, 1816.

Przywara, Erich. *Analogia Entis: Metaphysics: Original Structure and Universal Rhythm*. Translated by John Betz and David Bentley Hart. Grand Rapids: Wm. B. Eerdmans, 2013.

Quenstedt, Andreas. *Theologia Didactico-Polemica sive Systema Theologicum*. 2 vols. Wittenberg: Johannes Ludolphus Quenstedt et Elerdi Schumacheri Haeredes, 1685.

———. *Theologia Didactico-Polemica sive Systema Theologicum*. Vol. 1. Leipzig, 1715.

Rambach, Johann Jacob. *Institutions Hermeneutica Sacra*. Jena, 1723.

Reid, Thomas. *Essays on the Powers of the Human Mind; to Which Are Prefixed, an Essay on Quantity, and an Analysis of Aristotle's Logic*. 3 vols. Edinburgh: Bell and Bradfute, 1812.

———. *An Inquiry into the Human Mind, on the Principles of Common Sense*. Edinburgh: Bell and Bradfute, 1810.

Roberts, Alexander, and James Donaldson, eds. *Ante-Nicene Fathers*. 10 vols. Peabody, MA: Hendrickson Publishers, 2004.

Schaff, Philip, ed. *Nicene and Post-Nicene Fathers*. 14 vols. First Series. Peabody, MA: Hendrickson Publishers, 2004.

Schaff, Philip, and William Wace, eds. *Nicene and Post-Nicene Fathers*. 14 vols. Second Series. Peabody, MA: Hendrickson Publishers, 2004.

Simonetti, Manlio, ed. *Ancient Christian Commentaries on Scripture, New Testament: Matthew 14–28*. Downers Grove, IL: InterVarsity Press, 2002.

Spinoza, Baruch. *Theologico-Political Treatise*. Cambridge, UK: Cambridge University Press, 2007.

Strauss, David Friedrich. *Die Christliche Glaubenslehre*, vol. 1. Tübingen: C. F. Osiander, 1840.

———. *In Defense of My Life of Jesus Against the Hegelians*. Translated by Marilyn Chapin Massey. Hamden, CT: Archon Books, 1983.

———. *The Life of Jesus, Critically Examined*. Translated by George Eliot. Philadelphia: Fortress Press, 1972.

———. *The Old Faith and the New: A Confession*. Translated by Mathilde Blind. New York: Holt, 1873.

Tertullian. *Prescription against Heretics*. In *Ante-Nicene Fathers*, edited by Alexander Roberts and James Donaldson, 10 vols., 3:243–68. Peabody, MA: Hendrickson Publishers, 2004.

Thomas Aquinas. *Summa Theologiae*. 60 vols. Black Friars Edition. New York and London: McGraw-Hill, 1964–.

Tyconius. *The Book of Rules*. Translated by W. S. Babcock. Atlanta: Scholars Press, 1989.

Voltaire. *Candide*. New York: Dover Publications, 1991.

SECONDARY SOURCES

Abraham, William. *Canon and Criterion in Christian Theology: From the Fathers to Feminism*. Oxford: Oxford University Press, 1998.

———. *The Divine Inspiration of the Scriptures*. Oxford: Oxford University Press, 1981.

Alī Nāṣirī. *An Introduction to Hadith: History and Sources*. Translated by Mansoor Limba. London, MIU Press, 2013.

Alt, Albrecht. "God of the Fathers." In *Essays on Old Testament and Religion*, translated by R. A. Wilson, 3–66. Oxford: Basil Blackwell, 1966.

Althaus, Paul. *Faith and Fact in the Kerygma Today*. Translated by David Cairns. Philadelphia: Muhlenberg Press, 1959.

Anderson, Deland. *Hegel's Speculative Good Friday: The Death of God in Philosophical Perspective*. Missoula: Scholars Press, 1996.

Archer, Gleason. *A Survey of the Old Testament, Introduction*. Chicago: Moody Press, 1985.

Armstrong, Dave. *Biblical Proofs of an Infallible Church and Papacy*. Lulu.com, 2015.

Attridge, Harold. *The Epistle to the Hebrews: A Commentary on the Epistle to the Hebrews*. Philadelphia: Fortress Press, 1989.

Ayres, Lewis. *Nicaea and Its Legacy: An Approach to Fourth-Century Trinitarian Theology*. Oxford: Oxford University Press, 2006.

Bainton, Roland. *Here I Stand: A Life of Martin Luther*. 1950. Reprint. Nashville: Abingdon Press, 1978.

Balthasar, Hans Urs von. "God Is His Own Exegete." *Communio* 13, no. 4 (1986): 280–87.

———. *Theo-Drama*. Translated by Graham Harrison. 5 vols. San Francisco: Ignatius Press, 1983–98.

———. *Truth Is Symphonic: Aspects of Christian Pluralism*. Translated by Graham Harrison. San Francisco: Ignatius Press, 1987.

Barnard, Leslie William. *Athenagoras: A Study in Second Century Christian Apologetic*. Paris: Beauchesne, 1972.

Barr, James. *Holy Scripture: Canon, Authority, and Criticism*. Philadelphia: Westminster, 1983.

Barrett, C. K. "Shaliach and Apostle." In *Donum Gentilicium: New Testament Studies in Honour of David Daube*, edited H. Bammel and W. D. Davies, 88–102. Oxford: Clarendon Press, 1978.

Barth, Gerhard. "Matthew's Understanding of the Law." In Günther Bornkamm, Gerhard Barth, and Heinz Joachim Held, *Tradition and Interpretation in Matthew*, translated by Percy Scott, 58–164. Philadelphia: The Westminster Press, 1963.

Barth, Karl. *Church Dogmatics*. Translated by G. T. Thomason, G. W. Bromiley, and T. F. Torrance. 4 vols. Edinburgh: T&T Clark, 1936–77.

———. "Gospel and Law." In *Community, State and Church: Three Essays*, edited by Will Herberg, 71–100. New York: Doubleday, 1960.

Bauckham, Richard. *Jesus and the Eyewitnesses: The Gospels as Eyewitness Testimony*. Grand Rapids: Wm. B. Eerdmans, 2006.

———. *Jude, 2 Peter*. Word Biblical Commentary, vol. 50. Waco, TX: Word Publishing Group, 1983.

Baur, Ferdinand Christian. *History of Christian Dogma*. Translated by Peter Hodgson. New York: Oxford University Press, 2015.

Bayer, Oswald. *A Contemporary in Dissent: J. G. Hamann as Radical Enlightener*. Translated by Roy Harrisville. Grand Rapids: Wm. B. Eerdmans, 2012.

———. "Creation as History." In *The Gift of Grace: The Future of Lutheran Theology*, edited by Niels Hendrik Gregersen, Bo Holm, Ted Peters, and Peter Widmann, 253–63. Minneapolis: Augsburg Fortress, 2005.

———. "God as Author of My Life-History." *Lutheran Quarterly* 2 (1988): 437–56.

———. *Living by Faith: Justification and Sanctification*. Translated by Geoffrey Bromiley. Grand Rapids: Wm. B. Eerdmans, 2003.

——. *Martin Luther's Theology: A Contemporary Interpretation.* Translated by Thomas Trapp. Grand Rapids: Wm. B. Eerdmans, 2008.

——. "Poetological Doctrine of the Trinity." *Lutheran Quarterly* 15 (2001): 43–58.

——. *Promissio: Geschichte der reformatorischen Wende in Luthers Theologie.* Göttingen: Vandenhoeck & Ruprecht, 1971.

——. *Theology the Lutheran Way.* Translated by Jeffrey Silcock and Mark Mattes. Grand Rapids: Wm. B. Eerdmans, 2007.

——. "Worship and Theology." In *Worship and Ethics: Lutherans and Anglicans in Dialogue,* edited by Oswald Bayer and Alan Suggate, 148–62. New York: Walter de Gruyter, 1996.

Baynes, Leslie. *The Heavenly Book Motif in Judeo-Christian Apocalypses 200 BCE–200 CE.* Leiden: Brill, 2011.

Beale, G. K. *The Temple and the Church's Mission: A Biblical Theology of the Dwelling Place of God.* Downers Grove, IL: InterVarsity Press, 2004.

Becker, Matthew. *Fundamental Theology: A Protestant Perspective.* New York: T & T Clark, 2014.

——. *The Self-Giving God and Salvation History: The Trinitarian Theology of Johannes von Hofmann.* New York: T&T Clark International, 2004.

Beckwith, Carl. *The Holy Trinity.* Confessional Lutheran Dogmatics, vol. 3. St. Louis: The Luther Academy, 2016.

Beckwith, Roger. *The Old Testament Canon of the New Testament Church and Its Background in Early Judaism.* 1986. Reprint. Eugene, OR: Wipf & Stock, 2008.

Behe, Michael. *Darwin's Black Box: The Biochemical Challenge to Evolution.* New York: Free Press, 1996.

Berkhof, Louis. *Principles of Biblical Interpretation.* Grand Rapids: Baker Book House, 1950.

Berlinski, David. *The Devil's Delusion: Atheism and Its Scientific Pretensions.* New York: Basic Books, 2009.

Bidmead, Julye. *The Akitu Festival: Religious Continuity and Royal Legitimation in Mesopotamia.* Piscataway, NJ: Gorgias Press, 2002.

Black, Edwin. *War against the Weak: Eugenics and America's Campaign to Create a Master Race.* Washington, DC: Dialogue Press, 2012.

Blocher, Henri. "God and the Scripture Writers." In *The Enduring Authority of the Christian Scriptures,* edited by D. A. Carson, 497–541. Grand Rapids: Wm. B. Eerdmans, 2016.

Boehme, Armand. "The Smokescreen Vocabulary." *Concordia Theological Quarterly* 41 (1977): 25–40.

Boer, Harry. *A Short History of the Early Church.* Grand Rapids: Wm. B. Eerdmans, 1976.

Bohlmann, Ralph. *Principles of Biblical Interpretation in the Lutheran Confessions.* St. Louis: Concordia Publishing House, 1983.

Bornkamm, Günther, Gerhard Barth, and Heinz Joachim Held. *Tradition and Interpretation in Matthew.* Translated by Percy Scott. Philadelphia: The Westminster Press, 1963.

Bozeman, Theodore Dwight. *Protestants in the Age of Science: The Baconian Ideal and Antebellum Religious Thought.* Chapel Hill, NC: University of North Carolina Press, 1977.

Braaten, Carl. *The Principles of Lutheran Theology.* Philadelphia: Fortress Press, 1985.

Brighton, Louis. *Revelation*. St. Louis: Concordia Publishing House, 1998.

Bruce, F. F. *The Canon of Scripture*. Downers Grove, IL: InterVarsity Press, 1988.

Bucher, Richard. *The Ecumenical Luther: The Development and Use of His Doctrinal Hermeneutic*. St. Louis: Concordia Publishing House, 2003.

Buckley, Theodore Alois, trans. *The Canons and Decrees of the Council of Trent*. London: George Routledge & Co., 1851.

Bultmann, Rudolf. *Begriff der Offenbarung im Neuen Testament*. Tübingen: Mohr, 1929.

———. *Existence and Faith: Shorter Writings of Rudolf Bultmann*. Edited and translated by Schubert M. Ogden. New York: Living Age Books, 1960.

———. *History and Eschatology: The Presence of Eternity*. New York: Harper & Brothers, 1962.

———. "How Does God Speak to Us through the Bible?" In *Existence and Faith: Shorter Writings of Rudolf Bultmann*, edited and translated by Schubert M. Ogden, 166–70. New York: Living Age Books, 1960.

———. *Jesus and the Word*. Translated by Louise Pettibone Smith and Erminie Huntress Lantero. New York: Scribner, 1958.

———. *Jesus Christ and Mythology*. New York: Hymns Ancient and Modern Ltd., 2012.

———. "New Testament and Mythology." In *Kerygma and Myth: A Theological Debate*, edited by Hans Werner Bartsche, translated by Reginald Fuller, 1–44. London: SCPK, 1953.

———. *New Testament and Mythology, and Other Basic Writings*, edited and translated by Schubert M. Ogden. Minneapolis: Fortress Press, 1984.

———. "On the Problem of Demythologization (1952)." In Rudolf Bultmann, *New Testament and Mythology, and Other Basic Writings*, edited and translated by Schubert M. Ogden, 95–130. Minneapolis: Fortress Press, 1984.

———. *Theology of the New Testament*. Translated by Kendrick Grobel. 2 vols. Waco, TX: Baylor University Press, 2007.

Burghardt, Walter. "Assumption of Mary." In *Encyclopedia of Early Christianity*, edited by Everett Ferguson, 1:134–45. New York: Garland Publishing, 1997.

Callan, Terrance. "Use of the Letter of Jude by the Second Letter of Peter," *Biblica* 85, no. 1 (2004): 42–64.

Cardozo, Nathan T. Lopes. *The Oral and Written Torah: A Comprehensive Introduction*. New York: Rowman & Littlefield, 1998.

Carson, D. A. *Exegetical Fallacies*. Grand Rapids: Baker Academic, 1996.

———, ed. *The Enduring Authority of the Christian Scriptures*. Grand Rapids: Wm. B. Eerdmans, 2016.

Carson, D. A., and Douglas Moo. *Introducing the New Testament: A Short Guide to Its History and Message*. Grand Rapids: Zondervan, 2010.

Carvanos, Constantine. *The Hellenic-Christian Philosophical Tradition*. Belmont, MA: Institute for Byzantine and Modern Greek, 1989.

Cascione, Gioacchino Michael. *Repetition in the Bible*. Tucson: Redeemer Press, 2016.

Cassuto, Umberto. *The Documentary Hypothesis and the Composition of the Pentateuch*. Translated by Israel Abrahams. Jerusalem: Shalem Press, 2008.

Chilton, David. *The Days of Vengeance: An Exposition of the Book of Revelation*. Ft. Worth: Dominion Press, 1990.

Christensen, Duane L. "Josephus and the Twenty-Two-Book Canon of Sacred Scripture," *Journal of the Evangelical Theology Society* 29, no. 1 (1986): 37–46.

Clabeaux, J. J. *A Lost Edition of the Letters of Paul: A Reassessment of the Text of the Pauline Corpus Attested by Marcion*. Washington, DC: Catholic Biblical Association, 1989.

Congar, Yves. *A History of Theology*. Translated by Hunter Guthrie. Garden City, NY: Doubleday, 1968.

———. *Tradition and Traditions: A Historical and Theological Essay*. Translated by Michael Naseby and Thomas Rainborough. New York: Macmillan, 1966.

Copan, Paul, and William Lane Craig. *Creation Out of Nothing: A Biblical, Philosophical, and Scientific Exploration*. Grand Rapids: Baker Academic, 2004.

Coxon, Paul. *Exploring the New Exodus in John: A Biblical Theological Investigation of John Chapters 5–10*. Eugene, OR: Resource Publications, 2014.

Criswell, W. A. *Why I Preach the Bible Is Literally True*. Nashville: Broadman Press, 1969.

Cross, Richard. "Duns Scotus and Suarez at the Origins of Modernity." In *Deconstructing Radical Orthodoxy: Post-Modern Theology, Rhetoric, and Truth*, edited by Wayne Hankey and Douglas Hedley, 65–80. Burlington, VT: Ashgate Publishing, 2005.

Cullman, Oscar. *Christ and Time: The Primitive Christian Concept of Time and History*. Translated by Floyd Filson. London: SCM Press, 1962.

———. *Salvation in History*. New York: Harper & Row, 1967.

Daniélou, Jean. *Gospel Message and Hellenistic Culture*. Translated by John Austin Baker. Philadelphia: The Westminster Press, 1973.

———. *The Lord of History: Reflections on the Inner Meaning of History*. Translated by Nigel Abercrombie. London: H. Regnery, 1958.

Davies, Philip. "Ethics in the Old Testament." In *The Bible in Ethics: The Second Sheffield Colloquium*, edited by John Rogerson, Margaret Davies, and Mark Daniel Carroll, 164–73. Sheffield, UK: Sheffield Academic Press, 1995.

Davies, Rupert. *The Problem of Authority in the Continental Reformers: A Study in Luther, Zwingli, and Calvin*. London: Epworth Press, 1946.

Davis, Stephen. *The Debate about the Bible: Inerrancy versus Infallibility*. Philadelphia: Westminster Press, 1977.

De La Torre, Miguel A., ed. *Out of the Shadows, Into the Light: Christianity and Homosexuality*. Danvers, MA: Chalice Press, 2009.

De Lubac, Henri. *Medieval Exegesis: The Four Senses of Scripture*. Translated by Mark Sebanc and E. M. Macierowski. 3 vols. Grand Rapids: Wm. B. Eerdmans, 1998–2009.

Denzinger, Heinrich. *The Sources of Catholic Dogma*. Translated by Roy Deferrari. St. Louis: B. Herder, 1957.

Dimock, George. *The Unity of the Odyssey*. Amherst: University of Massachusetts Press, 1989.

Dowden, Ken. *Zeus*. New York: Routledge, 2006.

Drane, John. *Introducing the New Testament*. Oxford: Lion Hudson, 2010.

Duffy, Eamon. *What Catholics Believe about Mary*. London: Catholic Truth Society, 1989.

Dunn, James D. G., and John Rogerson, eds. *Eerdmans Commentary on the Bible*. Grand Rapids: Wm. B. Eerdmans, 2003.

Eaton, Elizabeth. "Speech to the ELCA Churchwide Assembly, 2013." http://on.aol.com/video/rev--elizabeth-eaton-speaks-about-being-first-female-lutheran-bishop-517899277 (accessed September 19, 2013).

Ebeling, Gerhard. "Disputatio de homine." In *Lutherstudien,* vol. 2. Pt. 1–2. Tübingen: Mohr Siebeck, 1977.

———. *Lutherstudien,* vol. 2. Pt. 1–2. Tübingen: Mohr Siebeck, 1977.

———. "The New Hermeneutic and the Early Luther." *Theology Today* 21 (1964): 34–46.

———. *The Problem of Historicity in the Church and Its Proclamation.* Translated by Grover Foley. Philadelphia: Fortress Press, 1967.

Ehrman, Bart. *Misquoting Jesus: The Story Behind Who Changed the Bible and Why.* San Francisco: HarperOne, 2007.

———. *The Orthodox Corruption of Scripture: The Effect of Early Christological Controversies on the Text of the New Testament.* Oxford: Oxford University Press, 2011.

Eichrodt, Walther. *Theology of the Old Testament.* Translated by J. A. Baker. 2 vols. Philadelphia: The Westminster Press, 1961–67.

Elert, Werner. *An Outline of Christian Doctrine.* Translated by Charles Jacobs. Philadelphia: United Lutheran Publication House, 1927.

———. *The Structure of Lutheranism: The Theology and Philosophy of Life of Lutheranism, Especially in the Sixteenth and Seventeenth Centuries,* vol. 1. Translated by Walter Hansen. St. Louis: Concordia Publishing House, 1962.

Eliade, Mircea. *The Myth of the Eternal Return: Cosmos and History.* Translated by Willard Trask. Princeton: Princeton University Press, 2005.

———. *The Sacred and the Profane: The Nature of Religion.* Translated by Willard Trask. Chicago: Harcourt, 1987.

Ellis, Earle. *The Making of the New Testament Documents.* Leiden: Brill, 2002.

Ellison, Marvin. "Practicing Safer Spirituality: Changing the Subject and Focusing on Justice." In *Out of the Shadows, Into the Light: Christianity and Homosexuality,* edited by Miguel A. De La Torre, 1–19. Danvers, MA: Chalice Press, 2009.

Erickson, Millard. *Christian Theology.* Grand Rapids: Baker Academic, 2009.

Erlandsson, Seth. *The Scroll of Isaiah.* Handen: XP Media, 2014.

Fagerberg, Holsten. *A New Look at the Lutheran Confessions, 1529–1537.* Translated by Gene Lund. St. Louis: Concordia Publishing House, 1972.

Fastiggi, Robert. "What Did the Protestant Reformers Teach about *Sola Scriptura*?" In *Not by Scripture Alone: A Catholic Critique of the Protestant Doctrine of Sola Scriptura,* edited by Robert Sungenis, 325–68. Santa Barbara: Queenship Publishing, 1997.

Feinberg, Paul. "The Meaning of Inerrancy." In *Inerrancy,* edited by Norman Geisler, 267–306. Grand Rapids: Zondervan, 1982.

Ferguson, Everett. *Encyclopedia of Early Christianity.* 2 vols. New York: Garland Publishing, 1997.

———. "Sacrifice." In *Encyclopedia of Early Christianity,* edited by Everett Ferguson, 2:1017. New York: Garland Publishing, 1997.

Ferreiro, Alberto. *Simon Magus in Patristic, Medieval, and Early Modern Traditions.* Leiden: Brill, 2005.

Fiore, Benjamin. *The Pastoral Epistles: First Timothy, Second Timothy, Titus.* Collegeville: Liturgical Press, 2006.

Firey, Abigail. *A New History of Penance.* Leiden: Brill, 2008.

Flesseman-van Leer, Ellen. *Tradition and Scripture in the Early Church.* Assen: Van Gorcum & Co., 1953.

Forbes, Christopher. *Prophecy and Inspired Speech in Early Christianity and Its Hellenistic Environment*. Tübingen: Mohr Siebeck, 1995.

Forde, Gerhard. *The Captivation of the Will: Luther vs. Erasmus on Freedom and Bondage*. Edited by Steven Paulson. Grand Rapids: Wm. B. Eerdmans, 2005.

Foster, Paul. "Ignatius of Antioch and the Writings That Later Formed the New Testament." In *The Reception of the New Testament in the Apostolic Fathers*, edited by Andrew Gregory and Christopher Tuckett, 159–86. Oxford: Oxford University Press, 2005.

Fraenkel, Peter. *Testimonia Patrum: The Function of Patristic Argument in the Theology of Philip Melanchthon*. Geneva: Librairie E. Droz, 1961.

Francisco, Adam. "Authority: The Holy Scriptures." In *Where Christ Is Present: A Theology for All Seasons on the 500th Anniversary of the Reformation*, edited by John Warwick Montgomery, Gene Edward Veith, Jr., Cameron A. MacKenzie, Adam Francisco, Rod Rosenbladt, Harold L. Senkbeil, Todd Wilken, Uwe Siemon-Netto, Craig A. Parton, Steven A. Hein, and Angus J. L. Menuge, 65–78. Irvine, CA: NRP Books, 2015.

Franklin, James. *The Science of Conjecture: Evidence and Probability before Pascal*. Baltimore: The Johns Hopkins University Press, 2001.

Franzmann, Martin. "The New Testament View of Inspiration." *Concordia Theological Monthly* 21, no. 10 (1954): 743–48.

Frei, Hans. *The Eclipse of the Biblical Narrative: A Study in Eighteenth and Nineteenth Century Hermeneutics*. New Haven: Yale University Press, 1974.

Friedman, Richard Elliot. *Who Wrote the Bible?* San Francisco: HarperOne, 1987.

Gagnon, Robert. *The Bible and Homosexual Practice: Texts and Hermeneutics*. Nashville: Abingdon Press, 2002.

———. *Homosexuality and the Bible: Two Views*. Minneapolis: Fortress Press, 2009.

Gallegos, Joseph. "What Did the Church Fathers Teach about Scripture, Tradition, and Church Authority?" In *Not by Scripture Alone: A Catholic Critique of the Protestant Doctrine of Sola Scriptura*, edited by Robert Sungenis, 389–486. Santa Barbara: Queenship Publishing, 1997.

Geisler, Norman. *Thomas Aquinas: An Evangelical Appraisal*. Eugene, OR: Wipf & Stock Publishers, 2003.

———. *When Critics Ask: A Popular Handbook on Bible Difficulties*. Grand Rapids: Baker Books, 1992.

———, ed. *Inerrancy*. Grand Rapids: Zondervan, 1982.

Gerberding, George Henry. *Lutheran Fundamentals*. Rock Island, IL: Augustana Book Concern, 1925.

Gerrish, B. A. "To the Unknown God: Luther and Calvin on the Hiddenness of God." *Journal of Religion* 53 (1973): 263–93.

———. "The Word of God and the Words of Scripture: Luther and Calvin on Biblical Authority." In *Protestantism Old and New: Essays on the Reformation Heritage*, 51–68. New York: T&T Clark International, 1982.

Gieschen, Charles. *Angelomorphic Christology: Antecedents and Early Evidence*. Leiden: Brill, 1998.

———. "The Divine Name in Ante-Nicene Christianity." *Viliae Christianae* 57 (2003): 115–58.

———. "The Real Presence of the Son before Christ: Revisiting an Old Approach to Old Testament Christology." *Concordia Theological Quarterly* 68 (2004): 105–26.

———. "The Relevance of the *Homologoumena* and *Antilegomena* Distinction for the New Testament Canon Today: Revelation as a Test Case." *Concordia Theological Quarterly* 79, no. 3–4 (2015): 279–300.

Gilbert, Christopher. *A Complete Introduction to the Bible.* New York: Paulist Press, 2009.

Glesne, David N. *Understanding Homosexuality: Perspectives for the Local Church.* Minneapolis: Kirk House, 2004.

Grabowski, Francis A. *Plato, Metaphysics, and the Theory of the Forms.* London: Bloomsbury Academic, 2008.

Graebner, A. L. *Outline of Doctrinal Theology.* St. Louis: Concordia Publishing House, 1949.

Grannan, Charles. *A General Introduction to the Bible,* vol. 3. St. Louis: Herder, 1921.

Grant, Robert. *The Formation of the New Testament.* New York: Harper & Row, 1965.

Green, Lowell. *Adventures in Law and Gospel: Lectures in Lutheran Dogmatics.* Ft. Wayne, IN: Concordia Theological Seminary Press, 1993.

———. *How Melanchthon Helped Luther Discover the Gospel.* Greenwood, SC: Attic Press, 1980.

Gregersen, Niels, Hendrik Bo Holm, Ted Peters, and Peter Widmann, eds. *The Gift of Grace: The Future of Lutheran Theology.* Minneapolis: Augsburg Fortress, 2005.

Grudem, Wayne. *Systematic Theology: An Introduction to Biblical Doctrine.* Grand Rapids: Zondervan, 1994.

Guthrie, Donald. *New Testament Introduction.* Downers Grove, IL: InterVarsity Press, 1990.

———. *The Pastoral Epistles: An Introduction and Commentary.* Grand Rapids: Wm. B. Eerdmans, 1990.

Habel, Norman. "The Form and Significance of the Call Narratives." *Zeitschrift für die Alttestamentliche Wissenschaft* 77 (1965): 297–323.

Habermas, Gary R., and Michael Licona. *The Case for the Resurrection of Jesus.* Grand Rapids: Kregel Publishers, 2004.

Hagner, Donald. *The New Testament: A Historical and Theological Introduction.* Grand Rapids: Baker Academic, 2012.

Hahn, Scott. *Covenant by Kinship: A Canonical Approach to the Fulfillment of God's Saving Promises.* New Haven: Yale University Press, 2009.

Hahn, Scott, Curtis Mitch, and Dennis Walters. *The Letter to the Hebrews.* San Francisco: Ignatius Press, 2007.

Hahn, Scott, and Benjamin Wiker. *Politicizing the Bible: The Roots of Historical Criticism and the Secularization of Scripture 1300–1700.* St. Louis: Herder & Herder, 2013.

Hall, Stuart. *Doctrine and Practice in the Early Church.* Eugene, OR: Wipf & Stock, 2011.

Hamilton, James. *God's Glory in Salvation through Judgment: A Biblical Theology.* Wheaton, IL: Crossway, 2010.

Hannah, John, ed. *Inerrancy and the Church.* Chicago: Moody Press, 1984.

Hanson, R. P. C. *The Search for the Christian Doctrine of God: The Arian Controversy, 318–381.* Grand Rapids: Baker Academic, 2006.

———. *Tradition in the Early Church.* London: SCM Press, 1962.

Harrison, R. K. *Introduction to the Old Testament.* Grand Rapids: Wm. B. Eerdmans, 1971.

Harrisville, Roy, and Walter Sundberg. *The Bible in Modern Culture: Baruch Spinoza to Brevard Childs*. Grand Rapids: Wm. B. Eerdmans, 2002.

Hart, David Bentley. *Atheist Delusions: The Christian Revolution and Its Fashionable Enemies*. New Haven: Yale University Press, 2009.

Hatab, Lawrence. *Nietzsche's Life Sentence: Coming to Terms with Eternal Recurrence*. New York: Routledge, 2005.

Hatch, Nathan. *The Democratization of American Christianity*. New Haven: Yale University Press, 1989.

Hayward, Robert. *Divine Name and Presence: The Memra*. Lanham, MD: Rowman & Littlefield, 1982.

Headley, John. *Luther's View of Church History*. New Haven: Yale University Press, 1963.

Heathers, Peter, and John Matthews. *The Goths of the Fourth Century*. Liverpool: Liverpool University Press, 1991.

Heidegger, Martin. "The Onto-theo-logical Constitution of Metaphysics." In *Identity and Difference*, translated by Joan Stambaugh, 42–74. New York: Harper and Row, 1969.

Heimbigner, Kent. "The Evolution of Luther's Reception of the Early Church Fathers in Eucharistic Controversy: A Consideration of Selected Works, 1518–1529." *Logia: A Journal of Lutheran Theology* 7, no. 1 (1998): 3–12.

Helmer, Christine. *The Trinity and Martin Luther*. Bellingham, WA: Lexham Press, 2017.

Hendriksen, William. *Exposition of the Pastoral Epistles*. Grand Rapids: Baker Book House, 1957.

Hengel, Martin. *The Four Gospels and the One Gospel of Jesus Christ: An Investigation of the Collection and Origin of the Canonical Gospels*. Translated by John Bowden. Harrisburg, PA: Trinity Press International, 2000.

Hengstenberg, E. W. *Christology of the Old Testament*. Translated by Theodore Meyer and James Martin. 4 vols. Grand Rapids: Kregel, 1956.

Henry, Carl F. *God, Revelation, and Authority*. 6 vols. Wheaton, IL: Crossway, 1999.

Heppe, Heinrich. *Reformed Dogmatics Set Out and Illustrated from the Sources*. Translated by G. T. Thomson. London: George Allen & Unwin, 1950.

Herrmann, Erik. "Luther's Absorption of Medieval Biblical Interpretation." In *The Oxford Handbook of Martin Luther's Theology*, edited by Robert Kolb, Irene Dingel, and L'Ubomir Batka, 71–90. New York: Oxford University Press, 2014.

Hill, Charles. "'The Truth above All Demonstration': Scripture in the Patristic Period to Augustine." In *The Enduring Authority of the Christian Scriptures*, edited by D. A. Carson, 43–88. Grand Rapids: Wm. B. Eerdmans, 2016.

———. *Who Chose the Gospels? Probing the Great Gospel Conspiracy*. New York: Oxford University Press, 2010.

Hinlicky, Paul. *Beloved Community: Critical Dogmatics after Christendom*. Grand Rapids: Wm. B. Eerdmans, 2015.

———. *Divine Complexity: The Rise of Creedal Christianity*. Minneapolis: Fortress Press, 2011.

———. *Divine Simplicity: Christ the Crisis of Metaphysics*. Grand Rapids: Baker Academic, 2016.

———. *Luther and the Beloved Community: A Path for Christian Theology after Christendom*. Grand Rapids: Wm. B. Eerdmans, 2010.

Hodgson, Peter. "Editor's Introduction: Strauss' Theological Development from 1825 to 1840." In David Friedrich Strauss, *The Life of Jesus, Critically Examined*, translated by George Eliot, xv–xlvii. Philadelphia: Fortress Press, 1972.

Hoenecke, Adolf. *Evangelical Lutheran Dogmatics.* Translated by Joel Fredrich, James L. Langebartels, Paul Prange, and Bill Tackmier. 4 vols. Milwaukee: Northwestern Publishing House, 1999–2009.

Hoffmeier, James. *The Archaeology of the Bible.* Oxford: Lion Hudson, 2008.

Holl, Karl. *Gesammelte Aufsätze.* 3 vols. Tübingen: Mohr, 1928.

Holmes, Michael. "Origen and the Inerrancy of Scripture." *Journal of the Evangelical Theology Society* 24, no. 3 (1981): 221–24.

———. "Polycarp's *Letter to the Philippians* and the Writings That Later Formed the New Testament." In *The Reception of the New Testament in the Apostolic Fathers*, edited by Andrew Gregory and Christopher Tuckett, 187–227. Oxford: Oxford University Press, 2005.

Horton, Michael. *The Christian Faith: A Systematic Theology for Pilgrims on the Way.* Grand Rapids: Zondervan, 2011.

———. *The Gospel Commission: Recovering God's Strategy for Making Disciples.* Grand Rapids: Baker Books, 2011.

Hove, Elling. *Christian Doctrine.* Minneapolis: Augsburg Publishing House, 1930.

Hummel, Horace. *The Word Becoming Flesh: An Introduction to the Origin, Purpose, and Meaning of the Old Testament.* St. Louis: Concordia Publishing House, 1979.

Hunsinger, George. *How to Read Karl Barth: The Shape of His Theology.* New York: Oxford University Press, 1993.

Hütter, Reinhard. *Suffering Divine Things: Theology as Church Practice.* Translated by Doug Stott. Grand Rapids: Wm. B. Eerdmans, 2000.

Israel, Jonathan. *Radical Enlightenment: Philosophy and the Making of Modernity, 1650–1750.* Oxford: Oxford University Press, 2001.

Jenson, Robert. "Can We Have a Story?" *First Things* 11 (March 2000): 16–17.

———. *Creed and Canon.* Louisville: Westminster/John Knox, 2010.

———. "How the World Lost Its Story." *First Things* 4 (October 1993): 19–24.

———. *On the Inspiration of Scripture.* Delhi, NY: ALPB Books, 2012.

———. *Story and Promise: A Brief Theology of the Gospel about Jesus.* Philadelphia: Fortress Press, 1973.

———. *Systematic Theology.* 2 vols. New York: Oxford University Press, 1997–98.

———. *The Unbaptized God: The Basic Flaw in Ecumenical Theology.* Minneapolis: Fortress Press, 1992.

Jeremias, Joachim. *Die Briefe an Timotheus und Titus.* Göttingen: Vandenhoeck & Ruprecht, 1953.

Johnson, John F. "Biblical Authority and Scholastic Theology." In *Inerrancy and the Church*, edited by John Hannah, 67–98. Chicago: Moody Press, 1984.

Johnson, Luke Timothy. *The First and Second Letters to Timothy: A New Translation with Introduction and Commentary.* New York: Doubleday, 2001.

———. *Hebrews: A Commentary.* Louisville: Westminster/John Knox, 2006.

———. *Letters to Paul's Delegates: 1 Timothy, 2 Timothy, Titus.* Valley Forge, PA: Trinity Press International, 1996.

Johnson, Philip E. *Darwin on Trial*. Downers Grove, IL: InterVarsity Press, 2010.

Jones, Edgar. *The Greatest Old Testament Words*. London: SCM Press, 1964.

Jowers, Dennis. "Observations on the Authenticity of the Pastoral Epistles." *Western Reformed Seminary Journal* 12, no. 2 (2005): 7–11.

Judisch, Douglas. *An Evaluation of Claims to the Charismatic Gifts*. Grand Rapids: Baker Book House, 1978.

Just, Arthur. *Luke*. 2 vols. St. Louis: Concordia Publishing House, 1996–97.

Kärkkäinen, Veli-Matti. *Pneumatology: The Holy Spirit in Ecumenical, International, and Contextual Perspective*. Grand Rapids: Baker Academic, 2002.

Keating, Karl. *Catholicism and Fundamentalism: The Attack on "Romanism" by "Bible Christians."* San Francisco: Ignatius Press, 1988.

Keener, Craig S. *The Gospel of John: A Commentary*. 2 vols. Peabody, MA: Hendrickson Publishers, 2003.

———. *Miracles: The Credibility of the New Testament Accounts*. 2 vols. Grand Rapids: Baker Academic, 2011.

Keil, Carl Friedrich, and Franz Delitzsch. *Biblical Commentary on the Old Testament*, vol. 3: *The Pentateuch*. Translated by James Martin. 1865. Reprint. Peabody, MA: Hendrickson Publishers, 1996.

Keller, Rudolf. *Der Schlüssel zur Schrift: Die Lehre vom Wort Gottes bei Matthias Flacius Illyricus*. Hannover: Lutherisches Verlagshaus, 1984.

Keller, Werner. *The Bible as History*. New York: Bantam, 1983.

Kelly, J. N. D. *Early Christian Creeds*. London: Continuum, 2006.

———. *Early Christian Doctrines*. San Francisco: HarperCollins, 1978.

Kilcrease, Jack. "Is *Sola Scriptura* Obsolete? An Examination and Critique of Christian Smith's *Scripture Made Impossible*." *Concordia Theological Quarterly* 82, no. 3–4 (2018): 213–34.

———. "Johann Gerhard's Reception of Thomas Aquinas' *Analogia Entis*." In *Aquinas among the Protestants,* edited by Carl Manfred Svensson and David VanDrunen, 109–28. Hoboken, NJ: Wiley-Blackwell, 2017.

———. "Kenosis and Vocation: Christ as the Author and Exemplar of Christian Freedom." *Logia: A Journal of Lutheran Theology* 19, no. 4 (2010): 21–34.

———. "The Life and Theological Contribution of Matthias Flacius Illyricus." In Matthias Flacius Illyricus, *How to Understand the Sacred Scriptures: From* Clavis Scripturae Sacrae, translated by Wade Johnston, 8–46. Saginaw, MI: Magdeburg Press, 2011.

———. "Review of Matthew Becker, *Fundamental Theology*." In *Logia Online*, April 8, 2015, accessible at www.logia.org/logia-online/book-review-fundamental-theology2015.

———. *The Self-Donation of God: A Contemporary Lutheran Approach to Christ and His Benefits*. Eugene, OR: Wipf & Stock, 2013.

———. "The Self-Donation of God: Gerhard Forde and the Question of Atonement in the Lutheran Tradition." Ph.D. diss., Marquette University, 2009.

———. "Thomas Aquinas and Martin Chemnitz on the Hypostatic Union." *Lutheran Quarterly* 27, no. 1 (2013): 1–32.

King, David, and William Webster. *Holy Scripture: The Ground and Pillar of Our Faith*. 3 vols. Battle Ground, WA: Christian Resources, Inc., 2001.

King, Leonard W. *Enuma Elish: The Seven Tablets of Creation; The Babylonian and Assyrian Legends Concerning the Creation of the World and Mankind*, vol. 1. New York: Cosimo Books, 2007.

Kistemaker, Simon. *Revelation*. Grand Rapids: Baker Academic, 2001.

Kitchen, K. A. *On the Reliability of the Old Testament*. Grand Rapids: Wm. B. Eerdmans, 2006.

Kleinig, John. *Leviticus*. St. Louis: Concordia Publishing House, 2003.

———. "*Oratio, Meditatio, Tentatio*: What Makes a Theologian?" *Concordia Theological Quarterly* 66, no. 3 (2002): 255–68.

Kline, Meredith. *The Structure of Biblical Authority*. Grand Rapids: Wm. B. Eerdmans, 1972.

———. *Treaty of the Great King: The Covenant Structure of Deuteronomy, Studies and Commentary*. Eugene, OR: Wipf & Stock, 2012.

Kloha, Jeffrey. "Herman Sasse Confesses the Doctrine *De Scriptura Sacra*." In *Scripture and the Church: Selected Essays of Hermann Sasse*, edited by Jeffrey Kloha and Ronald Feuerhahn, 337–424. St. Louis: Concordia Seminary, 1995.

———. "Theological and Hermeneutical Reflections on the Ongoing Revisions of the *Novum Testamentum Graece*." In *Listening to the Word of God: Exegetical Approaches*, edited by Achim Behrens and Jorg Christian Salzmann, 169–207. Göttingen: Edition Ruprecht, 2016.

Klug, Eugene. "Luther and Chemnitz on Scripture." *The Springfielder* 37, no. 3 (1973): 165–75.

Knight, George W., III. *The Pastoral Epistles: A Commentary on the Greek Text*. The New International Greek Testament Commentary. Grand Rapids: Wm. B. Eerdmans, 1992.

Koehler, J. P. "The Analogy of Faith." In *The Wauwatosa Theology*, 3 vols., edited by Curtis Jahn, 1:221–68. Milwaukee: Northwestern Publishing House, 1997.

Kolb, Robert. "The Bible in the Reformation and Protestant Orthodoxy." In *The Enduring Authority of the Christian Scriptures*, edited by D. A. Carson, 89–114. Grand Rapids: Wm. B. Eerdmans, 2016.

———. *Bound Choice, Election, and the Wittenberg Theological Method: From Martin Luther to the Formula of Concord*. Grand Rapids: Wm. B. Eerdmans, 2005.

———. *The Christian Faith: A Lutheran Exposition*. St. Louis: Concordia Publishing House, 1993.

———. "The Ordering of the *Loci Communes Theologici*: The Structuring of the Melanchthonian Dogmatic Tradition," *Concordia Journal* 23, no. 4 (1997): 317–37.

Koren, Ulrik Vilhelm. "The Inspiration of Holy Scripture." In *Truth Unchanged, Unchanging: Selected Sermons, Addresses, and Doctrinal Articles*, translated and edited by the Evangelical Lutheran Synod Translation Committee, 145–66. Lake Mills, IA: Graphic Publishing Company, 1978.

Köstenberger, Andreas J. *A Theology of John's Gospel and Letters*. Biblical Theology of the New Testament. Grand Rapids: Zondervan, 2009.

Köstenberger, Andreas J., L. Scott Kellum, and Charles L. Quarles. *The Cradle, the Cross, and the Crown: An Introduction to the New Testament*. Nashville: B & H Academic, 2009.

Kramm, H. H. *The Theology of Martin Luther*. Eugene, OR: Wipf & Stock, 2009.

Krauth, Charles Porterfield. *The Bible a Perfect Book*. Gettysburg, PA: Henry C. Neinstedt, 1857.

Kreeft, Peter. *Catholic Christianity: A Complete Catechism of Catholic Beliefs Based on the Catholic Catechism*. San Francisco: Ignatius Press, 2001.

Kruger, Michael. *The Question of the Canon: Challenging the Status Quo in the New Testament Debate*. Downers Grove, IL: InterVarsity Press, 2013.

Kuhn, Thomas. *The Structure of Scientific Revolutions*. Chicago: University of Chicago Press, 1996.

Küng, Hans. *Infallibility: An Inquiry*. New York: Doubleday, 1983.

Lane, Anthony. *John Calvin: Student of the Church Fathers*. Grand Rapids: Baker Book House, 2000.

Lapidge, Michael. "Stoic Cosmology." In *The Stoics,* edited by John Rist, 161–86. Cambridge, UK: Cambridge University Press, 1978.

Le Goff, Jacques. *The Birth of Purgatory*. Chicago: University of Chicago Press, 1986.

Leith, John. *An Introduction to the Reformed Tradition: A Way of Being the Christian Community*. Louisville, KY: Westminster/John Knox, 1980.

Leithart, Peter. *Deep Comedy: Trinity, Tragedy and Hope in Western Literature*. Moscow, ID: Canon Press, 2006.

———. *Deep Exegesis: The Mystery of Reading Scripture*. Waco, TX: Baylor University Press, 2009.

———. *A House for My Name: A Survey of the Old Testament*. Moscow, ID: Canon Press, 2000.

Lenski, R. C. H. *The Interpretation of the Epistles of St. Peter, St. John, and St. Jude*. Peabody, MA: Hendrickson Publishers, 1998.

———. *The Interpretation of Matthew's Gospel*. Peabody, MA: Hendrickson Publishers, 1998.

———. *The Interpretation of St. Mark's Gospel*. Peabody, MA: Hendrickson, 1998.

———. *The Interpretation of St. Paul's Epistles to the Colossians, to the Thessalonians, to Timothy, to Titus, and to Philemon*. Peabody, MA: Hendrickson Publishers, 1998.

———. *The Interpretation of St. Paul's First and Second Epistles to the Corinthians*. Peabody, MA: Hendrickson Publishers, 1998.

Leupp, Roderick T. *The Renewal of Trinitarian Theology: Themes, Patterns & Explorations*. Downers Grove, IL: InterVarsity Press, 1995.

Lewis, C. S. "Myth Became Fact." In *God in the Dock: Essays on Theology and Ethics,* 54–61. Grand Rapids: Wm. B. Eerdmans, 2014.

Licona, Michael. *The Resurrection of Jesus: A New Historiographical Approach*. Downers Grove, IL: InterVarsity Press, 2010.

Lienhard, Joseph. *The Bible, the Church, and Authority: The Canon of the Christian Bible in History and Theology*. Collegeville, MN: Liturgical Press, 1995.

Lindbeck, George. *The Nature of Doctrine: Religion and Theology in a Post-Liberal Age*. Philadelphia: The Westminster Press, 1984.

Lindberg, Conrad Emil. *Christian Dogmatics*. Rock Island, IL: Augustana Book Concern, 1928.

Little, C. H. *Disputed Doctrines: A Study in Biblical and Dogmatic Theology*. Burlington, IA: Lutheran Literary Board, 1933.

Lockwood, Gregory. *1 Corinthians*. St. Louis: Concordia Publishing House, 2000.

Lohse, Bernhard. *Martin Luther's Theology: Its Historical and Systematic Development.* Translated and edited by Roy A. Harrisville. Minneapolis: Fortress Press, 1999.

———. *A Short History of Christian Doctrine.* Translated by F. Ernest Stoeffler. Philadelphia: Fortress Press, 1985.

Lord, Albert. *The Singer of Tales.* Cambridge, MA: Harvard University Press, 1960.

Lyotard, Jean-François. *The Postmodern Condition: A Report on Knowledge.* Translated by Geoff Bennington and Brian Massumi. Minneapolis: University of Minnesota Press, 1984.

MacInytre, Alasdair. *Whose Justice? Which Rationality?* South Bend, IN: University of Notre Dame Press, 1988.

Marion, Jean-Luc. *God without Being.* Translated by Thomas Carlton. Chicago: University of Chicago Press, 1991.

Marquart, Kurt. *Anatomy of an Explosion: Missouri in Lutheran Perspective.* Ft. Wayne: Concordia Theological Seminary Press, 1977.

———. "Hermann Sasse and the Mystery of Sacred Scripture." In *Herman Sasse: A Man for Our Times?* Edited by John Stephenson and Thomas Winger, 167–93. St. Louis: Concordia Publishing House, 1998.

———. "Luther and Theosis." *Concordia Theological Quarterly* 64, no. 3 (2000): 182–205.

———. "The 'Realist Principle' of Theology." In *Doctrine Is Life: Essays on Justification and the Lutheran Confessions,* edited by Klemet I. Preus, 367–73. St. Louis: Concordia Publishing House, 2006.

Marsden, George. "Everyone's Own Interpretation? The Bible, Science, and Authority in Mid-Nineteenth-Century America." *The Bible in America,* edited by Nathan Hatch and Mark Noll, 79–100. New York: Oxford University Press, 1982.

Martensen, Hans. *Christian Dogmatics.* Edinburgh: T&T Clark, 1898.

Martin, John Stanley. *Ragnarök: An Investigation into Old Norse Concepts of the Fate of the Gods.* Assen: Van Gorcum, 1972.

Mathison, Keith. *A Reformed Approach to Science and Scripture.* Sanford, FL: Ligonier Ministries, 2013.

———. *The Shape of Sola Scriptura.* Moscow, ID: Canon Press, 2001.

Mayes, Benjamin. "The Mystical Sense of Scripture according to Johann Jacob Rambach." *Concordia Theological Quarterly* 72, no. 1 (2008): 45–70.

McArthur, John. *Why Believe in the Bible?* Ventura: Regal Publishers, 2007.

McBrien, Richard. *Catholicism.* 2 vols. Minneapolis: Winston Press, 1980.

McConkie, Bruce. *Mormon Doctrine.* Salt Lake City: Bookcraft, 1966.

McConville, J. Gordon. "God's Name and God's Glory." *Tyndale Bulletin* 30 (1979): 149–63.

McDonald, Lee Martin. *The Biblical Canon: Its Origin, Transmission, and Authority.* Grand Rapids: Baker Academic, 2011.

McGrath, Alister E. *Christian Theology: An Introduction.* Oxford: Blackwell, 2001.

———. *Iustitia Dei: A History of the Christian Doctrine of Justification.* 2d ed. Cambridge, UK: Cambridge University Press, 1998.

———. *Reformation Thought: An Introduction.* Oxford: Basil Blackwell, 1993.

———. *A Scientific Theology.* Vol. 1. *Nature.* Edinburgh: T&T Clark, 2003.

———. *A Scientific Theology.* Vol. 2. *Reality.* Edinburgh: T&T Clark, 2006.

Meens, Robert. *Penance in Medieval Europe, 600–1200.* Cambridge, UK: Cambridge University Press, 2014.

Menuge, Angus J. L. "The Cultural and Aesthetic Impact of Lutheranism." In *Where Christ Is Present: A Theology for All Seasons on the 500th Anniversary of the Reformation*, edited by John Warwick Montgomery, Gene Edward Veith, Jr., Cameron A. MacKenzie, Adam Francisco, Rod Rosenblatt, Harold L. Senkbeil, Todd Wilken, Uwe Siemon-Netto, Craig A. Parton, Steven A. Hein, and Angus J. L. Menuge, 209–32. Corona, CA: NRP Books, 2015.

Metso, Sarianna. *The Textual Development of the Qumran Community Rule*. Leiden: Brill, 1997.

Metzger, Bruce. *The Canon of the New Testament: Its Origin, Development, and Significance*. Oxford: Clarendon Press, 1987.

———. *The Text of the New Testament: Its Transmission, Corruption, and Restoration*. Oxford: Oxford University Press, 1992.

Meyendorff, John. *Christ in Eastern Christian Thought*. Washington, DC: Corpus Books, 1969.

Moltmann, Jürgen. *The Crucified God: The Cross of Christ as the Foundation and Criticism of Christian Theology*. Translated by R. A. Wilson and John Bowden. Minneapolis: Fortress Press, 1993.

Montgomery, John Warwick. *Crisis in Lutheran Theology*. 2 vols. Grand Rapids: Baker Book House, 1967.

———. "Lessons from Luther on the Inerrancy of Holy Writ." In *God's Inerrant Word*, edited by John Warwick Montgomery, 63–94. Minneapolis: Bethany Fellowship, 1974.

———. *Tracatus Logico-Theologicus*. Eugene, OR: Wipf & Stock, 2013.

———. *Where Is History Going? Essays in Support of the Historical Truth of the Christian Revelation*. Grand Rapids: Zondervan, 1969.

———. "You Are Looking for a Church Home—or Perhaps You Aren't." In *Where Christ Is Present: A Theology for All Seasons on the 500th Anniversary of the Reformation*, edited by John Warwick Montgomery, Gene Edward Veith, Jr., Cameron A. MacKenzie, Adam Francisco, Rod Rosenblatt, Harold L. Senkbeil, Todd Wilken, Uwe Siemon-Netto, Craig A. Parton, Steven A. Hein, and Angus J. L. Menuge, 1–16. Irvine, CA: NRP Books, 2015.

———, ed. *Myth, Allegory, and the Gospel: An Interpretation of J. R. R. Tolkien, C. S. Lewis, G. K. Chesterton, and Charles Williams*. Minneapolis: Bethany House, 1974.

Morgan, Kathryn. *Myth and Philosophy from the Presocratics to Plato*. Cambridge, UK: Cambridge University Press, 2004.

Motyer, Stephen. "The Rending of the Veil: A Markan Pentecost." *New Testament Studies* 33, no. 1 (1987): 155–57.

Muller, Richard. "Biblical Interpretation in the 16th and 17th Centuries." In *Historical Handbook of Major Biblical Interpreters*, edited by Donald K. McKim, 123–52. Downers Grove, IL: InterVarsity, 1998.

———. "John Calvin and Later Calvinism: The Identity of the Reformed Tradition." In *The Cambridge Companion to Reformation Theology*, edited by David Bagchi and David C. Steinmetz, 130–49. Cambridge: Cambridge University Press, 2004.

———. "A Note on 'Christocentricism' and the Imprudent Use of Such Terminology." *Calvin Theological Journal* 68 (2006): 253–60.

———. *Post-Reformation Reformed Dogmatics: The Rise and Development of Reformed Orthodoxy, Ca. 1520–1720.* 4 vols. Grand Rapids: Baker Academic, 2003.

———. *The Unaccommodated Calvin: Studies in the Foundation of a Theological Tradition.* New York: Oxford University Press, 2000.

Murphy, Francesca Aran. *1–2 Samuel.* Grand Rapids: Brazos Press, 2010.

Murray, Scott. "The Concept of *Diatheke* in the Letter to the Hebrews." *Concordia Theological Quarterly* 66, no. 1 (2002): 41–60.

———. *Law, Life, and the Living God: The Third Use of the Law in Modern American Lutheranism.* St. Louis: Concordia Publishing House, 2002.

Nafzger, Peter H., and Joel P. Okamoto. *"These Are Written": Toward a Cruciform Theology of Scripture.* Eugene, OR: Pickwick Publications, 2013.

Nagel, Norman. "Allegory." *The Springfielder* 35, no. 1 (1971): 41–54.

———. "The Authority of Scripture." *Concordia Theological Monthly* 27, no. 9 (1956): 693–706.

Nelson, Stephanie. *God and the Land: The Metaphysics of Farming in Hesiod and Vergil.* Oxford: Oxford University Press, 1998.

Newman, John Henry. *The Arians of the Fourth Century.* South Bend, IN: Notre Dame University Press, 2001.

———. *An Essay in Aid of a Grammar of Assent.* London: Longmans, Green, and Co., 1870.

———. *Essay on the Development of Christian Doctrine.* South Bend, IN: Notre Dame University Press, 1989.

———. "Private Judgment." In *Essays Critical and Historical*, vol. 2, 336–74. London: Basil, Montagu, Pickering, 1877.

Nicol, Martin. *Meditation bei Luther.* Göttingen: Vandenhoeck & Ruprecht, 1984.

Oberman, Heiko Augustinus. "*Quo Vadis, Petre?* Tradition from Irenaeus to *Humani Generis.*" In *The Dawn of the Reformation: Essays in Late Medieval and Early Reformation Thought,* 269–96. Grand Rapids: Wm. B. Eerdmans, 1992.

O'Collins, Gerald. *Believing in the Resurrection: The Meaning and Promise of the Risen Jesus.* New York: Paulist Press, 2012.

O'Connor, John Bonaventure. *Monasticism and Civilization.* New York: P. J. Kenedy & Sons, 1921.

Olsen, Arthur. "Martin Chemnitz and the Council of Trent." *Dialog* 2 (1963): 60–67.

Olson, Roger. *Arminian Theology: Myths and Realities.* Downers Grove, IL: InterVarsity Press, 2006.

———. *The Story of Christian Theology: Twenty Centuries of Tradition and Reform.* Downers Grove, IL: InterVarsity Press, 1999.

Orchard, Bernard. "The Matthean Tradition before A.D. 150." In Bernard Orchard and Harold Riley, *The Order of the Synoptics: Why Three Synoptic Gospels?* 118–22. Macon: Mercer University Press, 1987.

Orchard, Bernard, and Harold Riley. *The Order of the Synoptics: Why Three Synoptic Gospels?* Macon: Mercer University Press, 1987.

Ott, Ludwig. *Fundamentals of Catholic Dogma.* Rockford, IL: TAN Books, 1974.

Otto, Eckart. "Law and Ethics." In *Religions of the Ancient World: A Guide*, edited by Sarah Iles Johnston, 91. Cambridge, MA: Harvard University Press, 2004.

Ozment, Steven. *The Age of Reform, 1250–1550: An Intellectual and Religious History of Medieval and Reformation Europe*. New Haven: Yale University Press, 1980.

Pabel, Hilmar, and Mark Vessey. *Holy Scripture Speaks: The Production and Reception of Erasmus' Paraphrases on the New Testament*. Toronto: University of Toronto Press, 2002.

Pannenberg, Wolfhart. *Systematic Theology*. Translated by Geoffrey Bromiley. 3 vols. Grand Rapids: Wm B. Eerdmans, 1991–98.

Pannenberg, Wolfhart, Rolf Rendtorff, Trutz Rendtorff, and Ulrich Wilkens. *Revelation as History*. Edited by Wolfhart Pannenberg and translated by D. Granskou. New York: Macmillan, 1968.

Patton, Corrine. "Creation, Fall, and Salvation: Lyra's Commentary on Genesis 1–3." In *Nicholas of Lyra: The Senses of Scripture*, edited by Philip D. W. Krey and Lesley Janette Smith, 39. Leiden: Brill, 2000.

Paulus, Heinrich Eberhard Gottlieb. *Das Leben Jesu als Grundlage einer reinen Geschichte des Urchristentums*. 2 vols. Heidelberg: C. F. Winter, 1828.

Pelikan, Jaroslav. *The Christian Tradition: A History of the Development of Doctrine*. 5 vols. Chicago: University of Chicago Press, 1971–1989.

———. *Luther the Expositor: Introduction to the Reformer's Exegetical Writings*. St. Louis: Concordia Publishing House, 1959.

———. *Obedient Rebels: Catholic Substance and Protestant Principle in Luther's Reformation*. London: SCM Press, 1964.

Perkins, Pheme. *Reading the New Testament*. New York: Paulist Press, 1988.

Pieper, Francis. *Christian Dogmatics*. 3 vols. St. Louis: Concordia Publishing House, 1951.

Piepkorn, Arthur Carl. "Book Review: *The Inspiration of Scripture*." In *The Sacred Scriptures and the Lutheran Confessions*, vol. 2, edited by Philip Secker, 20–25. Mansfield, CT: CEC Press, 2007.

———. "The Position of the Church and Her Symbols." *Concordia Theological Monthly* 21, no. 10 (1954): 738–42.

———. "What Does 'Inerrancy' Mean?" In *The Sacred Scriptures and the Lutheran Confessions: Selected Writings of Arthur Carl Piepkorn*, edited by Philip J. Secker and Robert Kolb, 2:25–55. Mansfield, CT: CEC Press, 2007.

Pierson, Mark A. "Chemnitz's Pearls vs. Luther's Rose: A Comparison of Canonical Criteria in the Two Martins." In *Theologia et Apologia: Essays in Reformation Theology and Its Defense Presented to Rod Rosenbladt*, edited by Adam S. Francisco, Korey S. Maas, and Steven P. Mueller, 177–98. Eugene, OR: Wipf & Stock, 2007.

Plantinga, Alvin. "Is Naturalism Irrational?" In *The Analytical Theist: An Alvin Plantinga Reader*, edited by James Sennett, 72–96. Grand Rapids: Wm. B. Eerdmans, 1998.

Posset, Franz. *Pater Bernhardus: Martin Luther and Bernard of Clairvaux*. Kalamazoo: Cistercian Publications, 2000.

Powell, Mark. *Papal Infallibility: A Protestant Evaluation of an Ecumenical Issue*. Grand Rapids: Wm. B. Eerdmans, 2009.

Preus, J. A. O. *It Is Written*. St. Louis: Concordia Publishing House, 1971.

———. "The New Testament in the Lutheran Dogmaticians." *The Springfielder* 25, no. 1 (1961): 8–33.

Preus, James Samuel. *From Shadow to Promise: Old Testament Interpretation from Augustine to the Young Luther*. Cambridge, MA: Belknap Press of Harvard University Press, 1969.

———. *Spinoza and the Irrelevance of Biblical Authority.* Cambridge, UK: Cambridge University Press, 2009.

Preus, Robert D. *Doctrine Is Life: The Essays of Robert D. Preus on Justification and the Lutheran Confessions.* Edited by Klemet I. Preus St. Louis: Concordia Publishing House, 2006.

———. *Doctrine Is Life: The Essays of Robert D. Preus on Scripture.* Edited by Klemet I. Preus. St. Louis: Concordia Publishing House, 2006.

———. "The Hermeneutics of the Formula of Concord." In *Doctrine Is Life: The Essays of Robert D. Preus on Scripture,* edited by Klemet I. Preus, 215–42. St. Louis: Concordia Publishing House, 2006.

———. "How Is the Lutheran Church to Interpret and Use the Old and New Testaments?" *Lutheran Synod Quarterly* 14, no. 1 (1973): 1–52.

———. *The Inspiration of Scripture: A Study of the Theology of the Seventeenth Century Lutheran Dogmaticians.* St. Louis: Concordia Publishing House, 2003.

———. "Luther and Biblical Infallibility." In *Inerrancy and the Church,* edited by John Hannah, 99–142. Chicago: Moody, 1984.

———. "Notes on the Inerrancy of Scripture." *Concordia Theological Monthly* 38 (June 1967): 363–75.

———. *The Theology of Post-Reformation Lutheranism.* 2 vols. St. Louis: Concordia Publishing House, 1970–72.

———. "The Unity of Scripture." *Concordia Theological Quarterly* 54, no. 1 (1990): 1–23.

———. "The View of the Bible Held by the Church: The Early Church through Luther." In *Inerrancy,* edited by Norman Geisler, 357–84. Grand Rapids: Zondervan, 1982.

Preuss, Horst Dietrich. *Old Testament Theology.* Translated by Leo G. Perdue. 2 vols. Louisville: Westminster John Knox, 1995–96.

Rast, Lawrence, and Grant Knepper. "Collecting Autographs: Missouri's Assumption of Princeton's Doctrine of the *Autographa.*" In *All Theology Is Christology: Essays in Honor of David P. Scaer,* edited by Dean Wenthe, William Weinrich, Arthur Just, Daniel Gard, and Thomas Olson, 349–74. Ft. Wayne: Concordia Theological Seminary Press, 2000.

Ratzinger, Joseph. *Principles of Catholic Theology: Building Stones for a Fundamental Theology.* Translated by Mary Frances McCarthy. San Francisco: Ignatius Press, 1987.

Reicke, Bo. *Examining Paul's Letters: The History of the Pauline Correspondence.* Edinburgh: T&T Clark, 2001.

Reu, Johann Michael. *Christian Ethics.* Columbus: The Wartburg Press, 1935.

———. *An Explanation of Dr. Martin Luther's Small Catechism.* Minneapolis: Augsburg Publishing House, 1964.

———. *Luther and the Scriptures.* Columbus: The Wartburg Press, 1944.

———. *Lutheran Dogmatics.* Dubuque: Wartburg Theological Seminary, 1951.

Ritschl, Albrecht. *The Christian Doctrine of Justification and Reconciliation: The Positive Development of the Doctrine.* Vol. 3. Translated by H. R. McIntosh and A. B. Macaulay. 1902. Reprint. Clifton, NJ: Reference Book Publishers, 1966.

———. "Theology and Metaphysics." In *Three Essays,* translated by Philip Hefner, 149–217. Philadelphia: Fortress Press, 1972.

Robinson, John A. T. *The Priority of John.* London: Meyer-Stone Books, 1985.

———. *Redating the New Testament.* Eugene, OR: Wipf & Stock, 2000.

Rogers, Jack B., and Donald K. McKim. *The Authority and Interpretation of the Bible: An Historical Approach*. Eugene, OR: Wipf & Stock, 1999.

Rorty, Richard. *The Linguistic Turn: Essays in Philosophical Method*. Chicago: University of Chicago Press, 1992.

Rosa, Susan. "Seventeenth-Century Catholic Polemic and the Rise of Cultural Rationalism." *Journal of the History of Ideas* 57, no. 1 (1996): 87–107.

Roux, Sophie, and Daniel Garber, eds. *The Mechanization of Natural Philosophy*. New York: Springer, 2013.

Rudolph, Kurt. *Gnosis: The Nature and History of Gnosticism*. Translated by Robert McLachlan Wilson. San Francisco: HarperSanFrancisco, 1987.

Ruokanen, Miikka. *Doctrina Divinitus Inspirata: Martin Luther's Position in the Ecumenical Problem of Biblical Inspiration*. Helsinki: Luther-Agricola Society, 1985.

Russell, Bertram. *A History of Western Philosophy*. New York: Touchstone, 1967.

Sailhamer, John. *The Meaning of the Pentateuch: Revelation, Composition, and Interpretation*. Downers Grove, IL: InterVarsity Press, 2009.

Sanders, E. P. *Judaism: Practice and Belief 63 BCE–66 CE*. Valley Forge, PA: Trinity Press International, 1992.

Sandys, John Edwin. *A History of Classical Scholarship: The Eighteenth Century in Germany and the Nineteenth Century in Europe and the United States of America*. Cambridge, UK: Cambridge University Press, 2011.

Sasse, Hermann. "Additional Notes Concerning Holy Scripture." In *Scripture and the Church: Selected Essays of Hermann Sasse*, edited by Jeffrey Kloha and Ronald Feuerhahn, 158–88. St. Louis: Concordia Seminary, 1995.

———. "Augustine's Doctrine of Inspiration." In *Scripture and the Church: Selected Essays of Hermann Sasse*, edited by Jeffrey Kloha and Ronald Feuerhahn, 221–45. St. Louis: Concordia Seminary, 1995.

———. "The Church and the Word of God." In *The Lonely Way: Selected Essays and Letters, Volume 1 (1927–1939)*, translated by Matthew C. Harrison, Robert G. Bugbee, Lowell C. Green, Gerald S. Krispin, Maurice E. Schild, and John R. Stephenson, 147–58. Concordia Publishing House, 2001.

———. "Concerning the Bible's Inerrancy" (1966). In *Scripture and the Church: Selected Essays of Hermann Sasse*, edited by Jeffrey Kloha and Ronald Feuerhahn, 333–36. St. Louis: Concordia Seminary, 1995.

———. "Flight from Dogma: Remarks on Bultmann's 'Demythologization' of the New Testament." In *The Lonely Way: Selected Essays and Letters, Volume 2 (1941–1976)*, translated by Matthew C. Harrison, Paul N. Anderson, Charles J. Evanson, John W. Kleinig, and Norman E. Nagel, 93–116. Concordia Publishing House, 2002.

———. "Liturgy and Confession: A Brotherly Warning Against the 'High Church' Danger." In *The Lonely Way: Selected Essays and Letters, (1941–1976)*, translated by Matthew C. Harrison, Paul N. Anderson, Charles J. Evanson, John W. Kleinig, and Norman E. Nagel, 299–316. St. Louis: Concordia Publishing House, 2002.

———. *The Lonely Way: Selected Essays and Letters, Volume 1 (1927–1939)*, translated by Matthew C. Harrison, Robert G. Bugbee, Lowell C. Green, Gerald S. Krispin, Maurice E. Schild, and John R. Stephenson. Concordia Publishing House, 2001.

———. *The Lonely Way: Selected Essays and Letters, Volume 2 (1941–1976)*, translated by Matthew C. Harrison, Paul N. Anderson, Charles J. Evanson, John W. Kleinig, and Norman E. Nagel. St. Louis: Concordia Publishing House, 2002.

———. "On the Doctrine *De Scriptura Sacra*." In *Scripture and the Church: Selected Essays of Hermann Sasse*, edited by Jeffrey Kloha and Ronald Feuerhahn, 47–104. St. Louis: Concordia Seminary, 1995.

———. *Sacra Scriptura: Studien zur Lehre von der Heilgen Schrift*. Edited by Friedrich Wilhelm Hopf. Erlangen: Verlage der Evangelische-lutherisch Mission, 1981.

———. *Scripture and the Church: Selected Essays of Hermann Sasse*, edited by Jeffrey Kloha and Ronald Feuerhahn. St. Louis: Concordia Seminary, 1995.

———. "The Theology of the Cross." In *We Confess Anthology*, translated by Norman Nagel, 35–45. St. Louis: Concordia Publishing House, 1998.

———. "What Is the State?" (1932). Translated by Matthew Harrison. Unpublished manuscript, 2015.

Scaer, David P. *The Apostolic Scriptures*. Contemporary Theology Series. St. Louis: Concordia Publishing House, 1971.

———. "Apostolicity, Inspiration, and Canonicity." *Concordia Theological Quarterly* 44, no. 1 (1980): 46–49.

———. *Christology*. Confessional Lutheran Dogmatics, vol. 6. St. Louis: The Luther Academy, 1989.

———. *Discourses in Matthew: Jesus Teaches the Church*. St. Louis: Concordia Publishing House, 2004.

———. "Evangelical and Catholic: A Slogan in Search of a Definition." *Concordia Theological Quarterly* 65, no. 4 (2001): 323–44.

———. "The Historical Critical Method: A Short History Appraisal." *The Springfielder* 36, no. 4 (1973): 294–309.

———. "Inspiration in Trinitarian Perspective." *Pro Ecclesia* 14, no. 2 (2005): 143–60.

———. *James, Apostle of Faith: A Primary Christological Epistle for a Persecuted Church*. Eugene, OR: Wipf & Stock, 2004.

———. "The Law–Gospel Debate in the Missouri Synod Continued." *The Springfielder* 40, no. 2 (1976): 107–18.

———. "Ordaining Women: Has the Time Come?" *Logia: A Journal of Lutheran Theology* 4, no. 2 (1995): 83–85.

———. "2 Peter and the Canon." In *Mysteria Dei: Essays in Honor of Kurt Marquart*, edited by Paul McCain and John Stephenson, 269–86. Ft. Wayne, IN: Concordia Theological Seminary Press, 2000.

———. "The Theology of Robert David Preus and His Person: Making a Difference." *Concordia Theological Quarterly* 74, no. 1 (2010): 75–91.

Scaltsas, Theodore. *Substances and Universals in Aristotle's "Metaphysics."* Ithaca: Cornell University Press, 2010.

Schleiermacher, Friedrich. *The Christian Faith*. Translated by H. R. Mackintosh and J. S. Stewart. New York: T&T Clark, 1999.

Schmid, Heinrich. *The Doctrinal Theology of the Evangelical Lutheran Church*. Translated by Charles Hay and Henry Jacobs. Minneapolis: Augsburg Publishing House, 1961.

Schroeder, Edward. "Law–Gospel Reductionism in the History of The Lutheran Church—Missouri Synod." *Concordia Theological Monthly* 43, no. 4 (1972): 232–47.

Schroeder, H. J., trans. *The Canons and Decrees of the Council of Trent*. Rockford, IL: TAN Books, 1978.

Schröder, Richard. *Johann Gerhards lutherische Christologie und die aristotelische Metaphysik*. Tübingen: Mohr Siebeck, 1983.

Secker, Philip, ed. *The Sacred Scriptures and the Lutheran Confessions: Selected Writings of Arthur Carl Piepkorn.* Vol. 2. Mansfield, CT: CEC Press, 2007.

Shea, Mark. *By What Authority? An Evangelical Discovers Catholic Tradition.* Huntington, IN: Our Sunday Visitor Publishing, 1996.

Sherwin, Byron. *Kabbalah: An Introduction to Jewish Mysticism.* New York: Rowman & Littlefield, 2006.

Silcock, Jeffrey. "Jacob's Ladder—A Bridge between Heaven and Earth: Reading Genesis 28:10–22 against the Grain of Modernity." *Lutheran Theological Journal* 46, no. 3 (2012): 180.

Smalley, Beryl. *The Study of the Bible in the Middle Ages.* 2d ed. 1952. Reprint. South Bend, IN: Notre Dame University Press, 1989.

Smalley, S. S. "John's Revelation and John's Community." *Bulletin of the John Ryland Library* 69, no. 2 (1987): 549–71.

Solomon, Robert. *The Enduring Word: The Authority and Reliability of the Bible.* Singapore: Genesis Books, 2011.

Spear, Wayne. "Augustine's Doctrine of Biblical Infallibility." In *Inerrancy and the Church,* edited by John Hannah, 37–66. Chicago: Moody Press, 1984.

Stark, Rodney. *For the Glory of God: How Monotheism Led to Reformations, Science, Witch-Hunts, and the End of Slavery.* Princeton: Princeton University Press, 2004.

Steiger, Johan Anselm. "The *Communicatio Idiomatum* as the Axle and Motor of Luther's Theology." *Lutheran Quarterly* 14 (2000): 125–58.

———. "The Development of the Reformation Legacy: Hermeneutics and the Interpretation of Scripture in the Age of Orthodoxy." In *Hebrew Bible/Old Testament: The History of Its Interpretation: II: From the Renaissance to the Enlightenment,* edited by Christianus Brekelmans, Magne Sæbø, and Menahem Haran, 691–757. Göttingen: Vandenhoeck & Ruprecht, 2008.

Steiner, George. *The Death of Tragedy.* New York: Oxford University Press, 1961.

Steinhardt, P. J., and N. Turok. *Endless Universe.* New York: Doubleday, 2007.

Steinmann, Andrew. *Daniel.* St. Louis: Concordia Publishing House, 2008.

Steinmetz, David. "Luther and the Two Kingdoms." In *Luther in Context,* 112–25. Bloomington: University of Indiana Press, 1986.

Stephenson, John. *Eschatology.* Confessional Lutheran Dogmatics, vol. 13. Ft. Wayne, Indiana: The Luther Academy, 1993.

———. "Inerrancy." *Logia: A Journal of Lutheran Theology* 2, no. 4 (1993): 4–9.

Stephenson, John, and Thomas Winger, eds. *Herman Sasse: A Man for Our Times?* St. Louis: Concordia Publishing House, 1998.

Stewart, Quentin. *Lutheran Patristic Catholicity: The Vincentian Canon and the Consensus Patrum in Lutheran Orthodoxy.* Zürich: LIT Verlag, 2015.

Stone, Larry. *The Story of the Bible: The Fascinating History of Its Writing, Translation, and Effect on Civilization.* Nashville: Thomas Nelson, 2013.

Sundberg, Albert. "Towards a Revised History of the New Testament Canon." *Studia Evangelica* 4, no. 1 (1968): 452–61.

Sundberg, Walter. "The Development of Dogma as an Ecumenical Problem: Catholic-Protestant Conflict over the Authority and Historicity of Dogmatic Statements." Ph. D. diss., Princeton Theological Seminary, 1981.

Surburg, Raymond. "An Evaluation of the Law–Gospel Principle as a Hermeneutical Method." *The Springfielder* 36, no. 4 (1973): 280–93.

———. "The Presuppositions of the Historical-Grammatical Method as Employed by Historic Lutheranism." *The Springfielder* 38, no. 4 (1974): 278–88.

Tavard, George. *Holy Writ or Holy Church: The Crisis of the Protestant Reformation.* New York, Harper, 1960.

Thiemann, Ronald. *Revelation and Theology: The Gospel as Narrated Promise.* 1987. Reprint. Eugene, OR: Wipf & Stock, 2005.

Thomasius, Gottfried. *Christi: Person und Werk: Darstellung der Evangelisch-lutheranischen Dogmatik vom Mittelpunkt der Christologie Aus.* 2 vols. Erlangen: Andreas Deichert Verlag, 1886–88.

Thompson, Mark. *A Sure Ground on Which to Stand: The Relation of Authority and Interpretive Method of Luther's Approach to Scripture.* Carlisle, UK: Paternoster Press, 2004.

Tierney, Brian. *Origins of Papal Infallibility, 1150–1350: A Study on the Concepts of Infallibility, Sovereignty, and Tradition in the Middle Ages.* Leiden: Brill, 1972.

Tillich, Paul. *The History of Christian Thought: From Its Judaic and Hellenistic Origins to Existentialism.* Chicago: University of Chicago Press, 1972.

Trevett, Christine. *Montanism: Gender, Authority, and the New Prophecy.* Cambridge, UK: Cambridge University Press, 1996.

Tripolitis, Antonia. *Religions of the Hellenistic-Roman Age.* Grand Rapids: Wm. B. Eerdmans, 2002.

Tsumura, David Toshio. *Creation and Destruction: A Reappraisal of the* Chaoskampf *Theory in the Old Testament.* Winona Lake, IN: Eisenbrauns, 2005.

Turnbloom, David Farina. *Speaking with Aquinas: A Conversation about Grace, Virtue, and the Eucharist.* Collegeville, MN: Liturgical Press, 2017.

Turner, David. *Israel's Last Prophet: Jesus and the Jewish Leaders in Matthew 23.* Minneapolis: Fortress Press, 2015.

Turner, Nigel. *A Grammar of New Testament Greek.* 4 vols. Edinburgh: T&T Clark, 1980.

Van der Toorn, Karel. *Scribal Culture and the Making of the Hebrew Bible.* Cambridge, MA: Harvard University Press, 2009.

Vanhoozer, Kevin. *The Drama of Doctrine: A Canonical-Linguistic Approach to Christian Theology.* Louisville: Westminster/John Knox, 2005.

———. *Is There Meaning in the Text? The Bible, the Reader, and the Morality of Literary Knowledge.* Grand Rapids: Zondervan, 1998.

———. *Remythologizing Theology: Divine Action, Passion, and Authorship.* Cambridge, UK: Cambridge University Press, 2012.

Van Liere, Frans. *An Introduction to the Medieval Bible.* Cambridge, UK: Cambridge University Press, 2014.

Voelz, James. *What Does This Mean? Principles of Biblical Interpretation in the Post-Modern World.* St. Louis: Concordia Publishing House, 1997.

Von Harless, Adolf. *A System of Christian Ethics.* Translated by A. W. Morrison. Brighton, IA: Just & Sinner, 2014.

Von Leibniz, Gottfried. *Theodicy.* Translated by E. M. Huggard. New York: Cosmo Classics, 2010.

Von Loewenich, Walther. *Luthers Theologia Crucis.* München: Kaiser Verlag, 1954.

Von Rad, Gerhard. *Old Testament Theology: Single Volume Edition.* 2 vols. Translated by D. M. G. Stalker. Peabody, MA: Prince Press, 2005.

Walker, Williston, Richard A. Norris, David W. Lotz, and Robert T. Handy. *A History of the Christian Church*. 4th ed. New York: Simon & Schuster, 1985.

Wallace, Daniel. *Greek Grammar Beyond the Basics: An Exegetical Syntax of the New Testament*. Grand Rapids: Zondervan, 1996.

Waltke, Bruce. "Myth, History, and the Bible." In *The Enduring Authority of the Christian Scriptures*, edited by D. A. Carson, 542–76. Grand Rapids: Wm. B. Eerdmans, 2016.

Walton, John. *Ancient Near Eastern Thought and the Old Testament: Introducing the Conceptual World of the Hebrew Bible*. Grand Rapids: Baker Academic, 2006.

Warfield, Benjamin. *The Inspiration and Authority of the Bible*. Philadelphia: Presbyterian and Reformed Publishing Company, 1970.

Weber, Otto. *Foundations of Dogmatics*. Translated by Darrell Guder. 2 vols. Grand Rapids: Wm. B. Eerdmans, 1981.

Webster, John. *Holy Scripture: A Dogmatic Sketch*. Cambridge, UK: Cambridge University Press, 2007.

Webster, William. *The Church of Rome at the Bar of History*. Edinburgh: The Banner of Truth Trust, 1995.

Weikart, Richard. *From Darwin to Hitler: Evolutionary Ethics, Eugenics and Racism in Germany*. New York: Palgrave Macmillan, 2004.

Wellhausen, Julius. *Prolegomena to the History of Israel*. Translated by J. Sutherland Black. Edinburgh: Adam and Charles Black, 1885.

Wengert, Timothy. *Reading the Bible with Martin Luther: An Introductory Guide*. Grand Rapids: Baker Academic, 2013.

Wenham, John. "Christ's View of Scripture." In *Inerrancy*, edited by Norman Geisler, 3–38. Grand Rapids: Zondervan, 1982.

———. *Redating Matthew, Mark, and Luke: A Fresh Assault on the Synoptic Problem*. Downers Grove, IL: InterVarsity Press, 1992.

Wenthe, Dean, William Weinrich, Arthur Just, Daniel Gard, and Thomas Olson, eds. *All Theology Is Christology: Essays in Honor of David P. Scaer*. Ft. Wayne, IN: Concordia Theological Seminary Press, 2000.

Westphal, Merold. *Overcoming Onto-theology: Toward a Postmodern Christian Faith*. New York: Fordham University Press, 2001.

Where Christ Is Present: A Theology for All Seasons on the 500th Anniversary of the Reformation. Edited by John Warwick Montgomery, Gene Edward Veith, Jr., Cameron A. MacKenzie, Adam Francisco, Rod Rosenblatt, Harold L. Senkbeil, Todd Wilken, Uwe Siemon-Netto, Craig A. Parton, Steven A. Hein, and Angus J. L. Menuge. Irvine, CA: NRP Books, 2015

White, Benjamin. "How to Read a Book: Irenaeus and the Pastoral Epistles Reconsidered." *Vigiliae Christianae* 65 (2011): 125–49.

White, James. *Answers to Catholic Claims*. Southbridge, MA: Crowne Publications, 1990.

———. *The King James Only Controversy: Can You Trust the Modern Translations?* Minneapolis: Bethany House, 1995.

———. *The Roman Catholic Controversy: Catholics and Protestants—Do the Differences Still Matter?* Minneapolis: Bethany House, 1996.

———. *Sola Scriptura: Exploring the Bible's Accuracy, Authority, and Authenticity*. Minneapolis: Bethany House, 2001.

White, Thomas Joseph, ed. *The Analogy of Being: Invention of the Antichrist or the Wisdom of God?* Grand Rapids: Wm. B. Eerdmans, 2011.

Whybray, R. N. *The Making of the Pentateuch: A Methodological Study*. Sheffield: Sheffield Academic Press, 1987.

Williams, George H. *The Radical Reformation*. Kirksville, MO: Truman State University Press, 2000.

Williams, H. H. Drake. *Jesus, Tried and True: Why the Four Gospels Provide the Best Picture of Jesus*. Eugene, OR: Wipf & Stock, 2013.

Williams, Rowan. *Arius: Heresy and Tradition*. Grand Rapids: Wm. B. Eerdmans, 2002.

Wingren, Gustaf. *Creation and Law*. Translated by Ross McKenzie. Philadelphia: Muhlenberg Press, 1961.

———. *Gospel and Church*. Translated by Ross McKenzie. Philadelphia: Fortress Press, 1964.

———. *The Living Word: A Theological Study of Preaching and the Church*. Translated by Victor Pogue. Philadelphia: Muhlenberg Press, 1960.

Wink, Walter. "Homosexuality and the Bible." In *Homosexuality and Christian Faith: Questions of Conscience for the Churches,* edited by Walter Wink, 33–49. Minneapolis: Augsburg Fortress, 1999.

———, ed. *Homosexuality and Christian Faith: Questions of Conscience for the Churches*. Minneapolis: Augsburg Fortress, 1999.

Wiseman, P. J. *Ancient Records and the Structures of Genesis: A Case for Literary Unity*, edited by D. J. Wiseman. New York: Thomas Nelson Publishers, 1985.

Wissink, J. B. M., ed. *The Eternity of the World in the Thought of Thomas Aquinas and His Contemporaries*. Leiden: Brill, 1990.

Witherington, Ben, III. *New Testament Rhetoric: An Introductory Guide to the Art of Persuasion in and of the New Testament*. Eugene, OR: Cascade Books, 2009.

Wolterstorff, Nicholas. *Divine Discourse: Philosophical Reflections on the Claim That God Speaks*. Cambridge, UK: Cambridge University Press, 1995.

Wood, A. Skevington. *Captive to the Word: Martin Luther, Doctor of Sacred Scripture*. Grand Rapids: Wm. B. Eerdmans, 1969.

Wright, N. T. *Christian Origins and the Question of God*. 4 vols. Minneapolis: Fortress Press, 1992–2013.

Young, Edward. *Introduction to the Old Testament*. Grand Rapids: Wm. B. Eerdmans, 1989.

SACRED SCRIPTURE INDEX

LUTHERAN CONFESSIONS INDEX

NAME AND SUBJECT INDEX

www.ingramcontent.com/pod-product-compliance
Lightning Source LLC
Chambersburg PA
CBHW060006100426
42740CB00010B/1411